D1544632

Harley-Davidson Sportster
Service and Repair Manual

by Tom Schauwecker, Curt Choate, Penny Cox, Mike Stubblefield and Alan Ahlstrand

Models covered

XL, XLH, XLCH 883 Hugger, Sportster, Deluxe. 1970 to 1971, 1986 to 2003
XL, XLX-61, XLH, XLCH, XLS 1000 Sportster, Roadster, Anniversary. 1972 to 1985
XL, XLH 1100 Sportster. 1986 and 1987
XL. XLH 1200, 1200C, 1200S Sportster. 1998 to 2003

ABCDE
FGHIJ
KLMNO
PQRS

ISBN **1 56392 534 6**

British Library Cataloguing in Publication Data
A catalogue record for this book is available from the British Library.

Library of Congress Control Number 2004106127
Printed in the USA

Haynes Publishing
Sparkford, Nr Yeovil, Somerset BA22 7JJ, England

Haynes North America, Inc
861 Lawrence Drive, Newbury Park, California 91320, USA

04-232

Contents

LIVING WITH YOUR HARLEY-DAVIDSON SPORTSTER

Introduction

Daily (pre-ride) checks

MAINTENANCE

Routine maintenance and servicing

Contents

REPAIRS AND OVERHAUL

Engine, transmission and associated systems

Chassis and bodywork components

Electrical system

Wiring diagrams

REFERENCE

Index

Harley-Davidson
Milwaukee Magic

by Alan Ahlstrand

Milwaukee Magic

Late in the 1960s, on a typical warm summer California evening, a friend showed up at my house and announced, "Alan, if I can't make the payment, I'm coming to you for the money, because I'm *not* losing this bike."

He'd just traded his Suzuki X-6 - a 250cc 2-stroke twin with six-speed transmission, at that time being talked about as the new Harley-beater - for a new-to-him 1966 Sportster XLCH.

I'd ridden the Suzuki and laid it down on asphalt, so I wasn't invited onto the front seat of the Sportster. Instead, he gave complete instructions in back-seat riding technique for a torquey motorcycle without a sissy bar or grab strap for the passenger: "Put your hands around my waist and lock your fingers, or the bike will jet out from under you." Off we went,

ending up on newly-opened Highway 280 south of San Francisco, which was deserted at 2 a.m. Helmetless, ungoggled, dressed in jeans and t-shirts and unbridled by a sense of mortality, we cranked it up. After I'd had enough time to think "We're crazy, but yeee-haaa" more than once, he took one hand off the grip, turned around with one eye closed, the other half-closed and streaming tears, grinned, and held up one finger - we'd hit a hundred miles an hour.

Maybe the speedometer was optimistic, and it was really only 97.4 or so, but when the wind is shredding the shirt on your back and flapping your face like flags in a hurricane, the difference is academic.

Every Harley rider has done something like that - or will, when the time and place are right - and that Milwaukee magic has been the key to the company's modern success.

All of this started a century ago. In 1903

Arthur Davidson and William S. Harley finished a three-year project, building what amounted to a powered bicycle. The first Harley-Davidson engine had a single cylinder with a bore of 2-1/8 inches and a stroke of 2-7/8 inches, displacing 405 cc. The intake valve was not operated mechanically; rather, it was sucked open by the downward pull of the piston and pushed shut by the compressing fuel-air mixture on the piston's upward stroke, a design shared with contemporary automobile engines such as the Knox Porcupine. Power transmission was by a leather belt, assisted when necessary by bicycle pedals, a chain, sprockets and human effort. Braking was accomplished by pedaling backwards, bicycle-style. The front suspension was the leading-link design later to be improved and used in Springers, historic and modern. The rear suspension? There wasn't any - the bike's rigid, triangular rear frame section connected directly to the rear axle.

From 1903 to 1909, the company continued to grow, with steady improvements in the single-cylinder bike's design, steady increases in sales, and a move from the shed where the company started to a two-story factory in Milwaukee. In 1909 Harley's first V-twin, the model 5D, was introduced, and with it the company's enduring theme.

Despite diversions such as the Topper scooter and Aermacchi singles of the Sixties and Seventies, the theme continues to the present day. The heart of all Harleys, the key to what makes a motorcycle a Harley-Davidson, is the engine. The rest of the bike exists to keep the engine off the pavement. This function is performed in grand style, of course, with a near-infinite selection of customizing possibilities, but at the center of it all is a big-displacement, narrow-angle, uneven-firing, air-cooled V-twin that roars instead of wails. From the flatheads that succeeded the Model 5D, to the Knucklehead of 1936, to the Panhead of 1948, to the Shovelhead of 1966, to the Evolution of 1984, to the current Twin Cam 88, every important Harley-Davidson engine has fit that description.

(Actually, the only official designations in the list are Evolution and Twin Cam 88. Pan-head, Knucklehead and Shovelhead were

The 1975 FLH1200 (Shovelhead)

informal names, based on the appearance of the cylinder heads and valve covers. For that reason, the Twin Cam 88 came dangerously close to being dubbed "Fathead.")

In addition to big piston displacement and a V-twin configuration, Harley engines share some unique characteristics. The angle between the cylinders, or "V," is 45 degrees. The crankshaft has one crankpin, with both connecting rods mounted on it. This means that the cylinders fire 90-degrees apart (at 315 and 405 degrees of crankshaft rotation). This uneven firing sequence gives the engine its signature "potato-potato" idle. In addition to being mounted on a single crankpin, the connecting rods are mounted knife-and-fork style rather than side-by-side. In this design, the bottom end of one connecting rod is an inverted Y, with the bottom end of the other connecting rod centered between the Y's branches. This allows the engine to be narrow from side to side, while the small angle between the cylinders allows it to be narrow front-to-rear.

The company continued producing new products under family ownership until 1969, when it was bought by the conglomerate AMF. The AMF years, 1969 to 1981, were widely regarded as the company's Dark Ages - sales dropped, along with the bikes' reputation for quality. My friend replaced his 1966 Sportster with a 1979 model, and then replaced a series of tachs and speedometers because the needles kept breaking off from vibration. This era ended with the company's rescue in a buyout by company executives, led by Vaughn Beals. This is one of the most successful employee buyouts in corporate history, if the company's stock price and sales are any indication - the stock has multiplied in value many times, and Harley-Davidson has for years maintained the biggest market share in the cruiser and touring bike categories.

That almost didn't happen - and Harley-Davidson nearly ended up in the recycling bin of history, as a nostalgic brand name that would-be entrepreneurs could paste onto yet another corporate startup attempt.

The buyout coincided with a downturn in the motorcycle market. Along with that, competition from Japanese bikes had become well established. The Suzuki X-6 wasn't a Harley-beater, but there were now plenty of four-cylinder Japanese 750s that were. Worse yet, the major Japanese manufacturers began to build V-twin cruisers. Faced with imminent doom, Harley-Davidson turned to the US government for help. This came in the form of a tariff, beginning in 1983, on Japanese-built motorcycles with displacements over 700cc. The result was a sudden rash of Japanese bikes displacing 699cc, but it was enough to keep the company alive. Its fortunes even improved enough that it asked for an early end to the tariff in 1987.

The motorcycle market coasted along the bottom for several years, then finally began to

The 1974 XL1000 Sportster (Shovelhead)

The XL1200 Sportster (Evolution)

The 1993 FLSTC Heritage Softail (Evolution)

The 1993 XLH 883 Sportster Hugger (Evolution)

turn up significantly in the early 1990s. As the market revived, the audience was changing; motorcyclists were becoming older, richer, but more in need of a bad boy image (and increasingly, a bad girl image). They also needed bikes that were reliable and relatively comfortable to ride. Harley-Davidson had possessed the image for decades, even if Marlon Brando did ride a Triumph in "The Wild One." With the Evolution engine and improved quality control, the company was on its way to reliability. Comfort and simplicity had been evolving, and continued to do so.

Comfort and simplicity were no part of the Sportster XLCH, but in its day, the bike was enough of a thrill ride to make up for it. The kickstarter, operated in the wrong synchronicity with the twist-grip spark timing, could kick back and hurt you. The drum brakes stopped the bike far less capably than the engine made it go. The XLCH had no battery; its electrical system was powered by a magneto, which meant that the lights would dim if you let the engine idle. (Why no, officer, I wasn't speedshifting, I was just trying to keep the lights safely bright.)

The XLCH was intended for competition. Other Harleys were easier to ride, and had battery-based electrical systems. Electric start was introduced on the first Electra Glide in 1965. Final drive progressed from an exposed chain, to an enclosed chain, to a cogged belt that's still in use. Drum brakes were replaced by discs at front and rear. Rubber engine mounts were employed on touring bikes, and later on the Dyna. The hardtail look of early bikes was recreated with the Softail, but the Softail had a rear suspension. A well-designed sequential port fuel injection system was added as an option. Some models were designed with low seat heights to accommodate shorter riders.

The Evolution engine was a turning point in the company's history, even though it was essentially a refined top end on the Shovelhead bottom end. The iron cylinders and heads of the Shovelhead were replaced with aluminum components. The valve train's basic design was unchanged, with geardriven camshafts, hydraulic lifters, pushrods and rocker arms. The change to aluminum at the top end eliminated a major source of oil leaks, at the joints of the cylinders and crankcase, because the parts now expanded and contracted at the same rate as they heated and cooled. The combination of mechanical improvement and Harley tradition was enthusiastically received by customers, first in the Big Twins for 1984 and then in the Sportster for 1986.

The Evolution engine was superseded by the Twin Cam 88, in the Touring and Dyna chassis for the 1999 model year and in Softails for 2000 (the Evo is still used in the Sportster). Unlike the Evolution, the Twin Cam 88 was a completely new design, even while it retained the basics of the traditional Harley

A hundred years old, and stronger than ever - 100th Anniversary models sport a distinctive logo

Past meets future - the Sportster is essentially unchanged, while the V-Rod is radically new

engine. Despite the name, the engine did not have overhead cams. The Twin Cam designation came about because the wide spacing between the large cylinder bores made a single camshaft impractical. The solution was to use one camshaft for each cylinder. The camshafts are mounted in a support plate on the right side of the engine, below the cylinders. The rear camshaft is driven by the crankshaft through a chain and sprockets mounted outside the camshaft support plate. The rear camshaft drives the front camshaft through a second chain and sprockets, mounted inside the camshaft support plate. As with earlier Harley engines, the camshafts operate the valves through hydraulic lifters, pushrods and rocker arms.

Engine vibration in Dyna and Touring models was handled by rubber engine mounts. In the Softail, where the engine is solidly mounted to the chassis, another solution was needed. This was the Twin Cam 88B, the balancer-equipped version of the engine that appeared in Softails in 2000. The Twin Cam 88B is the same as non-counterbalanced versions from the crankshaft up. A pair of balance shafts, one behind the crankshaft and one in front, are driven by the crankshaft through a chain and sprockets.

Thus Harley-Davidson ends its first century with a very good product line and very good prospects. What's in store for Harley's next century? Logically, the company's future cruisers and touring motorcycles should be variations of the V-Rod sport bike. The V-Rod is an attractive mix of Harley tradition and modern technology. Like traditional Harleys, the V-Rod has a V-twin engine. Unlike traditional Harleys, the V-Rod employs overhead cams, four-valve heads and liquid cooling to produce an impressive 115 horsepower. And yet, Harley customers have left V-Rods on the sales floor in record numbers while buying more Twin Cam 88s every year.

Modern Japanese bikes and Sportsters tend to have four-figure price tags and five-figure redlines; Harleys, traditional and V-Rod, are the other way around. Modern Harleys are well built and reliable, but so are their competitors. Why, in the face of those facts, do traditional Harleys continue to dominate their market? When Milwaukee magic applies, logic doesn't. It's as simple, and as complicated, as that.

Acknowledgements

Our thanks are due to JIMS Tools, of Camarillo, California (www.jimsusa.com), for supplying the special tools used in some photographs. The introduction "Milwaukee Magic" was written by Alan Ahlstrand.

About this manual

The aim of this manual is to help you get the best value from your motorcycle. It can do so in several ways. It can help you decide what work must be done, even if you choose to have it done by a dealer; it provides information and procedures for routine maintenance and servicing; and it offers diagnostic and repair procedures to follow when trouble occurs.

We hope you use the manual to tackle the work yourself. For many simpler jobs, doing it yourself may be quicker than arranging an appointment to get the motorcycle into a dealer and making the trips to leave it and pick it up. More importantly, a lot of money can be saved by avoiding the expense the shop must pass on to you to cover its labor and overhead costs. An added benefit is the sense of satisfaction and accomplishment that you feel after doing the job yourself.

References to the left or right side of the motorcycle assume you are sitting on the seat, facing forward.

We take great pride in the accuracy of information given in this manual, but motorcycle manufacturers make alterations and design changes during the production run of a particular motorcycle of which they do not inform us. No liability can be accepted by the authors or publishers for loss, damage or injury caused by any errors in, or omissions from, the information given.

Buying spare parts

Once you have found all the identification numbers, record them for reference when buying parts. Since the manufacturers change specifications, parts and vendors (companies that manufacture various components on the machine), providing the ID numbers is the only way to be reasonably sure that you are buying the correct parts.

Whenever possible, take the worn part to the dealer so direct comparison with the new component can be made. Along the trail from the manufacturer to the parts shelf, there are numerous places that the part can end up with the wrong number or be listed incorrectly.

The two places to purchase new parts for your motorcycle - the accessory store and the franchised dealer - differ in the type of parts they carry. While dealers can obtain virtually every part for your motorcycle, the accessory dealer is usually limited to normal high wear items such as shock absorbers, tune-up parts, various engine gaskets, cables, chains, brake parts, etc. Rarely will an accessory outlet have major suspension components, cylinders, transmission gears, or cases.

Used parts can be obtained for considerably less than new ones, but you can't always be sure of what you're getting. Once again, take your worn part to the salvage yard for direct comparison.

Whether buying new, used or rebuilt parts, the best course is to deal directly with someone who specializes in parts for your particular make.

1 or 5	Market designation
HD	Harley-Davidson
1 or 4	Heavyweight or middleweight motorcycle
2 or 3 letters	Model designation
Single letter	Engine displacement
1 or 2	Introduction date or model
0 through 9 or X	Check digit
Single digit	Model year
Single letter	Location or manufacture
Six digits	Sequential serial number

Vehicle identification number details (typical)

Decoding the Vehicle Identification Number (VIN)

The frame serial number is stamped into the right side of the steering head and printed on a decal attached to the right frame downtube. An abbreviated frame serial number is stamped on the crankcase below the "V" of the cylinders. Both of these numbers should be recorded and kept in a safe place so they can be given to law enforcement officials in the event of a theft.

The frame serial number and engine serial number should also be kept in a handy place (such as with your driver's license) so they are always available when purchasing or ordering parts for your machine.

The Vehicle Identification Number (VIN) contains code letters and numbers that provide specific information about each motorcycle. The purpose of each letter or number is shown below. The letter and number codes are described below.

Market designation

1: Manufactured for USA
5: Manufactured for all other markets

Heavyweight motorcycle:

1: 901 cc or greater engine displacement

Middleweight motorcycle:

4: 351 through 900 cc or greater engine displacement

Model designation

1970 through 1978
2G: XLT
3A: XL or XLH
4A: XLCH
4D: XLA

1979 and 1980
3A: XLH
4A: XLCH
4E: XLS

1981 through 1985
CAH: XLX
CBH: XLS
CCH: XLX
CDH: XR-1000

1986 and 1987
CA: XLH 883, XLH 883 Deluxe, XLH 1100
CE: XLH 883 Hugger

1988 through 1998
CA: XLH 883, XLH 1200
CE: XLH 883 Hugger
CF: XLH 883 Deluxe
CG: XL1200C Custom
CH: XL1200S Sport

1999 and later
CAM: XLH 883
CEM: XLH 883 Hugger
CJM: XLH 883C Custom
CKM: XL 883R
CAP: XL1200
CGP: XL1200C Custom
CHP: XL1200S Sport

continued on next page

Introduction date and special models

1: Regular introduction date
2: Mid-year introduction date

3: California model
4: Anniversary model, or special edition

Engine Size

M: 883 cc

N: 1100 cc

P: 1200 cc

VIN check digit

Varies from 0 through 9 or X

Model year code (1983 and later)

D: 1983	K: 1989	R: 1994	X: 1999
E: 1984	L: 1990	S: 1995	Y: 2000
F: 1985	M: 1991	T: 1996	1: 2001
G: 1986	N: 1992	V: 1997	2: 2002
H: 1987	P: 1993	W: 1998	3: 2003
J: 1988			

Assembly plant

K: Kansas City, Missouri
Y: York, Pennsylvania

An abbreviated version of the VIN is stamped in the engine, below the "V" of the cylinders

The VIN is also printed on a decal on the right frame downtube

The VIN is stamped on the right side of the steering head

Professional mechanics are trained in safe working procedures. However enthusiastic you may be about getting on with the job at hand, take the time to ensure that your safety is not put at risk. A moment's lack of attention can result in an accident, as can failure to observe simple precautions.

There will always be new ways of having accidents, and the following is not a comprehensive list of all dangers; it is intended rather to make you aware of the risks and to encourage a safe approach to all work you carry out on your bike.

Asbestos

● Certain friction, insulating, sealing and other products - such as brake pads, clutch linings, gaskets, etc. - contain asbestos. Extreme care must be taken to avoid inhalation of dust from such products since it is hazardous to health. If in doubt, assume that they do contain asbestos.

Fire

● Remember at all times that gasoline is highly flammable. Never smoke or have any kind of naked flame around, when working on the vehicle. But the risk does not end there - a spark caused by an electrical short-circuit, by two metal surfaces contacting each other, by careless use of tools, or even by static electricity built up in your body under certain conditions, can ignite gasoline vapor, which in a confined space is highly explosive. Never use gasoline as a cleaning solvent. Use an approved safety solvent.

● Always disconnect the battery ground terminal before working on any part of the fuel or electrical system, and never risk spilling fuel on to a hot engine or exhaust.

● It is recommended that a fire extinguisher of a type suitable for fuel and electrical fires is kept handy in the garage or workplace at all times. Never try to extinguish a fuel or electrical fire with water.

Fumes

● Certain fumes are highly toxic and can quickly cause unconsciousness and even death if inhaled to any extent. Gasoline vapor comes into this category, as do the vapors from certain solvents such as trichloro-ethylene. Any draining or pouring of such volatile fluids should be done in a well ventilated area.

● When using cleaning fluids and solvents, read the instructions carefully. Never use materials from unmarked containers - they may give off poisonous vapors.

● Never run the engine of a motor vehicle in an enclosed space such as a garage. Exhaust fumes contain carbon monoxide which is extremely poisonous; if you need to run the engine, always do so in the open air or at least have the rear of the vehicle outside the workplace.

The battery

● Never cause a spark, or allow a naked light near the vehicle's battery. It will normally be giving off a certain amount of hydrogen gas, which is highly explosive.

● Always disconnect the battery ground terminal before working on the fuel or electrical systems (except where noted).

● If possible, loosen the filler plugs or cover when charging the battery from an external source. Do not charge at an excessive rate or the battery may burst.

● Take care when topping up, cleaning or carrying the battery. The acid electrolyte, even when diluted, is very corrosive and should not be allowed to contact the eyes or skin. Always wear rubber gloves and goggles or a face shield. If you ever need to prepare electrolyte yourself, always add the acid slowly to the water; never add the water to the acid.

Electricity

● When using an electric power tool, inspection light etc., always ensure that the appliance is correctly connected to its plug and that, where necessary, it is properly grounded. Do not use such appliances in damp conditions and, again, beware of creating a spark or applying excessive heat in the vicinity of fuel or fuel vapor. Also ensure that the appliances meet national safety standards.

● A severe electric shock can result from touching certain parts of the electrical system, such as the spark plug wires (HT leads), when the engine is running or being cranked, particularly if components are damp or the insulation is defective. Where an electronic ignition system is used, the secondary (HT) voltage is much higher and could prove fatal.

Remember...

✗ **Don't** start the engine without first ascertaining that the transmission is in neutral.

✗ **Don't** attempt to drain oil until you are sure it has cooled sufficiently to avoid scalding you.

✗ **Don't** grasp any part of the engine or exhaust system without first ascertaining that it is cool enough not to burn you.

✗ **Don't** allow brake fluid or antifreeze to contact the machine's paintwork or plastic components.

✗ **Don't** siphon toxic liquids such as fuel or hydraulic fluid by mouth, or allow them to remain on your skin.

✗ **Don't** inhale dust - it may be injurious to health (see Asbestos heading).

✗ **Don't** allow any spilled oil or grease to remain on the floor - wipe it up right away, before someone slips on it.

✗ **Don't** use ill-fitting wrenches or other tools which may slip and cause injury.

✗ **Don't** lift a heavy component which may be beyond your capability - get assistance.

✗ **Don't** rush to finish a job or take unverified short cuts.

✗ **Don't** allow children or animals in or around an unattended vehicle.

✗ **Don't** inflate a tire above the recommended pressure. Apart from overstressing the carcass, in extreme cases the tire may blow off forcibly.

✔ **Do** ensure that the machine is supported securely at all times. This is especially important when the machine is blocked up to aid wheel or fork removal.

✔ **Do** take care when attempting to loosen a stubborn nut or bolt. It is generally better to pull on a wrench, rather than push, so that if you slip, you fall away from the machine rather than onto it.

✔ **Do** wear eye protection when using power tools such as drill, sander, bench grinder etc.

✔ **Do** use a barrier cream on your hands prior to undertaking dirty jobs - it will protect your skin from infection as well as making the dirt easier to remove afterwards; but make sure your hands aren't left slippery. Note that long-term contact with used engine oil can be a health hazard.

✔ **Do** keep loose clothing (cuffs, ties etc. and long hair) well out of the way of moving mechanical parts.

✔ **Do** remove rings, wristwatch etc., before working on the vehicle - especially the electrical system.

✔ **Do** keep your work area tidy - it is only too easy to fall over articles left lying around.

✔ **Do** exercise caution when compressing springs for removal or installation. Ensure that the tension is applied and released in a controlled manner, using suitable tools which preclude the possibility of the spring escaping violently.

✔ **Do** ensure that any lifting tackle used has a safe working load rating adequate for the job.

✔ **Do** get someone to check periodically that all is well, when working alone on the vehicle.

✔ **Do** carry out work in a logical sequence and check that everything is correctly assembled and tightened afterwards.

✔ **Do** remember that your vehicle's safety affects that of yourself and others. If in doubt on any point, get professional advice.

● If in spite of following these precautions, you are unfortunate enough to injure yourself, seek medical attention as soon as possible.

1 Engine oil level check

Before you start:

Caution: Do not run the engine in an enclosed space such as a garage or workshop.

✔ Stop the engine and support the motorcycle on its sidestand. Allow it to stand undisturbed for a few minutes to allow the oil level to stabilize. Make sure the motorcycle is on level ground.

✔ Check the engine oil level with the bike on the sidestand. If the engine is cold, use the Cold check scale on the dipstick. If the engine is warm, let it idle for one or two minutes on the sidestand, then shut it off and check the oil.

✔ To check the oil level, remove the dipstick/filler cap from the oil tank (it's on the right side of the motorcycle on all models). Rock the cap back-and-forth to free the O-ring, then lift the dipstick out. Wipe the dipstick with a clean rag, set it back in the hole (don't push it all the way in), then lift it out and read the level on the dipstick scale.

✔ Don't confuse the engine oil cap with the transmission oil cap; the engine oil cap is above the transmission cap and is held in place by a rubber O-ring, while the transmission oil cap is unscrewed with an Allen wrench.

Bike care:

● If you have to add oil frequently, you should check whether you have any oil leaks. If there is no sign of oil leakage from the joints and gaskets the engine could be burning oil (see *Troubleshooting*).

The correct oil

● Modern, high-revving engines place great demands on their oil. It is very important that the correct oil for your bike is used.

● Always top up with a good quality oil of the specified type and viscosity and do not overfill the engine.

Shovelhead engine

Oil type	HD rating 360 or equivalent
Normal (20 to 90-degrees F	SAE 20W-50
Below 40-degrees F	SAE 30
Above 40-degrees F	SAE 40
Above 80-degrees F	SAE 60

Evolution engine

Oil type	H-D rating 360 or equivalent
Oil viscosity	
Below 40-degrees F (4-degrees C)	H.D. Multi-Grade, SAE 10W-40
Above 40-degrees F (4-degrees C)	H.D. Multi-Grade, SAE 20W-50
Above 60-degrees F (16-degrees C)	H.D. Regular Heavy, SAE 50
Above 80-degrees F (27-degrees C)	H.D. Extra Heavy, SAE 60

1 The engine oil filler cap is in the oil tank on the right side of the bike.

2 Rock the engine oil dipstick back-and-forth while pulling it out. Measure the oil level on the dipstick scale.

2 Suspension, steering and final drive checks

Suspension and Steering:
● Check that the front and rear suspension operate smoothly without binding.
● Check that the suspension is adjusted as required.
● Check that the steering moves smoothly from lock-to-lock.

Final drive:
● On chain drive models (1970 through 1985), check the drive chain slack isn't excessive and adjust it if necessary (see Chapter 1).
● On chain drive models without an automatic oiler, lubricate the chain if it looks dry (see Chapter 1).

● Check the drivebelt tension (1986 and later), with the belt cold, the bike on the sidestand and the weight of the rider on the seat. Using a tension gauge is the best way to check, but the gauge isn't absolutely necessary. If belt tension is incorrect, adjust it (see Chapter 1). On later Dyna models, the belt is visible through a hole in the belt guard.

1 Belt deflection can be viewed through a window on some models.

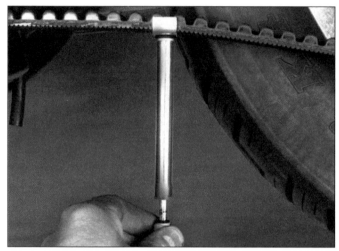

2 The rear drivebelt tension should be checked at the center of the lower run, with the bike on the sidestand. Apply 10-pounds force to the belt (ideally, using a tension gauge) and measure the belt deflection.

3 Legal and safety checks

Lighting and signalling:
● Take a minute to check that the headlight, tail light, brake light, instrument lights and turn signals all work correctly.
● Check that the horn sounds when the switch is operated.
● A working speedometer graduated in mph is a statutory requirement in the UK.

Safety:
● Check that the throttle grip rotates smoothly and snaps shut when released, in all steering positions. Also check for the correct amount of freeplay (see Chapter 1).
● Check that the engine shuts off when the kill switch is operated.
● Check that sidestand return spring holds the stand securely up when retracted.

Fuel:
● This may seem obvious, but check that you have enough fuel to complete your journey. If you notice signs of fuel leakage - rectify the cause immediately.
● Ensure you use the correct grade unleaded fuel - see Chapter 4 Specifications.

4 Brake fluid level checks

> ⚠ **Warning: Some early models used DOT 3 brake fluid. Later models use DOT 5. If you don't know which type your bike uses, drain all the brake fluid and have the system flushed before refilling. Refer to the manufacturer's fluid recommendation stamped on the reservoir cap or cover. Never mix DOT 3 and DOT 5 fluids or brake failure may occur.**

Before you start:

✔ Ensure the motorcycle is held vertical while checking the levels. Make sure the motorcycle is on level ground.

✔ Make sure you have the correct hydraulic fluid (see the **Warning** above). Never reuse old fluid.

✔ Wrap a rag around the reservoir being worked on to ensure that any spillage does not come into contact with painted surfaces.

Bike care:

● The fluid in the front and rear brake master cylinder reservoirs will drop slightly as the brake pads wear down.

● If any fluid reservoir requires repeated topping-up this is an indication of a hydraulic leak somewhere in the system, which should be investigated immediately.

● Check for signs of fluid leakage from the hydraulic hoses and components - if found, rectify immediately.

● Check the operation of both brakes before taking the machine on the road; if there is evidence of air in the system (spongy feel to lever or pedal), it must be bled as described in Chapter 7.

1 Check the front brake fluid level in the sight glass on top of the master cylinder. If the level is high enough, the sight glass will be dark. It lightens in color as the fluid level drops.

2 The rear master cylinder (located near the brake pedal) also has a sight glass. Fluid level is checked in the same way as for the front master cylinder.

3 If the fluid level is low in either master cylinder, remove the cover screws and lift off the cover and diaphragm. Top up to 1/8-inch (3 mm) from the gasket surface with the correct brake fluid only, then reinstall the cover and diaphragm.

5 Tire checks

The correct pressures:

● The tires must be checked when **cold**, not immediately after riding. Note that low tire pressures may cause the tire to slip on the rim or come off. High tire pressures will cause abnormal tread wear and unsafe handling.
● Use an accurate pressure gauge.
● Proper air pressure will increase tire life and provide maximum stability and ride comfort.

Tire care:

● Check the tires carefully for cuts, tears, embedded nails or other sharp objects and excessive wear. Operation of the motorcycle with excessively worn tires is extremely hazardous, as traction and handling are directly affected.
● Check the condition of the tire valve and ensure the dust cap is in place.
● Pick out any stones or nails which may have become embedded in the tire tread. If left, they will eventually penetrate through the casing and cause a puncture.
● If tire damage is apparent, or unexplained loss of pressure is experienced, seek the advice of a tire fitting specialist without delay.

Tire tread depth:

● Tires incorporate wear indicators in the tread. Identify the triangular pointer or 'TWI' mark on the tire sidewall to locate the indicator bar and replace the tire if the tread has worn down to the bar.

Tire pressures*

Tire pressures (COLD)

1970 through 1978
    Front .... 24 psi (1.66 Bars)
    Rear .... 30 psi (2.07 Bars)
1979 through 1985
    Front .... 26 psi (1.79 Bars)
    Rear .... 30 to 32 psi (2.07 to 2.21 Bars)*
1986-on
    883 cc engine through 1990
        Front .... 26 psi (1.79 Bars)
        Rear .... 30 to 32 psi (2.07 to 2.21 Bars)*
    1200cc engine and 1981-on 883 cc engine
        Front .... 30 psi (2.07 Bars)
        Rear .... 36 to 40 psi (2.48 to 2.76 Bars)*

Lower number up to 300 lbs (136 kg) load (rider, passenger and cargo). Higher number up to maximum rated load.

1 Check the tire pressures when the tires are **cold** and keep them properly inflated.

2 Measure tread depth at the center of the tire using a tread depth gauge.

3 Tire tread wear indicator bar and its location marking (usually either an arrow, a triangle or the letters TWI) on the sidewall.

Chapter 1
Tune-up and routine maintenance

Contents

Degrees of difficulty

Easy, suitable for novice with little experience	**Fairly easy,** suitable for beginner with some experience	**Fairly difficult,** suitable for competent DIY mechanic 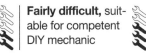	**Difficult,** suitable for experienced DIY mechanic 	**Very difficult,** suitable for expert DIY or professional

Specifications

Engine

Spark plugs
  Type
    1970 through 1979.. Harley-Davidson no. 4 or 4R (resistor type)
    1980 and 1981 .... Harley-Davidson no. 4-5
    1980 through 1985... Harley-Davidson no. 4R5 (resistor type)
    1986 and later .... Harley-Davidson no. 6R12 (no substitutes)
  Gap
    No. 4 and 4R
      1970 through 1978 .... 0.025 to 0.030 inch (0.635 to 0.762 mm)
      1979 .... 0.060 inch (1.524 mm)
    No. 4-5, 4R5 and 6R12 .... 0.038 to 0.043 inch (0.97 to 1.09 mm)
Valve clearance (Shovelhead engine only) .... No lash (pushrods just free to rotate)
Idle speed
  1970 through 1978 .... 900 to 1100 rpm
  1979 through 1987 .... 900 to 950 rpm
  1988 through1990 .... 1000 to 1050 rpm
  1991 and later .... 950 to 1050 rpm
Fast idle speed
  1979 through 1985 .... 1500 rpm
  1986 and 1987 .... 1500 to 1550 rpm
  1988 and later .... Not specified
Ignition timing speed
  1970 through 1982 .... Approximately 2000 rpm
  1983 through 1985 .... 1300 rpm
  1986 through 1994 all, 1995 US.................................. 1650 to 1950 rpm
  1995 international, all 1996 and later .... 1050 to 1500 rpm

Chassis

Drive chain freeplay
  1970 through 1985 .... 1/2-inch (12.70 mm)
  1986 and later .... 1/4-inch (6.350 mm)
Drive belt freeplay
  Through1999 .... 9/16 to 11/16-inch (14 to 17 mm)
  2000 and later
    883 Hugger, 883 Custom.. 1/4 to 5/16-inch (6.5 to 8 mm)
    883 standard, 1200 standard, 1200 Sport.................................... 5/16 to 3/8-inch (8 to 9.5mm)
Primary chain freeplay
  1970 through early 1984
    Cold engine.. 5/8 to 7/8 inch (15.9 to 22.2 mm)
    Hot engine.. 3/8 to 5/8 inch (9.5 to 15.9 mm)
  Late 1984 and later
    Cold engine.. 3/8 to 1/2-inch (9.53 to 12.7 mm)
    Hot engine.. 1/4 to 3/8-inch (6.35 to 9.53 mm)
Minimum brake lining thickness
  Drum brake shoes .... 0.080-inch (2 mm)
  Disc brake pads .... 1/16-inch (1.5 mm)
Tire pressures (COLD)
  1970 through 1978
    Front.. 24 psi (1.66 Bars)
    Rear... 30 psi (2.07 Bars)
  1979 through 1985
    Front.. 26 psi (1.79 Bars)
    Rear... 30 to 32 psi (2.07 to 2.21 Bars)
  1986 and later
    883 cc engine through 1990
      Front .... 26 psi (1.79 Bars)
      Rear .... 30 to 32 psi (2.07 to 2.21 Bars)
    1200 cc engine and 1991-on 883 cc engine
      Front .... 30 psi (2.07 Bars)
      Rear .... 36 to 40 psi 92.48 to 2.76 Bars)*
*Lower number up to 300 lbs (136 kg) load (rider, passenger and cargo). Higher number up to maximum rated load.
Tire tread depth (minimum)
  Front .... 1/16-inch (1.5 mm)
  Rear .... 3/32-inch (2.0 mm)

Torque specifications

Lifter adjusting locknut (Shovelhead engine only) .... 72 to 132 inch-lbs (8 to 15 Nm)
Primary chaincase drain plug .... 14 to 21 ft-lbs (19 to 28 Nm)
Outer clutch cover Torx bolts (later models) .... 84 to 108 inch-lbs (9 to 12 Nm)
Spark plugs
  Shovelhead engine.. 20 ft-lbs (27 Nm)
  Evolution engine.. 11 to 18 ft-lbs (15 to 24 Nm)
Rear axle nut... 60 to 65 ft-lbs (81 to 88 Nm)

Recommended lubricants and fluids

Engine oil

Shovelhead engine
  Oil type .... HD rating 360 or equivalent
  Normal 20 to 90-degrees F .... SAE 20W-50
  Below 40-degrees F... SAE 30
  Above 40-degrees F... SAE 40
  Above 80-degrees F... SAE 60
Evolution engine
  Oil type .... H-D rating 360 or equivalent
  Oil viscosity
    Below 40-degrees F (4-degrees C)... H.D. Multi-Grade, SAE 10W-40
    Above 40-degrees F (4-degrees C) .... H.D. Multi-Grade, SAE 20W-50
    Above 60-degrees F (16-degrees C) .... H.D. Regular Heavy, SAE 50
    Above 80-degrees F (27-degrees C) .... H.D. Extra Heavy, SAE 60
Oil capacity .... 3 US qt (2.8 liters)*
*If the motorcycle has a spin-on filter, subtract the amount poured into the filter before it was installed.

Transmission oil

Type

1970 through early 1984	Harley-Davidson Power Blend Super Premium or equivalent (20W-50 above 40-degrees F, 60W below 40-degrees F)
Late 1984 and 1985	Harley-Davidson Front Chaincase Lubricant (part no. 99887-84)
1986 and later	Harley-Davidson Sport Trans Fluid

Capacity

1970 through 1990	24 US fl oz (710 cc)
1991 through 1997	40 US fl oz (1183 cc)
1998 and later	32 US fl oz (946 cc)

Brake fluid

Type	DOT 3 (early models), DOT 5 (later models)

 Warning: Do not mix fluid types. If not known, fully drain the fluid and have the system flushed before refilling. Refer to the manufacturer's fluid recommendation stamped on the reservoir cap or cover.

Fork oil

Type

1970 through 1978	Harley-Davidson Type B fork oil or equivalent
1979 and later	Harley-Davidson Type E fork oil or equivalent

Amount

1970 through 1983

Drain and fill	5 fl oz (148 cc)
After overhaul	6 fl oz (177cc)

1984 through 1987

Drain and fill	5.4 fl oz (160 cc)
After overhaul	6.4 fl oz (189cc)

1988 and later

All except 1992 through 1998 883 Hugger and 1995-on XL1200S

Drain and fill	9 fl oz (266 cc)
After overhaul	10.2 fl oz (302cc)

1992 through 1998 883 Hugger and 1995-on XL1200S

Drain and fill	10.7 fl oz (316 cc)
After overhaul	12.1 fl oz (358cc)

Final drive chain

Conventional chain..	Harley-Davidson Chain Spray (part no. 99870-58) or High Performance Chain Lube Plus (part no. 99865-81)
O-ring chain...	High Performance Chain Lube Plus (part no. 99865-81) or API GL-5 gear lube SAE 80 or 90
Steering head bearings..	Harley-Davidson Special Purpose Grease or equivalent
Sidestand..	Loctite Aerosol Anti-Seize or equivalent
Swingarm pivot bearings	Medium weight, lithium-based multi-purpose grease
Throttle grip	Graphite grease
Cables and lever pivots	Harley-Davidson Super Oil or equivalent
Brake pedal/shift lever pivots	Medium weight, lithium-based multi-purpose grease

1

Component locations - right-hand side (late 1200 model shown)

1	Oil tank filler plug	3	Front brake fluid reservoir
2	Air cleaner	4	Right drivebelt adjuster

5	Rear brake master cylinder reservoir
6	Right fork leg drain plug

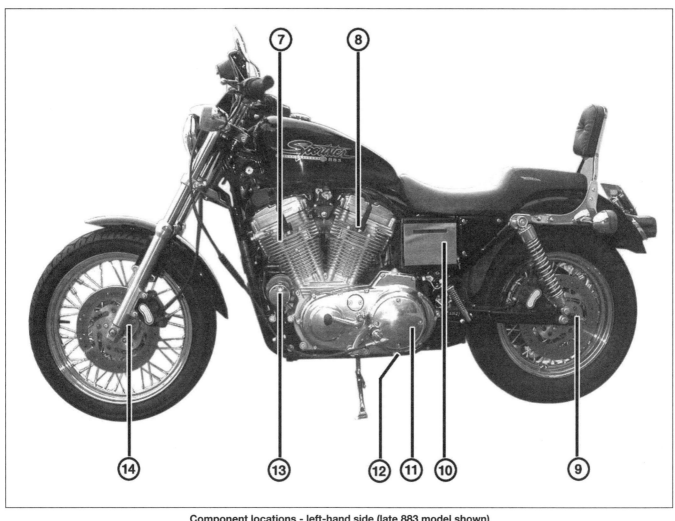

Component locations - left-hand side (late 883 model shown)

7	Front spark plug	10	Battery	13	Engine oil filter
8	Rear spark plug	11	Clutch inspection cover	14	Clutch cable adjuster
9	Left drivebelt adjuster	12	Transmission oil drain plug	15	Left fork leg drain plug

1

1 Harley Sportster - Routine maintenance intervals

Note: *The pre-ride inspection outlined in the owner's manual covers checks and maintenance that should be carried out on a daily basis. It's condensed and included here to remind you of its importance. Always perform the pre-ride inspection at every maintenance interval (in addition to the procedures listed).*

Daily or before riding

☐ Check the engine oil level
☐ Check the fuel level and inspect for leaks
☐ Check the operation of both brakes - also check the fluid level and look for leakage (disc brakes)
☐ Check the tires for damage, the presence of foreign objects and correct air pressure
☐ Check the throttle for smooth operation and correct freeplay
☐ Check the operation of the clutch - make sure the freeplay is correct
☐ Make sure the steering operates smoothly, without looseness and without binding
☐ Check for proper operation of the headlight, taillight, brake light, turn signals, indicator lights, speedometer and horn
☐ Make sure the sidestand returns to its fully up position and stays there under spring pressure
☐ Make sure the engine STOP switch works properly
☐ Lubricate the final drive chain (early models) and check play
☐ Check deflection of the final drive belt

After the initial 1,000 miles (1600 km)

This service is usually performed by a dealer service department, since the bike is still under warranty. It consists of all of the daily checks plus:
☐ All of the 5000 mile checks
☐ Fastener torque check
☐ Sidestand lubrication
☐ Check the condition of the contact breaker points (1970 through 1976 models only) (Section 11)

Every 300 miles (500 km)

☐ Lubricate the drive chain (without automatic oiler) and check play (chain drive models) (Section 3)
☐ Check engine oil level in the oil tank (Section 4)

Every 1,000 miles (1,600 km)

☐ Clean and oil the metal mesh air cleaner element (Section 5)
☐ Inspect the brakes and adjust drum brakes (Section 6)
☐ Check the automatic chain oiler (1970 through 1976 models) (Section 7)
☐ Inspect the wheel and tires (Section 8)

Every 2000 miles (3200 km)

☐ Change the engine oil and clean the filter (in-tank filter models) (Section 9)
☐ Adjust the valve clearance (Shovelhead models) (Section 10)
☐ Inspect and adjust the breaker points (Section 11)

Every 2,500 miles (4,000 km)

☐ Check transmission oil level (Section 4)
☐ Check the drive belt tension (Section 12)
☐ Inspect and clean the air filter element (1972 and later models) (Section 5)
☐ Check/adjust the throttle operation and freeplay (Section 13)
☐ Check/adjust choke knob tension (Section 14)
☐ Check the fuel system for leaks (Section 15)
☐ Check the evaporative emission control system (California models) (Section 16)
☐ Check the external oil lines for leaks (Section 17)
☐ Check tightness of all fasteners except head bolts (Section 18)
☐ Inspect the battery (Section 19)
☐ Operate and check all electrical equipment (Section 20)

Every 5,000 miles (8,000 km)

☐ Change the engine oil and replace the filter (spin-on filter models) (Section 9)
☐ Change the transmission/primary chaincase oil (Section 21)
☐ Check the primary chain deflection (Section 22)
☐ Adjust the clutch freeplay (Section 23)
☐ Check the drive belt and sprockets for wear (belt final drive models) (Section 12)
☐ Check the brake fluid level and condition (Section 4)
☐ Lubricate the steering head bearings through the grease fitting (Section 24)
☐ Lubricate the cables and lever pivots (Section 25)
☐ Inspect the spark plugs (Section 26)
☐ Check/adjust the idle speed (Section 27)
☐ Check/adjust ignition timing (electronic ignition models) (Section 28)

Every 10,000 miles (16,000 km)

All of the items above plus:
☐ Replace the spark plugs (Section 26)
☐ Check the exhaust system for leaks and check the tightness of the fasteners (Section 29)
☐ Check the steering head bearing adjustment (Section 30)
☐ Check the suspension (Section 31)
☐ Repack the swingarm and wheel bearings (Section 32)
☐ Inspect the fuel supply valve filter screen (Section 33)
☐ Change the fork oil (Section 34)

2 Introduction to tune-up and routine maintenance

1   This Chapter covers in detail the checks and procedures necessary for the tune-up and routine maintenance of your motorcycle. Section 1 includes the routine maintenance schedule, which is designed to keep the machine in proper running condition and prevent possible problems. The remaining Sections contain detailed procedures for carrying out the items listed on the maintenance schedule, as well as additional maintenance information designed to increase reliability.

2   Since routine maintenance plays such an important role in the safe and efficient operation of your motorcycle, it is presented here as a comprehensive checklist. For the rider who does all of the bike's maintenance, these lists outline the procedures and checks that should be done on a routine basis.

3   Maintenance and safety information is printed on decals in various locations on the motorcycle. If the information on the decals differs from that included here, use the information on the decal.

4   Deciding where to start or plug into the routine maintenance schedule depends on several factors. If you have a motorcycle whose warranty has recently expired, and if it has been maintained according to the warranty standards, you may want to pick up routine maintenance as it coincides with the next mileage or calendar interval. If you have owned the machine for some time but have never performed any maintenance on it, then you may want to start at the nearest interval and include some additional procedures to ensure that nothing important is overlooked. If you have just had a major engine overhaul, then you may want to start the maintenance routine from the beginning. If you have a used machine and have no knowledge of its history or maintenance record, you may desire to combine all the checks into one large service initially and then settle into the maintenance schedule prescribed.

5   The Sections which outline the inspection and maintenance procedures are written as step-by-step comprehensive guides to the performance of the work. They explain in detail each of the routine inspections and maintenance procedures on the check list. References to additional information in applicable Chapters are also included and should not be overlooked.

6   Before beginning any maintenance or repair, the machine should be cleaned thoroughly, especially around the oil filter, spark plugs, valve covers, side covers, carburetor, etc. Cleaning will help ensure that dirt does not contaminate the engine and will allow you to detect wear and damage that could otherwise easily go unnoticed.

Every 300 miles (500 km)

3 Final drive chain - check, adjustment and lubrication

1   Early models use chain final drive. Later models use a cogged belt.

Check

2   A neglected drive chain won't last long and can quickly damage the countershaft and rear wheel sprockets. Routine chain adjustment and lubrication isn't difficult and will ensure maximum chain and sprocket life.

3   To check the chain, place the motorcycle upright with a rider sitting on the seat and shift the transmission into Neutral. Make sure the ignition switch is Off.

4   Check for the specified freeplay (slack) at the lower chain run, midway between the sprockets. Chains usually don't wear evenly, so rotate the rear wheel and check the freeplay in a number of places. As wear occurs, the chain will actually get longer, which means that adjustment usually involves removing some slack from the chain. In some cases where lubrication has been neglected, corrosion and galling may cause the links to bind and kink, which effectively shortens the chain. If the chain is tight between the sprockets, rusty, or kinked, it's time to replace it with a new one.

5   After checking the slack, grasp the chain where it wraps around the rear sprocket and try to pull it away from the sprocket. If more than 1/4-inch of play is evident, the chain is excessively worn and should be replaced with a new one.

Adjustment

6   Rotate the rear wheel until the chain is positioned where the least amount of slack is present.

7   Loosen the axle nut **(see illustration)**. On 1977 and earlier models, loosen the brake anchor bolt also.

8   Turn the axle adjusting nuts on both sides of the rear wheel until the proper chain tension is attained. Be sure to turn both adjusting nuts the same amount to keep the rear wheel in alignment. If the adjusting nuts reach the end of their travel, the chain is probably excessively worn and should be replaced with a new one. An accurate method of checking the alignment of the rear wheel is to measure the center-to-center distance between the swingarm pivot bolt and the rear axle on both sides of the motorcycle. When the distances are equal, the rear wheel (and thus the chain and sprockets) should be properly aligned.

9   Tighten the axle nut and anchor bolt (where applicable). Recheck the chain tension.

Lubrication

10   Pre-1977 models are equipped with an automatic chain oiler; refer to Section 4 for maintenance and adjustment procedures.

Conventional chain

11   The best time to lubricate the chain is after the motorcycle has been ridden. When the chain is warm, the lubricant will penetrate the joints between the side plates, pins, bushings and rollers to provide lubrication of the internal load bearing areas. Use a good quality chain lubricant and apply to the area where the side plates overlap - not the mid-

3.7 Loosen the axle nut (1) and tighten the chain adjusters (2) to take slack out of the chain

1

dle of the rollers. After applying the lubricant, let it soak in for a few minutes before wiping off any excess.

12   If the chain is extremely dirty, it should be removed and cleaner before it's lubricated. Remove the master link retaining clip with pliers. Be careful not to bend or twist it. Slide out the master link and remove the chain from the sprockets. Clean the chain and master link thoroughly with solvent. Use a small brush to remove caked-on dirt. Wipe off the solvent, hang up the chain and allow it to dry.

O-ring chain

13   Later models (circa 1992) are equipped with an O-ring chain as standard equipment. Lubricant is sealed in the rollers by O-rings and thus, lubrication is only required on its outer working surfaces. Take care to use only a lubricant marked as suitable for O-ring chains - other lubricants will cause damage to the O-rings.

14   If the chain is excessively dirty, it can be detached from its sprockets and cleaned in kerosene - don't use any strong solvents or gasoline for cleaning, otherwise the O-rings will deteriorate. When dry apply fresh lubricant to the outer rollers and side plates.

Both chain types

15   Inspect the chain for wear and damage. Look for cracked rollers and side plates and check for excessive looseness between the links. To check for overall wear, lay the chain on a clean, flat surface in a straight line. Push the ends together to take up all the slack between the links, then measure the overall length. Pull the chain ends apart as far as possible and measure the overall length again. Subtract the two measurements to determine the difference in the compressed and stretched lengths. If the difference, which is an indication of wear, is greater

than 3 per cent of the chain's nominal length, it's excessively worn and should be replaced with a new one.

16   Check the master link, especially the clip, for damage. A new master link should be used whenever the chain is reassembled.

17   Check the sprockets for wear (see Chapter 5). Replace worn sprockets with new ones. Never put a new chain on worn sprockets or a worn chain on new sprockets. Both chain and sprockets must be in good condition or the new parts will wear rapidly.

18   Reposition the chain on the sprockets and insert the master link. This should be done with both ends of the chain adjacent to each other on the back side of the rear wheel sprocket. On O-ring chains, be careful to position the O-ring correctly when assembling the master link. **Note:** *Make sure the closed end of the master link clip points in the direction of chain travel* **(see illustration)**.

19   Lubricate and adjust the chain as previously described.

4   Fluid levels - check

Engine oil

1   Engine oil level should be checked before every ride as described in *Daily (pre-ride) checks* at the beginning of this manual, as well as at the specified maintenance intervals.

Transmission/chaincase oil

2   Transmission oil level should be checked at the specified maintenance intervals.

3   Support the bike securely upright.

4   Remove the oil fill plug and the level

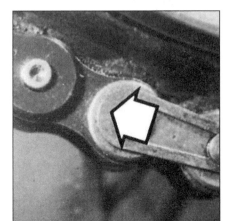

3.18 The closed end of the spring clip MUST face the direction of chain travel (arrow)

plug (if equipped) from the chaincase. On models through 1990 the level plug is positioned directly under the shift lever shaft, while on 1991 and later models it's at the rear of the chaincase **(see illustrations)**.

5   If the chaincase is equipped with a level plug, the oil level should be up to the bottom of the plug hole. On later models without an oil level plug, remove the outer clutch cover; the oil level should be up to the bottom of the clutch diaphragm spring.

6   If necessary, add oil of the type listed in this Chapter's Specifications. Don't overfill the transmission.

7   Tighten the oil fill plug (and level plug, if equipped) securely. If there's no level plug, tighten the outer clutch cover to the torque listed in the Chapter 2 Specifications.

Brake fluid (disc brake models)

8   Fluid level in the front and rear brake

4.4a The transmission/chaincase oil level should be at the bottom the opening with the motorcycle upright - models through 1990

1   Oil fill plug   *2   Oil level plug*

4.4b Transmission oil fill plug (1), level plug (some models) (2) and drain plug (3) - 1991 and later models

master cylinders should be checked before every ride as described in *Daily (pre-ride) checks* at the beginning of this manual, as well as at the specified maintenance intervals.

9   Also check the brake fluid for signs of contamination. If the fluid is contaminated, bleed all of it out and replace it with new fluid (see Chapter 6).

 Warning: Do not mix fluid types. If not known, fully drain the fluid and have the system flushed before refilling. Refer to the manufacturer's fluid recommendation stamped on the reservoir cap or cover.

Battery electrolyte (1970 through 1996)

 Warning: Be extremely careful when working around the battery. The electrolyte is very caustic and an explosive gas is given off when the battery is charging.

10   To check the electrolyte level in the battery, remove the side cover. The level should be between the upper and lower level marks printed on the outside of the battery case.

11   If the electrolyte is at or below the lower mark, the battery must be removed to add more water. If necessary, refer to Section 18

for this procedure.

12   With the battery removed form the motorcycle, remove each cell cap and add enough distilled water to each cell to bring the level up to the upper mark. Do not overfill. Also, do not use tap water, except in an emergency, as it will shorten the life of the battery. The cell holes are quite small so it may help to use a plastic squeeze bottle with a small spout to add the water. **Note:** *Be sure the vent hose is properly routed.*

13   The battery should periodically receive a thorough inspection, including a check of the electrolyte specific gravity. Refer to Section 18 for these procedures.

Every 1,000 miles (500 km)

5   Air filter element - servicing

 If you're using compressed air to clean the element, place your hand, a rag or a piece of cardboard on the inside of the element to keep dust and debris from being blown from one side of the element into the other.

1   Remove the cover screws or Allen bolts and lift off the air filter cover **(see illustrations)**. Some models have a baffle plate or seal band inside the cover.

2   The air cleaner element used on 1970 and 1971 models is made of metal mesh. It should be removed, washed in a non-flammable solvent and saturated with clean engine oil after it has been allowed to dry. This type of service should be performed at least every 1000 miles and more often in dusty conditions.

3   Wipe out the housing and cover with a

clean rag, then place a clean rag in the carburetor opening to keep out dirt.

4   Wash the element in soap and lukewarm water. Don't tap the element on a hard surface to remove the dirt. Finish cleaning by blowing low-pressure compressed air from the inside of the element to the outside, or else let it air dry.

5   After cleaning, hold the element up to a bright light. The light should pass evenly through the element (any darker areas are still dirty).

6   On 1972 through 1989 models, apply 1-1/4 tablespoons of engine oil to the element with an atomizer or work the oil into the foam by hand. Squeeze out any excess oil, then install the filter and other components.

7   Check the gasket, cover O-ring and breather tubes for damage or deterioration and replace them as needed. If you're working on a later California model, make sure the door for the evaporative emission control system moves freely.

8   Reinstall the filter by reversing the removal procedure. Make sure the element is seated properly and securely connected to

the breather tubes in the filter housing before installing the cover. On 1991 and later models, position the round holes in the back of the air cleaner over the bolts heads **(see illustration)**.

6   Brake system - check and adjustment

1   A routine general check of the brakes will ensure that any problems are discovered and remedied before the rider's safety is jeopardized.

2   Check the brake lever and pedal for loose connections, excessive play, bends, and other damage. Replace any damaged parts with new ones (see Chapter 6).

3   Make sure all brake fasteners are tight. On disc brake models, check the brake pads for wear as described below and make sure the fluid level in the reservoir is correct (see *Daily (pre-ride) checks* at the beginning of this manual). Look for leaks at the hose con-

1

5.1a Remove the cover screws or bolts and lift off the cover. . .

5.1b . . . for access to the air filter element

5.8 Circular holes in element rear surface must locate over bolt heads (1991-on models)

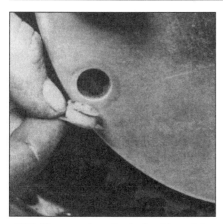

6.11 The rear drum brake backing plate has a small plug that can be removed to check the thickness of the brake shoe linings

6.12a On single-piston front calipers, pad lining thickness (arrows) can be checked without removing the caliper

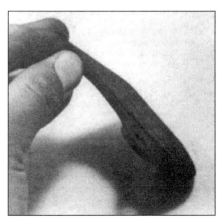

6.12b If the pads are allowed to wear to this extent, you risk damage to the disc(s)

6.12c On four-piston calipers, the front pads (arrow) are inspected from below and the rear pads are inspected from above

7.1 Automatic drive chain oiler (arrow)

nections and check for cracks in the hoses. If the lever is spongy, bleed the brakes as described in Chapter 6.

4   Make sure the brake light operates when the front brake lever is depressed.

5   Make sure the brake light is activated when the rear brake pedal is depressed.

6   On disc brake models, neither brake light switch is adjustable. If a front switch fails to operate properly, replace it with a new one (see Chapter 8). If a rear switch, which detects hydraulic pressure in the rear brake line, fails to operate properly, bleed the rear brake (see Chapter 6). If that doesn't solve the problem, replace the switch with a new one (see Chapter 8).

Drum brake adjustment

7   On front drum brakes, the brakes should begin to drag when the lever has reached about 1/4 of its travel. If not, loosen the cable locknut and turn the adjusting nut to achieve the correct amount of play, then tighten the locknut. Check to make sure the brakes release completely.

8   Operate the pedal while rolling the bike forward. The brake linings should begin to make contact with the drum when the pedal has been pressed 1-1/4 inches. Tighten or loosen the brake adjusting nut to achieve the specified travel.

Drum brake wear check

9   The front brake can be withdrawn from the front hub after the axle has been pulled out and the wheel removed from the forks. Refer to Chapter 6 for the front wheel removal procedures.

10   Examine the brake shoe linings. If they're thin or worn unevenly, they should be replaced with new ones.

11   Some drum brake models have an inspection hole in the backing plate - remove the plug (see illustration) and check the brake shoe lining thickness by looking through the hole. However, it's a good idea to remove the wheel to do a thorough inspection. Refer to Chapter 6 for the wheel

removal procedure. If the linings are worn unevenly or worn to the specified service limit, they should be replaced with new ones.

Disc brake wear check

12   Front brake pad wear can be checked without removing the calipers (see illustrations). The brake pads should have at least the specified minimum amount of lining material remaining on the metal backing plate.

13   If the pads are worn excessively, they must be replaced with new ones (see Chapter 6).

14   On 1979 through 1981 models, as well as 2000 and later models, refer to Steps 12 and 13 above to inspect the rear brake (the calipers are very similar). On 1982 through 1999 models, remove the calipers to examine the brake pads (see Chapter 6).

Rear disc brake pedal

15   Rear brake pedal position and play are not adjustable.

16   Operate the brake pedal and check for excessive play. If you find this problem,

bleed the brakes (see Chapter 6). If that doesn't help, overhaul the rear master cylinder and caliper (see Chapter 6).

---

7   Automatic drive chain oiler - maintenance and adjustment

1   Many 1970 through 1976 models are equipped with an automatic rear drive chain oiler (see illustration). The oiler is exposed to the elements so it must be kept clean and properly adjusted.

2   Loosen the locknut and turn the oiler adjusting screw until it bottoms on the seat. Note: Keep track of the number of turns required to bottom the adjuster.

3   Completely unscrew the adjuster and blow the orifice out with compressed air.

4   Install the adjusting screw and turn it in until it bottoms, then back it out to its original position (the same number of turns written down in Step 2). The normal setting is 1/4-turn open. Tighten the locknut.

5   The oiler should release two or three drops of oil per minute. Turn the adjusting screw in if less oil is desired; turn it out if more oil is needed.

8 Tires/wheels - general check

1   Routine tire and wheel checks should be made with the realization that your safety depends to a great extent on their condition.
2   Check the tires carefully for cuts, tears, embedded nails or other sharp objects and excessive wear. Operation of the motorcycle with excessively worn tires is extremely hazardous, as traction and handling are directly affected. Check the wear indicators molded into the tire, referring to the illustration in *Daily (pre-ride) checks* at the beginning of this manual, and replace worn tires with new ones when the indicators are worn away.
Note: *In the UK, tread depth must be at least 1 mm over 3/4 of the tread breadth all the way around the tire, with no bald patches. Many riders, however, consider 2 mm tread depth minimum to be a safer limit. German law requires a minimum of 1.6 mm.*
3   Repair or replace punctured tires as soon as damage is noted. Do not try to patch a torn tire, as wheel balance and tire reliability may be impaired.
4   Check the tire pressures when the tires are cold and keep them properly inflated. Proper air pressure will increase tire life and provide maximum stability and ride comfort. Keep in mind that low tire pressures may cause the tire to slip on the rim or come off, while high tire pressures will cause abnormal tread wear and unsafe handling.

Cast wheels

5   The cast wheels used on some models are virtually maintenance free, but they should be kept clean and checked periodically for cracks and other damage. Never attempt to repair damaged cast wheels; they must be replaced with new ones.
6   Check the valve stem locknuts to make sure they are tight. Also, make sure the valve stem cap is in place and tight. If it is missing, install a new one made of metal or hard plastic.

Wire wheels

7   The wire wheels used on some models

8.7 Check the tension of the spokes periodically, but don't over-tighten them

should be checked periodically for cracks, bending, loose spokes and corrosion. Never attempt to repair damaged wheels; they must be replaced with new ones. Loose spokes can be tightened with a spoke wrench **(see illustration)**, but be careful not to overtighten and distort the wheel rim.

Every 2,000 miles (3,200 km)

9 Engine oil and filter - change

1   Consistent routine oil and filter changes are the single most important maintenance procedure you can perform on a motorcycle. The oil not only lubricates the internal parts of the engine, transmission and clutch, but it also acts as a coolant, a cleaner, a sealant, and a protectant. Because of these demands, the oil takes a terrific amount of abuse and should be replaced often with new oil of the recommended grade and type. Saving a little money on the difference in cost between a good oil and a cheap oil won't pay off if the engine is damaged.
2   Before changing the oil and filter, warm up the engine so the oil will drain easily. Be careful when draining the oil, as the exhaust pipes, the engine, and the oil itself can cause severe burns.
3   Prop the motorcycle upright over a clean drain pan. Remove the oil filler cap/dipstick from the oil tank to act as a reminder that there is no oil in the engine (see *Daily (pre-ride) checks* at the front of this manual for dipstick location if necessary).
4   Remove the oil tank drain plug (if equipped) from the tank and allow the oil to drain into the pan **(see illustration)**. Discard the sealing washer on the drain plug; it should be replaced whenever the plug is removed. On later models without an oil tank drain plug, disconnect the oil tank drain hose form the lug at the rear muffler mount and lower the disconnected end of the hose into the drain pan.
5   On early models, lift the oil filter out of the tank after the oil has drained **(see illustration)**. The filter is housed in a cartridge and can be removed after detaching the filter clip and sealing washer from the upper end of the cartridge tube. The filter element should be replaced with a new one every time the oil is changed. When replacing the element, make sure the O-ring is positioned correctly on the cartridge tube flange. The correct order of assembly within the cartridge tube is: tube seal, spring, lower filter retainer, filter element, sealing washer and spring clip.
6   On later models, the oil filter is a conventional external spin-on type, mounted on a bracket between the engine and oil tank, on the lower left front engine bracket or

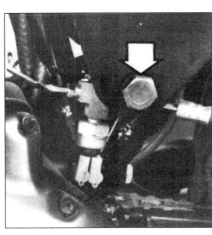

9.4 Typical oil tank drain location (arrow)

9.5 On early models, lift the filter cartridge out of the oil tank

1

9.6 The external oil filter is attached to the frame or engine, depending on year (1980-1981 model shown)

9.9 Smear a film of clean oil onto the gasket surface

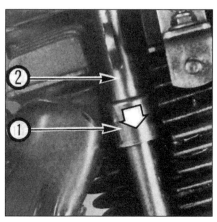

10.3 Push down on the spring retainer (1) and pull out the keeper (2) . . .

directly on the front of the engine (see illustration). Unscrew the filter with a filter wrench or strap wrench.

7   If additional maintenance is planned for this time period, check or service another component while the oil is allowed to drain completely.

8   Check the condition of the drain plug threads (if equipped with a drain plug). Replace the plug if they're damaged. Slip a new sealing washer over the drain plug, then install and tighten the plug to the torque listed in this Chapter's Specifications. Avoid overtightening, as damage to the oil tank will result.

 If the motorcycle has a spin-on filter, hold the filter with the open end upright and pour about four fl oz (120 cc) of clean engine oil into the filter. This will reduce the time required for the oil pressure light to go out.

9   If the motorcycle has a spin-on filter, wipe any remaining oil off the filter sealing area of the crankcase. Coat the gasket on a new filter with clean engine oil (see illustration). Install the filter and tighten it to the amount listed in this Chapter's Specifications.

 Before refilling the oil tank, check the old oil carefully. If the oil was drained into a clean pan, small pieces of metal or other material can be easily detected. If the oil is very metallic colored, then the engine is experiencing wear from break-in (new engine) or from insufficient lubrication. If there are flakes or chips of metal in the oil, then something is drastically wrong internally and the engine will have to be disassembled for inspection and repair.

10   If the inspection of the oil turns up nothing unusual, refill the oil tank to the proper level with the recommended oil and install the filler cap. Start the engine and let it run for two or three minutes. Shut it off, wait a few minutes, then check the oil level. If necessary, add more oil to bring the level up to

the Maximum mark. Check around the drain plug and filter housing for leaks.

11   The old oil drained from the engine cannot be reused in its present state and should be disposed of. Check with your local refuse disposal company, disposal facility or environmental agency to see whether they will accept the oil for recycling. Don't pour used oil into drains or onto the ground. After the oil has cooled, it can be drained into a suitable container (capped plastic jugs, topped bottles, milk cartons, etc.) for transport to one of these disposal sites.

10 Valve clearance adjustment (Shovelhead models only)

1   The valve clearances must be checked and adjusted with the engine cold.

2   Remove the spark plugs so the engine is easier to turn over.

3   Push down on the pushrod cover spring retainer and remove the keeper from the upper end to gain access to the lifters (see illustration).

4   The valve clearances are checked with the valves closed. This can be determined by turning the engine over by hand. Put the transmission in gear and turn the rear wheel forward while watching the lifters/pushrods for one particular cylinder - when the lifters move down in the bores and remain there, the valves for that cylinder are closed.

5   Hold the lower lifter cover up, out of the way (see illustration).

6   Loosen the locknut on the lifter adjusting screw.

7   Turn the adjusting screw into the lifter body until the pushrod can be moved up-and-down.

8   Slowly turn the adjusting screw out until the play between the adjusting screw and pushrod is nearly gone.

9   Tighten the locknut on the adjusting screw securely and check the pushrod. There should be no noticeable up-and-down play, but you should be able to rotate it with-

out any binding.

10   Adjust the remaining valve clearances in the same manner.

11   When all of the clearances are correct, install the pushrod covers. Installation is the reverse of removal - be sure the ends of the covers are seated properly against the washers.

11 Contact breaker points (1970 through 1978) - check and adjustment

1   If the contact breaker points are badly burned, pitted or worn, they should be replaced with a new set. This also applies if the fiber heel that rides on the breaker cam is badly worn.

2   Detach the point cover (see illustration). Prior to removal, mark the base plate in relation to the distributor body or engine side cover with a scribe or permanent felt-tip marker so the plate can be reinstalled in the same position. This will eliminate the need to retime the ignition after reassembly.

3   On 1970 models only, remove the two screws that secure the base plate to the distributor body. When the condenser wire and

10.5 . . . so the pushrod cover can be lifted up to get at the lifters (Shovelhead engine only)

11.2 The breaker point cover is retained by two screws

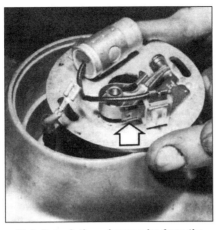

11.4 Detach the primary wire from the terminal (arrow), then remove the base plate with the points attached

11.7 Check the point gap with a feeler gauge - if the gap is correct, the feeler gauge will just slide between the contacts with a slight amount of drag

the external primary wire have been disconnected, the moving contact point will no longer be attached at the far end by its return spring so it can be lifted out of position. The fixed point can be detached by removing the screw that attaches it to the base plate. Note the arrangement of the various washers and insulators; if they're installed wrong, the points could short out, causing failure of the ignition system.

4 On 1971 and later models, remove the base plate mounting screws, lift out the base plate and disconnect the primary wire (see illustration).

5 Pull the condenser wire off the terminal post, unhooking the moving contact point return spring at the same time. Lift off the moving contact point and release the fixed contact by removing the single retaining screw through the base. Note the arrangement of the insulators and other washers to prevent them from being installed in the wrong order.

6 Installation is the reverse of the removal

steps. Make sure the insulators are installed in the correct positions. It's a good idea to place a small amount of distributor cam lube on the pivot pin before installing the moving contact arm.

7 Adjust the point gap with a feeler gauge when the points are completely opened by one of the cam lobes (see illustration).

8 Loosen the lock screw at the base of the fixed contact point and move the point by inserting a screwdriver into the adjusting slot and turning it (see illustration). Adjust the points until the specified gap is obtained, then retighten the lock screw and recheck the gap.

9 Turn the engine over until the points are completely opened by the other cam lobe and check the gap. The gap should be exactly the same for both cam lobes. If it isn't, the cam is worn and must be replaced with a new one.

11.8 Lockscrew (1) and breaker point adjusting slot (2) locations

1

Every 2,500 miles (4,000 km)

12 Final drive belt - tension check, adjustment and inspection

Check

1 Drive belt tension should be checked, and adjusted if necessary before every ride as described in *Daily (pre-ride) checks* at the beginning of this manual, as well as at the specified maintenance intervals.

2 The tension should be checked and adjusted with the bike on the ground and weight equivalent to the rider on the seat. The belt should be cold, so don't check tension or make the adjustment right after the bike has been ridden.

3 Harley-Davidson recommends using a

tension gauge to prevent the belt from being set too loose. This can allow the belt to jump one or more sprocket teeth, which will damage the belt.

4 To check belt tension, apply 10 lbs. (4.54 kg) upward pressure on the center of the lower belt run (at the point of the viewing window if equipped) and measure the amount the belt moves. Write this measurement down.

5 Roll the bike to change the belt position and repeat the measurement along every few inches of the belt. Do this along the entire belt until you locate the tightest point (where the belt moves least). At this point, compare the measurement to the range listed in this Chapter's Specifications.

6 If the belt is not within the specified range, adjust it.

Adjustment

7 Pull the cotter pin out of the axle nut, then loosen the nut.

8 Turn the belt adjuster bolts (at the rear of the swingarm, one on each side of the bike) in equal amounts until the belt tension is correct, then tighten the locknuts. Be sure to tighten or loosen the adjusters evenly so the rear wheel isn't cocked sideways.

9 Check the belt tension.

10 Tighten the rear axle locknut to the initial torque listed in this Chapter's Specifications, then install the cotter pin. If necessary, tighten the nut just enough to align the holes so the cotter pin can be installed, but don't exceed the maximum torque listed in this Chapter's Specifications.

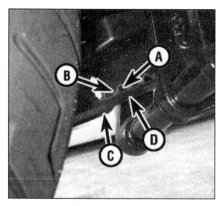

12.11 Check the drive belt for wear and damage

A) *Hairline cracks and minor chipping in the internal areas of the teeth (not the outer surface) are acceptable, but check the belt often*

B) *Cracks or other damage to the tooth surfaces require belt replacement*

C) *Frayed edges or a beveled outer edge are acceptable, but check the belt often*

D) *Stone damage in the center of the belt is acceptable, but replace the belt if stone damage is on the edge*

 Warning: Overtightening the nut could cause the rear wheel bearings to seize, resulting in loss of control of the motorcycle.

Inspection

11   Place the transmission in neutral and support the bike with the rear wheel off the ground. Rotate the rear wheel slowly and check each belt and sprocket tooth for wear or damage **(see illustration)**. The following conditions don't require belt replacement, but the belt should be given frequent, complete inspections:

a) *Hairline cracks in the internal portion of the belt teeth (if the cracks don't penetrate the outer layer of the tooth - the layer that contacts the sprocket)*

b) *Minor chips in the internal tooth material at the ends of teeth*

c) *Frayed fabric along the edges, with strands of cord exposed*

d) *Bevel wear of the outer edge of the belt*

e) *Stone damage in the middle of the belt*

12   The following conditions require belt replacement:

a) *Cracks that penetrate the outer layer of a tooth*

b) *Missing teeth*

c) *Hook (uneven) wear of teeth*

d) *Outer layer of teeth worn through*

e) *Stone damage on the edge of the belt*

13   Check the sprocket teeth for chips and other damage, especially if the damaged area has sharp edges. If the damage is severe enough that it has left a pattern on the belt, replace the belt and sprockets.

14   If teeth are missing or heavily damaged,

13.13a Slide back the rubber boots for access to the throttle cable adjusters

replace the belt and sprockets.

15   Check the chrome surface of the sprockets for wear. If you can't tell whether the chrome has worn off, drag a sharp tool (knife tip or nail) across the surface in the valley between two teeth. If the chrome is good, it won't be visibly scratched by the tool. If the chrome has worn away and the aluminum is exposed, the tool will leave a shiny scratch. In this case, replace the belt and sprockets.

13 Throttle operation/grip freeplay - check and adjustment

Check

1   With the engine stopped, make sure the throttle grip rotates easily from fully closed to fully open with the front wheel turned at various angles. The grip should return automatically from fully open to fully closed when released. If the throttle sticks, check the throttle cables for cracks or kinks in the housings. Also, make sure the inner cables are clean and well-lubricated.

2   Check for a small amount of freeplay at the grip and compare the freeplay to the value listed in this Chapter's Specifications.

Adjustment

Spiral throttle control

3   Early models use a spiral-type throttle control with a single throttle cable. It can be identified by the screw in the end of the grip (drum type throttle controls have an end cap, rather than an end screw).

4   When turned by hand and released, the throttle grip must return to the closed (idle) position. There should be 1/4-inch between the carburetor control clip and throttle control coil with the throttle closed. If not, or if the grip turns stiffly, the grip should be disassembled, cleaned and inspected (see Chapter 3).

Single cable, drum type throttle control

5   When turned by hand and released, the

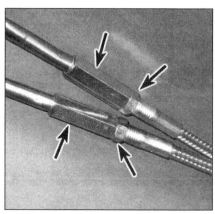

13.13b Loosen the locknuts (right arrows) and turn the adjusters (left arrows)

throttle grip must return to the closed (idle) position. If it doesn't return freely, back off the friction screw until it does.

6   If the throttle grip turns stiffly, or if backing off the friction screw doesn't cause it to return freely, it should be disassembled, cleaned and inspected (see Chapter 3).

7   Locate the throttle cable's connection at the carburetor. Watch it while turning the handlebars all the way from full left to full right lock. The inner cable should not pull on the carburetor lever as the handlebars are turned.

8   If it does, loosen the knurled round locknut on the cable adjuster (not the hex locknut on the elbow fitting). Turn the adjuster to change the cable's effective length, then tighten the locknut. Recheck as described in Step 7.

9   Center the front wheel in the straight-ahead position and open the throttle all the way. The carburetor throttle lever should reach the full-open position as the grip reaches the end of its travel. If not, adjust the stop screw on the underside of the grip with a 2 mm Allen wrench. Don't allow the grip to have remaining travel when the carburetor is all the way open, or the cable will be damaged by the strain.

Dual cables (1981 and later models)

Note: *These motorcycles use two throttle cables - a throttle (pull) cable and an idle (push) cable.*

10   Start freeplay adjustments at the throttle end of the cables. Loosen the locknut on each cable where it leaves the handlebar. Turn the adjusters to eliminate all throttle grip play, but leave the locknuts loose for the time being.

11   While holding the throttle wide open, make sure the cam on the throttle pulley just touches its stop. If necessary, turn the adjuster on the throttle cable to change the position of the throttle pulley cam. Once this is done, tighten the throttle cable locknut.

12   Release the throttle grip and turn the handlebars all the way to full right lock.

13   Turn the idle cable adjuster at the handlebar while watching the cable housing at the carburetor or throttle body **(see illustra-**

tions). The adjustment is correct when the cable housing just touches the spring inside the cable tube on the cable bracket.

14 Make sure the throttle pulley returns to idle when the throttle grip is in the closed throttle position.

! *Warning: Turn the handlebars all the way through their travel with the engine idling. Idle speed should not change. If it does, the cables may be routed incorrectly. Correct this condition before riding the bike.*

14 Choke knob - check

1 Inspect the choke knob and cable. The choke should pull out easily and stay out by itself.

2 If the knob doesn't operate correctly, loosen the hex nut behind the mounting bracket. Hold the cable with a wrench on the cable flats and adjust the knob's tension with the plastic knurled nut behind the knob. If this doesn't help, check the plunger bushing for wear or damage and replace as necessary. Don't lubricate the cable.

15 Fuel system - check

! *Warning: Gasoline is extremely flammable, so take extra precautions when you work on any part of the fuel system. Don't smoke or allow open flames or bare light bulbs near the work area, and don't work in a garage where a gas-type appliance (such as a water heater or clothes dryer) is present. If you spill any fuel on your skin, rinse it off immediately with soap and water. When you perform*

any kind of work on the fuel system, wear safety glasses and have a fire extinguisher suitable for a class B type fire (flammable liquids) on hand.

1 Check the fuel tank, the fuel supply valve on the underside of the fuel tank, the lines and the carburetor for leaks and evidence of damage (see illustration).

2 If carburetor gaskets are leaking, the carburetor(s) should be disassembled and rebuilt by referring to Chapter 3.

3 If the fuel supply valve is leaking at the lever, the valve should be disassembled and repaired or replaced with a new one.

4 If the fuel lines are cracked or otherwise deteriorated, replace them with new ones.

16 Evaporative emission control system (California models only) - check

1 This system, installed on California models to conform to stringent emission control standards, routes fuel vapors from the fuel system into the engine to be burned, instead of letting them evaporate into the atmosphere. When the engine isn't running, vapors are stored in a carbon canister.

Hoses

2 To begin the inspection of the system, remove the seat and fuel tank (see Chapters 3 and 7 if necessary). Inspect the hoses from the fuel tank, carburetor and air cleaner housing to the canister for cracking, kinks or other signs of deterioration.

Component inspection

3 Label and disconnect the hoses, then remove the canister from the machine (see Chapter 3).

4 Inspect the canister for cracks or other signs of damage. Tip the canister so the nozzles point down. If fuel runs out of the canister, the liquid/vapor separator is probably bad. The fuel inside the canister has probably caused damage, so it would be a good idea to replace it.

17 External oil lines - check

1 Follow the external lines from the oil tank to the engine and check them for leaks.

2 If the bike is equipped with rubber hoses, replace them if they're cracked or deteriorated. Use new hose clamps.

18 Fasteners - check

1 Since vibration of the machine tends to loosen fasteners, all nuts, bolts, screws, etc. should be periodically checked for proper tightness.

2 Pay particular attention to the following:
Spark plugs
Engine and transmission oil drain plugs
Oil filter
Gearshift lever
Footpegs and sidestand
Engine mount bolts
Shock absorber mount bolts
Front axle and clamp bolt(s)
Rear axle nut

3 If a torque wrench is available, use it along with the torque specifications at the beginning of this, or other, Chapters.

19 Battery - inspection

! *Warning: Be extremely careful when handling or working around the battery. The electrolyte is very caustic and an explosive gas (hydrogen) is given off when the battery is charging.*

Maintenance free battery

1 1997 and later models use a maintenance free battery. Do not open the cell caps at any time. If the electrolyte level is low, replace the battery.

2 Remove the seat (see Chapter 7).

3 Check the top of the battery for dirt, electrolyte and the white material that indicates oxidation (see illustration). If any of these are found, remove and clean the battery (see Chapter 8).

4 Check the terminals and cable ends for corrosion and damage. Clean or replace damaged parts. Make sure the cable ends are tight.

5 Check the battery case for damage, including cracks, warpage and leaks. Replace the battery if any of these problems are found.

15.1 Check the fuel lines to make sure they're secure and in good condition - replace leaking and deteriorated ones immediately!

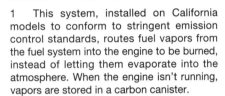

19.3 Check the top of the battery, the cable ends and the terminals for corrosion or dirt

Fillable battery

Warning: Be extremely careful when handling or working around the battery. The electrolyte is very caustic and an explosive gas (hydrogen) is given off when the battery is charging.

6   This procedure applies to fillable batteries, installed as original equipment on 1970 through 1996 models. The maintenance-free batteries used on later models do not require periodic checks of the electrolyte level.

7   On early models, where the battery is visible on the right side in front of the oil tank, remove the right side cover from above the battery.

8   Unbolt and move aside any electrical components mounted near the battery that obstruct battery removal, then unbolt the battery retainer and lift it off (see Chapter 8, if necessary). Note the position of the battery vent tube.

9   Remove the bolts securing the battery cables to the battery terminals (remove the negative cable first, positive cable last). Lift the battery out. The electrolyte level will now be visible through the translucent battery case - it should be between the Upper and Lower level marks.

10   If it is low, remove the cell caps and fill each cell to the upper level mark with distilled water. Do not use tap water (except in an emergency), and do not overfill. The cell holes are quite small, so it may help to use a plastic squeeze bottle with a small spout to add the water. If the level is within the marks on the case, additional water is not necessary.

11   Next, check the specific gravity of the electrolyte in each cell with a small hydrome-

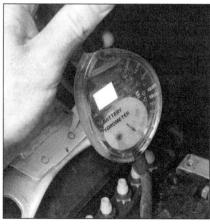

19.12 On fillable batteries, check the specific gravity with a hydrometer

ter made especially for motorcycle batteries. These are available from most dealer parts departments or motorcycle accessory stores.

12   Remove the caps, draw some electrolyte from the first cell into the hydrometer **(see illustration)** and note the specific gravity. Compare the reading to the Specifications listed in this Chapter. **Note:** *Add 0.004 points to the reading for every 10-degrees F above 68-degrees F (20-degrees C) - subtract 0.004 points from the reading for every 10-degrees below 68-degrees F (20-degrees C). Return the electrolyte to the appropriate cell and repeat the check for the remaining cells. When the check is complete, rinse the hydrometer thoroughly with clean water.*

13   If the specific gravity of the electrolyte in each cell is as specified, the battery is in good condition and is apparently being

charged by the machine's charging system.

14   If the specific gravity is low, the battery is not fully charged. This may be due to corroded battery terminals, a dirty battery case, a malfunctioning charging system, or loose or corroded wiring connections. On the other hand, it may be that the battery is worn out, especially if it is old, or that infrequent use of the motorcycle prevents normal charging from taking place.

15   Be sure to correct any problems and charge the battery if necessary. Refer to Chapter 8 for additional battery maintenance and charging procedures.

16   Install the battery cell caps, tightening them securely. Reconnect the cables to the battery, attaching the positive cable first and the negative cable last. Be very careful not to pinch or otherwise restrict the battery vent tube, as the battery may build up enough internal pressure during normal charging system operation to explode.

20 Electrical equipment check

1   Turn on the lights and make sure all of them work.

2   Operate the turn signals and make sure all of them blink steadily.

3   Sound the horn.

4   With the key on, operate the brake pedal and lever separately. Each of them should illuminate the brake light.

5   Check the instruments and indicator lamps for correct operation.

6   If any problems are found, repair them (see Chapter 8).

Every 5,000 miles (8,000 km)

21 Transmission and primary chaincase oil - change

1   The transmission and primary chaincase are lubricated by the same oil supply. Before changing the oil, warm up the transmission by riding the bike so the oil will drain easily. Be careful when draining the oil, as the exhaust pipes, the engine, and the oil itself can cause severe burns.

2   Prop the motorcycle upright over a clean drain pan. Remove the transmission/chaincase oil level plug to act as a reminder that there is no oil in the transmission.

3   Remove the transmission drain plug from the bottom of the primary chaincase and allow the oil to drain into the pan **(see**

illustration). Discard the sealing washer on the drain plug; it should be replaced whenever the plug is removed.

4   Check the condition of the drain plug threads.

5   Slip a new sealing washer over the drain plug, then install and tighten the plug to the torque listed in this Chapter's Specifications. Avoid overtightening, as damage to the transmission will result.

6   Before refilling the oil, check the old oil carefully. If the oil was drained into a clean pan, small pieces of metal or other material can be easily detected. If the oil is very metallic colored, then the transmission is experiencing wear from break-in (new transmission) or from insufficient lubrication. If there are flakes or chips of metal in the oil, then something is drastically wrong internally and the transmission will have to be disas-

21.3 Remove the drain plug from the bottom of the primary chaincase to drain the transmission oil

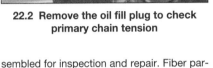

22.2 Remove the oil fill plug to check primary chain tension

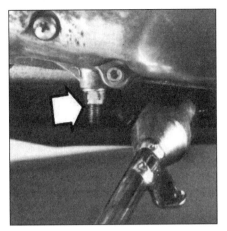

22.3 Primary chain adjusting screw location (arrow)

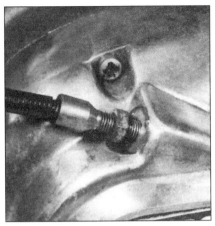

23.6 Loosen the clutch cable adjuster locknut at the primary chaincase

sembled for inspection and repair. Fiber particles in the oil indicate worn or damaged clutch plates.

7   If the inspection of the oil turns up nothing unusual, refill the transmission/chaincase until oil just starts to flow out of the level plug. Install the plug and tighten it securely.

8   The old oil drained from the transmission cannot be reused in its present state and should be disposed of. Check with your local refuse disposal company, disposal facility or environmental agency to see whether they will accept the oil for recycling. Don't pour used oil into drains or onto the ground. After the oil has cooled, it can be drained into a suitable container (capped plastic jugs, topped bottles, milk cartons, etc.) for transport to one of these disposal sites.

22 Primary chain deflection - check and adjustment

1   Support the motorcycle securely upright.
2   Remove the oil fill plug from the primary chaincase **(see illustration)**.
3   Loosen the adjusting screw locknut at the bottom of the chaincase, just in front of the sidestand **(see illustration)**.
4   Turn the adjusting screw in to tighten the chain and out to loosen it. When the tension is set to the value listed in this Chapter's Specifications, tighten the locknut.
5   Install the oil fill plug in the chaincase.
6   If the chain can't be adjusted tight enough, it's worn out or the adjuster is defective. Replace the faulty component.

23 Clutch - check and adjustment

1   Correct clutch freeplay is necessary to ensure proper clutch operation and reason-

able clutch service life. Freeplay normally changes because of cable stretch and clutch wear, so it should be checked and adjusted periodically.

1970 models

2   Loosen the release mechanism locknut located in the center of the sprocket cover and back the adjusting screw out (counterclockwise).
3   The release lever inside the cover should be heard to contact its stop when the handlebar lever is in the "at rest" position. Using the cable adjuster at the handlebar end, adjust so that the release lever does not quite return against its stop.
4   Turn the adjuster screw in the sprocket cover clockwise until there is 1/8-inch (3 mm) freeplay at the lever before the clutch comes into operation. At this point hold the adjuster screw steady while its locknut is tightened.
5   It is possible to adjust the spring tension of the clutch itself - refer to a Harley-Davidson dealer for details.

1971 through early 1984

6   Loosen the cable adjusting locknut where it enters the primary chaincase **(see illustration)**. Turn the cable adjuster lever in until the lever on the handlebar has plenty of freeplay.
7   Remove the clutch access plug from the primary chaincase, just behind the left footpeg **(see illustration)**.
8   Working through the opening in the chaincase, loosen the locknut and turn the adjusting screw clockwise until it becomes difficult to turn. From this point, turn the screw two more turns to be sure the clutch is disengaged.
9   Turn the cable adjuster out of the case until there's no freeplay in he cable. Don't put any tension on the cable. When there's no play at the hand lever, tighten the cable adjuster locknut.
10   Back off the clutch adjusting screw until it begins to turn easier (clutch is being engaged). Turn the screw back in until

there's no freeplay. Back the adjusting screw out 1/8 to 1/4 turn, then tighten the locknut while holding the adjusting screw stationary. This can be done with a Harley-Davidson special tool or by inserting a screwdriver through a deep socket with a hex head on its upper end.
11   There should be 1/16 inch of freeplay between the hand lever and the mounting bracket. If necessary, adjust the cable until the desired freeplay at the lever is obtained.

Late 1984 and later

12   On models through 1987 loosen the cable adjusting locknut where it enters the primary chaincase **(see illustration 23.6)**. Turn the adjuster in until the handlebar lever has plenty of play. The requirement is the same for 1988 and later models, but use the inline adjuster midway along the cable's length.
13   On models through 1993, remove the round access plug from the chaincase and lift out the spring and adjusting screw lockplate **(see illustrations)**. The procedure is the same on 1994 and later models except

23.7 Remove the access plug from the primary chaincase to adjust the clutch

1   Locknut
2   Adjusting screw

1

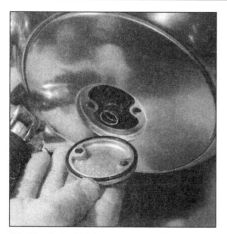

23.13a Late 1984-on - remove the access plug (shown) or outer cover and lift out the spring . . .

23.13b . . . then withdraw the adjusting screw lockplate

24.1 Steering grease nipple location - later models

that access is obtained by removing the four Torx screws that secure the outer clutch cover to the primary chaincase. Take the cover off without dislodging its O-ring.

14   Turn the adjusting screw out (counterclockwise) until it starts to turn hard (all freeplay removed).

15   Turn the adjusting screw in (1/4-turn counterclockwise), then install the lockplate and spring. If the lockplate hex doesn't match up with the recess in the chaincase cover, turn the adjusting screw clockwise slightly until it does. Install the access plug or outer clutch cover, making sure the O-ring is in its groove. Tighten the clutch cover Torx screws evenly, in a criss-cross pattern, to the torque listed in this Chapter's Specifications.

16   Use the cable adjuster previously loosened, to obtain 1/16-inch to 1/8-inch (1.5 to 3 mm) freeplay between the cable ferrule and the lever butt at the handlebar.

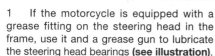

24 Steering head bearings - lubrication

1   If the motorcycle is equipped with a grease fitting on the steering head in the frame, use it and a grease gun to lubricate the steering head bearings (see illustration).
2   On all models, the steering head bearings should be periodically removed and repacked with grease (see Chapter 5).

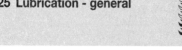

25 Lubrication - general

1   Since the controls, cables and various other components of a motorcycle are exposed to the elements, they should be lubricated periodically to ensure safe and trouble-free operation.
2   The footpegs, clutch and brake lever and sidestand pivot should be lubricated fre-

quently. In order for the lubricant to be applied where it will do the most good, the component should be disassembled. However, if chain and cable lubricant is being used, it can be applied to the pivot joint gaps and will usually work its way into the areas where friction occurs. If motor oil or light grease is being used, apply it sparingly as it may attract dirt (which could cause the controls to bind or wear at an accelerated rate). **Note:** *One of the best lubricants for the control lever pivots is a dry-film lubricant (available from many sources by different names).*
3   The clutch cable should be separated from the handlebar lever and bracket before it is lubricated (see Chapter 2). This is a convenient time to inspect the bushing at the end of the cable. The cable should be treated with motor oil or a commercially available cable lubricant which is specially formulated for use on motorcycle control cables. Small adapters for pressure lubricating the cables with spray can lubricants are available and ensure that the cable is lubricated along its entire length **(see illustration)**. If motor oil is being used, tape a funnel-shaped piece of heavy paper or plastic to the end of the cable, then pour oil into the funnel and suspend the end of the cable upright. Leave it until the oil runs down into the cable and out the other end. When attaching the cable to the lever, be sure to lubricate the barrel-shaped fitting at the end with high-temperature grease. **Note:** *While you're lubricating, check the barrel end of the cable for fraying. Replace frayed cables.*
4   To lubricate the throttle cables, disconnect the cables at the lower end, then lubricate the cable with a pressure lube adapter **(see illustration 26.3a)**.
5   The speedometer and tachometer cables (if equipped) should be removed from its housing and lubricated with motor oil or cable lubricant.
6   Refer to Chapter 5 for the swingarm bearing lubrication procedure where applicable.
7   Remove the brake pedal and lubricate the shaft with a light coat of Harley-Davidson Wheel Bearing Grease or equivalent.

26 Spark plugs - inspection and replacement

HAYNES HiNT *Stripped plug threads in the cylinder head can be repaired with a Heli-Coil thread insert - see 'Tools and Workshop Tips' in the Reference section.*

1   Disconnect the spark plug caps from the spark plugs **(see illustration)**. If available, use compressed air to blow any accumulated debris from around the spark plugs. Remove the plugs with a spark plug socket.
2   Inspect the electrodes for wear. Both the center and side electrodes should have square edges and the side electrode should be of uniform thickness. Look for excessive deposits and evidence of a cracked or chipped insulator around the center electrode. Compare your spark plugs to the color spark plug reading chart. Check the threads, the washer and the ceramic insulator body for cracks and other damage.
3   If the electrodes are not excessively worn, and if the deposits can be easily removed with electrical contact cleaner, the

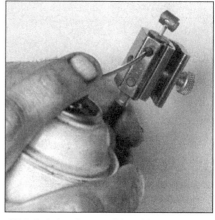

25.3 Lubricating a cable with a pressure lube adapter (make sure the tool seats around the inner cable)

26.1 Detach the plug wires (A) to remove the spark plugs

26.5a Spark plug manufacturers recommend using a wire type gauge when checking the gap - if the wire doesn't slide between the electrodes with a slight drag, adjustment is required

26.5b To change the gap, bend the side electrode only, as indicated by the arrows, and be very careful not to crack or chip the ceramic insulator surrounding the center electrode

plugs can be regapped and reused (if no cracks or chips are visible in the insulator). If in doubt concerning the condition of the plugs, replace them with new ones, as the expense is minimal.

4   If you're going to reuse the plugs, use a fine file to square the edges of the electrodes.

5   Before installing new plugs, make sure they are the correct type and heat range. Check the gap between the electrodes, as they are not preset. For best results, use a wire-type gauge rather than a flat gauge to check the gap (see illustration). If the gap must be adjusted, bend the side electrode only and be very careful not to chip or crack the insulator nose (see illustration). Make sure the washer is in place before installing each plug.

6   Since the cylinder heads are made of aluminum, which is soft and easily damaged, thread the plugs into the heads by hand. Since the plugs are quite recessed, slip a short length of hose over the end of the plug to use as a tool to thread it into place. The hose will grip the plug well enough to turn it, but will start to slip if the plug begins to

cross-thread in the hole - this will prevent damaged threads and the accompanying repair costs.

7   Once the plugs are finger tight, the job can be finished with a socket. If a torque wrench is available, tighten the spark plugs to the torque listed in this Chapter's Specifications. If you do not have a torque wrench, tighten the plugs finger tight (until the washers bottom on the cylinder head) then use a wrench to tighten them an additional 1/4 turn. Regardless of the method used, do not over-tighten them.

8   Reconnect the spark plug caps.

27 Idle speed - check and adjustment

1   The idle speed should be checked and adjusted at the specified maintenance intervals and when it is obviously too high or too

low. Before adjusting the idle speed, make sure the spark plug gaps are correct. Also, turn the handlebars back-and-forth and see if the idle speed changes as this is done. If it does, the accelerator cable may not be adjusted correctly, or it may be worn out. Be sure to correct this problem before proceeding.

2   The engine should be at normal operating temperature, which is usually reached after 10 to 15 minutes of stop and go riding. Prop the motorcycle securely upright. Make sure the transmission is in Neutral.

3   Connect a tune-up tachometer to the negative terminal of the ignition coil.

4   Start the engine and let it idle. Make sure the choke knob is pushed all the way in.

5   Turn the idle speed screw (see illustrations) until the idle speed listed in this Chapter's Specifications is obtained.

6   Snap the throttle open and shut a few times, then recheck the idle speed. If necessary, repeat the adjustment procedure.

7   If a smooth, steady idle can't be achieved, the fuel/air mixture may be incorrect. Refer to Chapter 3 for additional carburetor information.

28 Ignition timing - check and adjustment

1   A timing light is the best and most accurate way to check the ignition timing, since it is done with the engine running. The timing light leads should be attached to the front spark plug wire (initially) and the battery terminals. It's a good idea to replace the plug in the crankcase (left side on 1970 through 1990 models or right side on 1991 and later models) with the special clear plastic factory Timing Mark View Plug (part no. HD-96295 for 1970 through 1990 models, HD-96295-65D for 1991 and later models) (see illustrations). This will prevent oil spray

1

27.5a The throttle stop screw (arrow) is turned to change the idle speed (on the early model shown here, a stubby screwdriver will be required to reach it)

27.5b The idle speed screw on Keihin CV carburetors (arrow) can be reached with a long screwdriver

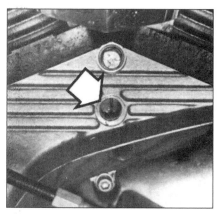

28.1a Install the special clear plastic plug in the timing inspection hole (arrow) here's the design used through 1990 . . .

28.1b . . . on 1991 and later models, the hole is on the right side of the engine (arrow)

while the engine is running. Make sure the plug doesn't touch the flywheel.

2   Run the engine at the timing speed listed in this Chapter's Specifications and observe the timing marks through the crankcase opening (see illustrations). The front cylinder timing mark should appear stationary in the opening. As the engine is revved up, the advance timing mark should move into view.

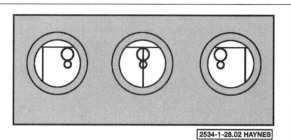

28.2a Here are the 1970 through 1978 timing marks - they should be centered in the opening

28.4a On later models with electronic ignition, drill out the rivet heads and remove the outer screw . . .

3   On 1970 models, the timing can be changed by turning the distributor body slightly after loosening the clamp. On other models with contact points, remove the point cover as described in Section 11 to get at the breaker point base plate.

4   On later models with electronic ignition, drill out the rivet heads (see illustration), and detach the outer cover, then remove the screws and take off the inner cover and gasket to get at the sensor plate (see illustration). Mark the sensor plate and cover with a felt-tip pen or scribe to ensure the sensor plate (ignition timing) can be returned to its original position if desired.

5   Adjustments can be made by loosening the contact breaker point base plate or electronic ignition sensor plate screws and rotating the plate very carefully, in small incre-

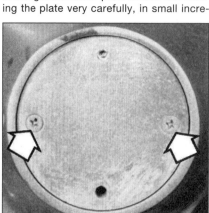

28.4b . . . then remove the screws (arrows) and detach the inner cover and gasket to get at the sensor plate

28.2b Timing marks
(late 1979 and later)

A   Front cylinder advance mark (late 1979 through early 1980) or front cylinder TDC mark (late 1980-on)
B   Front cylinder TDC mark(late 1979 through early 1980)
C   Front cylinder advance mark (late 1980 through 1994 all; 1995 US)
D   "Lazy 8" rear cylinder advance mark (some models)
E   Front cylinder advance mark (1995 international; 1996-on all)

ments, with a screwdriver inserted in the slot (see illustration). The ignition timing will change as the plate is moved. Note: When checking the ignition advance on later models, be sure to check the vacuum operated electric switch (VOES) also. With the engine idling, unplug the VOES hose from the carburetor and plug the carburetor fitting. The timing should retard - the engine speed should decrease. When the hose is reattached to the carburetor, the engine speed should increase (the timing should advance). If it doesn't, check the VOES wire connection at the ignition module and the VOES ground wire connection. If they appear to be OK, the VOES may be defective and should be replaced with a new one.

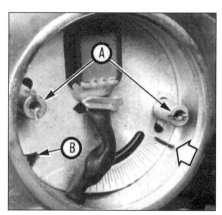

28.5 Mark the sensor plate (arrow), then loosen the screws (A) and insert a screwdriver into the slot (B) to change the position of the plate - move the plate a little at a time and recheck the timing

Every 10,000 miles (16,000 km)

29 Exhaust system - check

1 Periodically check all of the exhaust system joints for leaks and loose fasteners. If tightening the clamp bolts fails to stop any leaks, replace the gaskets with new ones (a procedure which requires disassembly of the system).
2 The exhaust pipe flange nuts at the cylinder heads are especially prone to loosening, which could cause damage to the head. Check them frequently and keep them tight.

30 Steering head bearings - check

1 The steering head in these motorcycles is equipped with ball bearings (1970 through 1974) or tapered roller steering head bearings (1975 and later) which can become dented, rough or loose during normal use of the machine. In extreme cases, worn or loose steering head bearings can cause steering wobble that is potentially dangerous.
2 To check the bearings, support the motorcycle securely upright. Block the machine so the front wheel is raised off the ground.
3 Point the wheel straight ahead and slowly move the handlebars from side-to-side. Dents or roughness in the bearing races will be felt and the bars will not move smoothly.
4 Next, grasp the fork legs and try to move the wheel forward and backward. Any looseness in the steering head bearings will be felt. If play is felt in the bearings, adjust them as described in Chapter 5.

31.3 Check above and below the fork seals (arrows) for signs of leakage

HAYNES HINT *Make sure you are not mistaking any movement between the bike and stand, or between the stand and the ground, for freeplay in the bearings. Do not pull or push the forks too hard - a gentle movement is all that is needed. Freeplay between the fork slider and the fork tube due to worn bushings can also be misinterpreted as steering head bearing play - don't confuse the two.*

31 Suspension - check

1 The suspension components must be maintained in top operating condition to ensure rider safety. Loose, worn or damaged suspension parts decrease the vehicle's stability and control.
2 While standing alongside the motorcycle, lock the front brake and push on the handlebars to compress the forks several times. See if they move up-and-down smoothly without binding. If binding is felt, the forks should be disassembled and inspected as described in Chapter 5.
3 Carefully inspect the area around the fork seals for any signs of fork oil leakage (see illustration). If leakage is evident, the seals must be replaced as described in Chapter 5.
4 Check the tightness of all suspension nuts and bolts to be sure none have worked loose.
5 Inspect the rear shock absorbers for fluid leakage and tightness of the mounting nuts. If leakage is found, the shocks should be replaced. Replace both shocks as a pair.
6 Prop the bike securely upright. Grab the swingarm on each side, just ahead of the axle. Rock the swingarm from side to side - there should be no discernible movement at

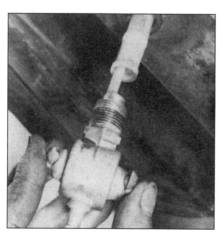
33.4 Unscrew the fuel valve from the tank

the rear. If there's a little movement or a slight clicking can be heard, make sure the pivot shaft nuts are tight. If the pivot nuts are tight but movement is still noticeable, the swingarm will have to be removed and the bearings replaced as described in Chapter 5.

32 Swingarm and wheel bearings - lubricate

1 The front wheel bearings should be removed, cleaned and repacked with grease (see Chapter 6).
2 The swingarm bearings should be removed, cleaned and repacked with grease (see Chapter 5).

33 Fuel valve filter screen - inspection and cleaning

1 Make sure the fuel control valve is in the Off position. Disconnect the hose from the fuel outlet fitting, then connect a length of hose to the fitting and place the end in an approved gasoline container.
2 Turn the fuel valve handle to reserve.
3 Disconnect the hose from the vacuum fitting and attach a vacuum pump to the fitting. Apply vacuum (1 to 10 inches Hg) to the fitting, which will allow the gasoline from the tank to flow into the drain hose.
Caution: Don't apply any more vacuum than necessary to make the gasoline flow.
4 Unscrew the hex nut on the bottom of the fuel tank, then remove the valve and filter screen (see illustration).
5 Thoroughly clean the filter. It can be removed from the valve to be cleaned or replaced if it's damaged.
6 If the fuel valve leaks, it's impractical to attempt to repair it. The complete unit should be replaced with a new one.
7 Apply thread sealant (Loctite Pipe Sealant with Teflon or equivalent) to the threads before installing the valve on the fuel tank.

34 Fork oil - replacement

1 This procedure applies to the damper rod forks used on all except Sportster 1200S (Sport) models. Changing the fork oil on cartridge forks (used on the Sportster 1200S models) requires partial disassembly of the fork (see Chapter 5).
2 Prop the motorcycle securely upright.

1

Position a jack with a block of wood on the jack head under the engine to support the motorcycle when the fork caps are removed.

 Warning: Do not rely on the jack alone to support the motorcycle. Be sure it is securely braced.

3   Unscrew the fork tube caps, taking care to release the spring pressure slowly **(see illustration)**.
4   Place a pan beneath the drain screw at the bottom of the fork leg, then remove the drain screw and washer.

 Warning: Do not allow the fork oil to contact the brake disc and pads (if equipped) or tire. If it does, clean the disc with brake system cleaner, wipe off the tire, and replace the pads with new ones before riding the motorcycle.

5   After most of the oil has drained, slowly compress and release the forks to pump out the remaining oil. An assistant will most likely be required to do this procedure.
6   Check the drain screw gasket for damage and replace it if necessary. Clean the threads of the drain screw with solvent and let it dry, then install the screw and gasket,

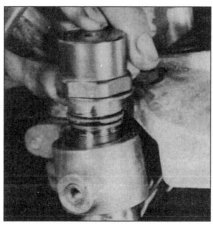

34.3 Unscrew the cap from the top of the fork leg

tightening it securely.
7   Pour the type and amount of fork oil, listed in this Chapter's Specifications, into the fork tube through the opening at the top **(see illustration)**. Remove the jack from under the engine and slowly pump the forks a few times to purge the air from the upper and lower chambers.
8   Check the plug seal and replace it if it's

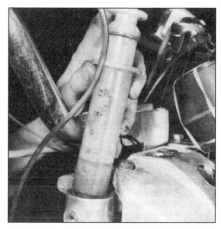

34.7 Fill the fork legs with the specified amount of fork oil (a baby bottle or measuring cup will make it easier)

damaged or deteriorated. Install the cap, push it down against the spring pressure, and tighten it to the torque listed in this Chapter's Specifications.
9   Repeat the procedure on the other fork. Note that it is essential that the oil quantity and level is identical in each fork.

Chapter 2 Part A
Engine

Contents

2

Degrees of difficulty

Easy, suitable for novice with little experience | **Fairly easy,** suitable for beginner with some experience | **Fairly difficult,** suitable for competent DIY mechanic | **Difficult,** suitable for experienced DIY mechanic | **Very difficult,** suitable for expert DIY or professional

Specifications

General

Engine type	45-degree V-twin, four-stroke
Bore	
1970 and 1971	3.00 inches (76.2 mm)
1972 through 1985	3.188 inches (81.0 mm)
1986 and later	
883 cc engine	3.00 inches (76.2 mm)
1100 cc engine	3.350 inches (85.09 mm)
1200 cc engine	3.498 inches (88.85 mm)
Stroke	3.812 inches (96.8 mm)

General (continued)

Displacement
    1970 and 1971 .... 883 cc (53.9 cubic inches)
    1972 through 1985 .... 997.5 cc (60.9 cubic inches)
    1986 and 1987 .... 883 cc (53.9 cubic inches) /1100 cc (67.2 cubic inches)
    1988 and later .... 883 cc (53.9 cubic inches)/1200 cc (73.3 cubic inches)
Oil pressure
  Shovelhead engine
    Under normal riding conditions .... 4 to 15 psi (0.27 to 1.04 Bars)
    At idle .... 4 to 7 psi (0.27 to 0.48 Bars)
  Evolution engine (1986 through 1990)
  Measured at adapter between tappet guide blocks
    At 2500 rpm... 5 to 30 psi (0.35 to 2.07 Bars)
    At idle .... 1 to 7 psi (0.07 to 0.48 Bars)
  Evolution engine (1991 and later)
  Measured at oil pressure switch union
    At 2500 rpm... 10 to 17 psi (0.69 to 1.17 Bars)
    At 1000 rpm... 7 to 12 psi (0.48 to 0.82 Bars)

Shovelhead engine

Valves and related components

Valve-to-guide clearance
  Standard
    Intake .... 0.0015 to 0.0035 inch (0.038 to 0.088 mm)
    Exhaust .... 0.0025 to 0.0045 inch (0.063 to 0.114 mm)
  Service limit
    Intake .... 0.006 inch (0.152 mm)
    Exhaust .... 0.007 inch (0.178 mm)
Valve spring free length
  Standard
    1970 through early 1983
      Inner.. 1-23/64 inch (34.54 mm)
      Outer... 1-1/2 inch (38.1 mm)
    Late 1983-on
      Inner.. 1-11/32 inch (34.13 mm)
      Outer... 1-9/16 inch (39.69 mm)
  Service limit
    1970 through early 1983
      Inner.. 1-19/64 inch (32.94 mm)
      Outer... 1-7/16 inch (36.51 mm)
    Late 1983-on
      Inner.. 1-5/16 inch (33.34mm)
      Outer... 1-1/2 inch (38.1 mm)
Rocker arm shaft-to-rocker box bushing clearance
  Standard .... 0.001 to 0.0025 inch(0.025 to 0.063 mm)
  Service limit .... 0.0035 inch (0.089 mm)
Valve timing (identical for both cylinders)
  1970 through 1979
    Intake valve opens .... 35.4 +/- 3-degrees BTDC
    Intake valve closes.. 41.2 +/- 3-degrees ABDC
    Exhaust valve opens .... 44.3 +/- 4-degrees BBDC
    Exhaust valve closes... 20.2 +/- 4-degrees ATDC
  1980-on
    Intake valve opens .... 7.5 +/- 3-degrees BTDC
    Intake valve closes.. 42.5 +/-3-degrees ABDC
    Exhaust valve opens .... 36.0 +/- 4-degrees BBDC
    Exhaust valve closes... 8.0 +/- 4-degrees ATDC

Lifters
    Fit in cam follower guide
        Standard .... 0.0005 to 0.001 inch (0.013 to 0.025 mm)
        Service limit.. 0.002 inch (0.05 mm)
    Roller fit
        Standard .... 0.0005 to 0.001 inch (0.013 to 0.025 mm)
        Service limit.. 0.0012 inch (0.03 mm)
    Roller end clearance
        Standard .... 0.008 to 0.010 inch (0.23 to 0.25 mm)
        Service limit.. 0.012 inch (0.03 mm)
Valve clearance (COLD engine) .... See Chapter 1

Pistons

Piston-to-cylinder clearance
Standard
    Late 1985 only... 0.0025 to 0.0035 inch (0.06 to 0.09 mm)
    All others .... 0.003 to 0.004 inch (0.076 to 0.101 mm)
Service limit
    Late 1985 only... 0.0055 inch (0.14 mm)
    All others .... 0.006 inch (0.15 mm)
Piston ring side clearance
    1970 through 1982 .... 0.0035 to 0.06 inch (0.088 to 0.15 mm)
    1983 and later .... 0.004 to 0.006 inch (0.10 to 0.15 mm)
Piston ring end gap
    Standard
        1970 through 1978.. 0.015 to 0.025 inch (0.38 to 0.63 mm)
        1979 through 1982 .... 0.010 inch (0.254 mm)
        1983 and later (compression rings) .... 0.008 inch (0.20 mm)
        1983 and later (oil control ring) .... 0.015 inch (0.38 mm)
    Service limit
        1970 through 1982 (compression rings) .... 0.031 inch (0.78 mm)
        1970 through 1982 (oil control ring)............................ 0.050 inch (1.27 mm)
        1983 and later (top compression ring) .... 0.022 inch (0.56 mm)
        1983 and later (second compression ring) .... 0.030 inch (0.76 mm)
        1983 and later (oil control ring) .... 0.055 inch (1.40 mm)

Crankshaft and connecting rods

Maximum flywheel runout.. 0.006 inch (0.15 mm) at rim
Maximum shaft runout.. 0.002 inch (0.051 mm)
Connecting rod end play
    1970 through 1978 .... 0.005 to 0.015 inch (0.127 to 0.381 mm)
    1979-on .... 0.005 to 0.030 inch (0.127 to 0.76 mm)

Camshafts

Idler gear shaft-to-bushing clearance .... 0.0005 to 0.003 inch (0.013 to 0.076 mm)
Camshaft-to-bushing clearance.. 0.0005 to 0.003 inch (0.013 to 0.076 mm)
Camshaft bearing clearance.. 0.0005 to 0.003 inch (0.013 to 0.076 mm)
Camshaft end play
    1970 through 1976 .... 0.001 to 0.005 inch (0.025 to 0.127 mm)
    1977 and 1978 (except rear intake)............................. 0.0005 to 0.012 inch (0.127 to 0.305 mm)
    1979-on (except rear intake) .... 0.005 to 0.025 inch (0.127 to 0.635 mm)
    Rear intake camshaft .... 0.004 to 0.010 inch (0.102 to 0.254 mm)
Camshaft gear backlash.. 0.0000 to 0.0005 inch (0.00 to 0.0127 mm)

Torque specifications

Gear shaft nut.. 100 to 120 ft-lbs (136 to 163 Nm)
Sprocket shaft nut .... 100 to 120 ft-lbs (136 to 163 Nm)
Crankpin nuts .... 150 to 175 ft-lbs (203 to 237 Nm)

2

Shovelhead engine

Torque specifications (continued)

Crankshaft gear nut (right end of crankshaft)	50 ft-lbs (68 Nm)
Through 1978	35 to 45 ft-lbs (47 to 61 Nm)
1979 and later	55 to 65 ft-lbs (75 to 88 Nm)
Cylinder head bolts	25 to 35 ft-lbs (34 to 47 Nm)
Cylinder base nuts	14 to19 ft-lbs (19 to 26 Nm)
Rocker arm cover bolts	6 to 11 ft-lbs (8 to 15 Nm)
Lifter adjusting locknut	16 to 24 ft-lbs (22 to 33 Nm)
Rear engine mount bolt/nut	110 to 150 ft-lbs (149 to 203 Nm)
Clutch center nut	Tighten securely
Compensating sprocket threaded collar	150 to 165 ft-lbs (203 to 224 Nm)
Primary drive (engine sprocket) bolt	35 to 65 ft-lbs (47 to 88 Nm)
Final drive sprocket nut	13 to 15 ft-lbs (18 to 20 Nm)
Transmission access cover bolts	14 to 21 ft-lbs (19 to 28 ft-lbs)
Primary chaincase drain plug	8 to 12 ft-lbs (11 to 16 Nm)
Primary chain tensioner stud nut	80 to 110 inch-lbs (9 to 12 Nm)
Primary chaincase cover screws	
Alternator stator mounting screws	
12-point socket head/slotted	20 to 35 inch-lbs (2.3 to 4 Nm)
Torx head	30 to 40 inch-lbs (3.4 to 5 Nm)
Engine mounting bolts/nuts (tighten in order listed)	
Rear	Not specified
Lower front mount to engine	Not specified
Lower front mount to frame	Not specified
Top center to engine	25 to 30 ft-lbs (34 to 41 Nm)
Top center to frame	30 to 35 ft-lbs (41 to 47 Nm)
Upper front bracket to engine	25 to 30 ft-lbs (34 to 41 Nm)
Upper front bracket to frame	30 to 35 ft-lbs (41 to 47 Nm)

Evolution engine

Valves and related components

Valve seat width	
Standard	0.040 to 0.062 inch (1.02 to 1.57 mm)
Service limit	0.090 inch (2.29 mm)
Valve stem protrusion (measured from spring pocket in head)	
Standard	1.975 to 2.011 inch (50.17 to 51.08 mm)
Service limit	2.031 inch (51.59 mm)
Valve-to-guide clearance	
Standard	
Intake	0.0008 to 0.0026 inch (0.020 to 0.066 mm)
Exhaust	0.0015 to 0.0033 inch (0.038 to 0.084 mm)
Service limit	
Intake	0.0035 inch (0.09 mm)
Exhaust	0.0040 inch (0.10 mm)
Valve spring free length	
Standard	
Outer spring	2.105 to 2.177 inch (53.47 to 55.30 mm)
Inner spring	1.926 to 1.996 inch (48.92 to 50.70 mm)
Service limit	
Outer spring	2.105 inch (53.47 mm)
Inner spring	1.926 inch (48.92 mm)
Rocker arm shaft-to-rocker arm bushing clearance	
Standard	0.0005 to 0.002 inch (0.0127 to 0.050 mm)
Service limit	0.0035 inch (0.089 mm)
Rocker arm end play	
Standard	0.003 to 0.013 inch (0.076 to 0.33 mm)
Service limit	0.025 inch (0.635 mm)
Rocker arm shaft-to-cover clearance	
Standard	0.0007 to 0.0022 inch (0.018 to 0.056 mm)
Service limit	0.0035 inch (0.09 mm)

Lifters
  Fit in guide
    Standard .... 0.0008 to 0.0023 inch (0.020 to 0.058 mm)
    Service limit .... 0.003 inch (0.076 mm)
  Roller fit .... 0.0006 to 0.0013 inch (0.015 to 0.033 mm)
  Roller end clearance .... 0.010 to 0.014 inch (0.25 to 0.36 mm)
  Cylinder head warpage limit .... 0.006 inch (0.152 mm)

Cylinders

Bore
  Diameter (standard - +/- 0.0002 inch)
    883 .... 3.0005 inch (76.213 mm)
    1100 .... 3.3505 inch (85.103 mm)
    1200 .... 3.4978 inch (88.844 mm)
Taper limit .... 0.002 inch (0.05 mm)
Out-of-round limit .... 0.003 inch (0.076 mm)
Gasket surface warpage limit
  Top (cylinder head) .... 0.006 inch (0.15 mm)
  Base .... 0.008 inch (0.20 mm)

Pistons

Piston ring end gap
  Standard
  Compression rings
    883 and 1100 .... 0.010 to 0.023 inch (0.254 to 0.58 mm)
    1200 .... 0.007 to 0.020 inch (0.178 to 0.508 mm)
  Oil control ring
    883 and 1100 .... 0.010 to 0.053 inch (0.25 to 1.35 mm)
    1200 .... 0.009 to 0.052 inch (0.15 to 1.32 mm)
  Service limit
    Compression rings .... 0.032 inch (0.81 mm)
    Oil control ring .... 0.065 inch (1.65 mm)
Piston ring side clearance
  Standard
  Compression rings
    883 and 1100 .... 0.002 to 0.0045 inch (0.05 to 0.11 mm)
    1200 (top ring) .... 0.002 to 0.0045 inch (0.05 to O.11 mm)
    1200 (second ring) .... 0.0016 to 0.0041 inch (0.04 to 0.10 mm)
  Oil control ring
    883 and 1100 .... 0.0014 to 0.0074 inch (0.036 to 0.188 mm)
    1200 .... 0.0016 to 0.0076 inch (0.04 to 0.193 mm)
  Service limit
    Compression rings .... 0.0065 inch (0.165 mm)
    Oil control ring .... 0.0094 inch (0.24 mm)

Crankshaft and connecting rods

Maximum flywheel runout .... 0.010 inch (0.25 mm) at rim
Maximum shaft runout .... 0.002 inch (0.051 mm)
Connecting rod side clearance .... 0.030 inch (0.127 mm) maximum
Crankshaft end play .... 0.001 to 0.005 inch (0.025 to 0.127 mm)

Camshafts

Camshaft-to-bushing clearance .... 0.0007 to 0.003 inch (0.018 to 0.076 mm)
Camshaft end play service limits
  Rear intake only .... 0.040 inch (1.02 mm) maximum
  All others .... 0.025 inch (0.64 mm) maximum

Primary drive side bearing

Outer race-to-crankcase .... 0.0004 to 0.0024 inch (0.010 to 0.061 mm)
Inner race-to-shaft .... 0.0002 to 0.0015 inch (0.005 to 0.038 mm)

2

Evolution engine (continued)

Torque specifications

Crankpin nuts	150 to 185 ft-lbs (203 to 250 Nm)
Crankshaft timing gear nut	35 to 45 ft-lbs (47 to 61 Nm)
Cylinder head bolts	
Step 1	7 to 9 ft-lbs (9 to 12 Nm)
Step 2	12 to 14 ft-lbs (16 to 19 Nm)
Step 3	Tighten an additional 90-degrees (1/4 turn)
Rocker arm cover bolts (through 1990)	
1/4-inch	10 to 13 ft-lbs (14 to 18 ft-lbs)
5/16-inch	15 to 18 ft-lbs (20 to 24 Nm)
Rocker arm cover bolts (1991-on)	
1/4-inch Allen head	90 to 120 inch-lbs (10 to 14 Nm)
1/4-inch hex head	10 to 13 ft-lbs (14 to 18 Nm)
5/16-inch	15 to 18 ft-lbs (20 to 24 Nm)
Lifter lockpin cover screw (1991-on)	86 to 110 inch-lbs (9 to 12 Nm)
Pushrod retaining plate screw (1991-on)	15 to 18 ft-lbs (20 to 24 Nm)
Final drive sprocket nut and lockscrew(s)	See Chapter 5 text
Engine mounting bolts/nuts (tighten in order listed)	
Rear	25 to 30 ft-lbs (34 to 41 Nm)
Lower front mount to engine	25 to 30 ft-lbs (34 to 41 Nm)
Lower front mount to frame	30 to 35 ft-lbs (41 to 47 Nm)
Top center to engine	25 to 30 ft-lbs (34 to 41 Nm)
Top center to frame	30 to 35 ft-lbs (41 to 47 Nm)
Upper front bracket to engine	25 to 30 ft-lbs (34 to 41 Nm)
Upper front bracket to frame	30 to 35 ft-lbs (41 to 47 Nm)

1 General information

The engine/transmission unit on all models is an air-cooled V-twin, with a 45-degree angle between the cylinders. The valves are operated by four separate camshafts (one for each valve), pushrods and rocker arms. The camshafts are gear driven off the crankshaft. The engine/transmission assembly is constructed from aluminum alloy. The crankcase is divided vertically.

The engine used in 1970 through 1985 models has cast iron cylinder heads and cylinders, and is popularly known as the Shovelhead due to the shape of the cylinder heads. The 1986 and later engine, called the Evolution, is basically the Shovelhead engine with aluminum cylinders and heads.

The crankcase incorporates a dry sump, pressure-fed lubrication system which uses an external oil tank, dual-rotor oil pump, oil filter, relief valve and oil pressure switch. The oil pump, which has separate rotors for scavenging and pressure feed, is driven directly by the crankshaft.

Power from the crankshaft is routed to the transmission via the primary drive chain and clutch. The clutch on 1970 models is a dry type, with coil springs. The clutch on later models is of the wet, multi-plate type. The transmission is a four- or five-speed, constant-mesh unit. The clutch and primary drive chain are contained in the primary drive housing on the left side of the engine. The transmission is mounted on the back of the engine. Service procedures for the clutch, primary drive and transmission are covered in Part B of this Chapter.

2 Cylinder compression - check

1   Among other things, poor engine performance may be caused by leaking valves, incorrect valve clearances, a leaking head gasket, or worn pistons, rings and/or cylinder walls. A cylinder compression check will help pinpoint these conditions and can also indicate the presence of excessive carbon deposits in the cylinder heads.

2   The only tools required are a compression gauge and a spark plug wrench. Depending on the outcome of the initial test, a squirt-type oil can may also be needed.

3   Run the engine until it reaches normal operating temperature. Place the motorcycle on the sidestand or prop it securely upright. Remove the spark plugs (see Chapter 1, if necessary). **Note:** *Remove only one plug from each cylinder on twin-plug models.* Work carefully - don't strip the spark plug hole threads and don't burn your hands.

4   Disable the ignition by unplugging the primary wires from the coils (see Chapter 4). Be sure to mark the locations of the wires before detaching them.

5   Install the compression gauge in one of the spark plug holes **(see illustration)**. Hold or block the throttle wide open.

6   Crank the engine over for five to seven revolutions (or until the gauge reading stops increasing) and observe the initial movement of the compression gauge needle as well as the final total gauge reading. Repeat the procedure for the other cylinder and compare the results to the value listed in this Chapter's Specifications.

7   If the compression in both cylinders built up quickly and evenly to the specified amount, you can assume the engine upper end is in reasonably good mechanical condition. Worn or sticking piston rings and worn cylinders will produce very little initial movement of the gauge needle, but compression will tend to build up gradually as the engine spins over. Valve and valve seat leakage, or head gasket leakage, is indicated by low initial compression which does not tend to build up.

8   To further confirm your findings, add a small amount of engine oil to each cylinder by inserting the nozzle of a squirt-type oil can through the spark plug holes. The oil will tend to seal the piston rings if they are leaking. Repeat the test for the other cylinder.

9   If the compression increases significantly after the addition of the oil, the piston rings and/or cylinders are definitely worn. If the compression does not increase, the pressure is leaking past the valves or the head gasket. Leakage past the valves may be due to insufficient valve clearances, burned, warped or cracked valves or valve seats, or valves that are hanging up in the guides.

10   If compression readings are considerably higher than specified, the combustion chambers are probably coated with excessive carbon deposits. It is possible (but not very likely) for carbon deposits to raise the compression enough to compensate for the effects of leakage past rings or valves. Remove the cylinder heads and carefully decarbonize the combustion chambers (see Section 14).

3 Operations possible with the engine in the frame

The components and assemblies listed below can be removed without having to remove the engine from the frame. If, however, a number of areas require attention at the same time, removal of the engine is recommended.

> *Clutch, primary drive and transmission (see Part B of this Chapter)*
> *Rocker arms, pushrods and lifters**
> *Cylinder head and valves*
> *Cylinders and pistons*
> *Cam gears and camshafts*
> *Oil pump*
> *Starter motor*
> *Generator or alternator*

*On Shovelhead engines, the rear cylinder rocker box must be removed as a unit with the cylinder head if the engine is in the motorcycle.

4 Operations requiring engine removal

1   It is necessary to remove the engine/transmission assembly from the frame and separate the crankcase halves to gain access to the following components:

> *Crankshaft, connecting rods and bearings*

5 Major engine repair - general note

1   It is not always easy to determine when

2.5 A compression gauge with a threaded fitting for the spark plug hole is preferred over the type that requires hand pressure to retain the seal

2

or if an engine should be completely over-hauled, as a number of factors must be considered.

2   High mileage is not necessarily an indication that an overhaul is needed, while low mileage, on the other hand, does not preclude the need for an overhaul. Frequency of servicing is probably the single most important consideration. An engine that has regular and frequent oil and filter changes, as well as other required maintenance, will most likely give many miles of reliable service. Conversely, a neglected engine, or one which has not been broken in properly, may require an overhaul very early in its life.

3   Exhaust smoke and excessive oil consumption are both indications that piston rings and/or valve guides are in need of attention. Make sure oil leaks are not responsible before deciding that the rings and guides are bad. Refer to Section 2 and perform a cylinder compression check to determine for certain the nature and extent of the work required.

4   If the engine is making obvious knocking or rumbling noises, the connecting rod and/or main bearings are probably at fault.

5   Loss of power, rough running, excessive valve train noise and high fuel consumption rates may also point to the need for an overhaul, especially if they are all present at the same time. If a complete tune-up does not remedy the situation, major mechanical work is the only solution.

6   An engine overhaul generally involves restoring the internal parts to the specifications of a new engine. During an overhaul the piston rings are replaced and the cylinder walls are bored and/or honed. If a rebore is done, then new pistons are also required. The crankshaft and connecting rods are replaced as a complete assembly if problems are found with any of them. Generally the valves are serviced as well, since they are usually in less than perfect condition at this point. While the engine is being overhauled, other components such as the carburetor (if equipped) and starter motor can

be rebuilt also. The end result should be a like-new engine that will give as many trouble-free miles as the original.

7   Before beginning the engine overhaul, read through all of the related procedures to familiarize yourself with the scope and requirements of the job. Overhauling an engine is not all that difficult, but it is time consuming. Plan on the motorcycle being tied up for a minimum of two weeks. Check on the availability of parts and make sure that any necessary special tools, equipment and supplies are obtained in advance.

8   Most work can be done with typical shop hand tools, although a number of precision measuring tools are required for inspecting parts to determine if they must be replaced. Often a dealer service department or motorcycle repair shop will handle the inspection of parts and offer advice concerning reconditioning and replacement. As a general rule, time is the primary cost of an overhaul so it doesn't pay to install worn or substandard parts.

9   As a final note, to ensure maximum life and minimum trouble from a rebuilt engine, everything must be assembled with care in a spotlessly clean environment.
Note: *These engines use a number of O-rings, some of them very close to each other in size. Make sure O-rings are labeled when you buy them, or else have the parts supplier label them for you. Don't remove the labels until you're ready to install the O-rings.*

6   Engine - removal and installation

> ⚠️ **Warning: The engine is VERY heavy. Engine removal and installation should be done with the aid of at least one strong assistant, though two are preferable, to avoid damage or personal injury that could occur if the engine is dropped. A**

hydraulic floor jack should be used to support and lower the engine if possible (they can be rented at low cost).

 Where options are given for removal of components not essential for engine removal, such as the starter motor or alternator rotor, bear in mind that although these do not weigh much by themselves, they add to the weight of the engine, and anything that can be removed to reduce the overall weight is a bonus.

Removal

1   Prop the motorcycle securely upright, so it can't be knocked over while you're loosening tight fasteners. Turn the fuel tank valve to the Off position. Disconnect the battery (negative cable first). Drain the oil from the oil tank and primary chaincase (see Chapter 1). If you're working on an early model, remove the crankcase drain plug as well as the oil tank drain plug **(see illustration)**.

2   Remove the seat (see Chapter 7).

3   Remove the fuel tank (see Chapter 3).

4   Label and disconnect the spark plug and ignition coil primary wires. Remove the ignition coil (see Chapter 4).

5   Remove the battery and battery box (see Chapter 8).

6   Remove the air cleaner and exhaust system (see Chapter 3).

7   Remove the oil tank (see Section 19).

8   Disconnect the starter wires.

9   If the vehicle has a rear drum brake, disconnect the brake linkage. If the vehicle has a rear disc brake, detach the master cylinder (leaving the brake line connected) and support it out of the way.

10   Remove the kickstarter lever (if equipped) (see Chapter 2B).

11   If you're working on a 1970 model, disconnect the clutch cable at the engine (see Chapter 2B).

12   If the bike has a mechanical speedometer cable, disconnect it at the sprocket cover

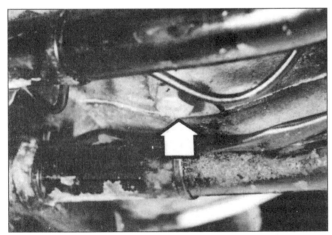

6.1   Location of the crankcase oil drain plug on early models

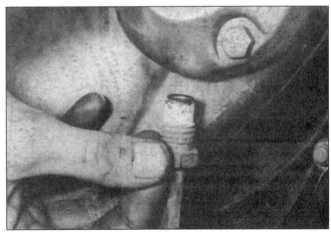

6.16   Disconnect the breather pipe from the base of the circular housing

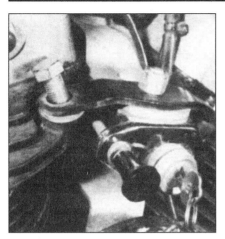

6.23a Note how the bracket is bolted to the head - early model shown

6.23b Note the arrangement of the washers at the frame connections - early model shown

6.26 Bolt up the front . . .

on the right-hand side of the engine.

13 Remove the sprocket cover from the right-hand side of the engine (on later models, remove the right footpeg and brake pedal at the same time). Remove the drive chain or belt (see Chapter 5).

14 On early models, remove the right footpeg and brake pedal.

15 If the motorcycle has a mechanical tachometer, disconnect the drive cable (see Chapter 8).

16 On early models, disconnect the breather pipe union from the timing cover **(see illustration)**.

17 Disconnect the wire from the oil pressure switch (at the base of the timing cover on early models and on the filter housing on later models).

18 Remove the carburetor and intake manifold (see Chapter 3).

19 Remove the left footpeg. On 1970 through 1974 models remove the brake pedal. On 1975 and later models, remove the shift lever.

20 Remove the primary chaincase (see Chapter 2B).

21 On 1970 through early 1984 models, remove the generator (see Chapter 8).

22 Remove the following from the upper engine steady bracket:

a) *Horn (1970 through1992)*
b) *Main key switch*
c) *Choke cable*

23 Note the positions of the washers and ground connections and remove the steady bracket **(see illustrations)**.

24 Disconnect the ignition module wiring harness and free it from any cable ties (see Chapter 4 if necessary).

25 On late 1984 and later models, disconnect the alternator wires (see Chapter 8 if necessary).

26 Support the engine. Note the positions of any washers and ground wires and remove the lower front engine mount **(see illustration)**. Place the bolts back in their holes so they won't be mixed up.

27 Unbolt the rear engine mount from the frame **(see illustration)**.

28 Make sure no wires or hoses are still attached to the engine.

29 With the help of at least one assistant, slowly and carefully guide the engine out the left side (1970 through 1985 models) or the right side (1986 and later models). It's a good idea to have a third person hold the frame steady as the engine is removed. Tilt the engine as necessary to ease removal, but be careful to control it so it doesn't tip all the way over.

Caution: Don't lay an Evolution engine down on the primary side or the clutch cable adjusting screw or cable fitting will be damaged.

Installation

30 Installation is the reverse of removal. Note the following points:

a) *Don't tighten any of the engine mounting bolts until they all have been installed.*
b) *Use new gaskets at all exhaust pipe connections.*
c) *Tighten the engine mounting bolts to the torque listed in this Chapter's Specifications.*

d) *Adjust the drive chain or belt, throttle cables and clutch cable following the procedures in Chapter 1.*
e) *Fill the oil tank and check the engine oil level (see Chapter 1).*

7 Engine disassembly and reassembly - general information

1 Before disassembling the engine, clean the exterior with a degreaser and rinse it with water. A clean engine will make the job easier and prevent the possibility of getting dirt into the internal areas of the engine.

2 In addition to the precision measuring tools mentioned earlier, you will need a torque wrench, a valve spring compressor, oil gallery brushes, a piston ring removal and installation tool, a piston ring compressor. Some new, clean engine oil of the correct grade and type, some engine assembly lube (or moly-based grease) and a tube of RTV (silicone) sealant will also be required.

3 An engine support stand made from short lengths of 2 x 4's bolted together will facilitate the disassembly and reassembly

2

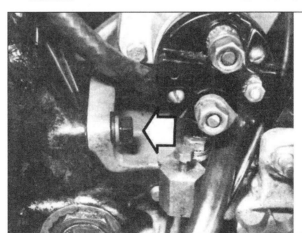

6.27 . . . and the rear engine mount (early model shown)

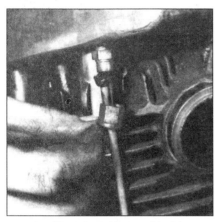

9.1 Note the rubber seal inside the union nut

9.2 External oil lines (Shovelhead engine) have a rubber seal under the union nut

10.4 After the bolts are removed, detach the rocker boxes (if they're stuck, dislodge them with a soft-faced hammer)

procedures. The perimeter of the mount should be just big enough to accommodate the engine crankcase. If you have an automotive-type engine stand, an adapter plate can be made from a piece of plate, some angle iron and some nuts and bolts.

4   When disassembling the engine, keep "mated" parts together (including gears, cylinders, pistons, etc. that have been in contact with each other during engine operation). These "mated" parts must be reused or replaced as an assembly.

5   Engine/transmission disassembly should be done in the following general order with reference to the appropriate Sections.

Remove the valve covers
Remove the breather
Remove the rocker arms, pushrods and lifters
Remove the cylinder heads
Remove the cylinders
Remove the pistons
Remove the camshafts
Remove the oil pump
Remove the primary drive housing (see Chapter 2B)
Remove the alternator rotor/stator coils and starter jackshaft (see Chapter 8)
Separate the crankcase halves
Remove the balancer chain and shafts
Remove the crankshaft and connecting rods
Remove the shift drum/forks

6   Reassembly is accomplished by reversing the general disassembly sequence.

8 Top Dead Center (TDC) - locating

1   Various procedures in this manual require placing one of the pistons at TDC on its compression stroke.
2   Remove the spark plugs (see Chapter 1).
3   Rotate the crankshaft as follows: With the primary cover installed, support the bike with the rear wheel off the ground. Place the transmission in fourth or fifth gear and turn the rear wheel in the forward direction.
4   Slip a screwdriver into the removal slot of the spring cap retainer on the intake pushrod (this is the pushrod closest to the center of the engine, on either front or rear cylinder). Push down on the screwdriver and pry outward to remove the spring cap retainer (see Section 10).
5   Lift the lower pushrod cover to expose the intake lifter. Place a finger on the lifter so you can feel it rise and fall, then rotate the crankshaft as described above. Let the intake lifter rise, then fall, indicating that the intake valve has closed, which means the piston has traveled downward on the intake stroke.
6   Place a finger over the spark plug hole and turn the engine as described above. This will cause air pressure to build up against your finger as the piston rises on the compression stroke. Keep turning until the pressure stops building, then look into the spark plug hole with a flashlight. Turn the engine back and forth slightly while watching the top of the piston, which will go up and down slightly. Center the piston at the top of its stroke.

9 External oil lines (Shovelhead engine) - removal and installation

1   Unscrew the fittings and remove the oil lines, taking care not to damage them **(see illustration)**.
2   Install new rubber seals on the oil lines **(see illustration)**.
Caution: Be sure the seals seat correctly, or oil flow to the cylinder heads may be cut off.
3   Position the oil lines and tighten the fitting nuts securely, but don't overtighten them and strip the threads.
4   Run the engine and check for leaks.

10 Cylinder heads, rocker arms, pushrods and lifters - removal and installation

Removal

Shovelhead engine

Note: *The rear cylinder rocker box must be removed together with the cylinder head if the engine is still in the motorcycle.*
1   Support the bike securely upright.
2   Remove the external oil lines (see Section 9).
3   Mark the rocker boxes for front or rear cylinder. Make sure the valves for the cylinder you're working on are closed (the cylinder is at TDC on the compression stroke) (see Section 8).
4   Loosen the rocker box bolts evenly, 1/4-turn at a time, until all seven are loose. Lift the rocker box off the head **(see illustration)**.
5   Mark the pushrods for location (front or rear cylinder, intake or exhaust). Lift them out of their tubes, then remove the pushrod tubes as complete assemblies **(see illustration)**.
6   To free the lifters, remove the single hex bolt securing the guide block and remove it. The guide block on 1970 through 1976 models is a press fit, as well as being bolted, so you'll need a small puller (Harley part no. HD 95724-57 or equivalent). The puller jaws need to engage the slots in the outside of the guide block.
7   Loosen the four cylinder head bolts in a criss-cross pattern, 1/8 turn at a time, until they're all loose, then unscrew them all the way and lift off the head **(see illustration)**. If the cylinder head won't come off, tap it gently with a soft face hammer. Don't pry it off, or fins will be broken. There's no need to mark the heads, since they won't fit on the wrong cylinder.

Evolution engine (1986 through 1990)

8   On 1986 through 1990 models, the

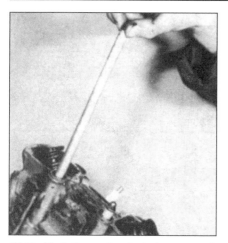

10.5a Mark the pushrods during removal - they must be installed in their original locations

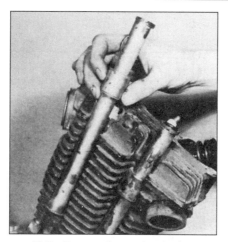

10.5b Remove the pushrod tubes as an assembly

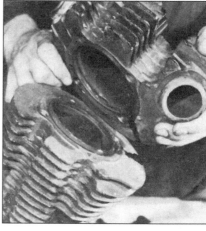

10.7 DO NOT pry the cylinder head off the barrel - damage could result

pushrod tubes are collapsible and are removed before the rocker boxes or heads. Push down on the front pushrod tube spring retainer, then remove the keeper and pull the upper tube out of the recess in the underside of the cylinder head (it's a good idea to start with the front head).

9   Repeat the procedure for the remaining pushrod tube.

10   To free the lifters, remove the single hex bolt securing the guide block and remove it.

All Evolution engines

11   On all Evolution models, remove the Allen screws and washers from the upper rocker arm cover, then detach the cover **(see illustration)**. If the cover is stuck, tap it gently with a soft-face hammer to break the gasket seal.

12   Remove the middle rocker arm cover **(see illustration)**. Remove and discard all rocker cover gaskets and use new ones during assembly.

13   Place the cylinder you're working on at TDC compression (see Section 8).

14   Remove the large bolts retaining the lower rocker arm cover **(see illustration)**.

1986 through 1990 Evolution engines

15   On 1986 through 1990 models, carefully tap the rocker arm shafts out of the lower rocker arm cover from the left side, then lift out the rocker arms and remove the pushrods and tubes. Be sure to mark all parts so they aren't mixed up.

All Evolution engines

16   On all Evolution models, remove the lower rocker arm cover-to-cylinder head bolts. There are two Allen bolts and three hex bolts.

17   Detach the lower rocker arm cover and gaskets. Discard the gaskets and use new ones during reassembly.

10.11 Remove the four Allen screws and detach the upper rocker cover (Evolution engine) . . .

2

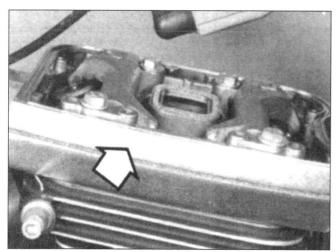

10.12 . . . then lift off the middle rocker arm cover and gasket (arrow)

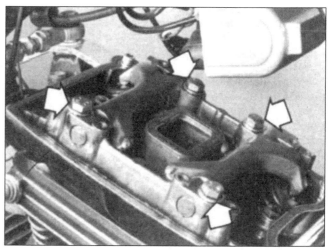

10.14 Remove the large bolts (arrows) (the two on the right retain the rocker shafts), then, with the valves closed, drive out the shafts from the left side to free the rocker arms

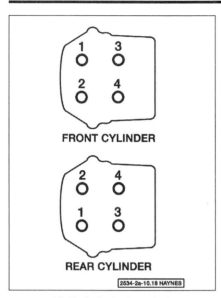

10.18 Cylinder head bolt tightening/loosening sequence (Evolution engine)

18   Loosen the cylinder head bolts in the specified sequence, 1/8 turn at a time, until they're all loose **(see illustration)**. Remove the bolts and any washers installed under them (on 1988 and later models, washers aren't used).

19   Carefully lift off the cylinder head, then remove the gasket and the O-rings around the dowel sleeves **(see illustration)**. Discard the gasket and O-rings and use new one during installation.

1991 and later Evolution engines

20   Lift the pushrods and tubes out of the crankcase and label them (front or rear cylinder, intake or exhaust).

21   On 1991 and later models, the rocker shafts can be removed from the lower rocker cover at this stage. Tap them out from the left side, then lift out the rocker arms.

22   To free the lifters on 1991 and later models, remove the triangular cover at the center of the pushrod bores and pull out the

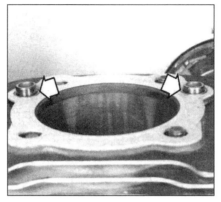

10.19 On Evolution engines, place the O-rings (arrows) over the dowels, then install the head gasket and make sure it's aligned correctly

tappet retaining pin, using pliers if necessary. Lift the lifters out of their bores and mark them so they don't get mixed up.

Inspection

Pushrods

23   Check the ends of the pushrods where they ride in the tappets and the rocker arms **(see illustration)**. Check for distortion by rolling them on a flat surface such as a pane of glass. If wear or distortion is evident, new pushrods should be installed.

Rocker arms

24   To disassemble a rocker box on Shovelhead engines, unscrew the rocker arm shaft end caps found on the right-hand side of each rocker box **(see illustrations)**.

25   Check the rocker arm bushings and the shafts for evidence of excessive wear and damage **(see illustrations)**.

26   Measure the outside diameter of the shaft (where it rides in the bushings) and the inside diameter of the rocker arm bushings. Subtract the diameter from the bushing diameter to obtain the clearance. If it's excessive, install new parts or have the bushings in the rocker arm(s) replaced by a

10.23 Check the pushrod ends for wear and make sure the oil holes (Evolution engine) are clear

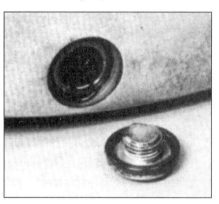

10.24a On Shovelhead engines, remove the rocker arm shaft end cap and . . .

dealer service department or other qualified shop.

27   Check each rocker arm where it contacts the pushrod and valve stem. If cracks, scuffing or breakthrough in the case hardened surface are evident, install a new rocker arm.

Lifters

28   Make sure the rollers on the lifters turn freely, with no play on their pins **(see illustration)**. If you find either problem, replace

10.24b . . . unscrew the acorn nut from the other end

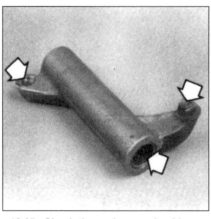

10.25a Check the rocker arm bushings, pushrod recesses and valve stem pads for wear and damage (arrows)

10.25b Check the rocker shafts for wear on the friction surfaces - the Evolution engine shafts have a cutout (arrow) for the bolt to pass through

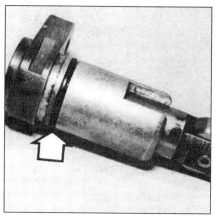

10.28 Check the lifters and guides carefully for wear - install a new O-ring (arrow) on each guide

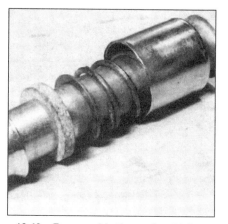

10.40a Reassemble the pushrod tubes using new seals

10.40b A new seal should be installed in each lifter housing

the lifter.

29   Measure the diameter of the lifters and lifter bores, using a micrometer and bore gauge. Calculate the difference and compare it to the value listed in this Chapter's Specifications. If it's beyond the specified range, replace the lifters or the crankcase, whichever is worn.

30   Check the lifters for worn pushrod sockets. Make sure the plunger inside the lifter is fully in contact with the lifter C-clip. Operate the plunger inside the lifter and make sure it moves freely. Replace the lifter if problems are found.

31   Place the lifters in clean engine oil and keep them in a covered container until they're reinstalled.

Installation

Shovelhead engine

32   Turn the adjustment screw assembly into the tappet body.

33   Install a new O-ring on the tappet guide and coat it with grease. Carefully push the lifter into the guide from below. Coat the lifter with fresh engine oil; be sure to apply plenty of oil to the roller needles.

34   Hold the lifter as high as possible in the lifter guide and position the assembly over

the gearcase. Turn the lifter guide so the mounting hole is aligned with the hole in the case, then turn the lifter so its roller is correctly aligned with the cam.

Caution: If the lifter roller isn't correctly aligned (crosswise to the camshaft) serious engine damage could occur.

35   Carefully press the lifter guide assembly into the crankcase. The guides are made of aluminum, so care must be taken not to damage them.

36   Install the guide retaining bolts and tighten them securely. On some earlier models, the rear bolt is also used to secure the starter motor retaining strap. On these models, the bolt can't be installed until the starter motor is installed.

37   Check the lifters for freedom of movement in the guide.

38   Place a new head gasket on top of each cylinder, without any sealant. Be sure the oil return holes in the gasket line up with the drain holes in the head.

39   Rotate the crankshaft until the lifters are at their lowest position.

40   Install the pushrod tubes in their bores, referring to the labels made during removal **(see illustrations)**. Use new seals on the tubes.

41   Carefully set the cylinder head in posi-

tion over the oil lines and the pushrod assemblies.

42   Install the cylinder head mounting bolts finger-tight.

43   Install the pushrods in their original locations, referring to the labels made during removal.

44   If the other cylinder head was removed, install it following the same procedure.

45   Attach the intake manifold to the cylinder heads (see Chapter 3).

46   Tighten the head bolts in three stages, in a criss-cross pattern, to the torque listed in this Chapter's Specifications.

47   Coat the rocker shafts with clean engine oil and install new O-rings on the right end, behind the acorn nuts. Install the rocker components in their original locations.

48   Rotate the crankshaft until both valves in the head being assembled are closed (tappets on camshaft base circles). This will prevent stress on the rocker box casting as it's bolted down.

49   Place new O-rings in each of the pushrod tube recesses **(see illustration)**.

50   Place a new rocker box gasket on top of the head without sealant. Carefully install the rocker box on the cylinder head **(see illustration)**. Be sure the pushrods engage

2

10.40c Be sure the pushrods engage in the lifters

10.49 Make sure the O-ring for each pushrod tube (arrow) is in place

10.50 Install the rocker box when the lifters are on the camshaft base circles, not the lobes (valve closed position)

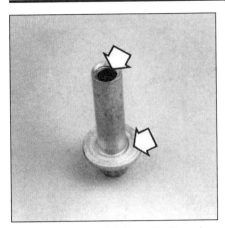

10.62 Clean and lubricate the threads and the underside of each head bolt (arrows) before installation

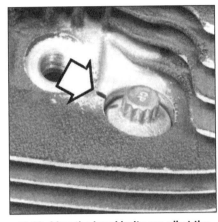

10.66 After the head bolts are all at the specified torque, make a mark on each bolt head flange and extend it onto the head (arrow)

10.67 Turn each head bolt an additional 90-degrees (1/4-turn) in an uninterrupted motion - this must be done exactly as described to prevent head gasket leaks

correctly with the ends of the rocker arms.

51 Tighten the rocker box retaining bolts in a criss-cross pattern, in three stages, to the torque listed in this Chapter's Specifications. The valves must be closed as this is done.

52 Reinstall the external oil lines (see Section 9).

53 Adjust the lifters (see Chapter 1).

Evolution engine

Note: *Before beginning this procedure, clean the cylinder head bolt threads, then lubricate them with a small amount of clean engine oil and thread the bolts onto the studs to maker sure they don't bind.*

1986 through 1990 Evolution engine

54 Install a new O-ring on the tappet guide and coat it with grease. Carefully push the lifter into the guide from below. Coat the lifter with fresh engine oil; be sure to apply plenty of oil to the roller needles.

55 Hold the lifter as high as possible in the lifter guide and position the assembly over the gearcase. Turn the lifter guide so the mounting hole is aligned with the hole in the case, then turn the lifter so its roller is correctly aligned with the cam.

Caution: If the lifter roller isn't correctly aligned (crosswise to the camshaft) serious engine damage could occur.

56 Carefully press the lifter guide assembly into the crankcase. The guides are made of aluminum, so care must be taken not to damage them.

57 Install the guide retaining bolts and tighten them securely.

58 Check the lifters for freedom of movement in the guide.

59 Rotate the crankshaft until the lifters are at their lowest position.

All Evolution engines

60 Install new O-rings over the dowel sleeves, then position the new head gasket on the cylinder barrel. No sealant is required on the head gaskets.

61 Make sure the bolt holes in the head are clean, then carefully lower it onto the cylinder

- the dowel sleeves must enter the holes and align the head.

62 Lubricate the threads and the underside of each bolt head with a small amount of engine oil **(see illustration)**.

63 Slip the washers (if used) over the studs, then install the bolts finger-tight.

Caution: The procedure for tightening the cylinder head bolts is extremely critical to prevent gasket leaks, stud failure and cylinder or head distortion.

64 Refer to the tightening sequence **(see illustration 10.18)** and tighten the bolts to the initial torque listed in this Chapter's Specifications.

65 Go through the tightening sequence again, this time tightening the bolts to the second torque setting listed in this Chapter's Specifications.

66 Mark each bolt and the cylinder head with a felt-tip pen **(see illustration)**.

67 Turn each bolt, in the specified sequence, an additional 1/4-turn **(see illustration)**.

1986 through 1990 Evolution engines

68 Install new rocker cover gaskets with the sealant beads facing UP.

69 Install new seals and reassemble the pushrod tubes, then slip the pushrods into the tubes and install them in their original locations. Make sure they're seated in the lifters.

Caution: The pushrods are color coded to ensure correct installation. Don't turn the pushrods end-for-end; they must be mated with the rocker arm or lifter just like they were originally.

If the valves and seats were reconditioned, or if valve train components were replaced with new ones, the pushrod length requirements very likely will change. Since a special gauge is required to determine the correct length pushrod(s) to use, have a Harley-Davidson dealer service department select

the parts for you.

70 Make sure the tappets for the cylinder being assembled are on the cam lobe base circles, not the lobes (turn the crankshaft if necessary to reposition them). **Note:** *If you're working on an early 1986 model, install the lower rocker arm cover now, but don't tighten the bolts completely (just snug them down). Don't install the two large bolts that retain the rocker arm shafts. Insert a 14-inch-long piece of 0.050 to 0.060 inch wire through the hollow pushrod and into the tappet. Depress the check valve in the tappet by pushing down on the wire, then push down on the pushrod to bleed down the tappet. Hold the pushrod down, pull out the wire and install the rocker arm and shaft. Repeat the procedure for the other valve and remaining cylinder. Tighten the lower rocker arm cover bolts to the torque listed in this Chapter's Specifications.*

1991 and later Evolution engines

71 Before installing the tappets rotate the engine so that the cam followers are on heir base circle (as viewed from the tappet bore). Liberally oil each tappet and insert so that its flats face the front and rear of the engine.

72 Insert the retaining pins, followed by a new O-ring and install the triangular plate. Install the washer and screw and tighten to the specified torque.

73 Install a new seal over the top of the pushrod tube and slide it down the tube together with the retaining plate. Fit a new O-ring on top of the tube and insert the tube into its location in the cylinder head underside. Maneuver the bottom of the tube into position and secure with the retaining plate (fit over the pin in the casing); tighten its screw to the specified torque. Install the pushrods in their original bores and the original way up.

All Evolution engines

74 Lubricate the rocker arm faces with moly-base grease, assemble the rocker arms

and shafts in the lower rocker arm cover and slip all the bolts through the holes. The cutouts in the shafts must be positioned so the bolts will pass through the cover and the cutouts to retain the shafts.

75 Position the lower rocker arm cover on the head and thread all the bolts into place finger-tight. Make sure the pushrods are engaged in the rocker arm sockets.

76 Tighten the bolts in 1/4-turn increments, following a criss-cross pattern, to the specified torque. This will allow the tappets to bleed down slowly.

77 Make sure the pushrods spin freely.

Caution: To avoid pushrod and rocker arm damage, do not operate the starter or turn the engine over by hand until both pushrods can be turned with your fingers.

78 Position new gaskets in the lower rocker arm cover, then install the middle rocker arm cover and a new gasket. On 1991-on models check the condition of the rubber umbrella valve in the middle rocker cover and renew it if it shows signs of deterioration. The valve is part of the crankcase breather system, and vents vapors passed up through the pushrod tubes into the intake system, via hollow bolts which mount the air cleaner to each cylinder.

79 Install the upper rocker arm cover and screws. Tighten the screws after making sure the middle rocker arm cover is positioned evenly on all sides.

11 Valves/valve seats/valve guides - servicing

1 Because of the complex nature of this job and the special tools and equipment required, servicing of the valves, the valve seats and the valve guides (commonly known as a valve job) is best left to a professional.

2 The home mechanic can, however, remove and disassemble the head, do the initial cleaning and inspection, then reassemble and deliver the head to a dealer service department or properly equipped motorcycle repair shop for the actual valve servicing. Refer to Section 12 for those procedures.

3 The dealer service department will remove the valves and springs, recondition or replace the valves and valve seats, replace the valve guides, check and replace the valve springs, spring retainers and keepers (as necessary), replace the valve seals with new ones and reassemble the valve components.

4 After the valve job has been performed, the head will be in like-new condition. When the head is returned, be sure to clean it again very thoroughly before installation on the engine to remove any metal particles or abrasive grit that may still be present from the valve service operations. Use compressed air, if available, to blow out all the holes and passages.

12.7a Compress the springs with a valve spring compressor, then remove the keepers (arrows) with a magnet or needle-nose pliers

12 Cylinder head and valves - disassembly, inspection and reassembly

1 As mentioned in the previous Section, valve servicing and valve guide replacement should be left to a dealer service department or motorcycle repair shop. However, disassembly, cleaning and inspection of the valves and related components can be done (if the necessary special tools are available) by the home mechanic. This way no expense is incurred if the inspection reveals that service work is not required at this time.

2 To properly disassemble the valve components without the risk of damaging them, a valve spring compressor is absolutely necessary. This special tool can usually be rented, but if it's not available, have a dealer service department or motorcycle repair shop handle the entire process of disassembly, inspection, service or repair (if required) and reassembly of the valves.

Disassembly

3 Remove the cylinder head from the engine (see Section 10).

4 Before the valves are removed, scrape away any traces of gasket material from the head gasket sealing surface. Work slowly and do not nick or gouge the soft aluminum of the head. Gasket removing solvents, which work very well, are available at most motorcycle shops and auto parts stores.

5 Carefully scrape all carbon deposits out of the combustion chamber area. A hand held wire brush or a piece of fine emery cloth can be used once the majority of deposits have been scraped away. Do not use a wire brush mounted in a drill motor, or one with extremely stiff bristles, as the head material is soft and may be eroded away or scratched by the wire brush.

6 Before proceeding, arrange to label and store the valves along with their related com-

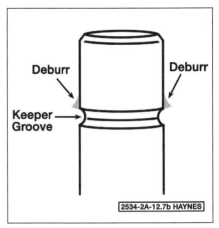

12.7b If the valve binds in the guide, deburr the area above the keeper groove

ponents so they can be kept separate and reinstalled in the same valve guides they are removed from (again, plastic bags work well for this).

7 Compress the valve spring on the first valve with a spring compressor, then remove the keepers and the retainer from the valve assembly **(see illustration)**. Do not compress the springs any more than is absolutely necessary. Carefully release the valve spring compressor and remove the springs and the valve from the head. If the valve binds in the guide (won't pull through), push it back into the head and deburr the area around the keeper groove with a very fine file or whetstone **(see illustration)**.

8 Repeat the procedure for the remaining valves. Remember to keep the parts for each valve together so they can be reinstalled in the same location.

9 Once the valves have been removed and labeled, pull off the valve stem seals with pliers and discard them (the old seals should never be reused), then remove the spring seats.

10 Next, clean the cylinder head with solvent and dry it thoroughly. Compressed air will speed the drying process and ensure that all holes and recessed areas are clean.

11 Clean all of the valve springs, keepers, retainers and spring seats with solvent and dry them thoroughly. Do the parts from one valve at a time so that no mixing of parts between valves occurs.

12 Scrape off any deposits that may have formed on the valve, then use a motorized wire brush to remove deposits from the valve heads and stems. Again, make sure the valves do not get mixed up.

Inspection

 Refer to Tools and Workshop Tips in the Reference section for details of how to read a micrometer and dial gauges.

13 Inspect the head very carefully for cracks and other damage. If cracks are found, a new head will be required.

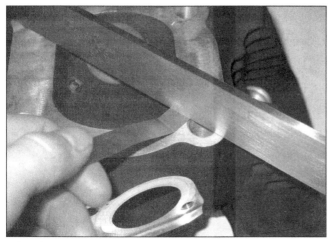

12.14 Lay a precision straightedge across the cylinder head and
try to slide a feeler gauge of the specified thickness (equal
to the maximum allowable warpage) under it

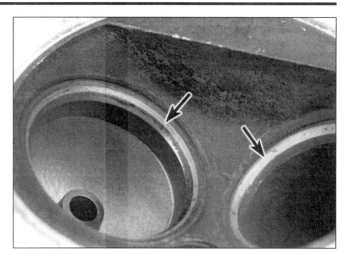

12.15a Check the valve seats (arrows) in each head - look for
pits, cracks and burned areas

12.15b Measuring the valve seat width

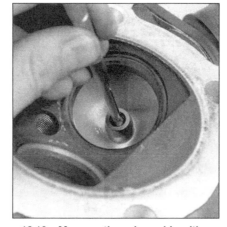

12.16a Measure the valve guide with a
small hole gauge . . .

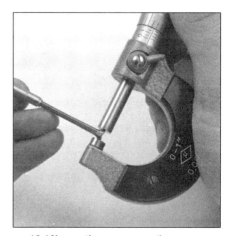

12.16b . . . then measure the gauge
with a micrometer

14   Using a precision straightedge and a feeler gauge, check the head gasket mating surface for warpage. Lay the straightedge lengthwise, across the head and diagonally (corner-to-corner), intersecting the head bolt holes. Try to slip a feeler gauge of the same thickness as the warpage limit listed in this Chapter's Specifications under it, on either side of the combustion chamber **(see illustration)**. If the feeler gauge can be inserted between the head and the straightedge, the head is warped and must either be machined or, if warpage is excessive, replaced with a new one.

15   Examine the valve seats **(see illustration)**. If they are pitted, cracked or burned, the head will require valve service that is beyond the scope of the home mechanic. Measure the valve seat width and compare it to this Chapter's Specifications **(see illustration)**. If it is not within the specified range, or if it varies around its circumference, valve service work is required.

16   Clean the valve guides to remove any carbon buildup, then measure the inside diameters of the guides (at both ends and the center of the guide) with a small hole

gauge and a 0-to-1-inch micrometer **(see illustrations)**. If the guides exceed the maximum value given in the Chapter's Specifications, they must be replaced. The guides are measured at the ends and at the center to determine if they are worn in a bell-mouth

12.17a Check the valve face and margin
for wear and cracks

pattern (more wear at the ends). If they are, guide replacement is an absolute must.

17   Carefully inspect each valve face for cracks, pits and burned spots **(see illustration)**. Check the valve stem and the keeper groove area for cracks **(see illustration)**.

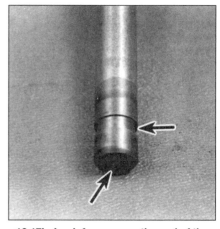

12.17b Look for wear on the end of the
valve stem and make sure the keeper
groove isn't distorted in any way

12.18 Measure the valve stem diameter
with a micrometer

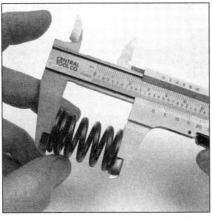

12.19a Measure the free length of the
valve springs

12.19b Check the valve springs
for squareness

Rotate the valve and check for any obvious indication that it is bent. Check the end of the stem for pitting and excessive wear. The presence of any of the above conditions indicates the need for valve servicing.

18 Measure the valve stem diameter and replace if it exceeds the minimum value listed in this Chapter's Specifications **(see illustration)**. Also check the valve stem for bending. Set the valve in a V-block with a dial indicator touching the middle of the stem. Rotate the valve and note the reading on the gauge. If the stem runout exceeds the value listed in this Chapter's Specifications, replace the valve.

19 Check the end of each valve spring for wear and pitting. Measure the free length **(see illustration)** and compare it to this Chapter's Specifications. Any springs that are shorter than specified have sagged and should not be reused. Stand the spring on a flat surface and check it for squareness **(see illustration)**.

20 Check the spring retainers and keepers for obvious wear and cracks. Any questionable parts should not be reused, as extensive damage will occur in the event of failure during engine operation.

21 If the inspection indicates that no ser-

vice work is required, the valve components can be reinstalled in the head.

Reassembly

22 Before installing the valves in the head, they should be lapped (1970 through 2002 models only) to ensure a positive seal between the valves and seats. The valves on 2003 models should not be lapped, as this will remove the interference fit (45-degree valve seat and 46-degree valve face angles). This procedure requires fine valve lapping compound (available at auto parts stores) and a valve lapping tool. If a lapping tool is not available, a piece of rubber or plastic hose can be slipped over the valve stem (after the valve has been installed in the guide) and used to turn the valve.

23 Apply a small amount of fine lapping compound to the valve face **(see illustration)**, then slip the valve into the guide. **Note:** *Make sure the valve is installed in the correct guide and be careful not to get any lapping compound on the valve stem.*

24 Attach the lapping tool (or hose) to the valve and rotate the tool between the palms of your hands **(see illustration)**. Use a back-and-forth motion rather than a circular motion. Lift the valve off the seat and turn it

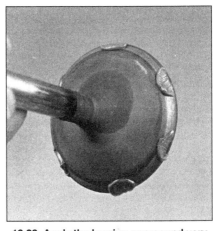

12.23 Apply the lapping compound very
sparingly, in small dabs, to the valve
face only (do not lap the valves
on 2003 models)

at regular intervals to distribute the lapping compound properly **(see illustration)**. Continue the lapping procedure until the valve face and seat contact area is of uniform width and unbroken around the entire circumference of the valve face and seat **(see illustrations)**.

2

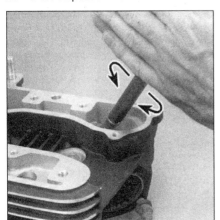

12.24a Rotate the lapping tool or hose
back-and-forth between the palms of
your hands

12.24b Lift the tool and valve periodically
to redistribute the lapping compound on
the valve face and seat

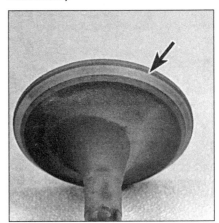

12.24c After lapping, the valve face
should exhibit a uniform, unbroken
contact pattern (arrow). . .

12.24d . . .and the seat should be the specified width (arrow) with a smooth, unbroken appearance

25 Carefully remove the valve from the guide and wipe off all traces of lapping compound. Use solvent to clean the valve and wipe the seat area thoroughly with a solvent soaked cloth. Repeat the procedure for the remaining valves.

26 Lay the spring seats in place in the cylinder head, then install new valve stem seals on each of the guides. Use an appropriate size deep socket to push the seals into place until they are properly seated. Don't twist or cock them, or they will not seal properly against the valve stems. Also, don't remove them again or they will be damaged.

27 Coat the valve stems with assembly lube or moly-based grease, then install one of them into its guide. Next, install the spring seats, springs and retainers, compress the springs and install the keepers. When compressing the springs with the valve spring compressor, depress them only as far as is absolutely necessary to slip the keepers into place. Apply a small amount of grease to the keepers **(see illustration)** to help hold them in place as the pressure is released from the springs. Make certain that the keepers are

12.27 A small dab of grease will help hold the keepers in place on the valve spring while the valve is released

securely locked in their retaining grooves.

28 Support the cylinder head on blocks so the valves can't contact the workbench top, then very gently tap each of the valve stems with a soft-faced hammer. This will help seat the keepers in their grooves.

29 Once all of the valves have been installed in the head, check for proper valve sealing by pouring a small amount of solvent into each of the valve ports. If the solvent leaks past the valve(s) into the combustion chamber area, disassemble the valve(s) and repeat the lapping procedure, then reinstall the valve(s) and repeat the check. Repeat the procedure until a satisfactory seal is obtained.

13 Cylinders - removal, inspection and installation

Removal

1 Before you start, obtain four six-inch lengths of 1/2-inch inside diameter tubing for each cylinder. You'll need these to slip over the studs.

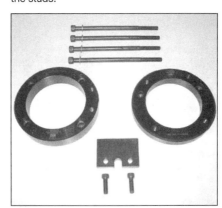

13.5a Accurate bore measurements on 2001 and later models require a set of torque plates to clamp the cylinder (this is the JIMS tool)

2 Following the procedure given in Section 10, remove the cylinder head and pushrods (the lifters don't have to be removed). Make sure the crankshaft is positioned at Top Dead Center (TDC) for the cylinder you're working on (see Section 8).

3 If you're working on a Shovelhead engine, remove the four cylinder base nuts. On all models, lift the cylinder straight up just until you can stuff clean shop towels around the piston, in the space between the cylinder and crankcase **(see illustration)**. If the cylinder is stuck, tap around its perimeter with a soft-faced hammer. Don't attempt to pry between the cylinder and the crankcase, as you will ruin the sealing surfaces.

4 Lift the cylinder straight off the studs. Remove the cylinder base gasket.

Inspection

Caution: Don't attempt to separate the liner from the cylinder.

5 Check the cylinder walls carefully for scratches and score marks.

Note: *On 2001 and later models, Harley-Davidson recommends using torque plates to compensate for cylinder distortion when measuring the bore. These are heavy metal plates that are attached to the top and bottom of the cylinder by studs that go through the cylinder stud passages. JIMS tools also supplies an equivalent tool (see illustrations). If you don't have these or the equivalent, or the necessary bore gauge, have the measurements done by a dealer service department or other qualified shop.*

6 Using the appropriate precision measuring tools, check each cylinder's diameter 1/2-inch down from the top, halfway down the ring travel area, and at the bottom of the ring travel area, parallel to the crankshaft axis **(see illustrations)**. Next, measure each cylinder's diameter at the same three locations across the crankshaft axis. Compare the results to this Chapter's Specifications. If the cylinder walls are tapered, out-of-round, worn beyond the specified limits, or badly scuffed or scored, have them rebored and honed by a dealer service department or a motorcycle

13.3 Carefully lift off the cylinder (after removing the base nuts on Shovelhead engines) - don't let the piston strike the crankcase

13.5b Lay one plate over the top of the cylinder . . .

13.5c . . . and attach the other plate and mounting base with the bolts, then tighten the nuts

13.6a Measure the cylinder bore with a micrometer

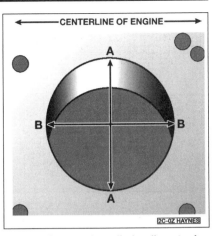

13.6b Measure the cylinder diameter in two directions, at the top, center and bottom of travel

repair shop. If a rebore is done, oversize pistons and rings will be required as well. Oversize pistons are listed in this Chapter's Specifications. Remove the torque plates after taking the measurements.

7 Lay a straightedge across the cylinder top surface and measure any gap between the straightedge and surface with a feeler gauge. Repeat the measurement on the cylinder bottom gasket surface. If either surface is warped beyond the limit listed in this Chapter's Specifications, replace the cylinder and piston.

8 If they are in reasonably good condition and not worn to the outside of the limits, and if the piston-to-cylinder clearances can be maintained properly (see Section 14), then the cylinders do not have to be rebored; honing is all that is necessary.

9 To perform the honing operation you will need the proper size flexible hone with fine stones, or a "bottle brush" type hone, plenty of light oil or honing oil, some shop towels and an electric drill motor. Harley-Davidson recommends a bottle-brush type hone with 240-grit stones. Hold the cylinder block in a vise (cushioned with soft jaws or wood blocks) when performing the honing operation. Mount the hone in the drill motor, compress the stones and slip the hone into the cylinder. Lubricate the cylinder thoroughly, turn on the drill and move the hone up and down in the cylinder at a pace which will produce a fine crosshatch pattern on the cylinder wall with the crosshatch lines intersecting at a 60-degree angle - the angle is important to obtain good ring seating. Be sure to use plenty of lubricant and do not take off any more material than is absolutely necessary to produce the desired effect. Do not withdraw the hone from the cylinder while it is running. Instead, shut off the drill and continue moving the hone up and down in the cylinder until it comes to a complete stop, then compress the stones and withdraw the hone. Wipe the oil out of the cylinder and repeat the procedure on the remaining cylinder. Remember, do not remove too

much material from the cylinder wall. If you do not have the tools, or do not desire to perform the honing operation, a dealer service department or motorcycle repair shop will generally do it for a reasonable fee.

10 Next, the cylinders must be thoroughly washed with warm soapy water to remove all traces of the abrasive grit produced during the honing operation. Be sure to run a brush through the bolt holes and flush them with running water. After rinsing, dry the cylinders thoroughly and apply a coat of light, rust-preventative oil to all machined surfaces.

Installation

11 Lubricate the cylinder bore, piston and rings with plenty of clean engine oil.

12 Install the new cylinder base gasket on the cylinder.

13 Slowly rotate the crankshaft until the piston is at top dead center.

14 Attach a piston ring compressor to the piston and compress the piston rings **(see illustration)**. A large hose clamp can be used instead - just make sure it doesn't scratch the piston, and don't tighten it too much.

15 Install the cylinder over the piston and carefully lower it down until the piston crown

fits into the cylinder liner **(see illustration)**. Push down on the cylinder, making sure the piston doesn't get cocked sideways, until the bottom of the cylinder liner slides down past the piston rings. A wood or plastic hammer handle can be used to gently tap the cylinder down, but don't use too much force or the piston will be damaged.

16 Remove the piston ring compressor or hose clamp, being careful not to scratch the piston. Raise the piston enough to remove the support tool.

17 The remainder of installation is the reverse of removal. If you're working on a Shovelhead, tighten the cylinder base nuts to the torque listed in this Chapter's Specifications.

14 Pistons - removal, inspection and installation

2

1 The pistons are attached to the connecting rods with piston pins that are a slip fit in the pistons and rods.

2 Before removing the pistons from the

13.14 A piston ring compressor . . .

13.15 . . . makes installation of the cylinders much easier

14.3a Using a sharp scribe, scratch the cylinder position (front or rear) into the piston crowns - if there isn't an arrow mark pointing to the front, make one

14.3b Wear eye protection and pry the circlip out of the groove with a pointed tool

14.3c Push the piston pin part-way out, then pull it the rest of the way

rods, stuff a clean shop towel into each crankcase hole, around the connecting rod. This will prevent the circlips from falling into the crankcase if they are inadvertently dropped.

Removal

3   Using a sharp scribe, scratch the position of each piston (front or rear cylinder) into its crown. Each piston should also have an arrow pointing toward the front of the engine **(see illustration)**. If not, scribe an arrow into the piston crown before removal. Support the piston and remove the circlip with needle-nose pliers or a pointed tool **(see illustration)**. Push the piston pin out with fingers **(see illustration)**. If the pin won't come out, fabricate a piston pin removal tool from threaded stock (stud), nuts, washers and a piece of pipe **(see illustration)**.

4   Push the piston pin out from the opposite end to free the piston from the rod. You may have to deburr the area around the groove to enable the pin to slide out (use a triangular file for this procedure). Repeat the procedure for the other piston.

Inspection

5   Before the inspection process can be carried out, the pistons must be cleaned and the old piston rings removed.

6   Using a piston ring installation tool, carefully remove the rings from the pistons **(see illustration)**. Do not nick or gouge the pistons in the process.

7   Scrape all traces of carbon from the tops of the pistons. A hand-held wire brush or a piece of fine emery cloth can be used once most of the deposits have been scraped away. Do not, under any circumstances, use a wire brush mounted in a drill motor to remove deposits from the pistons; the piston material is soft and will be eroded away by the wire brush.

8   Use a piston ring groove cleaning tool to remove any carbon deposits from the ring grooves. If a tool is not available, a piece

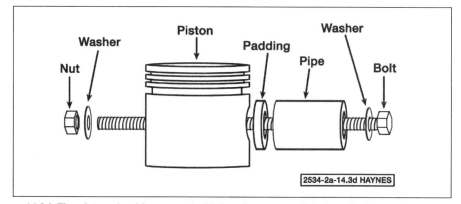

14.3d The piston should come out with hand pressure - if it doesn't, this tool can be fabricated from readily available parts

14.6 Remove the piston rings with a ring removal and installation tool

14.11 Check the piston pin bore and the piston skirt for wear, and make sure the internal holes are clear

broken off the old ring will do the job. Be very careful to remove only the carbon deposits. Do not remove any metal and do not nick or gouge the sides of the ring grooves.

9   Once the deposits have been removed, clean the pistons with solvent and dry them thoroughly. Make sure the oil return holes below the oil ring grooves are clear.

10   If the pistons are not damaged or worn excessively and if the cylinders are not

rebored, new pistons will not be necessary. Normal piston wear appears as even, vertical wear on the thrust surfaces of the piston and slight looseness of the top ring in its groove. New piston rings, on the other hand, should always be used when an engine is rebuilt.

11   Carefully inspect each piston for cracks around the skirt, at the pin bosses and at the ring lands **(see illustration)**.

14.13 Measure the piston ring-to-groove clearance with a feeler gauge

14.14 Measure the piston diameter with a micrometer

14.16 Slip the piston into the rod and try to rock it back-and-forth to check for looseness

14.18 Make sure both piston pin circlips are securely seated in the piston grooves

feeler gauge between the piston and cylinder on one of the thrust faces (90-degrees to the piston pin bore). The piston should slip through the cylinder (with the feeler gauge in place) with moderate pressure. If it falls through, or slides through easily, the clearance is excessive and a new piston will be required. If the piston binds at the lower end of the cylinder and is loose toward the top, the cylinder is tapered, and if tight spots are encountered as the feeler gauge is placed at different points around the cylinder, the cylinder is out-of-round. Repeat the procedure for the remaining piston and cylinder. Be sure to have the cylinders and pistons checked by a dealer service department or a motorcycle repair shop to confirm your findings before purchasing new parts.

15   Apply clean engine oil to the pin, insert it into the piston and check for freeplay by rocking the pin back-and-forth If the pin is loose, new pistons and pins must be installed.

16   Repeat Step 15, this time inserting the pin into the connecting rod (see illustration). If the pin is loose, measure the pin diameter and the pin bushing bore in the connecting rod (or have this done by a dealer service department or machine shop). Replace the piston and pin if the pin is worn; have the pin bushing pressed out and a new one pressed in if it's worn.

17   Refer to Section 17 and install the rings on the pistons.

Installation

18   Install the piston in its original location (front or rear cylinder) with the arrow pointing to the front of the engine. Lubricate the pin and the rod bore with clean engine oil. Install a new circlip in the piston groove on one side of the piston (don't reuse the old circlips). Push the pin into position from the opposite side and install a new circlip. Compress the circlips only enough for them to fit in the piston. Make sure the circlips are properly seated in the grooves (see illustration).

19   Repeat the procedure to install the other piston.

12   Look for scoring and scuffing on the thrust faces of the skirt, holes in the piston crown and burned areas at the edge of the crown. If the skirt is scored or scuffed, the engine may have been suffering from over-heating and/or abnormal combustion, which caused excessively high operating temperatures. The oil pump should be checked thoroughly. A hole in the piston crown, an extreme to be sure, is an indication that abnormal combustion (pre-ignition) was occurring. Burned areas at the edge of the piston crown are usually evidence of spark knock (detonation). If any of the above problems exist, the causes must be corrected or the damage will occur again.

13   Measure the piston ring-to-groove clearance by laying a new piston ring in the ring groove and slipping a feeler gauge in beside it (see illustration). Check the clearance at three or four locations around the groove. Be sure to use the correct ring for each groove; they are different. If the clearance is greater than specified, new pistons will have to be used when the engine is reassembled.

14   Check the piston-to-bore clearance by measuring the bore (see Section 13) and the

piston diameter. Make sure that the pistons and cylinders are correctly matched. On 1970 through 2002 models, measure the piston across the skirt on the thrust faces at a 90-degree angle to the piston pin, about 1/2-inch (13 mm) up from the bottom of the skirt (see illustration). On 2003 models, measure at the two small openings in the piston skirt (where the bare aluminum is exposed). These openings are very small, so you'll need anvil adapters for the micrometer. Subtract the piston diameter from the bore diameter to obtain the clearance. If it is greater than specified, the cylinders will have to be rebored and new oversized pistons and rings installed. If the appropriate precision measuring tools are not available, the piston-to-cylinder clearances can be obtained, though not quite as accurately, using feeler gauge stock. Feeler gauge stock comes in 12-inch lengths and various thicknesses and is generally available at auto parts stores. To check the clearance, select a piece of feeler gauge stock equal to the piston-to-cylinder clearance listed in this Chapter's Specifications. Slip the gauge into the cylinder alongside of the piston. The cylinder should be upside down and the piston must be positioned exactly as it normally would be. Place the

15 Piston rings - installation

1   Before installing the new piston rings, the ring end gaps must be checked.

2   Lay out the pistons and the new ring sets so the rings will be matched with the same piston and cylinder during the end gap measurement procedure and engine assembly.

3   Insert the top (No. 1) ring into the bottom of the cylinder and square it up with the cylinder walls by pushing it in with the top of the piston (see illustration). The ring should be about one inch above the bottom edge of the cylinder. To measure the end gap, slip a feeler gauge between the ends of the ring and compare the measurement to the Specifications.

4   If the gap is larger or smaller than specified, double check to make sure that you have the correct rings before proceeding.

5   If the gap is too small, it must be enlarged or the ring ends may come in contact with each other during engine operation, which can cause serious damage. The end gap can be increased by filing the ring ends very carefully with a fine file (see illustration). When performing this operation, file only from the outside in.

6   Excess end gap is not critical unless it is greater than 0.040 in (1 mm). Again, double check to make sure you have the correct rings for your engine.

7   Repeat the procedure for each ring that will be installed in the first cylinder and for each ring in the remaining cylinder. Remember to keep the rings, pistons and cylinders matched up.

8   Once the ring end gaps have been checked/corrected, the rings can be installed on the pistons.

9   The oil control ring (lowest on the pis-

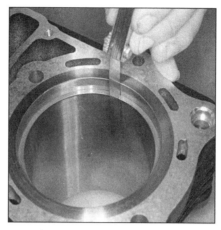

15.3 Check the piston ring end gap with a feeler gauge - measure at the bottom of the ring travel area if the cylinder looks worn

ton) is installed first. It is composed of three separate components. Slip the expander into the groove, then install the upper side rail (see illustrations). Do not use a piston ring installation tool on the oil ring side rails as they may be damaged. Instead, place one end of the side rail into the groove between the spacer expander and the ring land. Hold it firmly in place and slide a finger around the piston while pushing the rail into the groove. Next, install the lower side rail in the same manner.

10   After the three oil ring components have been installed, check to make sure that both the upper and lower side rails can be turned smoothly in the ring groove.

11   Install the second compression ring (middle ring) next. Do not mix the top and middle rings.

12   To avoid breaking the ring, use a piston ring installation tool and make sure that the identification mark is facing up. Fit the ring into the middle groove on the piston. Do not

expand the ring any more than is necessary to slide it into place.

13   Finally, install the top compression ring in the same manner. Make sure the identifying mark is facing up.

14   Repeat the procedure for the remaining piston and rings. Be very careful not to confuse the middle and top rings.

15   Once the rings have been properly installed, stagger the end gaps, including those of the oil ring side rails (see illustration 15.9).

16 Camshafts and timing gears - removal, inspection and installation

Removal

Caution: If the timing cover is not being removed as part of a general engine overhaul procedure, valve train pressure on the camshafts must be relieved (by removing the pushrods and tappets) before the timing cover or camshafts are disturbed.

1   If the engine is in the frame, drain the engine oil and remove any components which might prevent removal of the timing cover, such as the exhaust system and footpegs.

2   Camshaft end play should be checked before removing the timing cover. Rotate the engine by hand until the lobe of the first camshaft is visible in the tappet guide hole. Using a flat-bladed screwdriver, push the camshaft towards the timing cover and using a feeler blade, measure the clearance between the crankcase and the camshaft shoulder. Repeat on the other three camshafts and make a note of any which have excessive end play.

3   Remove the ignition components as described in Chapter 4.

15.5 If the end gap is too small, clamp a file in a vise and file the ring ends (from the outside in only) to enlarge the gap slightly

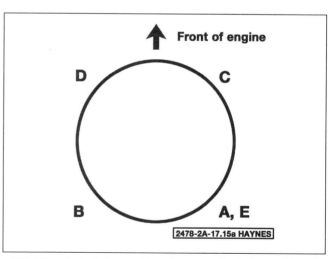

15.9 When installed, the piston ring gaps should be positioned as shown (120-degrees apart, and no closer than 10-degrees to the piston thrust surface)

16.4a Lift the cover off gently - don't pry it off

16.4b Note the shims on the camshaft gears

4   Place an oil drain tray beneath the timing cover. Remove all screws and bolts from the cover and withdraw it from the crankcase **(see illustration)**. It may require a few taps from a soft-faced hammer around its periphery to release the gasket seal - don't pry the cover free otherwise damage will result. On models with a rear chain oil feed, you may have to disconnect or bend the oil line to enable timing cover removal. Take care as the cover is withdrawn to spot any shims which have come detached from their shafts **(see illustration)**.

5   Note the exact location of any shims on the shaft ends and inspect the camshaft gears and crankshaft gear for alignment marks **(see illustrations)**. If the marks are faint, highlight them with a felt marker. Also check the camshafts for identification marks denoting their orientation; again if none are found make your own. When this information has been recorded, withdraw the camshafts. On models through early 1984, free the generator and remove its idler gear from the crankcase. Note the location of any washers or bearing retainer plates on the crankcase side; keep them with their respective shafts or mark them to ensure correct reassembly.

6   On early models, simply pull the crankshaft gear off the shaft, followed by the oil pump drive gear **(see illustrations)**. On later models, bend back the tab washer (models through 1987) and remove the nut (lock the crankshaft while it is loosened), followed by the crankshaft gear and oil pump drive gear. Note that a square-section key locates the oil pump and crankshaft gears on the shaft from 1988-on.

7   Where a shim is fitted below the oil pump drive gear, the oil pump body and gear shaft must be withdrawn before it can be removed **(see illustration)**.

Inspection

Note: *On all models, it is important when selecting a replacement timing cover, bushings, camshafts or timing gear, that the advice of a Harley-Davidson dealer is sought. Unless the replacement gears installed are suitably matched. and certain gears replaced in matched pairs, excessive gear noise and a pronounced wear rate will result.*

8   The timing gears are unlikely to require attention unless the engine has very high mileage or if there has been a lubrication failure. Wear will be evident in the form of excessive backlash between the individual gears, with a characteristic "clacking" noise.

9   The cam lobes should be checked for wear and damage in the form of pit marks, scuffing or flaking of the case hardened surfaces. Wear will be particularly evident on the flanks of the lobes, at the point where they begin to lift the tappet. If there's any doubt about the condition of the cam lobes, the camshafts should be replaced as a precaution.

10   If the cams are worn or damaged, more than likely the tappets will require attention,

16.5a Note the locations of the shims and bearing retainer plates under the cam gears

2

16.5b The camshaft gears are marked for correct valve timing (arrows) - be sure the marks align properly on assembly

16.6 The crankshaft gear can be pried off the shaft, along with the oil pump worm drive gear (early models only - on later models the gear is held on the shaft by a nut)

16.7 The large shim can't be removed until the oil pump is removed

16.16 Remove the Allen-head plug from the left side of the crankcase

16.17a Rotate the crankshaft until the TDC mark is in position

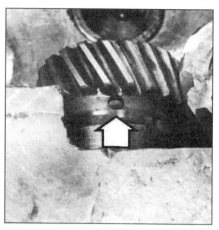

16.17b If the breather is timed correctly, the hole in the gear boss will be in this position

too (see Section 10).

11 Check the end of the tappet which bears on the pushrod; wear of its hardened surface will necessitate tappet replacement. Similarly check the pushrod ends as described in Section 10.

12 The needle roller bearings in the timing case should be replaced if there's any play evident or if there 's any sign of roughness. This also applies to any plain bushings. Replacement of the bearings should be done by a dealer service department, especially in the case of bushings, which may have to be reamed to size. Don't forget the timing cover, which has bushings also. The bushings are pegged in position and require expert attention when replacement is necessary.

13 On Shovelhead engines a figure is given for acceptable camshaft backlash (see Specifications). Backlash can be measured with a dial indicator. If there's excessive backlash between the gears, larger rear exhaust and front intake cam gears can be installed. If an increase of two or more color codes is required, a larger crankshaft gear should be installed also.

14 On Shovelhead engines, cam gear color codes can be used to provide information on the correct replacement part (see a Harley-

Davidson dealer for details). Each gear must be measured across opposite pins using a micrometer.

15 On Evolution engines, cam and timing gear replacement must be done by careful selection according to the color code of the individual gears or stamped letter, and the color code marking on the inside face of the timing cover, next to the shaft bushing locations. It is advised that the motorcycle or labeled component parts be taken to a Harley-Davidson dealer for inspection. If there's excessive backlash between the gears, larger rear exhaust and front intake cam gears can be installed. If an increase of two or more color codes is required, a larger crankshaft gear should be installed also.

Crankcase breather - timing (1976 and earlier models only)

16 Before the gear can be installed on the crankshaft, you'll have to time the crankcase breather, which forms part of the oil pump assembly. Proceed by removing the Allen-head plug in the left crankcase **(see illustration)**. It's located above the primary chaincase, between the two cylinders. When removed it will permit the edge of the

crankshaft flywheel to be seen.

17 Rotate the crankshaft until the TDC mark is exactly in the center of the hole **(see illustration)**. Slide the oil pump spiral gear over the splines on the right-hand end of the crankshaft with the marked side facing out. The oil pump gear that meshes with the spiral gear should be arranged so when the spiral gear is seated on the crankshaft, the timing hole in the oil pump/breather sleeve drive is facing forward **(see illustration)**. Make sure all the parts mentioned are in correct alignment, then install the crankshaft gear in front of the spiral gear, making sure it's completely seated.

18 Check the position of the gear on the end of the crankshaft. The gear outer face must be 5/16-inch from the timing cover mating surface.

19 Install the plug in the left crankcase.

Camshafts - installation

20 Install any shims originally fitted to the crankshaft end, followed by the oil pump drive gear and crankshaft gear; on 1988-on models the gears must locate with the shaft's key. If the oil pump body was withdrawn, this can now be installed. **Note:** *Refer to the procedure above for timing the crankcase breather on models through 1976.*

21 Secure the crankshaft gear with its retaining nut on later models. Note that on models through 1987 a new lock washer must be fitted under the nut. On 1988 through 1990 models apply a drop of Loctite 242 (blue) to the nut threads, and on 1991-on models apply a drop of Loctite 262 (red) to the nut threads. Tighten the nut to the specified torque and on models through 1987 secure with one of the lockwasher tabs.

22 Before the camshafts can be installed, you'll have to replace the bearing retainers and shims. These components should be marked to ensure they are replaced in their correct locations **(see illustration)**. Remember to apply a liberal coat of oil to the needle roller bearings and bushings before installing the camshafts.

16.17c Seat the crankshaft gear in front of the oil pump gear

16.22 Make sure the bearing retainers and shims are in position

16.25 The oil line to the final drive chain
(if equipped) must be securely connected

17.2a Remove the base plate to expose
the scavenge pump gears

17.2b Remove the circlip securing the oil
pump drive gear

23   The gears on the camshafts are clearly
marked and should be installed with all of the
timing marks aligned **(see illustration 16.5b)**.
24   Make sure all of the gears are exactly in
register to ensure the valve timing is correct.
Note that the idler gear is not marked - its
position isn't important. Install the rear chain
oiler oil line and gland nut (if equipped); it's
easier to install these components before the
timing cover is installed.
25   Make sure the oil line on the back of the
timing cover (models with automatic chain

17.2c Note how this gear is keyed
to the shaft

17.2d The second part of the body can
now be detached

oiler) is securely attached and in good condition **(see illustration)**.
26   If the check performed before removing
the timing cover confirmed camshaft end
play to be within the limits, refit any shims
present in their original positions. Seek the
advice of a Harley-Davidson dealer if adjustment needs to be made.
27   Install a new oil seal in the timing cover,
make sure both gasket surfaces are clean
and dry, then using a new cover gasket install
the timing cover. Install all screws and bolts
and tighten evenly in a criss-cross pattern.
28   Refit the ignition components as
described in Chapter 4. If the engine is in the
frame, refit all removed components and fill
the engine oil tank (see Chapter 1).

17 Oil pump - removal,
inspection and installation

1970 through 1976 models

1   The oil pump should not be removed
unless absolutely necessary. To remove it,
drain the oil tank first and unscrew the
crankcase drain plug. Detach the oil pressure switch by unscrewing it from the front of
the oil pump housing, after the wire has been

17.3a The feed pump idler gear will
remain attached to the shaft

removed. Disconnect the main oil feed line
and remove the five nuts and washers that
retain the oil pump on the studs that project
from the crankcase. The pump will probably
separate into three sections as it's withdrawn, although the upper two sections cannot be separated without further disassembly.
2   The base plate will lift off, exposing the
two scavenge pump gears **(see illustration)**.
The idler gear will lift out; the drive gear is
retained by two half rings or a circlip, which
will have to be pried out of position first **(see
illustration)**. It's keyed in position; don't lose
the small Woodruff key **(see illustration)**.
The second part of the body can now be
detached and the oil pump pressure switch
mount unscrewed to release the check valve
spring and ball bearing **(see illustration)**.
The feed pump idler gear will remain in the
top half of the housing, together with its
small detachable shaft.
3   The feed pump drive gear will probably
remain attached to the breather valve gear
and shaft, within the upper portion of the
pump assembly **(see illustration)**. Before the
breather valve gear and shaft can be lifted
out, it will be necessary to lift off the feed
pump drive gear and withdraw the small pin
that transfers the drive from the shaft to the
gear **(see illustration)**. Note there's a small

17.3b The pin through the shaft transmits
the drive to the gear

2

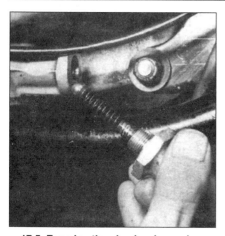

17.5 Examine the check valve spring, ball and seat

17.7 Note the small oil seal in this part of the oil pump body

wire screen around the breather valve, which should be cleaned prior to reassembly of the pump.

4   Damage is most likely to occur if some engine component has broken up and particles of metal have found their way into the pump. This will damage the oil pump gears, which will be obvious. Replacement gears will have to be obtained; the originals cannot be reused.

5   Unscrew the check valve assembly from the front of the oil pump body **(see illustration)**. Examine the check valve spring and ball bearing for wear. The free length of the spring should be 1-15/16 inch. If there's any doubt about the condition of either component, replace them with new ones.

6   Examine the ball valve seat. If only minor damage is evident, such as pit marks or dents, the seat can often be repaired by inserting the ball and giving it a sharp blow with a punch and hammer when it's resting on its seat. If damage is bad, a new pump body will be required. A badly seating check valve will cause oil to drain into the crankcase from the oil tank, making starting difficult and permitting the discharge of oil from the crankcase breather pipe.

7   Reassemble the pump by reversing the disassembly procedure using new gaskets and a new oil seal **(see illustration)** and circlip. All parts must be thoroughly cleaned with solvent and lightly oiled prior to reassembly. It's particularly important that each gasket is checked to ensure it does not mask off any oilways or obstruct the free movement of the pump gears. Don't use gasket cement at any of the joints. Tighten the pump mounting nuts a little at a time during reassembly and make sure it revolves freely at each stage. Keep checking to make sure the pump revolves freely, as uneven tension may cause it to misalign. Even a badly cut gasket can cause the gears to bind by fouling them during rotation. Note that during reassembly you'll have to remove the timing cover so the breather valve can be timed correctly, as described in Section 16. This is important.

8   Reconnect the oil line and install a new clamp. Check the line first, to ensure it isn't split or kinked.

1977 through 1990 models

9   The oil pump can be removed from the engine with the engine still in the frame. Label the oil lines to assist in reassembly, then disconnect them.

10   On early models, disconnect the wire from the oil pressure switch; on later models the switch is mounted on the oil filter adapter.

11   Remove the screws that secure the oil pump to the crankcase. Pull the oil pump away from the engine and throw away the old gasket.

12   Separate the cover from the body of the oil pump and remove the O-ring.

13   Lift the lower gerotor set off the gear shaft and pull the pin out of the gear shaft with needle-nose pliers.

14   Withdraw the outer plate, the plate seal, the spring washer, the inner plate and the outer gerotor (from the return set) from the gear shaft.

15   Remove the circlip from the gear shaft and lift the inner gerotor off the shaft.

16   Pull the remaining pin from the gear shaft and withdraw the shaft from the oil pump body.

17   On early models, press the check valve out the bottom of the pump housing by inserting a 5/16-inch pin punch through the oil pump outlet opening. Remove the O-rings from the check valve. On later models the check valve is installed in the oil filter.

18   Remove the oil seal from the outer plate and replace it with a new seal.

19   Check the spring loaded cup inside the check valve for binding and make sure it closes completely. Replace the valve if there's any doubt about it working properly.

20   Check the spring washer for damage such as broken or cracked fingers.

21   Clean all of the parts with solvent and dry them thoroughly. If available, use compressed air to blow out all of the passages.

22   Check the entire pump body and cover

for cracks and evidence of wear. Look closely for ridge wear on the gerotors and where the gerotors ride on the pump housing.

23   Place the inner gerotors inside of the outer gerotors and check the clearances with a feeler gauge. There should be no more than 0.004-inch clearance between the inner and outer gerotors.

24   Measure the thickness of the feed (lower) gerotors with a micrometer. If the thicknesses vary they must be replaced as a set.

25   Install the feed gerotors inside the cover and place a straightedge over the components. Insert a feeler gauge between the straightedge and the gerotor components. If the inner and outer gerotors aren't the same height, the cover is warped and must be replaced. The gerotors should extend out of the cover between 0.001 and 0.011-inch. If they extend less than 0.001-inch, the cover must be sanded down until the required measurements are obtained. To do the cover modification, place a piece of 280-grit sandpaper on a flat surface, such as a pane of glass, and invert the cover on the piece of sandpaper. Move the cover in a circular motion until the desired dimension is obtained. Finish the ridge of the cover with 400-grit sandpaper. Thoroughly clean the cover with solvent to prevent sand from getting into the oil. If the gerotors extend out of the cover more than 0.011-inch, the cover must be replaced with a new one.

26   Measure the clearances between the gear shaft and the two gear shaft bushings. It must be 0.005-inch. If the bushings are scored, damaged or worn, replace them.

27   The gear shaft bushings must be pressed into position. The bushing in the pump housing must be installed 0.100-inch below the surf ace, while the bushing in the cover must be installed 0.120-inch below the surface.

28   Inspect the teeth on the gear shaft for wear or damage and replace the shaft if necessary.

29   Assembly of the oil pump is essentially the reverse of disassembly. Be sure to lubricate all moving parts and the seals and O-rings with clean oil during assembly.

30   Place the new seal in the outer plate with the lip of the seal facing the feed (lower) gerotors. Secure the seal in the outer plate with Loctite Lock N' Seal Adhesive.

31   Install the spring plate with the fingers away from the inner plate.

32   When installing the outer plate, align the slot with the pin in the pump housing. Be sure the seal side faces in.

33   Install new O-rings on the check valve and the cover.

34   Place the new oil pump gasket in position with non-hardening gasket sealant.

1991 and later models

35   The oil pump can be removed with the engine in the frame, but first drain the engine

oil (see Chapter 1).

36   Disconnect the oil lines from the pump, labeling them FEED, RETURN and VENT to aid installation. Remove the two long Allen screws (those without washers) to free the complete pump from the crankcase. Peel off the gasket; a new one must be used on installation.

37   To disassemble the pump, remove the remaining two Allen screws (shorter) from its cover and lift the cover and its O-ring off the body. Slide the feed gerotor set (thinner), separator plate, and return gerotor set (thicker) off the gear shaft.

38   To remove the gear shaft from the pump body, remove the circlip and washer, and withdraw the gear shaft from the other side.

39   Clean all parts with solvent and dry thoroughly. If available, use compressed air to blow out all oil passages.

40   Inspect the gerotors for signs of excessive wear and scoring; replace if wear is excessive. Mesh each set of gerotors together and using a feeler blade, measure the clearance between their tips. If either set exceeds the service limit of 0.004 inches (0.10 mm) replace the rotors.

41   Using a micrometer, measure the thickness of the feed (thinner) gerotors; they must be exactly the same thickness.

42   The oil pump must be reassembled in clean conditions, using only new engine oil on the moving components. Slide the gear shaft into the body, install the washer and insert the circlip in its groove.

43   Lubricate and fit the inner return gerotor over the gear shaft, followed by its outer gerotor. Install the separator plate, aligning its cutouts with those of the body. Finally, install the feed gerotor set over the gear shaft end.

44   Using a new O-ring install the pump cover and secure with the two shorter screws, not forgetting their washers; tighten to 125 to 150 inch-lbs (14 to 17 Nm).

45   Using a new gasket install the pump on the crankcase, making sure that its gear engages correctly. Install the two long screws and tighten to 125 to 150 in-lbs (14 to 17 Nm). Reconnect the oil lines to their unions using new clamps.

46   Refill the oil tank and check for leaks. Check that oil pressure builds up to the correct level.

18 Oil pressure check and regulator valves - removal and installation

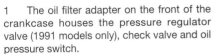

1   The oil filter adapter on the front of the crankcase houses the pressure regulator valve (1991 models only), check valve and oil pressure switch.

2   To gain access to the check valve, unscrew the oil filter and then unscrew the threaded boss from the center of the adapter. Lift out the ball and spring behind it

20.4   The right-hand crankcase will lift off the left-hand case (note the needle roller main bearing used on 1970 through 1976 models)

(see illustration 17.5).

3   The regulator valve can only be accessed after the gearcase has been removed. Unscrew its end plug, then remove the spring and valve.

4   Installation is the reverse of the removal steps.

19 Oil tank and lines - removal and installation

1   Drain the oil tank (see Chapter 1).

2   Remove the seat. Where necessary for access, remove the inner rear fender (see Chapter 7).

3   Remove the rear exhaust pipe (see Chapter 3).

4   Disconnect the oil lines from the tank.

5   Remove the oil tank mounting nut and bolt.

6   Remove the oil tank from the right side of the bike.

7   Installation is the reverse of the removal steps, with the following addition: Fill the oil tank and check oil level (see Chapter 1).

20 Crankcase - disassembly and reassembly

1   On early models with a compensating sprocket attached to the crankshaft, remove the sprocket shaft extension. Use a screwdriver to pry it off the crankshaft while tapping lightly around the outside with a soft-face hammer (see Chapter 2B). Don't use excessive force or drive the screwdriver into the gap between the collar and the crankcase itself - it's too easy to damage the bearing housing and oil seal located in front of the main bearing.

2   On models through 1990 remove the circlip (where fitted) from the crankshaft

20.6   Install the rear engine mount (on early models) before assembling the crankcases

right-hand end. On 1991 and later models detach the alternator stator from the left-hand crankcase (if not already done), referring to Chapter 8 for details. Loosening them evenly to avoid distortion, remove all crankcase bolts and stud nuts. On early models there will be five bolts and three stud nuts on the right side, two bolts and one stud nut on the left side and the engine rear mount bolts. On later models there will be three bolts and three nuts on the left side, eight bolts on the right side and the engine rear mount bolts. Disconnect the tachometer drive unit (if equipped). In all cases, two of the fasteners mentioned above will also secure the engine front mounting bracket.

3   On 1991 and later models, remove the four Allen-head bolts, and five hex-head bolts (two of these retain the engine front mounting bracket) from the crankcase left side.

4   With the engine resting on its left side (primary case), lift off the right-hand half to leave the crankshaft in the left-hand crankcase half (see illustration). If necessary, tap the crankcase gently with a soft-faced hammer to break the seal. Note: *As the crankcase leaves the right-hand main bearing on early models the bearing rollers will probably fall out of position; make sure that none are lost.*

5   If you have to remove the complete flywheel/crankshaft assembly (to replace the big-end bearings for example) the whole assembly must be pressed out of the left-hand crankcase with a special press. Don't hammer the flywheel assembly out of the left-hand crankcase - it will upset the alignment of the flywheels.

6   When the crankcases are parted on early models, it's possible to remove the rear engine mount (see illustration). It must be installed before the crankcases are rejoined; it cannot be installed afterwards.

7   If the flywheel assembly has been removed from the left-hand crankcase, reinsert it through the left-hand main bearing assembly, which requires special equipment.

2

20.9 Assemble the right roller bearing
assembly on the crankshaft -
early uncaged type

21.8a The crankshaft seal can be easily
pried out of position

21.8b Install new seals carefully to avoid
damage that could cause oil leaks

This should be done by a Harley-Davidson service department with the required service tools to pull the crankshaft through the bearing assembly without risk of damage. Install the sprocket shaft extension on the left-hand end of the crankshaft on early models so equipped.

8   Before joining the right-hand crankcase, make sure the mating surfaces are perfectly clean and apply a thin coat of gasket sealant. On all models through 1990, also make sure the rear engine mount is included with the parts for reassembly **(see illustration 20.6)**. It cannot be added after the crankcases are rejoined and bolted together.

9   Reassemble the right-hand needle roller bearing on the crankshaft (on models without caged bearings) **(see illustration)**, rather than in the crankcase bearing housing. Grease can be used to retain the uncaged rollers in place during reassembly.

10 Bolt the crankcases together, but before final tightening, make sure the crankshaft assembly revolves freely. Tighten the fasteners, then recheck it. Where fitted, replace the washer over the right-hand end of the crankshaft and the circlip in front of it.

21 Crankcase components - inspection and servicing

1   After thorough cleaning, the crankcases should be examined for cracks and other signs of damage that may ultimately cause failure. Minor cracks can be repaired by welding, but if more extensive damage is apparent, replacement is recommended.

2   Note that crankcases are always supplied as a matched pair and should never be replaced any other way. This is important - the crankcases are line bored in pairs, so the bearing housings are aligned correctly. Replacement of only one half will result in a mismatch, which may cause the crankshaft to run out of line and absorb a surprising

amount of power.

3   Make sure the mating surfaces are undamaged, otherwise oil leaks will be inevitable after reassembly. If there's any doubt about their ability to seal, use a liquid gasket sealer during reassembly.

4   Check the bearing housings to make sure they're undamaged. If they have worn as the result of a bearing rotating, it's possible to repair using a special bearing sealant such as red Loctite during reassembly. This can be used successfully only if the amount of wear is small.

5   Now is the opportunity to retap any of the threads, if they require attention. Most damage is caused by over-tightening the drain plugs. If necessary, threaded holes can be repaired by installing Helicoil thread inserts, which will permit the original drain plug to be reused. Most dealers can perform this type of repair.

Oil seals - inspection and replacement

6   Even after very careful examination it's difficult to determine whether an oil seal can be reused, especially if it has been disturbed during disassembly. Because an oil seal failure will necessitate another teardown at a later date, it's recommended that all the oil seals be replaced with new ones during an overhaul, as a precautionary measure.

7   Oil seals are very easily damaged during reassembly. Always be very careful when installing shafts and grease the lips of the seals.

8   The most important oil seals are those located around the drive side of the crankshaft assembly and around the transmission mainshaft behind the final drive sprocket (Shovelhead engine). The former is easily pried out of position **(see illustrations)**. The latter is retained by an oil seal retainer, held to the outer face of the right-hand crankcase with four screws and lockwashers.

22 Crankshaft and connecting rods - inspection

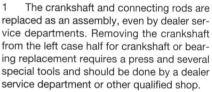

1   The crankshaft and connecting rods are replaced as an assembly, even by dealer service departments. Removing the crankshaft from the left case half for crankshaft and bearing replacement requires a press and several special tools and should be done by a dealer service department or other qualified shop.

2   Remove the engine and separate the crankcase halves (see Sections 6 and 20).

3   Measure side clearance of the connecting rods with a feeler gauge. If it's not within the limits listed in this Chapter's Specifications, replace the crankshaft and connecting rods as an assembly.

4   While an assistant supports the connecting rods, spin the crankshaft and check for roughness, looseness or noise in the bearings that support the left side. If problems are found, have the bearings replaced by a dealer service department or other qualified shop.

5   Installation is the reverse of the removal steps.

23 Initial start-up after overhaul

1   Make sure the engine oil level is correct, then remove the spark plugs from the engine. Place the engine STOP switch in the Off position and disconnect the primary wires from the ignition coil.

2   Turn on the key switch and crank the engine over with the starter until the oil pressure indicator light goes off (which indicates that oil pressure exists). Reinstall the spark plugs, connect the wires and turn the switch to On. **Note:** *If the oil pressure light won't go out on models with a screw-on oil filter, remove the filter (see Chapter 1). Hold the filter with the open end upright and pour oil*

into the center hole until the filter is full. Let the oil settle, then top it off again (you may need to do this twice). Reinstall the filter (a small amount of oil may leak out when you install it).

3   Make sure there is fuel in the tank, then turn the fuel tap to the On position and operate the choke.

4   Start the engine and allow it to run at a moderately fast idle until it reaches operating temperature.

 Warning: If the oil pressure indicator light doesn't go off, or it comes on while the engine is running, stop the engine immediately.

5   Check carefully for oil leaks and make sure the transmission and controls, especially the brakes, function properly before road testing the machine. Refer to Section 27 for the recommended break-in procedure.

24 Recommended break-in procedure

1   Any rebuilt engine needs time to break-in, even if parts have been installed in their original locations. For this reason, treat the machine gently for the first few miles to make sure oil has circulated throughout the engine and any new parts installed have started to seat.

2   Even greater care is necessary if the engine has been rebored or a new crankshaft has been installed. In the case of a rebore, the engine will have to be broken in as if the machine were new. This means greater use of the transmission and a restraining hand on the throttle until at least 500 miles (800 km) have been covered. There's no point in keeping to any set speed limit - the main idea is to keep from lugging the engine and to gradually increase performance until the 500 mile (800 km) mark is reached. These recommendations can be lessened to an extent when only a new crankshaft is installed. Experience is the best guide, since it's easy to tell when an engine is running freely.

3   If a lubrication failure is suspected, stop the engine immediately and try to find the cause. If an engine is run without oil, even for a short period of time, severe damage will occur.

2

Notes

Chapter 2 Part B
Primary drive, clutch and transmission

Contents

Degrees of difficulty

Easy, suitable for novice with little experience	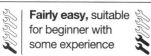	Fairly easy, suitable for beginner with some experience		Fairly difficult, suitable for competent DIY mechanic	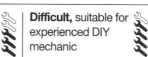	Difficult, suitable for experienced DIY mechanic		Very difficult, suitable for expert DIY or professional	

Specifications

Clutch

Type
  1970 .... Dry, multi-plate
  1971-on .... Wet, multi-plate
Number of plates
  1970 .... 7 plain, 7 friction
  1971 through early 1984 .... 8 plain, 8 friction
  Late 1984 through 1990.. 6 plain, 7 friction
  1991-on... 7 plain, 8 friction
Number of springs
  1970 .... Six
  1971 through early 1984 .... Two
  Late 1984-on.. One (diaphragm spring)
Spring adjustment
  1970 .... 3/16 in (5 mm) from inner surface of spring tension
                                                                                adjusting plate-to-outer surface of spring cup flange
  1971 through 1973... 11/32 in (9 mm) from outer surface of outer drive plate-
                                                                                outer surface of releasing disc
  1974 through early 1984 .... Fixed spacers; 1.53 in (39 mm)
Pushrod free play (1970 only)...................................... 0.095 to 0.115 in (2.42 to 2.92 mm)
Clutch plate thickness (late 1984 through 1990)
  Friction plate
    Standard .... 0.150 in (3.81 mm)
    Minimum .... 0.130 in (3.3 mm)
  Plain (steel) plate
    Standard .... 0.0629 in (1.60 mm)
    Minimum .... 0.060 in (1.52 mm)
    Warpage limit.. 0.010 in (0.254 mm)

2

Clutch (continued)

Clutch plate thickness (1991-on)
    Friction plate
        Standard ....   0.0866 + 0.0031 in (2.20 + 0.079 mm)
        Service limit (stacked together) ....   0.661 in (16.79 mm)
    Plain (steel) plate
        Standard ....   0.0629 + 0.0020 in +(1.598 + 0.051 mm)
        Warpage limit ....   0.006 in (0.152 mm)

Transmission

Type
    1970 through 1990 ....   Four-speed constant mesh
    1991-on ....   Five-speed constant mesh
Sprocket teeth
    Engine (primary drive)..   34 (4-speed), 35 (5-speed)
    Clutch (primary drive) 59 (4-speed), 56 (5-speed)
    Transmission (final drive)
        1970 and 1971 (XLCH only)   19
        1970 through 1972   20
        1973 through 1992 (chain drive)   21
        1991-on (belt drive 883)   27
        1991-on (belt drive 1200)   29
    Rear wheel (final drive)
        1970 through 1981   51
        1982 through 1992 (chain drive)   48
        1991-on (belt drive)...   61
Transmission oil capacity ....   See Chapter 1
Primary chain
Type..   See Chapter 1
Mainshaft clearances and wear limits (1970 through 1985)
    Clutch gear bearing-to-gear...   0.0009 in (0.023 mm) (tight)
    Clutch gear bearing-to-cover..   0.001 to 0.0012 in (0.025 to 0.030 mm) (loose)
    Clutch gear bushing-to-mainshaft ....   0.001 to 0.002 in (0.025 to 0.051 mm) (loose)
    Roller bearing assembly (right side)
        1970 through 1978..   0.0006 to 0.0014 in (0.015 to 0.036 mm) (loose)
        1979-on..   0.001 to 0.0034 in (0.025 to 0.086 mm) (loose)
    End play
        Without axial play (minimum)...   0.003 inch (0.076 mm) min
        With axial play (1979 through early 1984 only) ....   0.020 in (0.51 mm)
        Late 1984-on
            Minimum...   0.009 inch (0.229 mm)
            Maximum..   0.015 inch (0.381 mm)
    Third gear end play ....   0.012 to 0.030 inch (0.25 to 0.76 mm)
    Third gear-to-shaft ....   0.002 to 0.003 inch (0.051 to 0.076 mm) (loose)
Countershaft clearances and wear limits (1970 through 1985)
    Bearing clearance (shaft ends)...   0.0005 to 0.003 in (0.013 to 0.076 mm) (loose)
    Second gear-to-shaft..   0.001 to 0.0025 in (0.025 to 0.064 mm) (loose)
    First gear-to-shaft ....   0.0005 to 0.0016 in (0.013 to 0.041 mm) (loose)
    First gear end play ....   0.004 to 0.009 in (0.102 to 0.229 mm)
    Drive gear-to-shaft ....   0.0005 to 0.003 in (0.013 to 0.076 mm) (loose)
    Drive gear end play ....   0.004 to 0.009 in (0.102 to 0.229 mm)
    Countershaft end play ....   0.004 to 0.015 in (0.102 to 0.381 mm)
Clearance between gear faces (1970 through 1978)
    Countershaft First and Third gear ....   0.038 to 0.058 in (0.965 to 1.473 mm)
    Countershaft Second and Third gear..   0.038 to 0.058 in (0.965 to 1.473 mm)
    Mainshaft Second and Third gear ....   0.043 to 0.083 in (1.092 to 2.108 mm)
    Mainshaft Second and Fourth gear...   0.043 to 0.083 in (1.092 to 2.108 mm)
Clearance between gear faces (1979 through 1985)
    Countershaft First and Third gear ....   0.028 to 0.058 in (0.71 to 1.473 mm)
    Countershaft Second and Third gear..   0.028 to 0.058 in (0.71 to 1.473 mm)
    Mainshaft Second and Third gear ....   0.028 to 0.058 in (0.71 to 1.473 mm)
    Mainshaft Second and Fourth gear...   0.028 to 0.058 in (0.71 to 1.473 mm)
Shifter shaft end play (1970 through 1976) ....   0.010 to 0.030 in (0.254 to 0.762 mm)
Mainshaft clearances and wear limits (1986 through 1990)
    Clutch gear bearing-to-gear...   0.0009 in (0.023 mm) (tight)
    Clutch gear bearing-to-cover..   0.001 to 0.0012 in (0.025 to 0.030 mm) (loose)
    Roller bearing assembly (right side) ....   0.0004 to 0.0035 in (0.010 to 0.089 mm) (loose)

End play	
Minimum	0.006 in (0.152 mm)
Maximum	0.020 in (0.011 mm)
Third gear end play	0.006 to 0.020 in (0.152 to 0.011 mm)
Third gear-to-shaft	0.0027 to 0.004 in (0.069 to 0.102 mm) (loose)
Countershaft clearances and wear limits (1986 through 1990)	
Needle bearing journal diameter	
Access door end..	0.7490 in (19.02 mm) minimum
Right crankcase end	0.6865 in (17.44 mm) minimum
Second gear-to-shaft	0.001 to 0.0025 in (0.025 to 0.064 mm) (loose)
First gear needle bearing journal diameter......................................	0.6865 in (17.44 mm) minimum
Countershaft end play	0.004 to 0.015 in (0.102 to 0.381 mm)
Clearance between gear faces (1986 through 1990)	
Countershaft First and Third gear......................................	0.040 to 0.080 in (1.02 to 2.03 mm)
Countershaft Second and Third gear	0.040 to 0.080 in (1.02 to 2.03 mm)
Mainshaft Second and Third gear	0.040 to 0.080 in (1.02 to 2.03 mm)
Mainshaft Second and Fourth gear	0.040 to 0.080 in (1.02 to 2.03 mm)
Transmission access cover bolts	
Four-speed..	14 to 19 ft-lbs (19 to 26 Nm)
Five-speed...	13 to 17 ft-lbs (18 to 23 Nm)
Shifter shaft nuts...	90 to 110 inch-lbs (10 to 12 Nm)
Primary chaincase oil drain plug...	14 to 21 ft-lbs (19 to 28 ft-lbs)
Primary chain tensioner locknut	20 to 25 ft-lbs (27 to 34 Nm)
Primary chaincase main cover screws	80 to 110 inch-lbs (9 to 12 Nm)
Primary chaincase outer cover screws (1995-on)	30 to 40 inch-lbs (3.3 to 4.5 Nm)
Alternator stator screws...	30 to 40 inch-lbs (3.3 to 4.5 Nm)
Primary drive (engine sprocket) nut...	150 to 165 ft-lbs (203 to 224 Nm)
Clutch nut (1991-on)	70 to 80 ft-lbs (95 to 108 Nm)

1 General information

Power from the engine crankshaft is transmitted through the primary chain to the clutch, and then to the transmission. The clutch, primary chain, its tensioner and the compensating sprocket on the crankshaft (if equipped) are located in the primary drive housing, which is a removable unit located on the left side of the engine.

The transmission is mounted in the rear part of the engine crankcase casting. The gears are mounted on a mainshaft (input shaft) and countershaft (output shaft). The mainshaft is driven by the primary drive chain through the compensating sprocket, while the countershaft operates the rear wheel drive chain or belt through the chain or belt sprocket.

The transmission on models through 1990 has four forward gears; later models have five.

The gears consist of five pairs, one pair for each transmission ratio. Each pair is in constant mesh with its mating gear. When a particular ratio is selected, both gears for that ratio are locked to their shaft. One gear for each of the other ratios spins freely on its shaft, so that only one ratio is engaged at a time.

Shifting is accomplished by shift forks, which are moved by a shifter cam mounted in the transmission case.

2 Clutch cable - replacement

1 Loosen the cable adjuster to provide as much slack as possible in the cable (see Chapter 1).
2 Remove the snap-ring from the underside of the cable retaining pin at the handlebar lever, then pull out the pin and disconnect the upper end of the clutch cable from the lever.
3 Remove the transmission dipstick and

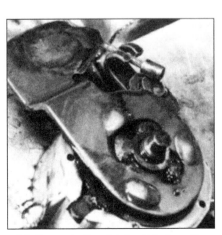

2.5 Separate the clutch cable from the operating arm inside the chaincase cover - the early type can be maneuvered out of the bracket . . .

drain the transmission oil (see Chapter 1).
4 If you're working on an early model without a small round clutch inspection cover in the primary chain case cover, remove the primary chaincase cover (see Section 3). If you're working on a motorcycle that does have a clutch inspection cover, remove it.
5 On early models, free the cable from the bracket **(see illustration)**.
6 On later models, you'll need to disassemble the release mechanism **(see illustration)**. Note the location of the gap in the retaining ring so it can be reinstalled in the same location, then remove the retaining ring. Take the inner ramp and coupling out of

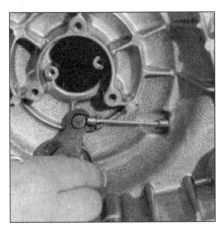

2.6 . . . but the later type requires disassembly of the mechanism to allow cable disconnection

2

the primary chaincase cover. Hold them together as you remove them so the coupling balls don't fall out.

7   Turn the inner ramp and disconnect the coupling from it, then detach the end of the cable from the coupling. Unscrew the cable fitting from the transmission cover and remove its O-ring.

8   Before removing the cable from the bike, tape the lower end of the new cable to the upper end of the old cable. Slowly pull the lower end of the old cable out, guiding the new cable down into position. Using this method will ensure the cable is routed correctly.

9   Installation is the reverse of the removal steps, with the following additions:

a) *Use a new O-ring on the clutch cable threaded fitting.*

b) *Position the retaining ring gap as noted during removal.*

c) *Use a new gasket on the clutch inspection cover (if equipped) and tighten its bolts to the torque listed in this Chapter's Specifications.*

d) *Lubricate and adjust the clutch cable (see Chapter 1).*

3   Clutch and primary drive - removal, inspection and installation

Removal

Primary chaincase cover

1   Loosen the primary chain adjuster locknut and back off the adjuster a few turns (see Chapter 1). On late 1984 and later models, remove the small inspection cover to gain access to the clutch adjuster mechanism. Lift out the spring and hex piece, then screw the adjuster all the way in so the nut can be withdrawn. On all models remove all of the chaincase screws and lift the chaincase off the crankcase **(see illustration)**. The case screws are of different lengths, so keep them in a cardboard template of the cover (the old gasket will do if it hasn't been destroyed dur-

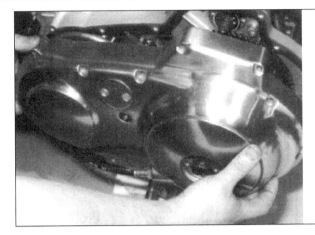

3.1a The primary chaincase cover can be removed without disconnecting the clutch cable

ing removal) to ensure that they are returned to their original locations. Note the thrust washer on the starter shaft of 1970 through 1980 models **(see illustration)**. To remove the cover completely you'll need to detach the clutch cable (see Section 2).

Primary chain, sprocket and clutch

2   Because a triple row endless chain is employed for the primary drive, the engine and clutch sprockets have to be lifted off together with the chain. This makes it necessary to remove the clutch and the primary drive sprocket (compensating sprocket on models produced before 1976) first. To do this, the transmission must be shifted into gear (temporarily install the shift lever) and the drive sprocket must be held with a chain wrench or other tool to keep it from turning as the nut/threaded collar is loosened. If the engine is in the frame, shift the transmission into gear and apply the rear brake with the rear tire in firm contact with the ground. Another way to lock the transmission, if the cylinders and heads are still in place, is to remove the spark plugs and rotate the engine to top dead center. Back the engine up about 1/8-revolution and fill the combustion chamber with nylon cord inserted through the spark plug hole until no more cord can be fed in. Be sure the end of the cord is still outside of the engine. On some 1992 and later models, a lockplate

3.1b On pre-1981 electric start models, the thrust washer on the starter motor shaft extension (arrow) is loose and easily lost

may be fitted over the sprocket nut; remove its lock screw and lift the plate off the sprocket nut before attempting nut removal.

3   On early models (with compensating sprocket), if the Harley-Davidson service tool is not available note that the threaded collar can be loosened with a large U-bolt and screwdriver or pry bar **(see illustration)**.

3.3a A large U-bolt can be used to unscrew the compensating sprocket threaded collar

3.3b The compensating spring pressure is released before the end of the collar threads

3.4 The primary drive sprocket is retained by a flanged nut on later models

3.6 Heavy springs require a great deal of caution when removing the release disc

3.8a Remove the inner circlip to release the clutch plates

3.8b The clutch plates will pull out from the center of the clutch

Unscrew the collar and remove the spring, outer collar and the splined sliding cam **(see illustration)**.

4   On later models, unscrew the sprocket nut fully and remove it from the crankshaft end (see **illustration**). **Note:** *This nut is very tight. Be sure that you have adequate means of locking the engine to prevent rotation.*

5   On all models the engine sprocket is now free to be removed from the shaft, but as stressed in Step 1, it must be withdrawn as a unit with the clutch and chain. Refer to the following procedures and remove the clutch from the mainshaft.

1970 through early 1984

6   Special care is needed when removing the clutch, as a very strong inner and outer spring applies pressure to the release disc **(see illustration)**. Never loosen the six nuts around the edge of the release disc without first taking adequate precautions. If the proper Harley-Davidson service tool isn't available, use a three-jaw gear puller to keep the release disc from moving while the six nuts are removed. The puller can then be loosened slowly, to relieve the spring pressure in a controlled fashion. Note that even

when the nuts are removed, the spring still exerts considerable pressure when the release disc has passed beyond the limit of the studs **(see illustration)**.

7   The 1970 clutch, which is designed to run dry, has a somewhat different arrangement. In this instance you have to remove the domed clutch cover, which acts as an oil excluder, by removing the twelve screws around its edge. Note that they're linked in pairs by a lock plate. The cover will then lift off, exposing the gasket. This type of clutch has six separate springs, which seat within the thimbles inserted into the release disc. Removal of the six retaining nuts (three long, three short) will permit the release disc to be removed without need for special precautions or service tools.

8   When the release disc has been removed, along with the internal circlip, the clutch plates and release disc can be pulled out of the clutch drum **(see illustrations)**. On 1970 models, take out the shouldered clutch release rod.

9   The clutch center is retained by a large nut, which is very tight. Bend back the tab washer, then use a tight-fitting socket on the nut, with a long extension, to jar the nut

loose. Hold the clutch center to keep it from turning as the nut is loosened **(see illustration)**.

10   The clutch center will now come off. It may be necessary to use a puller. Before removing the engine sprocket, primary chain and clutch sprocket as an assembly, detach the chain tensioner **(see illustration)**. They will then come off easily. Slide the clutch bushing off the end of the gear shaft sleeve.

Late 1984 and later

Note: *the clutch can be removed from the mainshaft as a complete unit as described below. Disassembly of the clutch, however, requires a Harley-Davidson serviced tool to safely compress its diaphragm spring while the large circlip is removed - no other means of dismantling the clutch should be used. It is recommended that the clutch be disassembled by a dealer service department or other qualified shop.*

11   Remove the circlip from the clutch boss and withdraw the adjuster assembly (composed of the small circlip, guide/release plate, bearing and adjuster screw) from the pressure plate **(see illustrations)**.

12   On models through 1990, remove the

3.9 A metal "sprag" can be used to lock the center of the clutch while the nut is loosened

3.10 Remove the chain tensioner (arrow) to increase the slack in the chain

3.11a Remove the circlip shown (not the large diaphragm spring circlip) ...

2

3.11b ... and lift off the adjuster assembly - 1991-on design shown

3.14a Remove the primary drive sprocket, the primary chain and the clutch drum as an assembly

external circlip and spacer from the main-shaft. On 1991 and later models remove the mainshaft nut (noting that it has left-hand threads and is loosened clockwise) and remove the conical washer. On all models, remove the clutch, engine sprocket and chain from the crankshaft and mainshaft as a single unit, noting that there will be some magnetic resistance as the alternator rotor and stator separate. On 1991 and later models, slide the spacer off the crankshaft end if it is loose.

13   If the alternator rotor requires removal from the rear of the clutch sprocket (models through 1990) or engine sprocket (1991 and later), refer to Chapter 8.

All models

14   Remove the primary sprocket, clutch sprocket and primary chain as an assembly **(see illustration)**. If you're working on an early model with a compensating sprocket, tap the sprocket collar to loosen it and pry if off the crankshaft **(see illustrations)**.

Clutch components - inspection

1970 through early 1984 models

15   Check the condition of the clutch sprocket, to ensure none of the teeth are chipped, broken or badly worn.

16   Clean the plates with solvent and make sure they are not warped or distorted. Remove all traces of clutch insert debris, otherwise a gradual build-up will occur and affect clutch action.

17   Visual inspection will reveal if the tongues of the clutch plates have been burred and whether corresponding indentations have formed in the slots in the clutch drum. Burrs should be removed with a file, which can also be used to dress the slots square, provided the depth of the indentations is not too great.

18   Check the thickness of the friction plates. When they have worn thin, they must be replaced. Always replace them as a complete set, irrespective of whether some may

not have reached the serviceable limit. Worn friction plates promote clutch slip.

19   Check the free length of the clutch springs and compare it to the Specifications Section of this Chapter. Do not stretch the springs if they have compressed. They must be replaced when the service limit has been reached.

20   Check the clutch pushrod for straight-ness, if necessary, by rolling it on a sheet of glass. Heavy action is often caused by a bent rod, which may hang up in its housing. Check the action of the clutch actuating mechanism that's located on the inside of the primary chaincase cover. It should give no trouble if greased regularly.

21   The bearings in the center of the pre-1971 clutch are needle roller type and a press fit. To gain access when replacement is necessary, remove the oil seal and rivets from the center of the outer drum and press out the bearing assembly, which includes two separate needle roller races, a large diameter washer of variable thickness and the starter clutch.

22   When reassembling, press the first bearing into place, pushing on the face on which the bearing number is inscribed. Press it in to a depth of 0.010 to 0.015-inch, mea-sured from the clutch drum to the inner face

of the bearing, then press the other bearing into position from the starter clutch side until it's flush with the first bearing. Position the roll pin and the large diameter washer, then the variable size washer. Lay the kickstarter ratchet on the back plate of the clutch and press down on it while a feeler gauge is inserted between it and the variable size washer. Adjustments should be made with different thicknesses of the variable size washer until a measured clearance of from 0.001 to 0.004-inch is obtained. Allow approximately 0.001-inch for the pull of the rivets. The rivets should not protrude more than 0.010-inch above the face of the kick-starter ratchet, after installing, and should be sealed off with a solvent-proof sealant. Do not forget to install the oil seal with the lip facing in.

23   Post-1970 clutches have a much sim-pler center bearing arrangement, composed of a roller bearing retained by a circlip. This is easily removed and replaced.

Late 1984-on models

Note: *Access to the clutch components requires disassembly of the clutch using the Harley-Davidson service tool. Due to the dangers involved in safely compressing the diaphragm spring, it is advised that the task*

3.14b Tap the compensating sprocket collar with a hammer to loosen it . . .

3.14c . . . then gently pull it off the end of the crankshaft

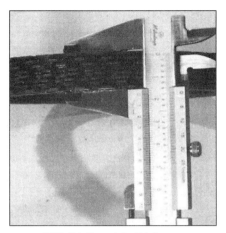

3.25 Friction plate thickness measurement - 1991 and later models

3.26 Check that the spring plate is correctly positioned in the plate pack

3.34a Install the compensating sprocket cam, followed by the spring and outer collar . . .

be entrusted to a *Harley-Davidson dealer. With the clutch disassembled, its components can be examined* as follows.

24 Check the sprocket teeth on the clutch sprocket, together with those of the engine sprocket. Severe wear is best remedied by replacement of both sprockets and chain. Also check the teeth of the starter ring gear.

25 Check the plates as described in Steps 2 to 4 of this Section, referring to the Specifications for minimum limits. When checking the friction plates for wear on 1991 and later models, wipe them free of oil then stack them together without the steel plates and spring plates and measure the overall thickness of the pack **(see illustration)**.

26 Note the position of the spring plate in the pack of plates; on models through 1990 it's between the 3rd and 4th friction plates from the outer drum, whereas on 1991-on models it's between the 4th and 5th friction plates from the outer drum **(see illustration)**.

27 Inspect the diaphragm spring for signs of cracking or bent tabs. Replace if either condition is found.

28 Rotate the clutch outer drum on the clutch center. If the bearing is excessively noisy it must be replaced. First remove the

circlip from the rear of the outer drum and separate the clutch center from the outer drum. Remove the circlip from the front of the outer drum and press out the bearing. Use new circlips on installation.

Primary drive components - inspection

29 Examine the teeth on the crankshaft and clutch drum sprockets. If any are chipped, hooked, or broken the sprocket must be replaced. It's a good idea to replace the clutch drum, the crankshaft sprocket and the primary chain together as a matched set. A badly worn sprocket will cause the chain to wear more rapidly and cause the engine to lose power.

30 On earlier models equipped with a compensating sprocket, check the condition of the splines on the sliding cam and the sprocket extension. If they are worn, the components should be replaced as a matched set. Although it's unlikely the sliding cam has worn to any great extent, it should be checked where it makes contact with the crankshaft sprocket.

31 The component most likely to wear on

models with a compensating sprocket is the sprocket spring, which will compress after extended use. Increased cam action is a sure sign that the spring is in need of replacement.

Installation

1970 through early 1984 models

32 Install the compensating sprocket collar (if equipped) on the end of the crankshaft **(see illustration 3.14c)**.

33 Assemble the clutch outer drum and sprocket, the engine sprocket and the primary chain, and attach them to their respective shafts as an assembly **(see illustration 3.14a)**.

34 If the motorcycle has a compensating sprocket, install the spring, then the threaded collar **(see illustrations)**. Lock the engine and tighten the collar or nut in a clockwise direction, using the method described in the removal procedure.

35 Install the clutch center, tab washer and large retaining nut. Install a new clutch pushrod seal (1970 models only). Using the same metal sprag used previously, tighten the nut **(see illustration)** and bend over the tab washer. The nut must be tight. Install the final drive sprocket temporarily and place the transmission in gear, locking the sprocket with a chain wrench wrapped around it. Reassemble the compensating sprocket and tighten the threaded collar to the specified torque while the engine is still locked.

36 The clutch can now be reassembled by reversing the disassembly procedure. Note that the 1970 clutch must remain oil tight, so a new gasket must be used under the domed cover. Remember to replace the shouldered clutch release rod before installing the pressure plate. In the case of the 1971 and later clutch, either the appropriate Harley-Davidson service tool or a three-jaw puller is needed to compress the two clutch center springs sufficiently for the release disc retaining nuts to be started on their threads **(see illustrations)**.

2

3.34b . . . and the threaded collar, which must be tightened securely

3.35 Install the clutch center and tighten the retaining nut to the specified torque

3.36a Make sure the spacers are in position on the clutch studs . . .

3.36b . . . and the circlip is installed to retain the clutch plates

3.36c The springs and pressure plate are installed last . . .

37   Install and adjust the primary chain tensioner, after checking to make sure it hasn't worn enough to require a new one (see Chapter 1). The primary chain should have the specified slack with the engine cold. When the adjustment is correct, rotate the crankshaft and check the slack at several points. Tighten the adjuster locknut when the correct adjustment has been obtained. Remove any equipment used to prevent engine rotation.

Late 1984-on models

Note: *This procedure describes clutch installation as a complete unit. If the clutch has been dismantled, it must be reassembled using the Harley-Davidson service tool.*
38   On 1991 and later models install the spacer on the end of the crankshaft (if it came off the shaft on removal). On all models, if the alternator rotor was detached from the clutch sprocket (models through 1990) or engine sprocket (1991-on) it should be installed as described in Chapter 8.
39   With the chain installed on the engine sprocket and clutch sprocket, install the assembly on the crankshaft and mainshaft,

being careful not to damage the stator coils as the rotor is moved into position. On models through 1990 install the washer on the mainshaft and secure with a new circlip. On 1991 and later models, install the conical washer on the mainshaft with the side marked OUT facing outwards. Clean the nut and shaft threads, apply a drop of Loctite 262 (red) to the shaft threads and tighten to the specified torque, remembering that the nut has a left-hand thread **(see illustration)**.
40   Install the adjuster assembly in the clutch pressure plate and secure with the circlip. On 1991 and later models note that the release plate ears must align with the cutouts in the pressure plate.
41   Clean the crankshaft and engine sprocket nut threads, then apply a drop of Loctite 242 (blue) thread-locking compound (Loctite 262 (red) on 1991-on models) to the shaft threads. With the engine locked, tighten the nut to the specified torque. Where a lockplate is fitted, install the plate over the nut and secure with the lockbolt.
42   Remove any equipment used to prevent engine rotation. Adjust the chain tension and clutch after the chaincase has been refitted.

4 Transmission components - removal and installation

1   Transmission components can be removed through the access cover in the left crankcase half. Remove the clutch and primary drive components (Section 3) and on late 1984 through 1990 models remove the alternator stator from the access cover (Chapter 8).

Removal

1970 through 1990 models (4-speed)

2   To remove the transmission as a complete unit, remove the four bolts around the outside of the square shaped access cover in the primary chaincase. The cover can then be pulled out, bringing with it the complete gear cluster and selector mechanism **(see illustration)**. The right-hand needle roller bearing, through which the mainshaft passes, will collapse as the bearings are uncaged **(see illustration)**. Don't lose any of them.

3.36d . . . using a gear puller to compress the springs and start the pressure plate nuts

3.39 Apply thread locking compound to the clutch nut on 1991 and later models - install the washer with the OUT mark facing outwards

4.2a After the access cover bolts are removed, the transmission can be withdrawn from the case as an assembly

4.2b The uncaged needle bearings will collapse on removal

4.3a Remove the bolt and tab washer to free the selector mechanism

4.3b Note the arrangement and number of shims installed

4.4 The small rollers on the selector fork pins are easily lost

4.5 The complete four-speed transmission gear cluster

3   To release the cam plate assembly, remove the single bolt that retains the assembly to the access plate (see illustration). The assembly has two dowels to locate the pawl carrier support and is shimmed. Note how many shims are installed and set them aside in a safe place for reassembly (see illustration).

4   It's also easy to lose the rollers that slip over the selector fork pins as they disengage from the cam plate tracks (see illustration). They should be taken off and kept in a safe place until reassembly. The selector forks will lift off the gears as the gear cluster is disassembled.

5   There's no need to disassemble the gear cluster unless examination shows obvious defects such as chipped or broken teeth, rounded dogs or worn bushings. See

Section 6 for further information (see illustration).

6   The foregoing information relates specifically to transmissions manufactured after 1971. Earlier transmissions differ in certain minor respects, although the same basic disassembly and reassembly techniques apply.

1991-on models (5-speed)

7   If you intend to dismantle the gear shafts, take this opportunity to loosen the Torx-head screw in the countershaft end while the shaft is locked in gear.

8   Release the detent lever spring from its anchor pin, but do not remove the lever's pivot bolt.

9   The shifter shaft is retained to the crankcase by two locknuts. Before removal, verify the claw arm-to-pin setting as a guide to reassembly. Release the spring clip from the end of the shift drum and withdraw the cam. Remove the two locknuts and washers and pull the shifter shaft free of the casing and drum pins.

10   Remove the five bolts from the access cover, and very gently pry the cover off the crankcase complete with gear shafts and shift drum/forks (see illustration).

11   The mainshaft 5th gear will remain in the right-hand crankcase (see illustration). It

4.10 Five-speed transmission - remove the gear shafts and shift drum as an assembly with the access cover

4.11 Special tools are required to remove the mainshaft 5th gear from the casing

2

4.13a Remove the cotter pins and then remove the guide pins from the forks

4.13b Remove the nut (arrow), followed by the reinforcing and locking plates . . .

4.13c . . . to allow removal of the detent lever pivot bolt

is a tight fit in its bearing and will require a press to draw it out of the bearing. Harley-Davidson has a service tool for this purpose (Part No HD-35316A and HD-3531691) which is essentially a long drawbolt that bears across the casing aperture and passes through the 5th gear, through a thick washer with a OD larger than the 5th gear boss, and then into a nut. As the nut is tightened the 5th gear is drawn into the casing. *Caution: It is advised that the correct tool is used due to the strain alternatives might place on the casing. Before attempting removal, first pry the blind seal out of the gear end and remove the spacer and sealing ring from the threaded portion. Oil seal removal is best done with the shaft removed.*

12 Examine the gear shafts as described above and if necessary dismantle them as described in Section 6.

13 To remove the gear shift drum, first position the drum in neutral (roll pin in right-hand end at 12 o'clock). Remove the cotter pins from the forks and using a magnetic rod, withdraw the shift guide pins from the fork bores. Remove the nut from the detent lever pivot bolt and lift out the reinforcing and locking plates from the drum groove (you

may have to pull the drum out of position slightly to clear the roll pin). Withdraw the shift drum from the forks and, having made note of their position, lift the forks off the gear shafts **(see illustrations)**.

Installation

1970 through 1990 models (4-speed)

14 Turn the engine over so the left side faces up. Make sure all the transmission bearings are in position and the gear shift shaft is located in its correct position. If the gear cluster has been disassembled, reassemble it by reversing the instructions in Section 6.

15 Oil the bearings, then slide the access cover and gear cluster into position making sure the end of the gear shift shaft engages correctly with the pawl carrier **(see illustration)**. Install and tighten the four access cover bolts to the specified torque (note that the shorter bolt goes in the upper right hole). Check that the shafts are able to revolve freely.

16 On late 1984 through 1990 models, reinstall the stator on the transmission access plate, referring to Chapter 8 for details.

1991-on models (5-speed)

17 If the gear cluster shift drum/forks or their bearings have been disassembled, reassemble them as described in Section 6.

18 If the mainshaft 5th gear was removed from the crankcase it must be pressed back into its bearing until its shoulder contacts the bearing inner race.

Caution: Use only the correct Harley-Davidson service tool to install the 5th gear, otherwise casing damage may result.

Working from the sprocket side of the 5th gear, insert a new blind seal in the end of the gear (it must be recessed to a depth of 0.03 to 0.06 inches (0.76 to 1 .52 mm). Fit a new sealing ring over the threaded part of the gear, followed by the spacer (chamfered end towards sealing ring). Lubricate the lips of the new oil seal and press it squarely into the casing until it is flush with the surface.

19 Insert the assembled access cover and gear cluster into the casing, engaging the mainshaft end in its 5th gear, and the countershaft and shifter drum ends in their respective casings. The access cover should fit flush with the crankcase; if not, remove the shafts for investigation.

4.13d Lift the shift drum and forks off the gear shafts

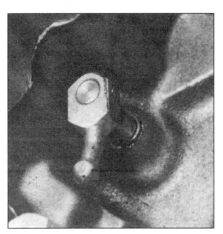

4.15 The end of the gear shift shaft must locate in the pawl carrier

4.21 Insert the shifter shaft into its crankcase bore and secure it lightly with its nuts

4.23 Install the cam correctly on the shifter drum end and secure it with a new retaining clip

4.24a Checking the shifter shaft claw alignment

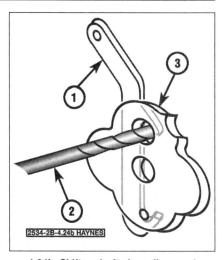

4.24b Shifter shaft claw alignment
1   *Shifter shaft claw*
2   *Drill bit*
3   *Cam*

20   Inspect the five access cover bolt threads - if they show signs of having stretched in use, replace them with new ones. Apply a few drops of Loctite 242 (blue) to the bolts and tighten them evenly to the specified torque. Check that the shafts are free to rotate when in neutral.
21   Engage the shifter shaft in its bore and loosely install its washers and nuts, having engaged the claw arm over the shifter drum pins. Do not tighten the nuts at this stage **(see illustration)**.
22   Loop the detent lever spring over its anchor pin.
23   Place the cam over the shifter drum pins, aligning its blind hole with the corresponding pin **(see illustration)**. Secure the cam with a new retaining clip.
24   The shifter shaft claw must be properly aligned with the drum pins. To ensure this, shift the transmission into 3rd gear and position a No. 32 (0.116 inch) drill bit through the hole at the top of the cam and between the top part of the claw and the drum pin **(see illustrations)**. At this point press down lightly on the top of the shifter shaft crank to remove all play between the claw and drill bit. At the same time, tighten the bottom

shifter shaft nut fully to the specified torque, then tighten the top nut to the same torque. Remove the drill bit.
25   If removed, install the Torx-head screw and bearing retainer in the countershaft end.

5   Transmission components - inspection

1   Give the transmission components a close visual examination for signs of wear or damage, such as chipped or broken teeth, worn dogs or splines or bent shift forks. If the transmission has shown a tendency to jump out of gear look for worn dogs on the back of the gears and wear in the shift mechanism; in the former case wear will be evident in the form of rounded corners or even a wedge-shaped profile in extreme cases. On models through 1990, the corners of the cam plate tracks will wear first, being characterized by a brightly polished surface.
2   The selector arms usually wear across the fork that engages with a gear, causing a certain amount of sloppiness in the gear

change movement. A bent selector will immediately be obvious, especially if overheating has blued the surface.
3   All transmission components that are worn or damaged must be replaced. There's no satisfactory method of repairing them.
4   Depending on the year of manufacture, it is possible to determine the condition of the gear shafts by direct measurement (see Specifications).

6   Transmission gear cluster - disassembly and reassembly

HAYNES HINT   *When disassembling the transmission shafts, place the components in order on a long rod.*

1970 through 1990 models (4-speed)

1   Assuming the selector mechanism and cam plate have been removed (as described in Section 4), withdraw the mainshaft (see **illustration**). Take off the tabbed thrust washer from the right-hand end and remove first gear. On the right-hand end of the mainshaft is the needle roller bearing that seats in the sleeve gear, a thrust washer and second gear, which will pull off. Before third gear can be released, remove and discard the snapring. The washer below should be lifted off, then the gear itself.
2   The sleeve gear will remain in position through the main bearing in the access cover and can be driven out if the access cover is supported and the gear driven through towards the inside of the cover. The bearing itself is retained by two snap-rings, which will have to be removed first **(see illustration)**. Warm the cover to simplify removal of the bearing.

6.1 Remove the mainshaft, leaving only the sleeve gear in position

6.2 Note the needle bearing inside the sleeve gear

2

3   The countershaft is disassembled by removing the thrust washers (note their number and arrangement), first gear, another washer and third gear **(see illustration)**. Reverting to the other (left-hand) end of the shaft, press the drive gear off the splined end of the countershaft. Remove the spacer, second gear and the thrust washer.

4   If required, the cam plate assembly can be disassembled by removing and discarding the snap-ring on the outer end of the cam plate shaft **(see illustration)**. This will give access to the pawl carrier and associated parts, all of which can be checked for wear **(see illustration)**. Don't forget the pawl carrier support, which should be checked for surface cracks **(see illustration)**. Check the two pawl carrier springs for damage caused by acids in the oil. **Note:** *On 1979 through 1985 models, do not install cadmium-plated, 14-coil pawl carrier springs. Use cadmium plated, 16-coil springs or black phosphatized springs (14 or 16-coil) only.*

5   Reassemble the shafts by reversing the disassembly order. Be sure to install new snap-rings and make sure all the shims and thrust washers are replaced in their original locations **(see illustrations)**. The shafts and gears must turn freely **(see illustration)**.

6   Before installing the transmission, have a Harley-Davidson dealer or a repair shop check the gear spacing and shaft end play. If it's not as specified, new pawl carrier support shims, shift forks or thrust washers may have to be installed. This is very important so let a qualified Harley-Davidson technician handle the job.

1991-on models (5-speed)

7   Disassembly of the transmission shafts is as follows. Place each component in order as it is removed as a guide to reassembly.

8   Remove the circlip from the end of the countershaft and remove its 5th gear. Next slide both the countershaft and mainshaft 2nd gears off their shafts, noting the split bearing inside the countershaft gear.

9   Slide the thrust washer off the countershaft and remove the circlip retaining the 3rd

6.3 Note the arrangement of the countershaft thrust washers

6.4a Remove the snap-ring so the cam plate can be withdrawn

6.4b Access is now available to the pawl carrier and spring assembly

gear; slide the 3rd gear off the shaft.

10   The mainshaft 3rd gear is retained on each side by a circlip and thrust washer. First displace the circlip between 3rd and 1st gears from its groove and move it and the thrust washer towards 1st gear. Then push the 3rd gear back towards 1st gear to provide clearance to remove the circlip from its front face. Slide the thrust washer, 3rd gear,

its split bearing and second thrust washer off the mainshaft.

11   At this point, the shafts should be pressed out of the access cover. Dealing first with the countershaft, check that the Torx screw and retainer plate have been removed from its end. Place a support between the 4th and 1st gears and press on the end of the countershaft (do not press on the inner

6.4c Check the pawl carrier support body for cracks

6.5a Reassemble by installing the shaft gears, thrust washers and snap-rings in the reverse order of disassembly

6.5b The mainshaft thrust washer has a projecting tab

6.5c Install the cam plate plunger, then check the action of the gear selector

6.5d All shafts should revolve freely before installation

7.1a If the bike has a direct-mounted shift pedal, remove the pinch bolt (arrow) to detach the pedal

7.1b If the bike has a forward-mounted shift pedal, remove the footpeg pivot bolt and nut, then unbolt the footpeg bracket and remove the pedal

A   Footpeg pivot bolt   B   Forward linkage adjuster

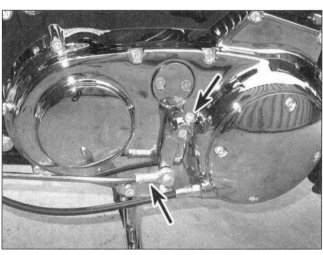

7.1c Loosen the pinch bolt (upper arrow) to remove the lever; unbolt the rear adjuster (lower arrow) to adjust the linkage

2

7.3 Pry out the seal (this can be done with the shaft installed) and drive in a new one

race of the bearing) to push it out of the access cover.

12   Once clear of the access cover, slide the angled spacer off its end, together with the 4th gear. The 1st gear is retained on both sides by a circlip and thrust washer; note its split bearing when removing.

13   Turning to the mainshaft, slide its 1st gear off the shaft. Place a support under its 4th gear and press the shaft from the access cover. Once free, remove the spacer, 4th gear and its split bearing. The remaining thrust washer and a clip can be removed if desired.

14   Reverse the disassembly sequence to assemble the gear shafts.

7 Shift pedal - removal, installation and adjustment

1   Mark the position of the shift pedal on

the shaft (see illustrations).

2   Remove the pedal pinch bolt and slide the pedal off the shaft. If the bike is equipped with a shift linkage, remove both pinch bolts and remove the shift pedal, linkage rod and shift lever.

3   Check the shift shaft seal for signs of oil leakage (see illustration). If necessary, pry it out of its bore and drive in a new one with a socket the same diameter as the seal.

4   Installation is the reverse of the removal steps.

Adjustment

5   Adjustment of the linkage on models so equipped shouldn't be necessary unless shifting becomes difficult. To make the adjustment, disconnect one end of the shift rod (see illustration 7.1c). Loosen the lock-nuts on the shift rod ends and turn the adjusters as needed to change shift rod length. Tighten the locknuts and reconnect the linkage.

8 Kickstarter - removal and installation

Removal

1   Remove the primary chaincase (see Section 3).

2   Rotate the kickstarter crank gear so the kickstarter ratchet gear can be lifted off the transmission sleeve gear assembly.

3   Remove the nut from the end of the kickstarter shaft (after bending back the tab washer) and tap the end of the shaft so it's driven through the center of the kickstarter crank gear. The kickstarter shaft can now be withdrawn, together with the oil seal, shims and thrust plate. Note the number of shims used - all of them must be replaced during reassembly.

Inspection

4   The kickstarter mechanism is extremely rugged. The problems most likely to develop are a broken kickstarter return spring, causing engagement of the mechanism while the engine is running, or slipping under load.

5   The kickstarter return spring is on the outside of the cover and is easily removed and replaced after the kickstarter lever has been removed. The spring is pre-tensioned, so it will return the kickstarter to an upright position when released.

6   Failure of the kickstarter mechanism to disengage after the engine has started can usually be traced to a bent kickstarter shaft, worn shaft bearings or excessive shaft end play, which should normally be within 0.001 to 0.007-inch. Shims of varying thicknesses are available to take up excess play.

7   Slippage is caused by worn or broken teeth on the kickstarter crank gear or the kickstarter ratchet gear with which it engages. It may also be caused by worn teeth on either the kickstarter ratchet found on the back of the clutch outer drum or on the face of the kickstarter ratchet gear. In all cases the worn parts are not repairable and must be replaced. In the case of the kickstarter ratchet, this will involve removing the rivets to release the worn component and re-riveting the replacement into position.

Installation

8   Install the kickstarter shaft. Grease the shaft before it's installed and make sure the thrust plate, shims and oil seals aren't left out.

9   Install the kickstarter crank gear and tighten the center retaining nut, bending over the tab washer to secure it. Install the spring, clutch sprocket spacer and kickstarter ratchet gear (the ratchet teeth should face out) over the transmission (input shaft) sleeve gear. The kickstarter crank gear must be located with the segment containing the teeth in the 6 to 8 o'clock position. This will permit the kickstarter ratchet gear to rest against the metal plate that covers the greater portion of the sprocket teeth.

10   The remainder of installation is the reverse of the removal steps.

Chapter 3
Fuel and exhaust systems

Contents

Degrees of difficulty

| Easy, suitable for novice with little experience | 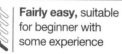 | Fairly easy, suitable for beginner with some experience | | Fairly difficult, suitable for competent DIY mechanic | 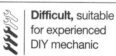 | Difficult, suitable for experienced DIY mechanic | | Very difficult, suitable for expert DIY or professional | |

Specifications

Carburetor

Type

1970 and 1971..	Tillotson
1972 through 1976	Bendix
1977 through 1987	Keihin non-CV
1988-on	Keihin CV

Adjustments

Idle speed	See Chapter 1
Fast idle speed	See Chapter 1
Float level..	See text

Main jet sizes

Tillotson	0.055, 0.057, 0.059, 0.061 and 0.063
Bendix...	90, 95, 100, 105, 110, 115, 120 and 125
Keihin	
1976 through 1978	1.60, 1.65, 1.70, 1.75, 1.80 and 1.85 mm
1979	165
1980 through 1985	160
1986	155
1987	
883..	155
1100..	150
1988	
California only	
883...	165
1200...	180

Main jet sizes (continued)
All others
883 170
1200 200
1989 - California only
883 155
1200 160
1990 and 1991 - California only
883 155
1200 160
1989 through 1991 (all others)
883 175
1200 175
1992 through 1994
883 160
1200 170
1995-on
883
California 170
49 states 160
International
Switzerland (1995) 160
Switzerland (1996-on) 190
1200 (except 1998 and 1999 XL1200S)
California 185
49 states 170
International 190
Through 1998 190
1999-on 200
Switzerland (1995) 160
Switzerland (1996 through 1998) 190
Switzerland (1999-on) 200
1998 and 1999 XL1200S (all) 195

Slow jet sizes (1979 and later models only)
1979 65
1980 through 1982 68
1983 through 1987 52
1988 35
1989 through 1991
California only 42
All others 45
1992 through 1994 40
1995
US and Switzerland 40
International 42
1996 and later 42

Torque specifications

Tillotson carburetor
Inlet needle valve seat .... 40 to 45 inch-lbs (4.5 to 5 Nm)
Diaphragm cover plug .... 23 to 28 inch-lbs (2.6 to 3 Nm)

Keihin carburetor (1977 through 1985)
Carburetor mounting nuts .... 19 ft-lbs (26 Nm)

Keihin carburetor (1986 and 1987)
Carburetor-to-intake manifold bolts .... 15 to 17 ft-lbs (20 to 23 Nm)
Intake manifold flange-to-cylinder head nuts/bolts .... 72 to 120 inch-lbs (8 to 14 Nm)
Air cleaner backplate
To engine bolts .... 120 to 144 inch-lbs (14 to 16 Nm)
To carburetor bolts .... 36 to 60 inch-lbs (4 to 7 Nm)
Air cleaner cover screws .... 36 to 60 inch-lbs (4 to 7 Nm)

Keihin carburetor (1988-on)
Intake manifold flange-to-cylinder head nuts/bolts
Through 2001 .... 72 to 120 inch-lbs (8 to 14 Nm)
2002 and later .... 96 to 144 inch-lbs (10.9 to 16.3 Nm)
Carburetor clamp screw .... 10 to 15 inch-lbs (1.1 to1.7 Nm)

1 Fuel system - general information

The fuel system consists of the fuel tank, the control valve, the fuel line and the carburetor. Gasoline is fed by gravity to the carburetor through the control valve, which contains a built-in filter. The control valve has three positions; On, Off and Reserve. The reserve position provides a small amount of fuel after the main supply has run out, so the engine will still run for a short time.

Three different makes of carburetors were installed on the motorcycles covered by this manual. Tillotson carburetors were used on 1970 and 1971 models, Bendix carburetors were used on 1972 through 1976 models and Keihin carburetors were used on 1977 and later models. Beginning in 1988, a constant velocity (CV) version of the Keihin carburetor was standard equipment.

All carburetors have a butterfly throttle (CV carburetors also have a slide, but it's vacuum operated and responds to throttle butterfly movement) and incorporate an accelerator pump. The Bendix and Keihin carburetors have an integral float chamber. Each carburetor has a manual choke to facilitate easy starting in low outside temperatures.

A large capacity air cleaner is attached to the carburetor intake on all models. Refer to Chapter 1 for filter maintenance instructions.

All 1986 and later California models are equipped with an evaporative emission control system to reduce air pollution that stems from evaporation of gasoline in the fuel tank when the motorcycle is parked.

Several fuel system routine maintenance procedures are included in Chapter 1.

2 Fuel tank - removal and installation

Warning: Gasoline is extremely flammable, so take extra precautions when you work on any part of the fuel system. Don't smoke or allow open flames or bare light bulbs near the work area, and don't work in a garage where a gas-type appliance (such as a water heater or clothes dryer) is present. Since gasoline is carcinogenic, wear fuel-resistant gloves when there's a possibility of being exposed to fuel, and, if you spill any fuel on your skin, rinse it off immediately with soap and water. Mop up any spills immediately and do not store fuel-soaked rags where they could ignite. When you perform any kind of work on the fuel system, wear safety glasses and have a fire extinguisher suitable for a Class B type fire (flammable liquids) on hand.

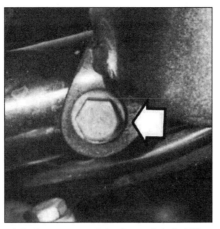

2.5 On most models, the tank is held in place by nuts/bolts at both ends

Removal

1   Turn the fuel control valve to the Off position and disconnect the fuel line from the carburetor. Some hose clamps installed at the factory must be cut or pried off and can't be reused.

2   Insert the end of the fuel line into a clean gasoline container and turn the fuel valve to the Reserve position to drain the tank. Use a funnel to direct the gasoline into the container.

3   On some tanks, the crossover hose, which connects the two lower portions of the tank, must be disconnected from one of the fittings. Release the clamp and slide it down the hose. Some clamps have to be cut off with wire cutters and can't be reused - install a worm-drive clamp when the hose is reinstalled.

4   On 1983 and later XLS models, remove the three screws, disconnect the tachometer, remove the gas tank cap and detach the center panel.

5   On most models, the fuel tank is attached to the upper frame rail at the front and rear by a nut and bolt. The bolts pass through flanges on the tank and lugs on the frame **(see illustration)**. On some models, the rear of the tank is secured by a strap and spring-loaded clip.

6   On some models, the front tank mount is also used to secure the ignition coil and horn with brackets and spacers **(see illustration)**. When the front mounting bolt is removed, the coil assembly should be held in place to prevent it from dropping down onto the engine, possibly causing damage.

7   Remove the nuts/bolts securing the fuel tank to the frame. Support the ignition coil, if necessary. Lift the fuel tank away from the frame and store it in a safe place, away from sparks and flames. **Note:** *On later models with an evaporative emission system, the vent hose must be detached from the fitting on the tank.*

Installation

8   When installing the tank, reverse the

2.6 The front fuel tank bolt also secures the ignition coil on early models

removal procedure. Make sure the coil and horn mounting brackets and spacers are correctly reinstalled at the front fuel tank mount. Don't pinch the wiring harness between the tank and frame. Position the horn so it doesn't touch the coil bracket or frame.

3 Fuel control valve - removal and installation

Warning: Gasoline is extremely flammable, so take extra precautions when you work on any part of the fuel system. Don't smoke or allow open flames or bare light bulbs near the work area, and don't work in a garage where a gas-type appliance (such as a water heater or clothes dryer) is present. Since gasoline is carcinogenic, wear fuel-resistant gloves when there's a possibility of being exposed to fuel, and, if you spill any fuel on your skin, rinse it off immediately with soap and water. Mop up any spills immediately and do not store fuel-soaked rags where they could ignite. When you perform any kind of work on the fuel system, wear safety glasses and have a fire extinguisher suitable for a Class B type fire (flammable liquids) on hand.

1   If the control valve is leaking or the filter must be cleaned, the valve must be detached from the bottom of the tank. Drain the fuel into a clean gasoline container first (see Section 2), then detach the fuel line from the valve. Most hose clamps installed at the factory must be pried or cut off and can't be reused.

2   Unscrew the large nut and detach the valve from the bottom of the fuel tank **(see illustration)**.

3   Refer to Chapter 1 for instructions on cleaning and replacing the fuel filter.

4   If the valve leaks badly or doesn't work correctly, it must be replaced with a new

3

3.2 Make sure the tank is empty, then unscrew the fuel control valve with a wrench on the large hex nut (arrow)

one. The control valve on later models can be disassembled by removing the two screws from each side of the lever.

5   The lever, spring and nylon valve can be removed after the screws are removed.

6   Before installing the valve in the fuel tank, apply Teflon tape or sealant that's resistant to gasoline to the tank threads. On 1975 and later models, the valve has a left-hand thread and the fitting on the bottom of the fuel tank has a right-hand thread. As the large nut is tightened, the fuel valve and the tank are drawn together.

7   When the fuel valve is securely fastened to the tank, connect the fuel line to it. Install a new hose clamp if necessary.

4   Carburetor - removal and installation

Warning: Gasoline is extremely flammable, so take extra precautions when you work on any part of the fuel system. Don't smoke or allow open flames or bare light bulbs near the work area, and don't work in a garage where a gas-type appliance (such as a water heater or clothes dryer) is present. Since gasoline is carcinogenic, wear fuel-resistant gloves when there's a possibility of being exposed to fuel, and, if you spill any fuel on your skin, rinse it off immediately with soap and water. Mop up any spills immediately and do not store fuel-soaked rags where they could ignite. When you perform any kind of work on the fuel system, wear safety glasses and have a fire extinguisher suitable for a Class B type fire (flammable liquids) on hand.

Note: *Although it isn't absolutely necessary, you probably will find it easier to remove the carburetor if the fuel tank is removed first (see Section 2).*

1   Refer to Section 8 and remove the air cleaner assembly.

2   Turn the fuel control valve to the Off position and disconnect the fuel line from the carburetor. Most hose clamps installed at the factory must be pried or cut off and can't be reused.

3   Disconnect the throttle cable(s) from the carburetor. Tillotson and Bendix carburetors use set screws to secure the throttle cable. To disconnect the cable(s) from a Keihin carburetor, turn the throttle valve open by hand and pull the cable ferrule out of the hole in the throttle lever. On 1981 and later models, there are two cables attached to the throttle lever.

4   Disconnect the choke cable from the carburetor - it's attached with a set screw on all carburetors. **Note:** *The CV carburetor used on 1988 and later models doesn't have a choke. It has an enrichener valve that's cable-operated just like the choke. To detach it, unscrew the fitting and pull the valve out of the left (rear) side of the carburetor. Be careful not to damage the end of the valve while it's exposed.*

5   Disconnect the vacuum and EVAP (emission) system hose(s) from the carburetor (some later California models only).

6   On all but 1988 and later models (CV carburetor), remove the nuts and bolts that secure the carburetor to the intake manifold. **Note:** *On 1983 and later models, remove the nut and washer and detach the VOES bracket from the carburetor mounting stud. Remove the stud and lower bolt. Carefully separate the carburetor from the intake manifold. On 1977 and 1978 Keihin carburetors, an O-ring seal is installed between the carburetor and intake manifold. All other models have a gasket.*

7   On 1988 and later models, simply loosen the hose clamp and pull the carburetor out of the intake manifold.

8   Installation is the reverse of the removal procedure, but be sure to install a new gasket or O-ring between the intake manifold and carburetor.

9   Replace the gasket between the air cleaner baseplate and the carburetor with a new one.

5   Carburetor overhaul - general information

1   Poor engine performance, hesitation and little or no engine response to idle fuel/air mixture adjustments are all signs that major carburetor maintenance is required.

2   Keep in mind that many so-called carburetor problems are really not carburetor problems at all, but mechanical problems in the engine or ignition system faults. Establish for certain that the carburetor needs maintenance before assuming an overhaul is necessary.

3   For example, fuel starvation is often mistaken for a carburetor problem. Make sure the fuel filter, the fuel line and the gas

tank cap vent hole are not plugged before blaming the carburetor for this relatively common malfunction.

4   Most carburetor problems are caused by dirt particles, varnish and other deposits which build up in and block the fuel and air passages. Also, in time, gaskets and O-rings shrink and cause fuel and air leaks which lead to poor performance.

5   When the carburetor is overhauled, it's generally disassembled completely and the metal components are soaked in carburetor cleaner (which dissolves gasoline deposits, varnish, dirt and sludge).

Caution: Don't soak any rubber parts (especially the vacuum piston diaphragm on the CV carburetor) in carburetor cleaning solvents. They will be damaged if you do.

The parts are then rinsed thoroughly with solvent and dried with compressed air. The fuel and air passages are also blown out with compressed air to force out any dirt that may have been loosened but not removed by the carburetor cleaner. Once the cleaning process is complete, the carburetor is reassembled using new gaskets, O-rings, diaphragms and, generally, a new inlet needle and seat.

6   Before taking the carburetor apart, make sure you have all of the necessary O-rings and other parts, some carburetor cleaner, solvent, a supply of rags, some means of blowing out the carburetor passages and a clean place to work.

7   Some of the carburetor settings, such as the sizes of the jets and the internal passageways, are predetermined by the manufacturer after extensive tests. Under normal circumstances, they won't have to be changed or modified. If a change appears necessary, it can often be attributed to a developing engine problem.

6   Carburetor - disassembly, inspection and reassembly

Warning: Gasoline is extremely flammable, so take extra precautions when you work on any part of the fuel system. Don't smoke or allow open flames or bare light bulbs near the work area, and don't work in a garage where a gas-type appliance (such as a water heater or clothes dryer) is present. Since gasoline is carcinogenic, wear fuel-resistant gloves when there's a possibility of being exposed to fuel, and, if you spill any fuel on your skin, rinse it off immediately with soap and water. Mop up any spills immediately and do not store fuel-soaked rags where they could ignite. When you perform any kind of work on the fuel system, wear safety glasses and have a fire extinguisher suitable for a Class B type fire (flammable liquids) on hand.

6.19 Check the inlet needle valve for a groove or ridge in the tapered area (arrow)

6.25 Disconnect the lever and remove the accelerator pump (Bendix carburetor)

6.27 Unscrew and withdraw the idle tube (Bendix carburetor)

1   Before disassembling the carburetor, clean the outside with solvent and lay it on a clean sheet of paper or a shop towel.

2   After it's been completely disassembled, submerge the metal components in carburetor cleaner and allow them to soak for approximately 30 minutes. Do not place any plastic or rubber parts in it - they'll be damaged or dissolved. Also, don't allow carburetor cleaner to get on your skin.

3   After the carburetor has soaked long enough for the cleaner to loosen and dissolve the varnish and other deposits, rinse it thoroughly with solvent and blow it dry with compressed air. Also, blow out all the fuel and air passages in the carburetor body.

Caution: Never clean the jets or passages with a piece of wire or drill bit - they could be enlarged, causing the fuel and air metering rates to be upset.

Tillotson carburetor

4   Carefully turn the idle mixture adjustment screw in until it bottoms, while counting the number of turns, then remove it, along with the spring. Record the number of turns - you'll need to refer to it later. Remove the intermediate mixture adjusting screw in the same manner. By counting the number of turns until they bottom, the adjustment screws can be returned to their original positions and adjustments will be kept to a minimum.

5   Note the position of the throttle valve before removing it to ensure it's reinstalled in the same position. Remove the two screws securing the throttle valve to the shaft and detach the valve.

6   Remove the screw securing the throttle shaft and accelerator pump. Pull the throttle shaft out of the carburetor body along with the throttle shaft spring and washers, then remove the dust seals from both sides of the carburetor body.

7   Invert the carburetor and remove the screws securing the diaphragm cover. Carefully lift off the cover, then remove the diaphragm and gasket. Separate the diaphragm from the gasket by peeling them apart.

8   Take out the screw that secures the accelerator pump plunger, then withdraw the plunger.

9   Remove the plug screw from the diaphragm cover.

10   Remove the inlet control lever screw. This will permit the control lever pin, the control lever and the inlet needle to be removed. These parts are very small and easily lost if you aren't careful. Remove the control lever tension spring from below the assembly.

11   Remove the inlet needle valve seat and gasket with a thin-wall 3/8-inch socket. Note the position of the seat insert with the smooth side toward the inside of the cage. The gasket can be lifted out with a scribe.

12   Unscrew the main jet plug, then remove the main jet and gasket.

13   Drill a 1/8-inch hole in the center of the main nozzle welch plug. Be careful not to drill beyond the welch plug, since damage to the main nozzle can result. Insert a small punch through the hole and carefully pry the plug out of the casting.

14   Remove the idle port welch plug as described in the previous Step.

15   Using a small punch, remove the welch plug over the economizer check ball and let the check ball roll out.

16   Remove the screws securing the choke valve and lift out the bottom part of the valve.

17   Slide the choke shaft assembly out of the carburetor (when this is done, the upper part of the choke valve will be released and can be removed). Remove the choke spring and the choke shaft friction ball and spring. Pry the choke shaft dust seal out of the carburetor body.

18   Clean and inspect the parts as described in Steps 2 and 3 of this Section. Inspect the carburetor body for cracks and make sure the throttle shaft turns freely without excessive play. If it's sloppy, a new carburetor will be needed (although sometimes the throttle shaft bores can be reamed out and bushings installed - check with a dealer service department).

19   Make sure the inlet control lever rotates freely on the pin and the forked end of the lever engages with the slot in the inlet needle valve. Check the end of the control lever for wear and burrs. Check the spring to be sure it isn't stretched or distorted. Check the inlet needle valve and seat for nicks and a pronounced groove or ridge on the tapered end of the valve **(see illustration)**. If there is one, a new needle and seat should be used when the carburetor is reassembled.

20   Examine the rest of the parts for wear and damage.

21   Reassemble the carburetor by reversing the disassembly sequence. Use a new diaphragm as well as new gaskets and seals and don't overtighten any of the small fasteners or they may break off.

22   Seat the new welch plugs by striking them with a punch slightly smaller than the plug itself. When the plug is seated, it should be flat, not concave. This will ensure a tight fit around the edge of the casting opening.

23   The inlet control lever tension spring should be installed in the carburetor body. Be sure it attaches to the protrusion on the inlet control lever. Bend the diaphragm end of the control lever so when the lever is installed, it's flush with the floor of the metering chamber.

24   Be sure to tighten the inlet needle valve seat and the diaphragm cover plug to the torques listed in this Chapter's Specifications.

Bendix carburetor

25   Remove the screw securing the accelerator pump lever to the throttle shaft. Disconnect the accelerator pump boot from the float bowl. Remove the accelerator pump and lever **(see illustration)**.

26   Compress the spring on the accelerator pump shaft, rotate the pump lever 1/4-turn and disengage the pin at the top of the shaft from the lever.

27   On 1972 through 1974 models, unscrew the idle tube from the top of the carburetor body and detach the gasket at the same time **(see illustration)**.

3

6.28 Unscrew the main jet and tube assembly from the float bowl (Bendix carburetor)

6.29a Note the position of the float spring before removing the pivot pin (Bendix carburetor)

6.29b Lift out the inlet needle valve with the retaining clip attached (Bendix carburetor)

28 Unscrew the main jet and tube assembly from the bottom of the float bowl (see illustration). This will release the float bowl. Remove the O-ring and fiber washer from the main jet assembly.

29 Note how the float spring is positioned (see illustration), then push the float pivot pin out of the throttle body. You may have to use a small punch to push the pin out. Remove the float assembly along with the inlet needle valve and the float spring (see illustration). Remove the float bowl gasket.

30 Carefully screw the idle mixture adjusting screw in until it bottoms, while counting the number of turns, then remove it along with the spring. Remove the throttle stop screw and spring in the same manner. Counting and recording the number of turns required to bottom the screws will enable you to return them to their original positions and minimize the amount of adjustment required after reassembly.

31 Close the choke and remove the screws securing the choke valve to the shaft. Pull the choke shaft and lever out, releasing the spring and the plunger.

32 Pry the choke shaft seal and retainer out of the carburetor body. Remove the choke shaft cup plug only if it's damaged and must be replaced.

33 Close the throttle valve and remove the two screws securing it to the shaft. Remove the valve, then slide the shaft out of the carburetor body. Release the spring from the throttle shaft.

34 Pry the throttle shaft retainers and seals out of both sides of the carburetor body.

35 Clean and inspect the parts as described in Steps 2 and 3 of this Section. Make sure the throttle shaft turns freely without excessive play. If it's sloppy, a new carburetor will be needed (although sometimes the throttle shaft bores can be reamed out and bushings installed - check with a dealer service department). Check the inlet needle valve and seat for nicks and a pronounced groove or ridge on the tapered end of the valve (see illustration 6.19). If there is one, a

6.40 Be sure the inlet needle valve is correctly seated during reassembly - the retainer clip fits over the tab on the float (arrow) (Bendix carburetor)

new needle and seat should be used when the carburetor is reassembled. Check the float pivot pin and its bores for wear - if the pin is a sloppy fit in the bores, excessive amounts of fuel will enter the float bowl and flooding will occur. Shake the float to see if there's gasoline in it. If there is, install a new one.

36 Reassembly is the reverse of disassembly. Use new gaskets and seals. Whenever an O-ring or seal is installed, lubricate it with grease or oil. Don't overtighten any of the small fasteners or they may break off.

37 Position the throttle shaft so the flat section is facing out and install the throttle valve (leave the screws slightly loose). Open and close the throttle a few times to center the valve on the shaft. Hold the valve firmly in place while tightening the screws.

38 Insert the choke shaft seal and seal retainer into the choke shaft hole and stake the retainer in place with a small punch.

39 Connect the choke valve to the choke shaft in the same manner as the throttle valve.

40 When the inlet needle valve assembly is installed, be sure the clip is attached to the

6.42 The long end of the float spring (arrow) must be positioned as shown (Bendix carburetor)

float tab (see illustration). Check and adjust the float level as described in Section 7.

41 Turn the idle mixture adjusting screw and the throttle stop screw in until they bottom and back each one out the number of turns required to restore them to their original positions.

42 Invert the carburetor and rotate the long end of the float spring up, against the float. Position the float bowl carefully over the throttle body, releasing the float spring so the long end of the spring is pressed against the side of the float bowl (see illustration).

43 Install the main jet and tube assembly through the bottom of the float bowl and into the throttle body. Tighten it securely.

Keihin carburetor (except CV type)

44 Remove the screws securing the float bowl to the bottom of the throttle body and detach the float bowl (see illustration).

45 Loosen the float retaining screw and slide the pivot pin out (see illustration), then carefully separate the float assembly from the carburetor.

6.44 Remove the screws securing the float bowl (Keihin non-CV carburetor)

6.45 Loosen the retaining screw to release the float pin (Keihin non-CV carburetor)

6.47 Disconnect the accelerator pump rod from the rocker arm (Keihin non-CV carburetor)

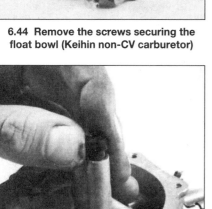

6.48 Remove the low speed jet plug (Keihin non-CV carburetor)

6.49 Remove the main jet (Keihin non-CV carburetor)

6.50a Remove the throttle cable pulley mounting nut (Keihin non-CV carburetor)

46   Remove the inlet needle valve and retaining clip from the float assembly.
47   Separate the rubber boot from the float bowl, then disengage the accelerator pump rod from the rocker arm **(see illustration)**.
48   Remove the plug from the bottom of the throttle body to gain access to the low speed jet. On some models, the low speed jet is accessible only after removing the main jet and main nozzle as described below.

49   Unscrew the main jet **(see illustration)**. On 1976 through 1978 models, tip the throttle body to remove the main nozzle, then unscrew the low speed jet.
50   Unscrew the nut securing the throttle cable pulley or the fast idle cam assembly in place (see **illustration**). Remove the throttle cable pulley and the return spring from the throttle shaft **(see illustration)**.

51   Remove the screws and detach the choke and throttle cable brackets **(see illustration)**.
52   Remove the low speed mixture adjusting screw (1975 through 1979 models only) and the throttle stop screw as described in Step 30 **(see illustration)**. **Note:** *Late 1977 through 1979 models have a limiter cap on the low speed mixture screw that must be*

3

6.50b Disconnect the throttle return spring from the throttle shaft (Keihin non-CV carburetor)

6.51 Locations of the throttle cable (1) and choke cable (2) brackets (Keihin non-CV carburetor)

6.52 Remove the throttle stop screw (Keihin non-CV carburetor)

6.59a Remove the cover screws (Keihin CV carburetor) . . .

6.59b . . . lift off the cover and remove the spring and diaphragm

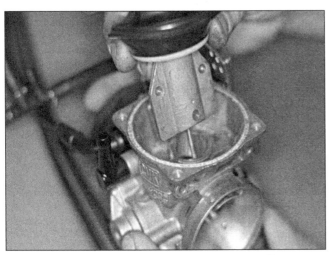

6.60 Lift out the vacuum piston and jet needle
(Keihin CV carburetor)

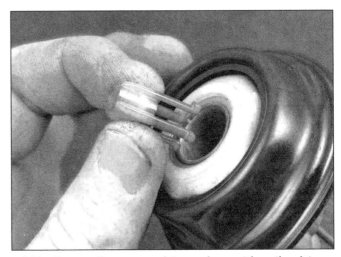

6.61a Remove the vacuum piston spring seat from the piston
(Keihin CV carburetor)

*pried off to remove the screw. Models built
after 1979 don't have a low speed mixture
screw - the idle mixture is preset and can't
be changed.*
53   Don't disassemble the throttle valve -
it's matched to the carburetor and isn't
replaceable. If there's a problem with the
valve, the carburetor must be replaced with a
new one.
54   Clean and inspect the parts as
described in Step 35.
55   Check the accelerator pump boot for
cracks, the rod for distortion and the
diaphragm for holes, cracks and other
defects. If any wear or damage is evident,
replace the pump components with new
ones.
56   Reassembly is the reverse of disassembly. Use new gaskets and seals. Whenever
an O-ring or seal is installed, lubricate it with
grease or oil. Don't overtighten any of the
small fasteners or they may break off. Check
the float level (Section 7) before installing the
float bowl.
57   Turn the low speed mixture adjusting
screw (if used) and the throttle stop screw in

until they bottom and back each one out the
number of turns required to restore them to
their original positions.

Keihin CV carburetor

58   Remove the carburetor from the
machine as described in Section 4. Set the
assembly on a clean working surface.
59   Remove the four screws securing the
top cover to the carburetor body **(see illustration)**. Lift the cover off and remove the
piston spring **(see illustration)**.
60   Peel the diaphragm away from its
groove in the carburetor body, being careful
not to tear it. Lift out the diaphragm/piston
assembly **(see illustration)**.
61   Remove the piston spring seat and separate the needle from the piston **(see illustrations)**.
62   Refer to the accompanying illustration
and note the following **(see illustration)**:
63   Make sure the screwdrivers fit their
slots.
64   Remove the float chamber cover and O-
ring for access to the jets and floats. Hold
the needle jet holder with a wrench while you

unscrew the main jet. Note which way the
needle jet goes in the bore **(see illustration)**.
65   Push out the float pin to remove the
floats.
66   When removing the diaphragm covers,

6.61b Remove the needle from the piston
(Keihin CV carburetor)

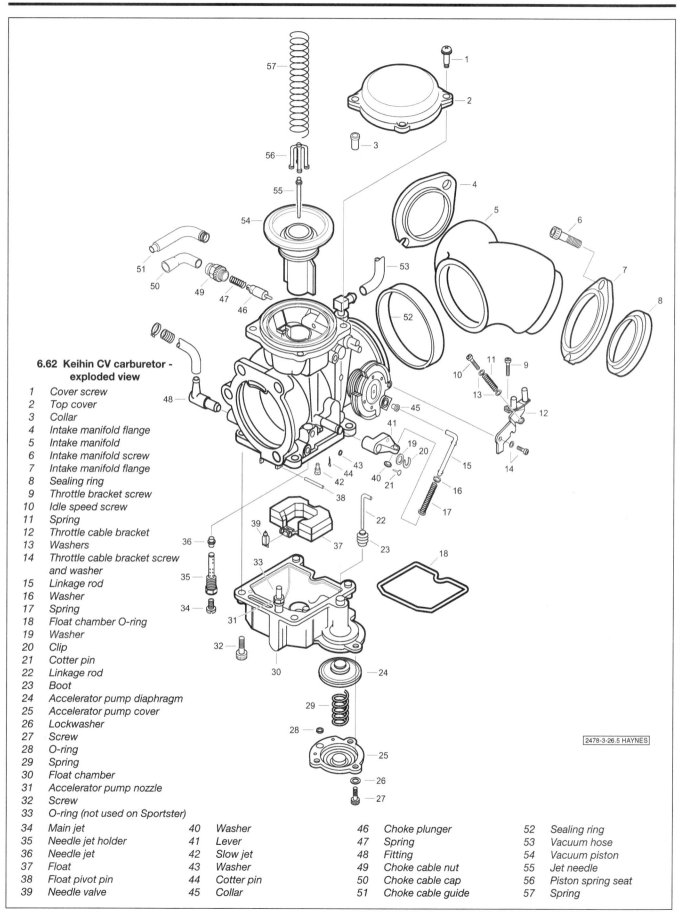

6.62 Keihin CV carburetor - exploded view

1   Cover screw
2   Top cover
3   Collar
4   Intake manifold flange
5   Intake manifold
6   Intake manifold screw
7   Intake manifold flange
8   Sealing ring
9   Throttle bracket screw
10 Idle speed screw
11 Spring
12 Throttle cable bracket
13 Washers
14 Throttle cable bracket screw
    and washer
15 Linkage rod
16 Washer
17 Spring
18 Float chamber O-ring
19 Washer
20 Clip
21 Cotter pin
22 Linkage rod
23 Boot
24 Accelerator pump diaphragm
25 Accelerator pump cover
26 Lockwasher
27 Screw
28 O-ring
29 Spring
30 Float chamber
31 Accelerator pump nozzle
32 Screw
33 O-ring (not used on Sportster)

34	Main jet	40	Washer	46	Choke plunger
35	Needle jet holder	41	Lever	47	Spring
36	Needle jet	42	Slow jet	48	Fitting
37	Float	43	Washer	49	Choke cable nut
38	Float pivot pin	44	Cotter pin	50	Choke cable cap
39	Needle valve	45	Collar	51	Choke cable guide

52	Sealing ring
53	Vacuum hose
54	Vacuum piston
55	Jet needle
56	Piston spring seat
57	Spring

2478-3-26.5 HAYNES

3

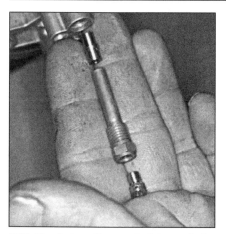

6.64 Here's how the needle jet, needle jet holder and main jet are arranged (Keihin CV carburetor)

6.67a Unscrew the starter valve from the carburetor and compress the spring . . .

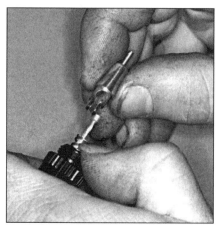

6.67b . . . then slip the cable end out of the plunger to separate the plunger from the cable (Keihin CV carburetor)

do not lose the small O-ring in the passage next to the diaphragm.

67 The choke plunger is part of the choke cable **(see illustration)**. To remove it, unscrew it from the carburetor, then compress the spring and slip the cable end out of the plunger **(see illustration)**.

68 Remove the accelerator pump diaphragm screws **(see illustration 6.64)**. Take out the pump cover, noting the location of the O-ring. Take out the spring and diaphragm.

69 Check the operation of the choke plunger. If it doesn't move smoothly, replace it, along with the return spring. Check the tapered end of plunger for wear and replace if it's worn **(see illustration)**.

70 Check the carburetor body, float bowl and top cover for cracks, distorted sealing surfaces and other damage. If any defects are found, replace the faulty component, although replacement of the entire carburetor will probably be necessary (check with your parts supplier for the availability of separate components).

71 Check the diaphragms for splits, holes and general deterioration. Holding them up

to a light will help to reveal problems of this nature.

72 Insert the vacuum piston in the carburetor body and see that it moves up-and-down smoothly. Check the surface of the piston for wear. If it's worn excessively or doesn't move smoothly in the bore, replace the carburetor.

73 Check the jet needle for straightness by rolling it on a flat surface (such as a piece of glass). Replace it if it's bent or if the tip is worn.

74 Check the tip of the fuel inlet valve needle. If it has grooves or scratches in it, it must be replaced. Push in on the rod in the other end of the needle, then release it - if it doesn't spring back, replace the valve needle.

75 Check the O-rings. Replace them if they're damaged.

76 Operate the throttle shaft to make sure the throttle butterfly valve opens and closes smoothly. If it doesn't, replace the carburetor.

77 Check the floats for damage. This will usually be apparent by the presence of fuel inside one of the floats. If the floats are damaged, they must be replaced.

78 Assembly is the reverse of disassembly, with the following additions.

79 Be sure the jet needle's spring doesn't cover the hole at the bottom of the vacuum piston - reposition it if necessary **(see illustration)**.

80 When installing the diaphragm, make sure the bead is seated in the groove and the diaphragm isn't distorted or kinked **(see illustration 6.59b)**. If the diaphragm doesn't want to seat in the groove, place the top cover over the diaphragm, insert your finger into the throat of the carburetor and push up on the vacuum piston. Push down gently on the top cover - it should drop into place, indicating that the diaphragm has seated in its groove. Install the top cover, tightening the screws to the torque listed in this Chapter's Specifications.

7 Carburetor - adjustments

Tillotson carburetor

1 Carburetor adjustments should be made with the engine at normal operating temperature. Also, be sure the air filter element is clean and the air cleaner assembly is installed securely. Adjustments cannot be done accurately unless the air cleaner assembly is in place.

2 Make sure the twist grip closes the throttle lever on the carburetor completely. Turn the idle mixture screw in until it seats lightly, then back it out 7/8 turn. Adjust the intermediate mixture screw in a similar fashion.

3 Start the engine and adjust the throttle stop screw until the engine is running at approximately 2000 rpm. Turn the intermediate mixture screw in both directions until the highest engine speed is obtained without any misfiring or surging. Turn the screw an additional 1/8-turn counterclockwise.

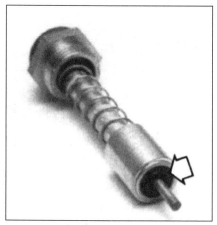

6.69 Check the plunger tip and seal (arrow) for wear (Keihin CV carburetor)

6.79 Don't let the jet needle retainer block the vacuum hole (arrow) (Keihin CV carburetor)

7.6 Locations of the throttle stop screw (1) and the idle mixture adjusting screw (2) (Bendix carburetor)

7.11a Measure the float level with the carburetor held vertically (1979 through 1987 Keihin carburetor)

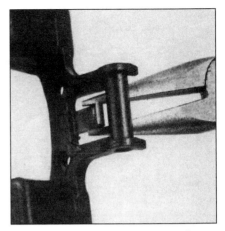

7.11b Bend the tab to adjust the float level (Keihin non-CV carburetor)

4   Turn the throttle stop screw to adjust the idle to the recommended speed.

Bendix carburetor

5   The float level must be adjusted before anything else is done to the carburetor. The carburetor must be removed and the float bowl detached to adjust the float level. Refer to Section 4 for carburetor removal and Section 6 for removal of the float bowl. Invert the carburetor and measure the distance between the lower edge of the float, opposite the pivot pin, and the gasket mating surface. The distance should be 3/16-inch (insert a 3/16-inch drill bit between the gasket surface and the float as a gauge). If adjustment is necessary, bend the tab that contacts the inlet needle valve with needle-nose pliers. Reassemble and install the carburetor.

6   Run the engine until it reaches normal operating temperature, then shut it off. Carefully turn the idle mixture adjusting screw in until it seats lightly **(see illustration)**. On 1972 and 1973 models, back it out 1-1/2 turns. On 1974 through 1976 models, back it out 2-1/4 turns. Adjust the engine speed by turning the throttle stop screw until it runs at 700 to 900 rpm with the twist grip closed.

7   Adjust the idle mixture screw until the engine will run smoothly at idle speed and accelerate crisply. If necessary, adjust the throttle stop screw until the engine idles at 700 to 900 rpm.

8   Remember, all adjustments must be made with the engine at normal operating temperature and the air cleaner securely in place.

Keihin carburetor (except CV type)

Float level (1977 and 1978 models)

9   These models must have the float level measured in both the open and closed positions. Hold the carburetor upside-down and measure the distance between the gasket

surface and the upper edge of the float. The distance should be 35/64 to 5/8-inch (14 to 16 mm).

10   Hold the carburetor right side up and measure the distance between the gasket surface and the lower edge of the float while it's suspended. The distance should be 1-3/32 to 1-3/16-inches (28 to 30 mm). Bend the tabs on the float, as necessary, to obtain the proper float levels.

Float level (1979 through 1987 models)

11   Hold the carburetor vertically with the float pivot pin at the top. Measure the distance between the outside edge of the float and the gasket surface **(see illustration)**. The distance should be 0.630 to 0.670-inch (16 to 17 mm). If necessary, bend the tab on the float until the desired float level is attained **(see illustration)**.

Low speed mixture adjustment (1977 and 1978 models)

12   Adjustments should be made with the engine at normal operating temperature and the air cleaner securely mounted.

13   Turn the low speed mixture adjusting screw in (clockwise) carefully until it seats lightly, then back it out 7/8-turn.

14   Adjust the throttle stop screw until the engine runs at 700 to 900 rpm. Turn the low speed mixture screw until the engine runs smoothly or until it reaches its highest rpm. Readjust the throttle stop screw, if necessary, to obtain the specified idle speed.

Low speed mixture adjustment (1979 models)

15   There's a limiter cap installed over the low speed mixture adjusting screw on these models. Normally the limiter cap shouldn't be removed. The low speed mixture screw should be turned only within the limits of the cap. If necessary, the limiter cap can be removed and the mixture can be altered.

16   Turn the mixture screw in until it seats

lightly, then back it out 1-1/4 turns. Reinstall the limiter cap in the center position on the adjusting screw.

17   Adjust the idle speed with the throttle stop screw to 900 rpm. Turn the limiter cap to the leanest setting that still permits the engine to run smoothly. **Note:** *Turn the limiter cap counterclockwise for a richer mixture and clockwise for a leaner mixture.*

18   Readjust the idle speed, if necessary, to the specified setting.

Low speed mixture adjustment (1980 and later models)

19   The low speed mixture for 1980 and later models is set at the factory and sealed - it's not possible to adjust it.

20   Adjust the idle speed with the choke completely open. Turn the throttle stop screw until the engine is idling at the speed listed in this Chapter's Specifications.

21   Pull the choke out to the second position and turn the fast idle adjusting screw **(see illustration)** until the engine is idling at the specified speed.

7.21 Fast idle adjusting screw (arrow) (1981 through 1987 Keihin carburetor, 1980 similar)

8.3 Remove the bolts holding the backplate to the carburetor (arrows) - some models also have nuts (arrows) holding the backplate to brackets

8.4 After the backplate has been separated from the carburetor, detach the hose from the fitting on the back side

Keihin CV carburetor

Float level (1988 through 1991 models)

22   The carburetor must be removed and the float bowl detached when checking the float level. Make sure the floats are aligned with each other - bend them carefully to realign them if necessary.
23   Invert the carburetor and measure the distance from the float bowl mounting surface to the very bottom (curved) side of the float(s) with a dial or vernier caliper. Don't push down on the float(s) as this is done. It should be 0.725 to 0.730 inch (18.4 to 18.5 mm) on 1988 through 1990 models, and 0.690 to 0.730 inch (17.5 to 18.5 mm) on 1991 models.
24   If the level is incorrect, carefully bend the tab on the float that contacts the inlet needle valve until it is correct.
25   Reinstall the float bowl and the carburetor.

Float level (1992 and later models)

26   Remove the carburetor and detach the float bowl. Place the carburetor body face down on a flat surface, on its engine manifold side.
27   Tilt the body at an angle of 15 to 20 degrees until the float tang is seen to just contact the needle valve tip, but not compress it. Do not tilt any more or less than the specified angle or the reading will be inaccurate.
28   Measure the distance from the top of the float to the bowl mounting surface; it should be within 0.413 to 0.453 inches (10.5 to 11.5 mm).
29   If the level requires adjustment, carefully bend the tab on the float that contacts the inlet needle valve, then recheck the setting.
30   Reinstall the float bowl and carburetor.

Enrichener valve cable

31   The enrichener valve control knob should open, remain open and close without

binding. The knurled plastic nut behind the knob controls the amount of resistance the cable offers.
32   If adjustment is required, loosen the locknut at the back of the cable bracket, then detach the cable from the bracket.
33   Grip the flats on the cable housing with an adjustable wrench, then turn the knurled plastic nut until the enrichener operates as described in Step 26.
34   Reattach the cable to the bracket and tighten the locknut. Do not lubricate the cable or housing - it must have a certain amount of resistance to work properly.
35   When the knob is closed, make sure the valve at the carburetor is closed completely.

Slow idle

36   With the engine at normal operating temperature and the enrichener valve fully closed, turn the throttle stop screw until the idle speed is correct (see this Chapter's Specifications). If the motorcycle doesn't have a tachometer, a hand-held instrument will be needed to measure the engine rpm.

8   Air cleaner - removal and installation

Note: *Although the air cleaners used on the models and years covered by this manual differ slightly in some details, they are all basically the same. They consist of a backplate, fastened to the carburetor with screws and a gasket. mounting bracket(s), a filter element and a cover. The following procedure is typical of what must be done to completely remove the air cleaner assembly - take notes, label parts and make a simple sketch of the mounting bracket(s) if the air cleaner on the machine you have appears different from the one described in the text. Make sure the gasket between the backplate and carburetor is in place and in good condition and hook up*

all hoses during installation. Use thread locking compound on the backplate mounting screws/bolts to prevent the screws from backing out during engine operation.
1   Remove the screws or bolts securing the outer cover to the air cleaner assembly. Pull the cover off.
2   Remove the filter (see Chapter 1).
3   Unscrew the bolts securing the air cleaner backplate to the carburetor. Some models also have two nuts attached to backplate mounting brackets that must be removed **(see illustration)**. Later models have two Allen-head bolts which attach the backplate directly to each cylinder head; from 1991 on these bolts are hollow and form part of the crankcase ventilation passage.
4   Some models have a vent hose attached to the rear of the backplate, which must be disconnected **(see illustration).**
5   Installation is the reverse of removal. Be sure to install a new gasket between the backplate and carburetor.

9   Evaporative emission control system - general information

1   This system, installed on all 1986 and later California models only, is virtually maintenance-free and shouldn't be tampered with unless a new canister, hoses or valves are required because of leaks or deterioration.
2   An occasional check to make sure the hoses are routed properly, secured to the fittings and not kinked or blocked should be sufficient. Make sure the hoses don't come too close to or touch the exhaust system components. Also, check all canister and valve mounting fasteners to see if they're tight. On 1988 through 1991 models, check the reed valves in the air cleaner assembly backplate to make sure they aren't cracked or broken off.

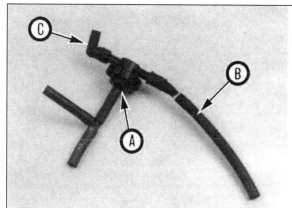

9.5 Vacuum operated valve port locations (1988 through 1991 California models) - see text

10.3 Connect the throttle cable(s) (single cable shown)

3 The system is designed to prevent fuel vapor from escaping from the tank into the atmosphere when the engine is off. The vapor is directed from the tank through a hose and valve to a charcoal-filled canister (mounted on a frame front tube or under the swingarm, depending on the model), where it's absorbed by the charcoal. When the engine is started, the vapor is drawn from the canister into the carburetor and then into the engine, where it's burned in the cylinders. A large diameter hose also purges the canister with fresh air from the air cleaner during engine operation. The vapor valve prevents raw fuel from entering the vent hose when the motorcycle is at extreme angles.

4 1988 through 1991 models also have a Vacuum Operated Electric Switch (VOES - see Chapter 4) and a vacuum operated valve. The VOES directs vacuum to the vacuum operated valve, which seals off the carburetor float bowl vent when the engine's off (it also vents it to the atmosphere when the engine's running). If the diaphragm in the vacuum valve starts to leak, the fuel/air mixture would be upset (leaned out) at high speeds.

5 To check the valve, apply a small vacuum (1 to 2 in-Hg only) to port A **(see illustration)**. The vacuum should remain steady and the valve should be open (you should be able to blow through port B or C - air should pass through). Release the vacuum and make sure the valve is closed (no air should pass through when blowing into port B or C). If the valve doesn't function as described, install a new one.

6 1992 and later models retain the VOES described above, but venting of the carburetor vent hose is controlled electrically by a solenoid-operated butterfly valve, clamped to the rear of the air cleaner baseplate. The butterfly valve itself resides in a housing at the bottom of the air cleaner and if functioning correctly, should remain closed when the engine is stopped, yet open when the starter circuit operates and stay open until the engine is stopped. If failure is suspected, check first the mechanical linkage from the valve pivot to the solenoid plunger. If this is in order, check the solenoid operation as described in Chapter 8.

10 Throttle cable and grip - removal, installation and adjustment

Removal

1 On early models with a spiral-type throttle grip, remove the handlebar end screw, screw spring and grip sleeve. Remove the roller pin and the rollers from the throttle cable plunger. Disconnect the throttle cable from the carburetor, then pull the plunger from the end of the handlebar with the cable still attached to it. Loosen the setscrew that secures the cable end to the control coil plunger and detach the cable.

2 On later models with a drum-type throttle, remove the screws that hold the bottom and top halves of the throttle assembly together. Separate the housing halves and detach the end of each cable from the pulley.

3 Detach the cable from the carburetor. If the bike has a single throttle cable, loosen the setscrew and disconnect the cable from the throttle lever **(see illustration)**. If the bike has dual cables, label them (pull cable and idle cable). Lift each cable out of its pulley groove, rotate the cable to align with the slot and slip the cable end out of the pulley.

Installation

4 Route the cable(s) into place. Make sure they don't interfere with any other components and aren't kinked or bent sharply.

5 If you're working on a dual-cable model, lubricate the end of the pull cable with multi-purpose grease and connect into the throttle pulley at the carburetor. Pass the inner cable through the slot in the bracket, then seat the cable housing in the bracket. Repeat the procedure to install the other cable.

6 Lubricate the throttle grip friction area on the handlebar with graphite grease. If you're working on a drum-type throttle grip (dual or single cable) lubricate the inner surfaces of the upper and lower throttle housing halves where they contact the throttle grip.

7 Reverse the disassembly procedure to reassemble the throttle grip on the handlebar.

Adjustment

8 Adjust cable freeplay as described in Chapter 1.

9 Turn the handlebars back and forth to make sure the cable(s) don't cause the steering to bind.

10 Operate the throttle and check the cable action. The cable(s) should move freely and the throttle pulley or lever at the carburetor should move back and forth in repose to both acceleration and deceleration. If this isn't the case, find and fix the problem before you operate the motorcycle.

 Warning: Do not over-tighten the throttle grip friction screw. Riding with the friction screw too tight is not recommended because of the danger involved when the engine won't return to idle automatically in an emergency.

11 Start the engine. With the engine idling, turn the handlebars all the way to left and right while listening for changes in idle speed. If idle speed increases as the handlebars turn, the cables are improperly routed. This is dangerous. Find the problem and fix it before riding the bike.

11 Choke knob and cable - removal and installation

1 On all except Keihin CV carburetors, loosen the setscrew that secures the choke cable to the carburetor **(see illustration)**.

2 On Keihin CV carburetors, unscrew the starter plunger and remove it from the carburetor **(see illustration 6.62)**.

3 Unscrew the nut that secures the choke knob to the bracket and remove the knob together with the cable.

4 Installation is the reverse of the removal steps.

3

11.1 On all except Keihin CV carburetors, attach the choke cable and secure it with the setscrew

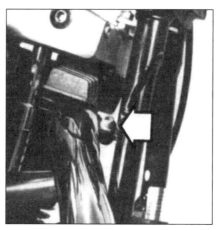

12.2 The exhaust pipes and mufflers are retained by clamps on early models (arrow)

12.3 Note how the muffler clamp is attached to the frame

12 Exhaust system - removal and installation

1   Loosen the clamps and remove the heat shields.

2   On early models, remove the clamps at the cylinder head **(see illustration)**. On later models, unscrew the exhaust pipe-to-cylinder head nuts.

3   Unbolt the mufflers **(see illustration)**.

4   Remove the exhaust system as a unit, then disassemble it as needed.

5   Installation is the reverse of the removal steps. Tighten all of the fasteners securely, but don't overtighten them and strip the threads.

Chapter 4
Ignition system

Contents

Degrees of difficulty

Easy, suitable for novice with little experience	**Fairly easy,** suitable for beginner with some experience	**Fairly difficult,** suitable for competent DIY mechanic	**Difficult,** suitable for experienced DIY mechanic	**Very difficult,** suitable for expert DIY or professional

Specifications

Ignition system type
1970 through 1978 .... Mechanical contact breaker point
1979 and later... Breakerless inductive discharge (electronic)

Air gap
1979 only .... 0.004 to 0.006 inch (0.102 to 0.152 mm)

Ignition coil resistance
1970 through 1978
    Primary .... 4.7 to 5.7 ohms
    Secondary .... 16,000 to 20,000 ohms
1979
    Primary .... 4.7 to 5.7 ohms
    Secondary .... 16,500 to 20,000 ohms
1980 through 1985
    Primary .... 3.3 to 3.7 ohms
    Secondary .... 16,500 to 19,500 ohms
1986 and later
    Primary
        All except 1998 and 1999 XL1200S............................ 2.5 to 3.1 ohms
        1998 and 1999 XL1200S .... 0.4 to 0.6 ohms
    Secondary
        1986 through 1990... Not specified
        1991 and 1992 .... 11,250 to 13,750 ohms
        1993 and later (except 1998 and later XL1200S)......... 10,000 to 12,500 ohms
        1998 and later XL1200S .... 11,500 to 12,700 ohms

4

1 General information

In order for the engine to run correctly, an electrical spark must ignite the fuel/air mixture in the combustion chambers at exactly the right moment in relation to engine speed and load. The ignition system operation is based on feeding low tension (primary) voltage from the battery to the coil where it's converted to high tension (secondary) voltage by a process known as induction. The secondary voltage is powerful enough to jump the spark plug gap in the cylinders many times a second under high compression pressures, provided the system is in good condition and all adjustments are correct.

The ignition system installed on 1970 through 1978 models as standard equipment is a mechanical contact breaker point type. The points are contained in a distributor (1970 models) or in a housing in the right engine cover (1971 through 1978 models).

The system installed on 1979 and later models is a breakerless inductive discharge system (electronic ignition).

Both systems are divided into two circuits: the primary (low tension) circuit and the secondary (high tension) circuit. The primary circuit consists of the battery, the contact breaker points (early models), the control module (1979 only) or the computerized control module (1980-on), the primary coil, the ignition switch and the wires connecting the components.

The secondary circuit consists of the secondary coil, the spark plugs and the wires. All models except the 1988 and later XL1200S (Sportster Sport) use one spark plug per cylinder. XL1200S models use two plugs per cylinder. On all except the XL1200S, the ignition coil fires both plugs at the same time. Since one cylinder is on the exhaust stroke, the spark in this cylinder doesn't have any effect. This is called a "waste spark" system. On the XL1200S, the electronic control system fires the plugs in "single-fire mode," or one cylinder at a time, when the cylinder is nearing TDC on the compression stroke.

Mechanical flyweights are incorporated in the ignition systems on pre-1980 models to advance the ignition timing mechanically. On 1980 and later models, the computer (control module) advances the timing electronically. On 1983 and later models, a Vacuum Operated Electric Switch (VOES) senses vacuum in the intake manifold and sends a signal to the computer, which advances or retards the ignition timing as needed.

2 Ignition coil - check, removal and installation

1   Detach the wires from the coil and connect an ohmmeter to the coil primary wire

2.3a The ignition coil is located under the fuel tank; here's an early model . . .

1   Primary terminals
2   Spark plug wires
3   Mounting nuts

terminals. The primary resistance should be as listed in this Chapter's Specifications - if it isn't, the coil is probably defective. If an ohmmeter isn't available, take the coil to a dealer service department to have it checked or temporarily install a known good coil.

Caution: Be sure to connect the wires to the correct terminals to avoid damaging other ignition components. If the ignition system trouble is eliminated by the temporary installation of the new coil, install it permanently.

2   Pre-1979 models with contact breaker point ignitions should be checked to make sure the condenser is good before replacing the coil. A bad condenser can act just like a defective coil, but the condenser is much more likely to fail. **Note:** *The easiest way to check for a defective condenser is to substitute a known good component. If the ignition system problem goes away when the new condenser is installed, the original condenser is defective.*

3   The coil is mounted under the front of the fuel tank **(see illustrations)**. On 1988 and later XL1200S models, remove the fuel tank (see Chapter 3).

4   Label the primary (small) wires and coil terminals, then disconnect the wires. Detach each spark plug wire from the coil by pulling the boot back, grasping the wire as close to the coil as possible and pulling the wire out of the coil. Note the routing of the dual plug wires on 1998 and later XL1200S models.

5   Remove the bolts/nuts and detach the coil.

6   If a new coil is being installed, make sure it's the right one.

Caution: 1980 and later models must have a coil marked "Electronic Advance". Installing the wrong type of coil could result in failure of the electronic components.

7   Installation of the coil is the reverse of removal. Be sure the spark plug wire boots are seated on the coil towers to keep dirt and

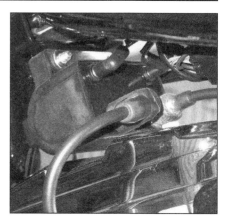

2.3b . . . on later models the coil is farther forward

moisture away from the terminals. Install new boots if the originals are cracked or torn.

3 Condenser - removal and installation

1   A condenser is included in the primary circuit of 1970 through 1978 models to prevent arcing across the contact breaker points as they open. If it fails, the ignition system will malfunction.

2   If the engine is difficult to start, or if misfiring occurs, it's possible the condenser is defective. To check it, separate the contact breaker points by hand when the ignition switch is on. If a spark occurs across the points and they appear to be discolored and burned, the condenser is defective.

3   It isn't possible to check the condenser without special test equipment. Since the cost is minimal, install a new condenser to see the effect on engine performance.

4   Because the condenser and contact breaker points supply a spark to both cylinders, it's virtually impossible for a faulty condenser to cause a misfire on one cylinder only.

5   The condenser is attached to the contact breaker baseplate by a clamp and screw. If the wire is disconnected and the screw removed, the condenser can be detached from the baseplate.

6   When installing the new condenser, be sure the clip around the body (which forms the ground connection) makes good contact with the baseplate. Tighten the mounting screw securely.

4 Air gap (1979 models) - check and adjustment

1   On 1979 models, the air gap between the trigger rotor and sensor is adjustable.

2   Remove the ignition component covers from the right side of the engine (see Chapter 2).

5.1 A simple spark test tool can be made from a block of wood, a large alligator clip, two nails, a screw and a piece of wire

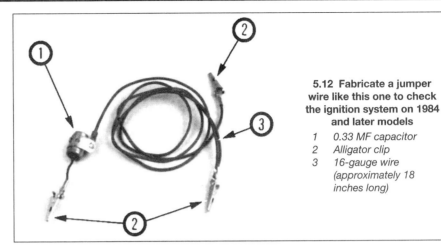

5.12 Fabricate a jumper wire like this one to check the ignition system on 1984 and later models

1 0.33 MF capacitor
2 Alligator clip
3 16-gauge wire (approximately 18 inches long)

3   Remove the spark plugs and rotate the crankshaft until the wide lobe on the trigger rotor is centered in the sensor.

4   Insert a feeler gauge of the specified thickness between the lobe of the rotor and the sensor. If the air gap isn't correct, loosen the screws securing the sensor and move it until the specified gap is obtained. Rotate the crankshaft 180-degrees until the other lobe of the rotor is centered in the sensor and measure the gap to be sure it's the same.

5 Electronic ignition system - check

All models

1   Check the condition of the spark plugs and the spark plug wires as described in Chapter 1. One way to check the ability of the ignition system to produce a strong enough spark is to construct a simple home-made test tool (see **illustration**) and hook it up to the plug wires, one at a time (with the alligator clip grounded on the engine), to see if the spark will jump the gap. Another way, though less conclusive, is to attach a spark plug that's known to be good to the spark plug wires and ground the plug against the engine. Crank the engine over and check for spark. If there is a spark, the coil and ignition system are working properly. Check the choke and the carburetor and replace the spark plugs with new ones if the engine doesn't run right.

2   If no spark is obtained, attach a volt-meter to the battery (black lead to the negative terminal, red lead to positive) and turn the ignition switch and the engine stop switch to the On position. The reading on the voltmeter should be at least 11.5 volts.

3   Measure the air gap (1979 models only) between the sensor and both trigger rotor lobes (refer to Section 4). If the gap between both rotor lobes can't be adjusted within the range given, replace the trigger rotor and/or

the timer mechanism.

4   Make sure the ground cable from the battery is secure and making good contact.

5   Check the ground for the module at the timer plate on the engine (1979 models) or at the frame (1980 and later models). It should be clean and tight to ensure a good connection.

6   Attach a voltmeter between the positive terminal of the coil and ground (red lead to the coil, black lead to ground). Rotate the crankshaft until the lobes of the trigger rotor (1979 models) or the slots in the rotor (1980 and later models) are equal distances from the center of the sensor. Turn the ignition switch and the engine kill switch to the On position and read the voltage on the meter. It should be within 1/2-volt of the battery voltage. If not, the trouble is somewhere between the battery and the coil. Check the connections at the ignition switch, the engine kill switch and the circuit breaker.

7   Disconnect the blue wire (pink wire 1991-on) from the negative terminal of the ignition coil and attach a voltmeter between the terminal and ground. With the ignition and kill switches on, the voltage should be the same as the battery. If the voltage is different, the coil should be replaced with a new one (after checking the resistance as described in Section 3).

1979 models only

8   Reconnect the blue wire to the negative terminal of the coil, then connect the volt-meter between ground and the negative terminal of the coil. The voltmeter should read 1.0 to 2.0 volts. Place the blade of a screwdriver against the face of the sensor and read the voltmeter. The reading should be between 11.5 and 13.0 volts. By removing the screwdriver, the voltage should drop to 1.0 to 2.0 volts. If not, the ignition module is defective and must be replaced with a new one.

9   Attach a known good spark plug to the plug wire and ground the plug against the engine. Check for spark each time the screwdriver is placed against the face of the sensor. If there is no spark, the ignition coil should be replaced with a new one.

1980 through 1985 models only

10   Unplug the connector between the module and the sensor plate. Connect a volt-meter between the red and black wires in the connector on the module side (positive volt-meter lead to the red wire, negative lead to black). Turn the ignition and the engine kill switches on and read the voltmeter. It should indicate 4.5 to 5.5 volts. If not, the ignition module is defective and should be replaced with a new unit.

11   A special jumper cable test adapter is needed to do the following test. It's available from a Harley-Davidson dealer (part number HD 94465-81). Attach the test adapter to the connector halves between the module and sensor. Be careful not to let the exposed wire touch a grounded component or each other or damage to the module will result. Recheck the voltage between the red and black wires. Connect the voltmeter between the green and black wires to test the sensor output (voltmeter positive lead to the green wire, negative lead to the black wire). The volt-meter should read 4.5 to 5.5 volts with the rotor slots away from the sensor, and zero to 1.0 volt with the slot aligned with the sensor. If either of these voltage readings is not attained, the sensor plate must be replaced with a new unit.

1986 and later models only

12   Assemble a jumper wire from 16-gauge wire, a 0.33 microfarad capacitor and three alligator clips (see illustration). A known good condenser from a breaker point ignition system can be used if a capacitor isn't available.

13   Attach a known good spark plug (or the home-made test tool) to one of the plug wires and ground the plug or tool on the engine.

14   Connect the jumper wire with the capacitor in it to the negative coil primary terminal (the blue wire [pink wire 1991-on] was disconnected from the terminal in Step 7). Attach the jumper wire common alli-gator clip to a good ground.

15   Momentarily touch the remaining

4

jumper wire alligator clip to the negative terminal on the ignition coil - when you do, a spark should occur at the plug or test tool.

16   If not, replace the ignition coil - it's defective. If a spark occurred, proceed to Step 17.

17   Follow the instructions in Step 10 above. If the voltage readings are not as specified, check the ignition module power and ground wires for loose and dirty connections. On 1991-on models note that the black wire described is black/white, and that the expected result is 12V+/-0.5V.

18   If the wires and connections are okay, turn the ignition and kill switches on and momentarily connect the black (black/white 1991-on) and green wire connector pins in the module wire connector with a jumper wire or a screwdriver. If a spark occurs at the plug or test tool when the screwdriver or jumper wire is disconnected, the sensor is probably defective (check the sensor resistance as described below before buying a new one).

19   If no spark occurred during the test in Step 18, check the module resistance (as described below) and install a new one if the resistance isn't as specified.

Intermittent ignition problem check

20   Check the battery terminals and the module ground connection to make sure they're clean and tight.

21   Disconnect the white wire from the ignition coil primary terminal (not the white wire that goes to the module from the same terminal).

22   Connect a 16-gauge jumper wire with alligator clips to the positive battery post and the terminal on the coil the white wire was disconnected from.

23   Start the engine and see if the problem is eliminated. If it is, the problem is possibly in the starter safety switch connections (they're probable loose).

Caution: The engine won't stop running until the jumper wire is removed.

24   If the intermittent problem still exists, remove the ignition component covers to gain access to the ignition sensor.

25   Start the engine and spray canned compressed air (available from electronics or computer supply stores) on the sensor - be sure to wear safety glasses or a face shield as this is done! **Note:** *Turn the can upside down for the maximum effect.*

 Warning: Avoid skin contact and don't breathe the vapors.

26   If the engine dies, the sensor is temperature sensitive (to cold) and should be replaced with a new one.

27   If the engine keeps running, allow it to reach normal operating temperature, then use a blow dryer to apply heat to the sensor. If the engine stops, the sensor is temperature sensitive (to excess heat) and should be replaced with a new one.

28   If the engine doesn't stop, apply heat to

the ignition module. If the engine stops. the module is defective and should be replaced.

Sensor resistance check

Note: *The following resistance test applies to 1986 through 1990 models - no resistance test details are available for 1991-on models.*

29   Position the ohmmeter selector switch on the Rx1 scale. Unplug the sensor wire harness connector and attach the positive (red) lead from the ohmmeter to each of the sensor harness terminals in the connector, one at a time, with the negative (black) ohmmeter lead connected to a good ground (use the sensor plate). If each terminal reading indicates infinite resistance, the sensor is good. If any of the terminal connections produce a resistance reading, the sensor is bad.

30   Connect the positive ohmmeter lead to the green sensor wire and the negative lead to the black sensor wire. If the ohmmeter indicates infinite resistance, the sensor is good. If a resistance reading is produced, the sensor is bad.

31   Reverse the ohmmeter leads. If the ohmmeter reads 300-to-750 K-ohms, the sensor is good. If it indicates infinite resistance, the sensor is defective.

Ignition module resistance check

32   Position the ohmmeter selector switch on the Rx1 scale. Unplug the ignition sensor-to-module wire harness connector and on 1986 through 1990 models, attach the positive (red) lead from the ohmmeter to the black wire terminal in the module side of the connector - the negative (black) ohmmeter lead should be connected to the black module ground wire. On 1991-on models attach the positive meter lead to the black/white wire terminal and the negative lead to ground on the frame. If the ohmmeter indicates 0-to-1 ohm, the module is good. if it indicates more than 1 ohm, replace the module.

33   The following resistance tests apply to 1986 through 1990 models only. No similar data is available for 1991-on models; if a fault is suspected with the module and all other ignition components checked out, including the wiring, then replacement of the module is the only solution.

34   Connect the positive ohmmeter lead to the white module wire at the ignition coil (disconnect it from the coil first) and check the meter reading again. If it's 800-to-1300 K-ohms, the module is good. If it indicates infinite resistance, the module is defective.

35   Reverse the ohmmeter leads (red lead to ground, black lead to the white module wire at the coil). If the ohmmeter indicates infinite resistance, the module is good. If it indicates any resistance, the module is bad.

36   Attach the positive ohmmeter lead to the blue module wire at the coil (disconnect it from the coil first) and attach the negative lead to the black module ground wire. If the meter indicates infinite resistance, the module is good. If it indicates any resistance, the module is bad.

37   Reverse the ohmmeter leads. If the

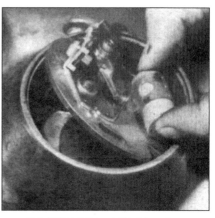

6.5 Lift out the contact breaker point assembly

ohmmeter indicates 400-to-800 K-ohms, the module is good. If infinite resistance is indicated, the module is defective.

38   If the module fails any of the tests, replace it with a new one.

6   Ignition components - removal and installation

1   Lay the engine on its left side, with the timing cover facing up. Make sure the surface the engine is resting on is clean, otherwise there's a risk of damaging the primary chaincase mating surface, resulting in oil leaks.

2   Remove the circular ignition cover from the timing cover. The circular ignition cover is held in place with screws on 1971 through 1979 models and is riveted in place on 1980 and later models. 1970 models have a separate distributor, which is dealt with later in this Section.

1970

3   The contact breaker assembly is contained within the distributor, mounted in the top of the timing cover. The distributor is retained by a clamp, which is released by removing the two screws. When the clamp is detached, the distributor can be lifted out of the timing cover (see Section 8).

1971 through 1978

4   Remove the center retaining bolt that secures the contact breaker cam and the two screws that secure the contact breaker baseplate assembly.

5   Scribe a line across the baseplate and the gearcase, then pull out the baseplate **(see illustration)**. The scribed line is to assist in reassembly so it won't be necessary to retime the ignition.

6   Pull off the contact breaker cam and the mechanical advance unit **(see illustration)**.

1979

7   Lift the ignition module out of the case after the outer cover is removed.

6.6 Pull off the mechanical advance unit under the contact breaker point assembly

8   Remove the screws securing the timer plate, then remove the bolt from the center of the trigger rotor.

9   Disconnect the sensor from the timer plate and the wire from the module to the timer plate.

10   Lift the timer plate out of position and pull the trigger rotor off the advance assembly. The advance assembly can now be removed from the gearcase cover.

1980 and later

11   These systems can be disassembled in basically the same way, the only difference being the addition of a vacuum operated electric switch (VOES) on 1983 and later models.

12   Use a 3/8-inch drill bit to remove the rivets securing the outer cover and detach the cover. Remove the screws holding the inner cover in place. Remove the inner cover and the gasket.

13   Unplug the electrical connector between the sensor plate and the ignition module. Mark the wires and their locations in the connector, then remove the wires from the connector on the sensor plate side.

14   Remove the screws securing the sensor plate to the gearcase and lift it out of position. Pull the wires through the opening in the gearcase one at a time.

15   Remove the screw and washer from the center of the rotor and detach the rotor.

16   If necessary, the camshaft oil seal can be pried out carefully and replaced with a new one.

17   The VOES on 1983 and later models doesn't have to be removed or disconnected to remove the ignition components from the gearcase.

Electronic ignition module

18   The electronic ignition system module is mounted as follows:

a) *1980 and 1981 - on the bottom of the battery carrier/oil tank.*

b) *1982 through 1997 - on the frame next to the battery (under the side cover).*

6.18 Ignition module location - 1982 through 1987 models

c) *1998 and later (except XL 1200S) - on the right side of the engine, in the rear case cover.*

d) *1998 and later XL 1200S - under the seat.*

7   Vacuum Operated Electric Switch (VOES) - check and replacement

1   The Vacuum Operated Electric Switch is controlled by intake manifold vacuum, sensed through an opening in the carburetor body. Under low vacuum conditions, such as hard acceleration, the switch is open, which causes the ignition module to retard the timing, reducing detonation. When high vacuum is present in the intake manifold, the ignition module switches to the advanced timing mode for better fuel economy and performance.

Check

2   Set the ignition timing with a timing light (see Chapter 1).

3   With the engine idling, detach the VOES vacuum hose from the carburetor and plug the carburetor fitting. The ignition module will select the retard mode and engine rpm should drop.

4   Reconnect the vacuum hose. Engine speed should increase and the timing mark should reappear in the timing plug hole.

5   If the engine speed doesn't change when the hose is disconnected and reconnected, check the wire between the VOES and the ignition module and the VOES ground wire.

Replacement

6   Detach the air cleaner cover and backplate, then remove the rear fuel tank mounting bolt and raise the rear of the tank to get at the VOES (see Chapter 3).

7   Disconnect the wire from the VOES to the ignition module.

8   Disconnect the VOES ground wire (to

the engine).

9   Detach the vacuum hose from the VOES (and the carburetor or T-fitting, if necessary).

10   Remove the nut, bolt and washer and detach the VOES from the bracket.

11   Installation is the reverse of removal. Make sure the ground wire is securely attached to the engine bracket with the VOES mounting bolt. Position the high-temperature conduit sleeve over the wire connectors and secure them to the frame with the nylon strap. The VOES and wires must not come in contact with the engine rocker arm covers - heat and vibration from the engine could damage them.

8   Distributor (1970 models only) - general information

1   The distributor used on 1970 models isn't a true distributor, in that it doesn't distribute the spark to the cylinders. However, it does contain the contact breaker points and condensers, as well as the flyweights that advance ignition timing. The distributor should operate reliably for a long time and require inspection at infrequent intervals. Problems will occur if the drive gear is damaged or if excessive end or side play develops as the result of worn bearings, which will allow oil to contaminate the contact breaker points. End play must not exceed 0.008-inch.

2   The mechanical advance flyweights must be free to move on the pivot pins and the springs must be in good condition. Clean and lubricate the flyweight bores and pivot pins and make sure the springs are properly attached. Make sure the point cam is free on the shaft.

3   While it's possible to disassemble and repair a worn distributor, it isn't recommended. Replace the distributor with a new one instead.

4   To remove the distributor, detach the primary wire from the terminal on the outside of the distributor and remove the clamp bolts.

5   When installing the distributor in the engine, make sure the external primary wire Terminal faces the rear of the machine so the contact breaker points are positioned toward the outside of the engine. This will allow easier access for adjustments. Always recheck the ignition timing before and after tightening the distributor clamp bolts.

9   Bank angle sensor (1998 and later models) - check and replacement

1   The bank angle sensor is mounted on the back of the battery tray. It consists of a magnet in a fluid-filled channel. If the bike's

4

lean angle exceeds 80 degrees, the magnet moves from its normal position, causing an open in the ignition module circuit. When the module detects this open, it shuts off the ignition system.

Check

2   Carefully pull off the left side cover (it's clipped onto the frame; there are no fasteners).
3   Start the engine.
4   Locate the bank angle sensor on the backside of the battery tray. Put a magnet on top of the bank angle sensor. If the sensor is operating correctly, the magnet inside the sensor will move, cause an open circuit, shut off the ignition system and stop the engine. Remove the magnet and turn the ignition switch to OFF. This resets the bank angle sensor (unless it was defective).
5   If the bank angle sensor fails to operate as described, replace it.

Replacement

6   Remove the bank angle sensor retaining screw.
7   Disconnect the bank angle sensor electrical connector.
8   Installation is the reverse of removal. Make sure that the locating pin on the sensor body is correctly aligned with the hole before tightening the sensor retaining screw.
9   Install the left side cover.

10 Ignition system (XL1200S models) - general information

1   The ignition system on XL Sport models is different from other late-model Sportsters. It consists of a timing rotor, a cam position sensor, a manifold absolute pressure (MAP) sensor, an ignition module, a dual-coil unit, and a bank angle sensor (see Section 12).
2   Ignition timing is handled by the timing rotor, the cam position sensor, the module and the MAP sensor. The rotor, which is mounted on the end of the camshaft, rotates at one-half crankshaft speed. As it rotates, slots in the rotor's circumference break the magnetic field of a Hall-effect device in the ignition module. The voltage output of the Hall-effect device provides accurate ignition timing even at very slow crank speed.
3   The MAP sensor, which is mounted on a bracket on the frame backbone under the fuel tank, monitors pressure in the intake manifold and provides an analog signal to the ignition module in response to changes in the intake manifold pressure.
4   The ignition module, which is located under the seat, turns battery voltage to the ignition coil on and off in response to the signal it receives from the Hall-effect device. The module also computes the correct spark advance in response to changes in the manifold absolute pressure.

Diagnostic trouble codes

5   The XL1200S ignition system has some self-diagnostic capabilities. When the engine is running, the module monitors the MAP sensor, battery voltage, the ignition coils, the tachometer, the cam sensor, the bank angle sensor, random access memory/read-only memory (RAM/ROM), electronic erasable programmable read-only memory (EE-PROM), and the module itself. If a malfunction occurs in one of these circuits, the module stores a diagnostic trouble code and turns on the Check Engine Lamp.
6   When the ignition key is turned to ON (after it's been turned to OFF for 10 or more seconds), and the engine kill switch in the RUN position, the Check Engine Lamp lights up for about four seconds, then goes out.
7   If the Check Engine Lamp does not come on when the ignition key is turned to ON, or if it fails to go out after four seconds, there is a malfunction in one or more of the monitored circuits in the ignition system.
8   There are two ways to output any diagnostic trouble code(s) stored in the ignition module. Harley-Davidson dealers use a portable scan tool known as a "Scanalyzer" which interfaces directly with the ignition module through the Data Link Connector. This method is beyond the scope of the home mechanic. The other method, which can be done at home, requires no fancy tools. This method is simply a matter of determining the two-digit trouble code(s) by counting the number of flashes of the Check Engine Lamp.
9   Fabricate a two-inch jumper wire from 18-gauge wire with the correct terminal (Harley part no. 72191-94) on each end.
10   Locate the Data Link Connector on the electrical bracket under the left side cover. The Data Link Connector has four wires (light green/red, black, violet/red. white/black) on one side of the connector, and none on the other side. Bridge terminals 1 and 2 (light green/red and black wires) with the jumper wire.
11   Turn the ignition switch key to IGNI-TION and wait about eight seconds for the Check Engine Lamp to begin flashing.
12   Each stored code is preceded by a series of rapid flashes (about three per second), followed by a two-second pause (lamp is off), followed by the code. (If the lamp continues to flash at the faster rate, no codes are stored).
13   The lamp indicates the first digit of the trouble code by flashing one or more times. Each flash is about one second in duration, followed by a one-second pause (lamp off). To determine the first digit, simply count the number of times the lamp flashes (it could be one, two, three, four or five flashes). Write down this number.
14   After the lamp has flashed the first digit of the code, there is another two-second pause (lamp off). The lamp then flashes one or more times to indicate the second digit of the code (two, four. five or six flashes).

Code	Description
12	MAP sensor
16	Battery voltage
24	Front coil
25	Rear coil
35	Tachometer
41	Cam sync failure
44	Bank angel sensor
52	RAM/ROM failure
54	EEPROM failure
55	Module failure

2534-4-10.17 HAYNES

10.17 trouble codes (XL1200S models)

15   After the lamp has flashed the second digit of the code, there is another two-second pause. Then, if there are no other codes stored, the lamp will repeat this trouble code again. If there is more than one code stored, the lamp will flash out the second stored code, in the same manner as the first. Again, jot down the code. This will be followed by another two-second pause, then the lamp will either repeat the first two codes again or, if there is a third code, it will display that code.
16   After the lamp has completed its output of all stored codes, it repeats, starting with the first code again. Once you note that the lamp is repeating itself, there is no need for further observation. (You may wish to record them a second time just to be sure that you counted the correct number of flashes for each digit of each code the first time.)
17   Compare the displayed trouble codes to the accompanying table (see illustration). You now know which circuit(s) has/have a problem.
18   The first things to check in any circuit with an apparent problem are the connectors and the wires. Make sure that all connectors are clean, dry, corrosion-free and tight. Inspect each wire in the circuit and make sure that it's not grounded, open or shorted. If all the connectors and wires are in good shape, take the bike to a Harley-Davidson dealer service department. No further diagnosis is possible at home.
19   To take the ignition module out of diagnostic mode, remove the jumper wire from the Data Link Connector and turn the ignition switch to OFF. Once any problems have been corrected, the trouble codes can be cleared in one of two ways. The convenient method requires the Scanalyzer. The other method is not convenient, but can be done at home if necessary. It requires 50 "start-and-run" cycles (each start-and-run cycle consists of starting the engine, allowing it to run for at least 30 seconds, then turning it off).

Chapter 5
Steering, suspension and final drive

Contents

Degrees of difficulty

| Easy, suitable for novice with little experience | | Fairly easy, suitable for beginner with some experience | | Fairly difficult, suitable for competent DIY mechanic | | Difficult, suitable for experienced DIY mechanic | | Very difficult, suitable for expert DIY or professional | |

Specifications

Fork oil capacity .... See Chapter 1

Torque specifications
Handlebar clamp bolts (1999 and later) .... 12 to 15 ft-lbs (16 to 20 Nm)
Steering stem pinch bolt
  1970 through 1978... 20 to 25 ft-lbs (27 to 34 Nm)
  1979 through 1985... 21 to 27 ft-lbs (28 to 37 Nm)
  1986 through 1989... 25 to 30 ft-lbs (34 to 41 Nm)
  1999 and later .... 30 to 35 ft-lbs (41 to 47 Nm)
Upper triple clamp pinch bolts
  1970 through 1985... Not applicable
  1986 and 1987... 21 to 27 ft-lbs (28 to 37 Nm)
  1988 through 1990... 25 to 30 ft-lbs (34 to 41 Nm)
  1991 and later .... 30 to 35 ft-lbs (41 to 47 Nm)
Lower triple clamp pinch bolts
  1970 through 1978... 35 ft-lbs (47 Nm)
  1979 through 1987... 30 to 35 ft-lbs (41 to 47 Nm)
  1988 and later 883 models.. 30 to 35 ft-lbs (41 to 47 Nm)
  1988 through 1990 1200 models .... 25 to 30 ft-lbs (34 to 41 Nm)
  1991 and later 1200 models.. 30 to 35 ft-lbs (41 to 47 Nm)
Swingarm pivot shaft (1979 through 1985).. 50 ft-lbs (68 Nm)
Swingarm Allen bolts (1986 and later) .... 50 ft-lbs (68 Nm)

5

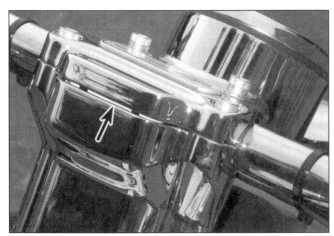

2.3 Remove the four Allen-head screws (arrows) securing the handlebar clamp

1 General information

The front suspension on all Sportster models is conventional, consisting of oil damped, telescopic forks. Cartridge forks are used on the XL1200S.

The rear suspension is also conventional, composed of a swingarm and two hydraulically-damped shock absorbers with adjustable spring rates.

2 Handlebars - removal and installation

1   These motorcycles use a one-piece handlebar, clamped in risers that extend upward from the fork legs.
2   Before removing the handlebars, look for a punch mark indicating the position of the handlebar in the brackets. Make your own mark if you can't see one.
3   If the handlebars must be removed for access to other components, such as the forks or the steering head, simply remove the clamp bolts and lift the handlebar off **(see illustration)**. It's not necessary to disconnect the cables, wires or hoses, but it is a good idea to support the assembly with a piece of wire or rope, to avoid unnecessary strain on the cables, wires and (on the right side) the brake hose.
4   Check the handlebar for cracks and distortion and replace it if any undesirable conditions are found.
5   If the handlebar risers need to be removed, unscrew their bolts from the underside of the upper triple clamp. Pull the riser out and immediately reinstall its hardware in the correct order so you don't forget how it goes.
6   Installation is the reverse of the removal steps. Tighten the clamp bolts to the torque listed in this Chapter's Specifications, but don't overtighten them or the brackets may break. On 1999 and later models, the manufacturer specifies tightening in sequence as described below.
7   On all except Custom models, tighten the two rear clamp bolts to the torque listed in this Chapter's Specifications, then tighten the two front bolts. On Custom models, tighten the two front bolts first to the torque listed in this Chapter's Specifications, then tighten the rear bolts. This will leave a gap between the riser(s) and clamp **(see illustration)**.

Caution: Don't overtighten the bolts trying to close the gap or they will strip out or break.

3 Forks - removal and installation

Removal

1   The forks can be removed very simply by separating the fork tubes from the yokes. Don't disassemble the steering head components unless the bearings require attention (Section 9).
2   Raise the front of the machine until the front wheel is off the ground. Support the machine securely on blocks. This will require a little forethought and care because the lower frame tubes are close together and the machine won't be very stable unless it has some side support.
3   Remove the front wheel as described in Chapter 6.
4   Remove the front fender (see Chapter 7).
5   On models with front disc brakes, remove the clamp securing the hydraulic lines to the fork legs. Disconnect the caliper(s) from the fork leg(s) and tie the caliper(s) to the frame, out of the way.
6   Remove the cap that retains the handlebars (see Section 2).
7   The handlebars can usually be moved out of the way without disconnecting any of the control cables or electrical wires. If necessary, disconnect the control cables and the electrical wires from the handlebar controls, or remove the control cables and electrical wires with their respective controls still attached. The shape of the handlebars and the length of the cables will dictate the best approach. It's a good idea to disconnect the battery before starting this operation. Be sure to keep the front brake master cylinder (on front disc brake models) level to keep air from entering the system.
8   On early models with the instruments attached to the top of the fork legs, remove the instruments and mounting brackets (see Chapter 8).
9   Unscrew the fork leg bolt from the top of each fork leg, but don't remove it at this point.
10   Loosen the pinch bolts in the lower triple clamp, under the plated cover **(see illustration)**. Remove the two bolts that secure the mounting bracket between the upper and lower yokes and remove the bracket (not used on all models) **(see illustration)**. On later models, remove the fork pinch bolts from the upper triple clamp **(see illustration 3.9)**.

2.7 Don't overtighten the bolts trying to close the gap (arrow) (Custom shown)

3.10a Remove the cover screws (if equipped), raise the cover and loosen the pinch bolts under the cover

3.10b On later models, remove the upper and lower triple clamp pinch bolts (arrows)

11   The upper ends of the fork legs are tapered and mate with a matching taper in the upper triple clamp. To break the taper, give the loosened fork leg bolts a sharp rap with a hammer and block of wood **(see illustration)**. Do not use excessive force or the

3.11 Drive the forks through the yokes with a hammer and wood block

3.13 Pull the fork legs through the lower yoke (don't compress the tube and slide or oil may spurt out)

3.10c Remove the bracket (if equipped) from the fork yokes

internal threads in the fork tube may be damaged. If the fork legs are a tight fit, try tapping up on the upper fork yoke at the same time.
12   After the forks are free from the upper yoke, remove the fork leg bolts from the top of each fork leg (except 1995 and later XL1200S models).
13   Remove the fork legs from the lower yoke by pulling only on the fork tubes **(see illustration)**.

Caution: Do not compress the fork tube and slider or oil may spurt out of the open end of the tube. Keep the fork leg upright until the bolts (caps) are installed (also, store them in an upright position).

Installation

14   Install the fork legs in the steering head yokes by reversing the removal procedure. Where tapered fork tubes are fitted, ensure that they mate fully with the matching taper in the fork yoke. Later models have parallel-sided fork tubes, which must be installed to a height of 0.42 to 0.50 inch (11 to 13 mm) from the top of the top bolt to the fork yoke surface. Be sure to push only on the fork

tubes as the fork legs are slipped into the yokes and don't compress the fork tube and slider until the bolts (caps) are in place.
15   Tighten the lower yoke pinch bolts temporarily, then add the specified amount of fork oil to each fork leg (see Chapter 1).
16   Install the fork leg bolts, loosen the lower yoke pinch bolts, tighten the fork leg bolts securely, then tighten the lower yoke pinch bolts (and on later models, the upper yoke fork pinch bolts) to the specified torque (where given).
17   Install the instruments and handlebars, then attach the fender to the forks. Refer to Chapter 6 and install the front wheel and related components.

4 Forks - disassembly, inspection and reassembly

1   Remove the fork legs from the steering head yokes as described in Section 3.
2   Always disassemble one fork leg at a time to avoid mixing up parts.

Disassembly (except 1995-on XL 1200S models)

All models

3   Turn the fork leg upside-down and drain the oil into a container. Keep in mind that when the fork is inverted the spring will slide out - don't let it fall. Compress the fork tube and slider a few times to ensure that it drains completely.
4   When most of the oil has drained, slide out the spring (and spring guide on 1972 through 1974 models) and wipe off as much of the oil as possible **(see illustration)**.
5   Secure the slider in a vise equipped with soft jaws. Clamp it very lightly - just enough to prevent it from rotating while the Allen-head screw is removed from the end of the slider **(see illustration)**. You may find that once loosened, the damper tube turns inside the fork tube, preventing removal of

4.4 Remove the fork spring (all models) and guide (1972 through 1974 models) from the fork tube

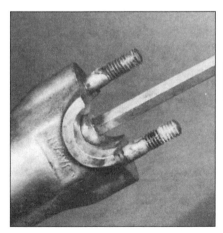

4.5a Remove the damper retaining bolt from the bottom of the fork slider

5

4.5b To make a damper rod holder, thread two nuts onto a bolt with a head that will wedge inside the damper rod and tighten the nuts against each other . . .

4.5c . . . then install the nut-end into a socket (connected to a long extension) and tape it into place

the Allen screw. Try installing the fork spring and cap and compressing the fork to apply pressure to the damper rod head to hold it still. If this fails, obtain either the Harley-Davidson service tool, or make your own **(see illustrations)**. With the exposed section of the tool held tightly, unscrew the Allen screw.

6 Withdraw the dust cover or gaiter from the slider **(see illustration)**. Separate the fork tube from the slider, on 1984-on models noting the procedure described in Step 10.

1970 through 1974

7 To detach the damper unit, remove the snap-ring from the lower end of the fork tube **(see illustration)**.

8 The damper unit is then free to be drawn out. It's a built-up assembly that can be disassembled if parts are worn and require replacement **(see illustrations)**.

9 There's an oil seal in the upper portion of each slider. If the retaining ring is removed, the oil seal can be pried out of position **(see illustrations)**. Do not disturb it

4.6 Separate the dust cover from the fork leg

unless it has to be replaced or if access is required to the two inner bushings (pre-1973 models), which will have to be replaced when play develops in the fork legs.

4.7 The damper unit is held in the slider with a snap-ring

1975 and later

10 Refer to the accompanying illustrations to disassemble the fork **(see illustrations)**.

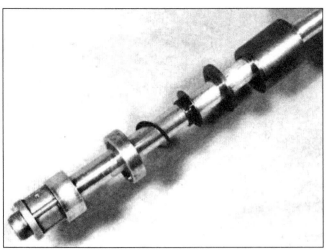

4.8 The damper unit will pull out as a complete assembly

4.9a The oil seal is held in place with a retaining ring

4.9b Don't disturb the oil seal unless it's going to be replaced with a new one

4.10a Pry the dust seal out of the fork slider with a small screwdriver

4.10b Pry the oil seal retaining ring out of its groove

Disassembly (1995-on XL 1200S)

11 Stand the fork upright and hold the inner fork tube with one hand. Unscrew the fork cap bolt from the inner tube, then lower the tube into the outer tube. The upper part of the spring will now be exposed.

12 Remove the stopper ring from the groove at the top of the fork, then remove the rebound adjuster and adjuster plate from the fork cap bolt.

13 To undo the fork cap bolt from the damper rod, you'll need to loosen the hex portion of the cap bolt. This requires compressing the spring and holding it compressed, so there will be room to place wrenches on the cap bolt hex and the flats at the bottom of the cap bolt (the flats are in the rebound adjuster portion of the cap bolt assembly). The spring is held in the compressed position by a slotted plate which is slipped under the locknut (see illustration). There's a special Harley tool available to compress the spring (HD-41549). If you don't

have the special tool you can fabricate a substitute; just be sure it grips the spring securely, so it won't slip out. You'll probably need an assistant to slip the holder into position while you hold the spring compressed.

14 With the spring compressed, place a socket or wrench on the hex at the top of the cap bolt. Place an open-end wrench on the flats at the bottom of the cap bolt. Hold the open-end wrench (don't let it turn) and unscrew the hex portion of the cap bolt. **Note:** *Don't unscrew the rebound adjuster (the part you're holding with the open-end wrench) from the damper rod unless the damper or the rebound adjuster needs to be replaced.*

15 Remove the upper spacer, spring collar and lower spacer from the top of the spring. Take the spring out of the fork.

16 Place the fork in a vise, clamped just tight enough to keep the fork tube from turning. Unscrew the Allen bolt from the bottom of the fork leg, then pull the damper out of the fork tube.

17 Refer to illustrations **4.20a, 4.20b and 4.20c** to complete disassembly of the fork.

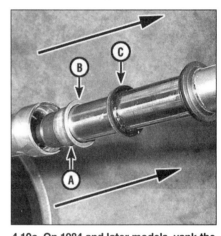

4.10c On 1984 and later models, yank the slider and tube apart until they separate; the slider bushing (A), back-up ring (B) and oil seal (C) will pop out of the slider

Inspection

18 On models fitted with fork bushings, wear will taken by the bushings themselves,

4.10d Remove the damper rod base from the damper rod (if it's not there, it's probably in the bottom of the slider) . . .

4.10e . . . remove the damper rod (and on 1984 and later models, the rebound spring) from the other (upper) end of the fork tube; don't remove the Teflon rings unless you plan to replace them

4.13 After you've unscrewed the fork cap, loosen the locknut, then remove the special tool or washer

5

4.20a The fork tube bushing (A) and slider bushing (B) are on the bottom of the fork tube

4.20b Pry the fork tube bushing apart at the slit just enough to slide it off . . .

4.20c . . . the slider bushing can now be slid off the fork tube

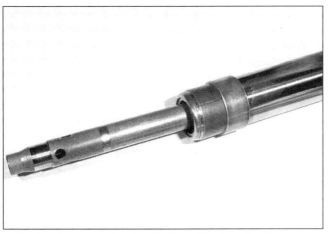

4.28a Put the rebound spring (1984 and later) on the damper rod, then (all models) place the damper rod in the fork tube so it protrudes from the lower end like this

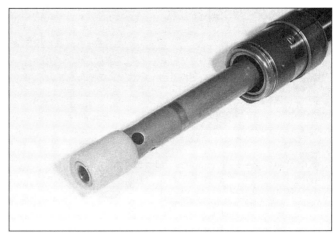

4.28b Install the damper rod base on the damper rod

otherwise it will be present on the working surfaces of the fork tube and slider. Wear can be felt as shuddering when the front brake is applied and the increased amount of play can be detected by pulling and pushing on the handlebars when the front brake is applied hard (do not confuse this with steering head play though).

19   On models through 1974 replacing the bushings is a difficult operation, as the new bushings have to be reamed to size after installation; this should be done by a dealer service department or other qualified shop.

20   On 1984 and later models the slider bushing is displaced during disassembly and a new one installed relatively easily. Only remove the fork tube bushing if it requires replacement - pry it apart at its split sufficiently to ease it off the end of the fork tube, followed by the slider bushing (see illustrations). Install the new slider bushing, then ease the new fork tube bushing over the end of the fork tube (see illustrations).

21   New oil seals must be fitted in the slider every time the fork is dismantled. A wire

retaining clip secures each seal in the top of the slider. Take note of any washers present and install them in their original position.

22   Apply fork oil to the oil seal lips to prevent damage during fork reassembly.

23   If fork damping action decreases, the damper assembly (pre-1975 models) should be examined carefully and the damper pistons replaced. On 1975-on models replace the damper tube wear rings if damping problems are evident and check that all holes in the damper tube are clear.

24   Before reassembling the forks, check the sliding surfaces of the fork tubes. If they're scuffed, scored or badly worn, they should be replaced, in conjunction with the fork bushings (if equipped).

25   It's not possible to straighten forks that have been bent in an accident, even if a repair service is available. There's no way of knowing whether the parts concerned have been overstressed. The tubes should always be checked for straightness by rolling them on a flat surface.

26   The fork yokes are also liable to twist or

distort in an accident. As in the case of the fork tubes, they should be replaced and not repaired, especially since they are far more difficult to align correctly.

4.28c The damper rod, base and damper rod bolt fit together like this in the lower end of the fork slider (slider removed for clarity)

4.28d Install the slider bushing (1984 and later) and back-up ring on the fork tube

4.28e Using a seal driver or equivalent tool . . .

4.28f . . . tap down gently and repeatedly to seat the slider bushing firmly against the shoulder inside the slider

Reassembly (except 1995 and later XL 1200S models)

1970 through 1983

27   Reassembly is the reverse of disassembly. Be sure to install new O-rings and seals and coat them with fork oil before assembly.

1984 and later

28   Refer to the accompanying illustrations to reassemble the fork (see illustrations).

Reassembly (1995 and later XL1200S models)

29   Reassembly is the reverse of the disas-

sembly steps, with the following additions:

a) Coat the bushings and oil seal with Harley Type E fork oil before assembly.
b) Install the guide bushing with its slit to one side of the fork, not facing front or rear.

4.28g If you don't have a bushing driver, you can use a section of pipe (be sure to tape the ends of the pipe so it doesn't scratch the fork tube)

4.28h Coat the inner lip and the outer circumference of the new seal with fork oil . . .

4.28i . . . and install the seal on the fork tube; don't let the upper edge of the fork tube damage the seal lip

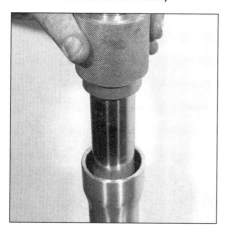

4.28j Tap the seal gently with a driver just until it's fully seated

4.28k This is the JIMS seal driver

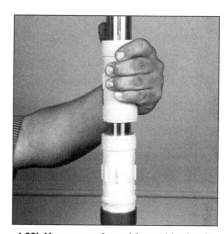

4.28l You can make a driver with plastic plumbing fittings; place one fitting on the seal and strike it with the other piece

5

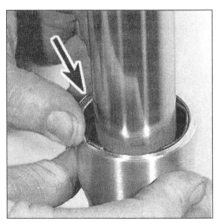

4.28m Compress the retaining ring and fit it securely into its groove in the fork slider

c) If you unscrewed the rebound adjuster from the damper rod, hold down the detent ball with a thumb and turn the rebound adjuster knob all the way counterclockwise, then turn it 13 clicks clockwise. Thread the locknut all the way onto the damper rod, then thread the rebound adjuster all the way on with fingers only. Tighten the locknut against the adjuster without letting the adjuster rotate.

d) Use a new sealing washer on the Alien bolt and tighten it to the torque listed in this Chapter's Specifications.

e) Pour half of the specified amount of fork oil into the fork, then slowly pump the damper rod at least 10 times and leave it compressed.

f) Add the remaining fork oil, then measure the distance from the top of the oil to the top of the fork tube with a stiff tape measure. Add or remove oil to obtain the level listed in this Chapter's Specifications.

g) Install the fork spring with its tight coils downward.

h) Install the flat spacers above and below the spring collar with their sharp edges toward the collar.

i) Tighten the fork cap onto the rebound adjuster, then into the fork tube, to the torques listed in this Chapter's Specifications.

j) Use new O-rings on the rebound adjuster and coat them with fork oil.

5 Steering head bearings - adjustment, removal, inspection and installation

Adjustment

1 Adjustment of the steering head bearings is critical. They should be tightened sufficiently to eliminate all play, but they must not be over-tightened. Note that it is possible to place a load of several tons on the bearings by over-tightening and yet still be able to turn the handlebars. Adjustment is done by tightening the nut or bolt at the top of the steering head, immediately above the upper triple clamp **(see illustrations)**. When the adjustment is correct, there should be no play in the bearings and, when the front wheel is raised off the ground, a light tap on the end of the handlebar should cause the forks to swing to the full lock position.

2 Over-tightened bearings in the steering head will cause the machine to roll at slow speeds, while loose bearings will cause front fork shudder when the front brake is applied.

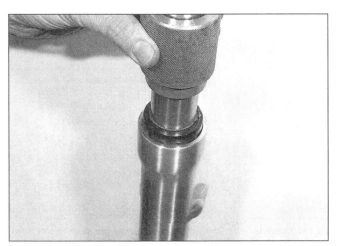

4.28n Use any of the tools previously shown to drive the dust seal (1984 and later) into place

5.1a Loosen the steering head pinch bolt (arrow) . . .

5.1b . . . and turn the adjusting bolt (arrow) to adjust the bearings . . .

5.1c . . . on some models, the bolt is under a decorative cover (arrow)

5.8a Place a box under the steering head to catch loose ball bearings, then lower the steering stem out of the head

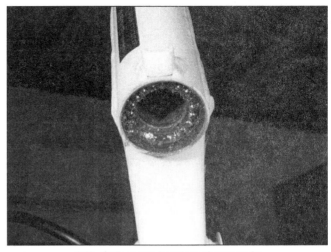

5.8b Collect any bearings that remain in the steering head

Removal

3   If the steering head bearing check (Chapter 1) reveals excessive play in the steering head bearings, the entire front end must be disassembled and the bearings and races replaced with new ones.

4   Refer to Chapter 6 and remove the front wheel.

5   Remove the forks from the triple clamps as described in Section 3.

6   Remove the two bolts that secure the small cowl and warning light console to the upper triple clamp. The cowl and headlight can be suspended without disconnecting the wires.

7   Loosen the pinch bolt through the rear of the upper triple clamp and remove the large nut or bolt and washer from the top of the steering head (see illustrations 5.1a, 5.1b and 5.1c).

8   1970 through 1974 models have uncaged ball bearings in the steering head, so precautions should be taken to catch the bearings as they fall out. As the upper triple clamp is being removed, the steering head

bearings on 1970 through 1974 models will begin to fall out (see illustrations). Usually only the lower bearings will be disturbed and the bearings in the top cup usually stay in place (see illustration).

9   Support the lower triple clamp while the upper triple clamp is removed, to prevent it from falling out of the steering head. Then lower the lower triple clamp/steering stem out of the steering head and remove the upper bearing seal and cone (see illustration).

Inspection

10   Clean and examine the bearings and races or cups and cones. They should have a polished appearance with no dents or tracks if they are going to be reused.

11   If replacement is necessary, the bearing races (cups and cones on 1970 through 1974 models) should be replaced as matched sets. The cups or races are a tight fit in the steering head and will have to be driven out. The lower bearing cone is a tight fit on the base of the steering stem, but can usually be removed

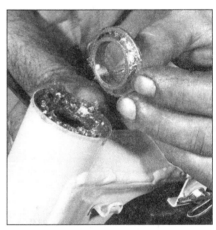

5.8c Lift the top race off the upper bearing assembly and remove the ball bearings

with the careful use of a chisel.

12   Clean and examine the bearings, which should also be highly polished with no signs of wear, pitting or surface cracks. If any of

5.9a Lower the steering stem and bearing out of the steering head

5.9b Lift off the bearing cover and upper bearing

5

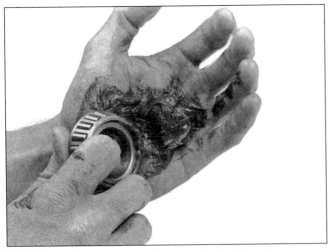

5.14 Drive the grease seal and bearing lower race on with a hollow driver (or equivalent piece of pipe) and a hammer

the ball bearings (used on 1970 through 1974 models) are unusable, replace the entire set. Again, if the bearings are replaced, the bearing cups or races should also be replaced as a matched set.

Installation

13 Since the bearing races are an interference fit in the steering head, installation will be easier if the new races are left overnight in a refrigerator. This will cause them to contract and slip into place in the frame with very little effort. Before installing the races, coat the outsides of the races with clean engine oil. Tap them gently into place with a hammer and bearing driver or a large socket. Do not strike the bearing surface or the race will be damaged.

14 Install the grease seal and lower bearing onto the steering stem using a section of pipe with diameter the same as the inner race of the bearing **(see illustration)**. Drive the bearing on until it is fully seated.

Caution: On tapered roller bearings, don't use a piece of pipe bigger than the inner race, or the bearing case will be damaged.

15 When reassembling the steering head bearings, pack the cups or races and the bearing cones with grease **(see illustration)**. This will simplify the assembly of the ball bearing steering head used on 1970 through 1974 models. Note that on 1970 through 1974 models, the bearing cup shouldn't be full of bearings. There should be room to insert an extra ball bearing, a necessary arrangement to prevent the bearings from skidding on each other and wearing out prematurely. There is a total of 28 ball bearings - 14 bearings in each cup.

16 Install the forks as described in Section 7 and the front wheel as described in Chapter 6.

17 Adjust steering head bearing play (see Step 1).

6 Rear shock absorbers - removal and installation

1 Raise the motorcycle and support it securely on blocks with the rear wheel slightly off the ground. If blocks aren't available, remove one shock absorber at a time. The other shock will hold the rear of the motorcycle in place.

2 Remove the passenger footpegs on 1970 through 1978 models.

3 Remove the mounting nuts (later models use bolts and nuts) securing the shock absorbers to the swingarm and frame **(see illustration)**. Carefully separate the shock absorbers from the frame and swingarm. When the shock absorbers are removed, the rear wheel and swingarm will drop to the ground if not supported.

4 The rear shock absorbers can't be disassembled or rebuilt. If they're worn out or leaking fluid, they must be replaced with new ones.

5 It is possible to replace the springs or transfer the springs to new shock absorbers. Compress the spring with an approved spring compressor and remove the keepers at the top of the shock absorber assembly (early models have a split key type of keeper, while later models have a one-piece keeper). Detach the shroud and the spring seat (if equipped) from the top of the spring.

6 Carefully release the tension on the spring compressor until the compressor can be removed. Lift the spring off the shock absorber assembly and remove all of the mounting hardware. Note the locations of the hardware to simplify reassembly.

7 Clean and inspect all of the components for wear and damage, especially the rubber parts. Replace any defective components with new parts.

8 Reassemble the shock absorber and spring in the reverse order of disassembly. Be sure the adjustment cams on both shock absorbers are positioned at the same level. Compress the spring until the spring keeper(s) can be installed, then slowly release the spring compressor.

9 Have an assistant lift the rear wheel and swingarm to the correct level to install the first shock absorber. With one shock absorber in place, the swingarm should be in the correct position to install the other shock.

10 Tighten the nuts (and bolts) securely and lower the motorcycle off the support blocks.

5.15 Work the grease completely into the rollers

6.3 Remove the upper and lower mounting bolts (arrows) to detach the shock absorber

8.10a Remove the swingarm pivot bolt . . .

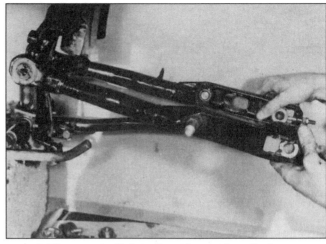

8.10b . . . and withdraw the swingarm from the frame

7 Swingarm bearings - check

1   The swingarm pivots on bearings, which rarely wear out.
2   Raise the rear of the motorcycle off the ground and support it securely on blocks. Grab the swingarm in front of the axle and move it from side-to-side. If there's any discernible movement, the bearings may be worn out.
3   The swingarm should be removed and inspected as described in the following Section.

8 Swingarm - removal, inspection and installation

1   Block the motorcycle up so the rear wheel is slightly off the ground. Position the blocks under the frame.
2   On chain final drive models, disconnect the final drive chain by removing the master link. Move the chain out of the way of the swingarm, but don't remove it from the front sprocket. On belt drive models, loosen the axle nut and belt adjusters to allow the wheel to be moved fully forwards in the swingarm; slip the belt off the rear sprocket.
3   Remove the rear wheel as described in Chapter 6.

Removal
1970 through 1978
4   Remove the rear brake assembly from the swingarm as described in Chapter 6.
5   Remove the rear exhaust pipe and muffler. Some models require the removal of the complete exhaust system.
6   Unscrew the passenger footpegs to release the lower shock absorber mounts. Support the swingarm and remove the shock absorbers from it.

1979 and later
7   Detach the rear disc brake caliper from the swingarm. You don't have to disconnect the brake line or drain the brake fluid. Hang the brake caliper from the frame with a piece of wire, away from the swingarm.

 Warning: Do not let the caliper hang by the brake line.

8   Support the swingarm and remove the lower shock absorber mounting bolts.
9   Remove the chain guard from the swingarm on 1979 through 1981 models. On 1982 models, remove both the front and rear chain guards. On 1983 and later chain drive models, remove only the rear chain guard. On all belt drive models, remove the rear belt guard and the debris deflector.

All models
10   On 1970 through 1985 models, unscrew the pivot bolt. On 1986 and later models, hold the pivot bolt with a wrench and remove the Allen-head bolt from the left end of the pivot bolt. Support the swingarm and pull out the pivot bolt **(see illustration)**.

Pull the swingarm to the rear, away from the frame **(see illustration)**.

Inspection
1970 through 1981
11   Disassembly of the swingarm should be done on a clean workbench. Remove the screw securing the lockplate on the right side of the swingarm **(see illustration)**.
12   Remove the bearing locknut and the outer spacer behind it. This will give access to the right-hand bearing.
13   Working from the left side of the swingarm, loosen the bearing lock ring with a punch until it can be unscrewed by hand.
14   Remove the pivot nut. This will give access to the left-hand bearing. Pry the bearing dust shields out from the inside of the swingarm **(see illustration)**.
15   Working inside the swingarm, drive or press out the bearing and bearing spacer by applying pressure to the spacer **(see illustrations)**. Although it isn't necessary unless the bearing is being replaced, the bearing outer race can be pressed out from the inside **(see illustration)**.
16   If the bearing is replaced, the race should be replaced with it as a matched set.

8.11 Remove the screw securing the lockplate to the bearing locknut (early models only)

8.14 Carefully pry out the bearing dust shield

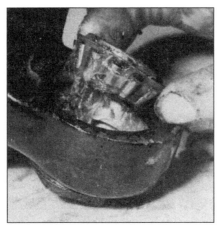

8.15a Lift out the bearing . . .

8.15b . . . and the bearing spacer

1982-on

17 The bearing components should not be interchanged. If any bearings are defective, the complete bearing assembly should be replaced with a new one.

18 You'll have to take the swingarm to a Harley-Davidson dealer or an automotive machine shop to have the bearing races or bushings pressed out and the new bearing races or bushings installed. Make sure the spacer is installed between the inner bearing races or bearing failure could occur.

All models

19 Clean and examine the tapered roller bearings for signs of wear and damage (which should be evident). If there is any doubt about the suitability of the bearings for further use, replace them with new ones. Most bearings fail as a result of pitting, which occurs on the inner and outer races.

Installation

1970 through 1981

20 Reassemble the swingarm in the reverse order of disassembly. Make sure the bearings are liberally packed with grease. When inserting the bearing spacers, the shouldered por-

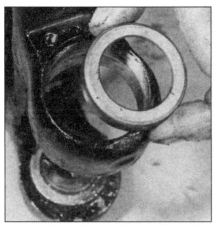

8.15c The bearing outer race must be pressed out

tion must face IN. The wide side of each bearing outer race must face OUT. Tighten the right-hand bearing locknut first. then loosen it one-half turn. On the left-hand side, insert the pivot bolt nut so it will align with the area in the back of the primary chaincase that it's recessed into after the swingarm has been replaced. Install and tighten the lock ring and stake it in three places.

21 After the pivot bolt has been installed, you'll have to pre-load the tapered roller bearings. This is done by attaching a spring balance to the extreme end of one of the arms, before the shock absorbers are installed. Take the reading (in pounds) necessary to make the swingarm turn on the pivot. Loosen the lock plate of the right-hand bearing locknut and tighten the locknut until the drag on the spring balance is increased by about two pounds. Install the lock plate and tighten the retaining screw.

22 Lubricate the components with grease as they're assembled.

23 The chamfered end of the spacer in the bushing (left-hand side) must face out. Insert the main pivot bolt in through the swingarm and, having applied a drop of thread-locking compound to its threads, install the Allen-head bolt in the end of the pivot bolt.

24 Tighten the Allen-head bolt to the specified torque.

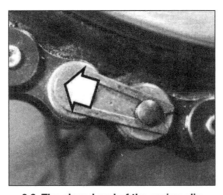

9.3 The closed end of the spring clip MUST face the direction of chain travel (arrow)

All models

25 Install the shock absorbers and the rear wheel brake components.

26 Install the rear wheel and connect the drive chain or slip the belt over the sprocket (as applicable). Be sure the closed end of the master link faces the direction of chain travel. Adjust the chain or belt (as applicable) as described in Chapter 1.

27 Readjust the brake on drum brake models and make sure all of the nuts and bolts are tight.

---

9 Drive chain - removal, cleaning, inspection and installation

Removal

1 Remove the chain guard.

2 Loosen the chain adjusters to create slack in the chain (see Chapter 1).

3 Remove the master link retaining clip with pliers **(see illustration)**. Be careful not to bend or twist it. Slide out the master link and remove the chain from the sprockets.

4 Check the chain guard on the swingarm for wear or damage and replace it as necessary.

Cleaning and inspection

5 Soak the chain in a high flash point solvent for approximately five or six minutes. Use a brush to work the solvent into the spaces between the links and plates.

6 Wipe the chain dry, then check it carefully for worn or damaged links. Replace the chain if wear or damage is found at any point.

7 Stretch the chain taut and measure its length. Then carefully compress all the links together and measure the length again. If the difference between the measurements is more than one inch, the chain is worn enough to need replacement. If the chain needs to be replaced, refer to Section 10 and check the sprockets. If they're worn, replace them also. If a new chain is installed on worn sprockets, it will wear out quickly.

8 Lubricate the chain as described in Chapter 1.

Installation

9 Installation is the reverse of the removal steps. Position the master link clip with its open end facing rearward (away from the direction of chain travel). Refer to Chapter 1 and adjust the chain.

10 Drive belt - removal, inspection and installation

1 Jack up the rear end of the motorcycle and support it securely.
2 Remove the exhaust system (see Chapter 3).
3 Detach the rear master cylinder and its fluid line from the front sprocket cover (see Chapter 6 if necessary). Loosen the pushrod locknut and turn the master cylinder pushrod until it separates.
4 Detach the sprocket cover from the engine and remove it together with the brake pedal.
5 Loosen the drive belt (see Chapter 1).
6 Unscrew the right shock absorber's lower mounting bolt.
7 Remove the belt guard from the motorcycle. Mark the belt with an arrow indicating its direction of rotation (see illustration).
8 Take the belt off the sprockets.
9 Installation is the reverse of the removal steps. Tighten the shock absorber bolt and master cylinder mounting bolts to the torque listed in this Chapter's Specifications.

11 Sprockets - check and replacement

1 Support the bike securely so it can't be knocked over during this procedure.
2 Whenever the sprockets are inspected, the chain should be inspected also and replaced if it's worn. Installing a worn chain on new sprockets will cause them to wear quickly.

3 If the engine is in the frame, remove the exhaust system, footpeg and rear brake master cylinder (if equipped). Remove the front sprocket cover.

Chain final drive

4 Check the teeth on the front and rear sprockets for wear. With the chain tension correctly adjusted, try to pull the chain away from the rear sprocket where the chain wraps around the sprocket. If you can make a gap of more than 1/4-inch between the chain and sprocket, the chain and sprockets should be replaced.

Belt final drive

5 Check the sprocket teeth for wear and for chips or other damage (see Chapter 1).

All models

6 If the sprockets are worn, remove the rear wheel (see Chapter 6) and the chain or belt (Section 9 or 10).

Rear sprocket (drum brake models)

Note: *Special tools are required to install a new sprocket on drum brake models. Read the procedure before beginning removal - you may decide to have a Harley-Davidson dealer do the job.*

7 The rear wheel sprocket is riveted to the brake drum. If examination indicates some of the teeth are chipped, broken or hooked, the brake drum must be removed from the wheel. It's attached to the wheel by five bolts.
8 Remove the bolts securing the brake drum to the hub.
9 The sprocket is attached to the brake drum with rivets. Using a sharp chisel, cut the heads off the rivets and dowel pins.
10 If the rivet holes aren't worn or elongated, the new rivets can be installed in the same holes. However, if they're worn or elongated, a new set of holes should be drilled midway between the existing holes and the dowel pin holes. A 9/64-inch drill bit is required to bore the holes.
11 New dowel pin holes should be drilled also (use a 3/16-inch drill bit). The dowel pins must be a tight fit. Use the new sprocket as a template.

12 Drill a rivet hole, then place the sprocket in position on the drum. Insert a rivet through the hole but don't head the rivet. Drill another hole across from the first rivet and insert another rivet. Again, don't head the rivet.
13 Drill the remaining holes, then drill the four dowel pin holes.
14 Remove the sprocket from the brake drum and deburr the newly drilled holes.
15 Position the drum and sprocket on the center support of the riveting jig (special tool no. 95600-33A).
16 The dowel pins are installed first, followed by the rivets. The dowel pins and the rivets must be installed through the brake drum side.
17 Using a hollow driver, seat the dowel pin and rivet simultaneously, driving the sprocket and hub flange together.
18 Using a concave punch, flare the end of the dowel pin. Head the end of the rivet until it extends 3/64-inch above the face of the sprocket.
19 Repeat Steps 11 through 13, seating the rivets and dowel pins on the opposite side of the hub until all of them are in place. This will prevent distortion of the sprocket as the rivets are installed.
20 Install the brake drum on the hub and reinstall the rear wheel as described in Chapter 6.

Rear sprocket (disc brake models)

21 The sprocket is attached to the rear wheel hub with five bolts.
22 On chain drive models, if examination of the sprocket indicates the teeth are chipped, broken or hooked, the sprocket should be replaced with a new one. If the rear wheel sprocket is worn, the final drive sprocket on the transmission is probably worn also. It's a good idea to replace both sprockets at the same time, as well as the chain. This will alleviate rapid wear that results from mixing old and new parts.
23 On belt drive models, examine the sprocket teeth and flange for signs of damage (see Chapter 1). The sprocket will not wear to the same extent as chain drive models, it being more likely that the belt itself will require replacement.
24 Remove the bolts securing the sprocket to the hub (see illustration). Lift the sprocket off and place the new one in position.
25 Install the sprocket mounting bolts and washers (having applied a drop of threadlocking compound to the bolt threads) and tighten the bolts to the torque listed in this Chapter's Specifications.
26 Install the rear wheel as described in Chapter 6.

Front sprocket (all models)

27 Either bend back the lockwasher and unscrew the nut, remove the lock screw, or remove the screws and lock plate depending on the model being worked on (see illustrations). Pull the sprocket off the transmission shaft, using a puller if necessary (see illustration).

11.24 Unbolt the rear sprocket from the wheel (arrows) (belt drive models)

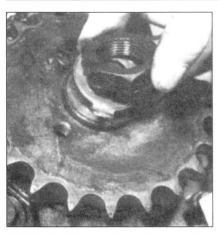

11.27a Lock the engine and unscrew the sprocket retaining nut (early chain drive models)

11.27b On belt drive models, remove the locking plate bolts (arrows), then unscrew the nut and remove the sprocket

11.27c Use a puller if the sprocket is a tight fit

28   On 1970 through early 1984 models, inspect the seal behind the front sprocket **(see illustration)**. If it has been leaking, remove the seal cover and gasket **(see illustration)**. Pry the seal out (taking care not to scratch the seal bore) and tap in a new seal with a socket the same diameter as the seal. Reinstall the cover, using a new gasket.

29   On late 1984 and later models, the mainshaft oil seal behind the sprocket is exposed when the sprocket is removed. Pry the seal out (taking care not to scratch the seal bore) and tap in a new seal with a socket the same diameter as the seal.

30   Install the retainer (if applicable), then slip the final drive sprocket over the splined mainshaft. The sprocket presses into the center of the oil seal on early models **(see illustration)**.

31   Install the tab washer behind the nut that secures the sprocket. You'll have to lock the engine to tighten the nut. When the nut is tight, bend the tab washer over the nut to lock it in place. Later models have a lock screw instead of a tab washer.

Late 1984 through 1990 models

32   Install the sprocket on the mainshaft and secure with its nut. Lock the engine and tighten the nut to 35 to 65 ft-lbs (47 to 88 Nm), check if one of the three holes for the lockscrew aligns with any of the nut flats. If none align, continue tightening (do not exceed maximum of 90 ft-lbs, 122 Nm) until one of the holes aligns. At this point, apply a drop of thread locking compound to the lock screw and tighten it to 50 to 60 in-lbs (6 to 7 Nm).

1991-on models

33   Install the spacer on the mainshaft with its chamfered side inwards, followed by the sprocket.

34   Apply a few drops of Loctite 262 (red) thread locking compound to the nut threads and install the nut on the mainshaft, remembering that it has a left-hand thread. Tighten to 110 to 120 ft-lbs (149 to 163 Nm).

35   On all chain drive models and 1991 belt drive models, align one of the sprocket lock screw holes as described in Step 4, not exceeding the maximum torque of 150 ft-lbs

(203 Nm). Apply a drop of Loctite 242 (blue) to the lock screw threads and tighten it to 50 to 60 in-lbs (6 to 7 Nm).

36   On 1992 through 1994 models with belt drive, fit the lock plate over the nut in such a way that it can be secured diagonally by the two lock screws (tighten the nut further if necessary as described above). Apply a drop of Loctite 242 (blue) to the lock screw threads and tighten them to 80 to 110 in-lbs (9 to 12 Nm) **(see illustration)**.

37   On 1995 and later models, install the nut as described in Step 5, but tighten it only to 50 ft-lbs (68 Nm). Draw a line across the nut and sprocket with a felt pen. Tighten another 30 to 40-degrees, aligning two of the lock plate holes with the holes in the sprocket. Try repositioning the lock plate if the holes don't line up; the lock plate holes are offset. If the holes can't be lined up within the 40-degree range, tighten further, but not more than a total of 45-degrees (1/8-turn) from the felt pen mark. Don't loosen the nut to line up the holes. Once the holes are aligned, install the lock plate Allen bolts and tighten to 80 to 110 in-lbs (9 to 12 Nm). The

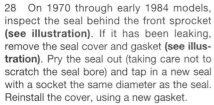

11.28a Remove the retainer to replace the oil seal on 1970 through early 1984 models

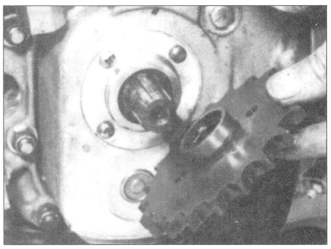

11.28b The final drive sprocket fits through the center of the oil seal on 1970 through early 1984 models

11.36 The sprocket lockplate (1992 and later) must be installed so the bolt holes align

Allen bolts come from the factory with a spot of Loctite on the threads and can be reinstalled three to five times. If you aren't sure how many times they've been installed, use new ones.

38   The remainder of installation is the reverse of the removal steps, with the following additions:

a) *Refer to Chapter 1 and adjust the chain or belt.*

b) *If you removed the seal cover (1970 through early 1984 models), check the engine oil level and add some if necessary* (see Chapter 1).

5

Notes

Chapter 6
Brakes, wheels and tires

Contents

Degrees of difficulty

Easy, suitable for novice with little experience		**Fairly easy,** suitable for beginner with some experience		**Fairly difficult,** suitable for competent DIY mechanic		**Difficult,** suitable for experienced DIY mechanic		**Very difficult,** suitable for expert DIY or professional	

Specifications

Wheels

Size (diameter)
    1970 through 1979
        Front.. 19 inches
        Rear .... 16 inches
    1980 and later
        Front.. 19 or 21 inches
        Rear .... 16 inches
Wheel bearing end play
    1970 through mid-1991.. 0.004 to 0.018 inch (0.10 to 0.46 mm)
    Mid-1991 through 1999.. 0.002 to 0.006 inch (0.05 to 0.15 mm)
    2000 and later .... 0.002 inch (0.05 mm) or less
Rim runout (front and rear)
    Spoke wheel.. 1/32 inch (0.79 mm)
    Cast wheel
        Lateral (axial)... 3/64 inch (1.19 mm)
        Radial .... 1/32 inch (0.79 mm)

Brakes

Minimum lining thickness	See Chapter 1
Maximum disc runout..	0.008 inch (0.2 mm)
Minimum disc thickness*	
Front	
1973 through 1977..	0.188 inch (4.78 mm)
1978 through 1985..	0.160 inch (4.06 mm)
1986 through 2001..	0.180 inch (4.57 mm)
2002 and later..	0.200 inch (5.08 mm)
Rear	
2001 and earlier...	0.205 inch (5.21 mm)
2002 and later..	0.230 inch (5.84 mm)
Caliper piston travel..	0.020 to 0.025 inch (0.51 to 0.63 mm)
Rear brake pedal freeplay..	See Chapter 1

If the minimum thickness is stamped in the disc, it supersedes the information printed here.

Tires

Air pressure..	See Chapter 1
Minimum tread depth	See Chapter 1

Torque specifications

Axle nut	
Front	
1970 through 1987..	50 ft-lbs (68 Nm)
1988 and later..	50 to 55 ft-lbs (68 to 75 Nm)
Rear..	60 to 65 ft-lbs (81 to 88 Nm)
Axle pinch bolt	
1970 through 1972..	11 ft-lbs (15 Nm)
1988 and later..	21 to 27 ft-lbs (28 to 37 Nm)
Brake caliper mounting bolts	
Front	
1973 through 1978..	35 Nm (47 ft-lbs)
1979 through 1983..	80 to 90 inch-lbs (9 to 10 Nm)
1984 and later..	25 to 30 ft-lbs (34 to 41 Nm)
Rear	
1979 through 1985..	155 to 190 inch-lbs (18 to 21 Nm)
1986 through early 1987	13 to 16 ft-lbs (18 to 22 Nm)
Late 1987 and later..	15 to 20 ft-lbs (20 to 27 Nm)
Brake hose-to-caliper banjo fitting bolts	
With copper washers	30 to 35 Nm (41 to 47 ft-lbs)
With steel and rubber washers..	17 to 22 ft-lbs (23 to 30 Nm)
Front disc mounting bolts/screws	
1973	35 ft-lbs (47 Nm)
1974 through 1983	
Spoke wheel	16 to 19 ft-lbs (22 to 28 ft-lbs)
Cast wheel	14 to 16 ft-lbs (19 to 22 Nm)
1984 through 1990 (both types)	16 to 18 ft-lbs (22 to 33 Nm)
1991 and later (both types)	16 to 24 ft-lbs (22 to 33 Nm)
Brake disc to rear hub bolts	
Through 1991	23 to 27 Nm (31 to 37 ft-lbs)
1992 and later	30 to 45 Nm (41 to 61 ft-lbs)
Rear brake master cylinder mounting bolts	
Through 1990	13 to 16 ft-lbs (18 to 22 Nm)
1991 and later	155 to 190 inch-lbs (18 to 21 Nm)
Brake drum to rear hub bolts..	25 ft-lbs (34 Nm)
Rear sprocket mounting bolts	
1970 through 1983	45 to 50 ft-lbs (61 to 68 Nm)
1984 and 1985	
Spoke wheel	45 to 50 ft-lbs (61 to 68 Nm)
Cast wheel	50 to 55 ft-lbs (68 to 75 Nm)
1986 through 1990	50 to 55 ft-lbs (68 to 75 Nm)
1991 and later spoke wheel	45 to 50 ft-lbs (51 to 68 Nm)
1991 cast wheel	50 to 55 ft-lbs (68 to 75 Nm)
1992 cast wheel	45 to 55 ft-lbs (61 to 75 Nm)
1993 and later cast wheel	55 to 65 ft-lbs (75 to 88 Nm)

1 General information

Depending on the model, either wire spoke wheels or cast alloy wheels are standard equipment. Wire wheels require frequent inspection and maintenance, while cast alloy wheels are virtually maintenance-free.

The brakes are different types, depending on year and model. Early models (through 1972) were equipped with drum brakes on both wheels. Models produced from 1973 through 1977 had a single disc brake at the front and a drum brake at the rear. Models produced in 1978 had dual front discs and a drum rear brake. Machines from 1979-on had either single or dual discs at the front and a single disc at the rear.

 Warning: Dust created by the brake system is harmful to your health. Never blow it out with compressed air and don't inhale any of it. An approved filtering mask should be worn when working on the brakes. Do not, under any circumstances, use petroleum-based solvents to clean brake parts. Use brake system cleaner or denatured alcohol only!

Tires are conventional, requiring an inner tube with spoke wheels. Models with cast wheels have tubeless tires.

2 Wheels - inspection and repair

Spoke (wire) wheels

1   Wire wheels should be inspected frequently to ensure the wheel runs true and to prevent potential damage from loose or broken spokes.
2   Clean the wheels thoroughly to remove mud and dirt, then make a general check of the wheels and spokes as described in Chapter 1.
3   Raise the motorcycle so the front wheel is off the ground and support it securely with blocks. Because the frame is very narrow under the engine, be sure to support the motorcycle so it can't fall over sideways. Attach a dial indicator to the fork slider and position the stem against the side of the rim. Spin the wheel slowly and check the side-to-side (axial) runout of the rim. In order to accurately check the radial runout with the dial indicator, the wheel would have to be removed from the machine and the tire removed from the wheel. With the axle clamped in a vise, the wheel can be rotated to check the runout.
4   An easier, though slightly less accurate, method is to attach a stiff wire pointer to the fork slider and position the end a fraction of

an inch from the wheel (where the wheel and tire join). If the wheel is true, the distance from the pointer to the rim will be constant as the wheel is rotated. Repeat the procedure to check the rear wheel.
5   A wheel that wobbles from side-to-side can be trued by loosening the spokes that lead to the hub from the high side of the rim and tightening the spokes that lead to the hub from the low side. This in effect will pull the bulge out of the rim. Always tighten/loosen spokes in small increments to avoid distorting the rim and make sure all the spokes are uniformly tight (see Chapter 1).
6   An out-of-round wheel can be trued by loosening the spokes (both sides of the hub) that lead to the low area, and tightening the spokes that lead to the high or bulged-out area.
7   Generally, the wheels will probably have a combination of side-to-side wobble and out-of-roundness. Keep in mind that tightening and loosening spokes will affect wheel runout in both directions. Wheel truing requires patience and practice to develop any degree of skill, so it's best left to a dealer service department or motorcycle repair shop.
8   If the inspection reveals a bent, cracked, or otherwise damaged rim, the entire wheel will have to be rebuilt using a new rim and spokes. This is a complicated task requiring experience and skills beyond those of the average home mechanic and should be done by a dealer service department or motorcycle repair shop.

Cast alloy wheels

9   Cast alloy wheels should be visually inspected for cracks, flat spots on the rim and other damage. Check the axial and radial runout as described previously for wire wheels.
10 If damage is evident, or if runout in either direction is excessive, the wheel will have to be replaced with a new one. Never attempt to repair a damaged cast wheel.

3 Front wheel - removal and installation

Caution: Do not operate the brake lever after the front wheel is removed from a disc brake model - the piston in the caliper might be forced out. If the piston is forced out of the bore, the caliper will have to be completely disassembled and rebuilt.

Removal

1   Raise the front wheel off the ground and support the machine securely on blocks. Be sure it's stable from side-to-side. The frame under the engine is very narrow, so you may have to support the sides of the motorcycle.
Note: *Pay close attention to any spacers*

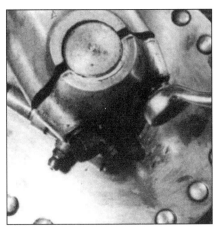

3.7 Loosen the slider cap nuts (shown), bolts or pinch bolt before attempting to remove the axle

used on the front axle. Be sure to reinstall them in their original location(s).

1970 through 1972

2   Disconnect the front brake cable from the front wheel by removing the clevis pin through the brake operating arm. Remove the brake plate anchor bolt and lock washer.
3   Unscrew the nut from the end of the axle.
4   Loosen the pinch bolts (at the bottom of each fork leg) that secure the axle to the forks.
5   Tap the axle out and remove the front wheel.

1973 only

6   Remove the axle nut and washer from the front axle.
7   Loosen the nuts securing the axle retaining cap to the bottom of the right fork slider **(see illustration)**.
8   Tap the axle out and lower the front wheel. Pull the speedometer drive out of the hub (see Chapter 8). Leave the speedometer drive unit connected to the speedometer cable and tie them up out of the way.

1974 through 1977

9   Remove the brake caliper mounting bolt, washers and locknut.
10 Remove the axle nut, washer and lock washer.
11 Loosen the bolts securing the axle retaining caps to the bottom of each fork slider.
12 Tap the end of the axle to loosen it, then pull it out of the forks and front hub.
13 Lower the front wheel until the speedometer drive unit can be disengaged from the front hub. Tie the speedometer drive unit and cable out of the way.
14 Remove the front wheel.

1978 through 1987

15 Detach the front brake caliper(s) from the fork leg(s) and tie them up out of the way.

6

16   Remove the nut, washer and lock washer from the axle.
17   Loosen the slider cap nuts at the bottom of each fork leg. **Note:** *On 1986 and 1987 models, detach the cable from the speedometer, then turn it counterclockwise to separate it from the speedometer drive at the wheel.*
18   Tap the end of the axle to loosen it, then pull it out of the front wheel.
19   Lower the wheel from the forks and remove the speedometer drive unit from the hub. Remove the front wheel.

1988 and later

20   Remove the axle nut and washers **(see illustration)**.
21   Loosen the pinch bolt and pull the axle out.
22   Lower the wheel until the brake disc clears the caliper, then remove the wheel and separate it from the speedometer drive unit (mechanical speedometer) or spacer (electronic speedometer).

Installation

23   Installation of the front wheel is the reverse of the removal procedure. Note the following important points:

   a) *On disc brake models with a mechanical speedometer, be sure the speedometer drive unit engages properly in the hub.*
   b) *On 1973 models, position the brake pads so the brake disc fits between them during installation.*
   c) *Tighten the axle nut to the specified torque before tightening the slider cap nuts or pinch bolt.*
   d) *Caution: The calipers on some later models are secured with locknuts. When the locknuts are removed, they're destroyed and must be replaced with new ones!*
   e) *Check the front wheel bearing end play and compare it to the Specifications in this Chapter. If end play doesn't fall within the specified limits it will be necessary to install a different length hub bearing spacer on models through mid-1991, or a different thickness spacer shim on models from mid-1991-on. Refer to Section 20 for access to spacer or shim and to a Harley-Davidson dealer for the appropriate replacement part.*

4 Front drum brake - inspection and brake shoe replacement

1   Drum brakes don't usually require frequent maintenance, but they should be checked periodically to ensure proper operation. If the linkage is properly adjusted, the brake shoes aren't contaminated or worn out and the return springs and cables are in good condition, the brakes should work fine.
2   Check the cable ends to make sure they aren't frayed and check the lever pivot

3.20 Remove the axle nut and washer (right arrow) and the speedometer drive unit or spacer (left arrow)

for binding and excessive play. As a general rule, the cable should be adjusted so the brake shoes don't drag when the lever is released and the lever doesn't touch the handlebar when the brake is applied.
3   If the lever doesn't operate smoothly, lubricate the cable, the cable ends and the pivot (refer to Chapter 1). If the brakes still don't operate smoothly, the problem is in the shoe actuating mechanism.
4   If the brake shoe wear check (refer to Chapter 1) indicates the shoes are near the wear limit, refer to Section 3 and remove the front wheel. Measure the thickness of the brake shoe lining and compare it to the Specifications in Chapter 1. If the shoes have worn beyond the allowable limits, or if they're worn unevenly, they must be replaced with new ones.
5   If the linings are acceptable as far as thickness is concerned, check them for glazing, high spots and hard areas. A light touch-up with a file or emery paper will restore them to usable condition. If the linings are extremely glazed, they have probably been dragging. Be sure to properly adjust the lever free play to prevent further glazing.
6   Occasionally the linings may become contaminated with grease from the wheel bearings or brake cam. If this happens, and it's not too severe, cleaning the shoes with a brake system solvent (available at auto parts stores) may restore them. Better yet, replace the shoes with new ones - the cost is minimal.
7   To remove the shoes from the backing plate, remove the pivot stud bolt, the operating shaft nut and the operating lever **(see illustration 4.4)**. Tap on the operating shaft and pull out the shaft, the pivot stud, the brake shoes and the return springs as an assembly.
8   Remove the return springs from the shoes and check the springs for cracks and distortion. Replace them with new ones if defects are noted.
9   Clean the backing plate with solvent to remove brake dust and dirt. Also, clean the

operating shaft and pivot stud. If compressed air is available, use it to dry the parts thoroughly.
10   Check the operating shaft and the hole in the backing plate for excessive wear. Slide the operating shaft back into the hole and make sure it turns smoothly without binding. If excessive side play is evident, the backing plate should be replaced with a new one. Check the shoe contact areas of the cam for wear also.
11   Before installing the new shoes, file a taper on their leading edges. Install the return springs, then apply a thin coat of high-temperature grease to the shoe contact areas of the cam and pivot stud.
12   Slip the brake shoe assembly into position in the backing plate, then install the pivot stud bolt and washer and the operating lever and shaft nut.
13   Clean the brake drum out with a wet rag. Don't use solvent in the brake drum because the rubber seals in the hub will be damaged by it.

 Warning: Don't blow the brake drum out with compressed air - the brake dust can damage your lungs if inhaled.

14   Check the drum for rough spots, rust and evidence of excessive wear. If the outer edge of the drum has a pronounced ridge, excessive wear has occurred. Measure the diameter of the drum at several places to determine if it's worn out-of-round. Excessive wear and out-of-roundness indicate the need for a new hub/drum. Slight rough spots and roughness can be removed with fine emery paper. Use one of the brake shoes as a sanding block so low spots aren't created in the drum.
15   Insert the brake shoe assembly into the brake drum and install the front wheel as described in Section 3.
16   Check the adjustment of the brake as described in Step 2 of this Section. If the brake needs adjusting, loosen the locknut on the adjusting sleeve, then turn the adjusting sleeve nut until the lever moves freely for about one-quarter of its full movement before the brakes begin to drag. Tighten the locknut against the adjusting sleeve.
17   If the adjustment is correct, but the brakes drag, the brake shoes must be centered in the brake drum. Loosen the pivot stud bolt and the axle nut, then spin the front wheel. While the wheel is spinning, apply the brake and tighten the pivot stud bolt and the axle nut. Recheck the adjustment.

5 Front disc brake pad replacement

Caution 1: Do not operate the brake lever while the caliper is apart - the piston will be forced out of the caliper. Always replace all pads in the front brake

5.1 Remove the screw securing the brake hose to the fender or fork leg

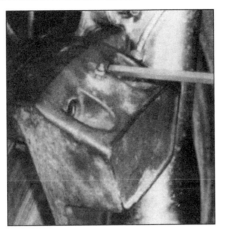

5.5a Remove the Allen-head bolts . . .

5.5b . . . and separate the caliper sections to get at the brake pads on 1973 models

caliper(s) at the same time; never replace only one pad or the pads in only one caliper on dual disc models.*

Caution 2: Ensure that only the correct parts are fitted when replacing pads or discs. Modifications to the pad and disc material from 1992-on prevent the mixing of early and late model components.

Removal

1973

1   Remove the clamp securing the brake hose to the fork leg **(see illustration)**.
2   Unscrew the bolts holding the caliper together, then separate the outer half and the

damper spring from the rest of the caliper.
3   Remove the mounting pin and the inner half of the caliper.
4   Disengage the brake pad mounting pins and detach the brake pads.

1974 through 1976

5   Remove the Allen-head bolts and lock-nuts holding the caliper together **(see illustration)**. Separate the two caliper halves **(see illustration)**.
6   Remove the brake pads and check them for wear.

1978 through 1983

7   Using a socket, universal joint and extension, loosen the bolt securing the two

halves of one of the calipers together **(see illustration)**. Work from the back side of the caliper to loosen the bolt.
8   Remove the Allen-head bolts and nuts attaching the caliper to the lower fork leg.
9   Detach the caliper from the forks and separate the two halves. Remove the brake pads from the guide pins **(see illustrations)**.
10   Repeat the procedure for the remaining caliper.

5.9a Remove the bolt holding the caliper sections together . . .

5.9b . . . then lift off the inner caliper half and remove the pads and shims

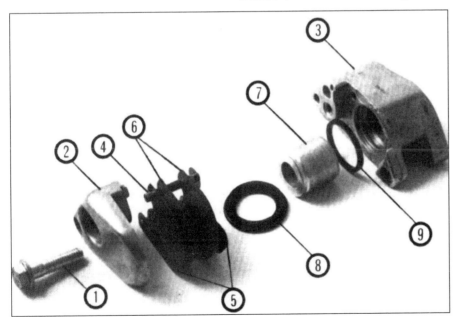

5.7 Front disc brake caliper components (1978 through 1983) - exploded view

1	Caliper bolt (holds caliper sections together)	5	Pad shims
		6	Brake pads
2	Inner caliper half	7	Piston
3	Outer caliper half	8	Boot
4	Pad guide pin (2)	9	Seal

6

5.12 On 1984 and later single-piston calipers, remove the upper mounting bolt and lower mounting pin to detach the caliper

1. *Caliper mounting bolt*
2. *Caliper mounting pin*
3. *Brake hose-to-caliper banjo fitting bolt (12-point head)*

5.14 This is what the outer brake pad and spring clip look like when correctly installed in the pad holder

5.15a Four-piston caliper mounting details (front caliper, left side)

1. *Mounting bolts*
2. *Pad pins*
3. *Brake hose banjo fitting bolt*

5.15b Four-piston caliper mounting details (front caliper, right side)

1. *Mounting bolts*
2. *Pad pins*
3. *Brake hose banjo fitting bolt*

1984 through 1999

11 Loosen the pad retainer screw at the back (inner) side of the caliper.

12 Remove the upper mounting bolt and the lower mounting pin **(see illustration)**. Move the caliper to the rear and down slightly, away from the fork slider, then remove the outer pad, pad holder and spring clip from the caliper as an assembly. Pull out the bushing the upper mounting bolt threads into, then slide the caliper off the brake disc.

13 Note how the pad retainer is installed in the caliper, then remove the screw and detach the pad retainer and inner brake pad.

14 Note how the pad and spring clip are positioned in the holder **(see illustration)**. Push the pad out of the clip to remove it from the holder.

2000 and later

15 Loosen the pad pins but don't remove them yet **(see illustrations)**. Remove the caliper mounting bolts. Slide the caliper and pads off the disc. **Note:** *If you're removing*

the caliper only to replace the pads, you can leave the brake hose connected to the caliper.

16 Support the caliper with rope or wire so it doesn't hang by the brake hose. It's a good

5.17a Unscrew the pad pins (arrows) . . .

idea to wrap the caliper with rags and tape to protect the caliper and wheel from scratches.

17 Remove the pad pins, then remove the brake pads **(see illustrations)**. If the pad

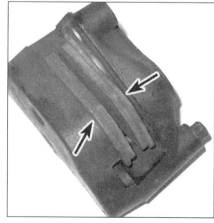

5.17b . . . then remove the pads (arrows)

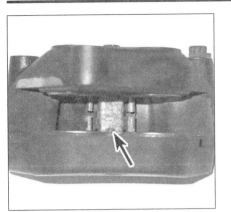

5.18 Remove the anti-rattle spring (arrow) from the caliper cavity

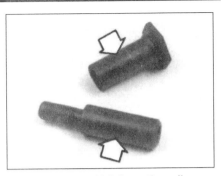

5.23 Clean and lubricate the caliper pins/bushings before assembly (1984 through 1999 shown)

pins are visibly worn, replace them.

18 Remove the anti-rattle spring **(see illustration)**. If it appears damaged, replace it.

Installation

All models

19 Clean the disc surface with brake system cleaner, lacquer thinner or acetone.

 Warning: Do not use petroleum-based solvents.

Check the condition of the brake disc (see Section 6). If it is in need of machining or replacement, follow the procedure in that Section to remove it. If it is okay, de-glaze it with sandpaper or emery cloth, using a swirling motion.

20 Remove the cap from the master cylinder reservoir and siphon out some fluid. Push the piston(s) into the caliper as far as possible, while checking to make sure that the master cylinder reservoir doesn't overflow. If you can't depress the pistons with thumb pressure, try using a C-clamp. If the pistons stick, remove the caliper and overhaul it (see Section 8).

1973 models

21 On 1973 through 1978 models only, check the movement of the piston in the outer caliper half while the caliper is apart. Mount a dial indicator on the back of the outer caliper, so the plunger rests on the piston face. Apply the handlebar lever gently until the piston is extended and set the indicator to zero. Release the brake lever. If the piston isn't restricted, it should move from 0.020 to 0.025-inch. Reassemble the caliper with the new pads in the reverse order of disassembly.

1974 through 1983 models

22 Apply a smear of high-temperature disc brake grease to the friction surfaces of the pad pins. Assemble the caliper with new pads in the reverse order of disassembly, using new locknuts.

1984 through 1999 models

23 Apply a smear of high-temperature disc brake grease to the friction surfaces of the pad pins **(see illustration)**.

24 Position the spring clip and install the pad with the insulator backing material in the pad holder. The pad lining (friction face) and spring clip loop must face away from the caliper piston **(see illustration 5.14)**.

25 On 1993 through 1999 models, install the upper mounting bolt threaded bushing with its flanged head under the pad holder rivet and one of its cutout slots over the rivet body **(see illustration)**.

2000 and later models

26 Install the new inner pad in the caliper with the curved portion toward the rear of the motorcycle **(see illustration)**, then install the outer pad. The inner and outer pads are different shapes **(see illustration)**. On the left side of the bike, the pad with two tabs is installed in the outer position and the pad with one tab is installed in the inner position. On the right side of the bike, it's the opposite; the pad with two tabs is installed in the inner position and the pad with one tab is installed in the outer position. **Note:** *The pads on four-piston front calipers are inter-*

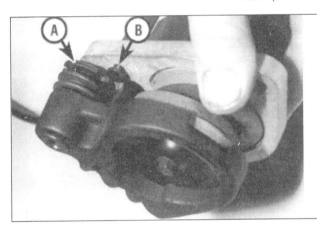

5.25 Caliper mounting bolt bushing flanged head (A) and rivet (B)

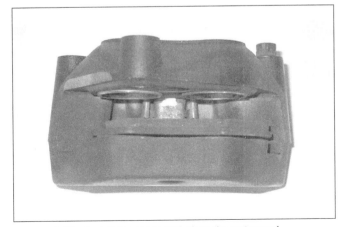

5.26a Install the inner pad, then the outer pad . . .

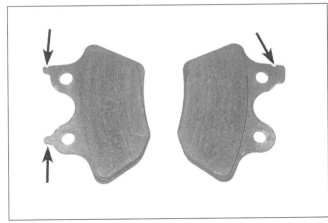

5.26b . . . the number of tabs (arrows) determines which pad goes in the inner or outer position (see text)

6

changeable with the pads on four-piston rear calipers.

27   Install the pad pins until you hear them click, but don't tighten them yet **(see illustration)**. **Note:** *If the pins won't go in, push the pads firmly against the anti-rattle clip and try again. If that doesn't work, make sure the anti-rattle clip is installed correctly.*

28   Install the caliper on the fork leg (see Section 5). If you're working on a bike with dual four-pin calipers at the front, align the calipers after installation (see Section 7). Once the calipers are installed, tighten the pad pins to the torque listed in this Chapter's Specifications.

29   Refill the master cylinder reservoir (see Chapter 1) and install the diaphragm and cap.

30   Operate the brake lever several times to bring the pads into contact with the disc. Check the operation of the brakes carefully before riding the motorcycle.

31   Check the brake fluid level in the master cylinder after the new pads are installed. Top up if necessary (see Chapter 1).

---

6   Front brake disc - inspection, removal and installation

Inspection

1   Prop the bike securely with the front wheel off the ground.

2   Visually inspect the surface of the disc for score marks and other damage. Light scratches are normal after use and won't affect brake operation, but deep grooves and heavy score marks will reduce braking efficiency and accelerate pad wear. If the disc is badly grooved it must be machined or replaced.

3   To check disc runout, mount a dial indicator to a fork leg (front disc) with the plunger on the indicator touching the surface of the disc about 1/2-inch from the outer edge. Slowly turn the wheel and watch the indicator needle, comparing your reading with the limit listed in this Chapter's Specifications. If the runout is greater than allowed, check the hub bearings for play. If the bearings are worn, replace them and repeat this check. If the disc still has too much runout, it will have to be replaced.

4   The disc must not be machined or allowed to wear down to a thickness less than the minimum allowable thickness listed in this Chapter's Specifications. The thickness of the disc can be checked with a micrometer. If the thickness of the disc is less than the minimum, it must be replaced. The minimum thickness is also stamped into the disc **(see illustration)**. On dual-disc models, the word RIGHT or LEFT is stamped below the serial number.

Removal

5   Remove the front wheel as described in Section 3.

5.27 Install the pad pins until they click, but don't screw them in yet (arrows)

6   Remove the bolts or screws and separate the disc from the hub. Some models may have Allen-head or Torx-head bolts which require a special tool for removal and installation.

Installation

7   Before installing the disc, be sure the threads on the bolts (and in the hub) are clean and undamaged. On later models, align the square notch on the disc inner surface with the corresponding cutout in the hub. It is recommended that new screws be used when installing the disc; unless the new screws are supplied with a patch of locking compound on them, apply a few drops of thread-locking compound yourself. Install the bolts and tighten them in a criss-cross pattern until the specified torque is reached. **Note:** *New bolts containing the locking patch can be removed and installed up to three times, then they should be replaced.*

---

7   Front disc brake caliper - removal and installation

1973

1   The caliper is held in place by the four bolts that secure the two caliper halves together.

2   Remove the clamp securing the brake hose to the fork leg, then remove the four caliper bolts.

3   The caliper can be removed by sliding the mounting pins out of the fork slider bushings after separating the outer caliper half from the inner half (see Section 5).

1974 through 1977

4   Remove the two Allen-head bolts and locknuts holding the caliper halves together **(see illustration 5.5a)**, then detach the caliper by pulling out on it until the pin is disengaged from the torque arm **(see illustration)**.

6.4 The minimum disc brake thickness is stamped near one of the mounting bolts

1978 through 1983

5   Loosen the bolt securing the two caliper halves together **(see illustration 5.9a)**. If both calipers are being removed, loosen the bolt in each caliper.

6   Remove the Allen-head bolts and nuts attaching the caliper(s) to the fork leg(s), then detach the caliper(s).

1984-on

7   Loosen the brake hose-to-caliper banjo fitting bolt, but don't unscrew it. A 12-point socket will be required to fit the bolt head.

8   If you're working on a 1984 through 1999 model, remove the upper mounting bolt and the lower mounting pin. If you're working on a 2000 or later model, remove the upper and lower mounting bolts, using a 12-point, 10 mm socket.

9   Detach the caliper.

All models

Caution: *While the caliper is apart or removed from the brake disc, do not operate the front brake lever - it will force the piston out of the caliper bore.*

10   Unscrew the brake line union or banjo

7.4 On 1974 through 1977 models, pull the caliper straight out until the pin (arrow) clears the torque arm

8.16 On 1978 through 1983 models, the piston can be pried out of the caliper bore very carefully with two screwdrivers

fitting bolt at the caliper. Plug the end of the brake line and the opening in the caliper to prevent dirt from entering the hydraulic system.

11 Installation of the caliper is the reverse of the removal procedure. Apply Teflon tape to the threads of the brake line fitting before attaching the line to the caliper. On later models, discard the original washers used at the brake line banjo fitting and install new ones.

12 On 1974 through 1977 models, be sure the locating pin at the bottom of the outer caliper engages the backing plate for the brake pad as well as the torque arm **(see illustration 7.4)**.

13 On 2000 and later models equipped with two front calipers, align the calipers to the discs as follows:

a) *Tighten the front axle nut to 50 to 55 ft-lbs, then loosen the nuts on the axle pinch bolts.*

b) *Locate the hole in the end of the axle where it protrudes from the fork leg. Insert the shank end of a 7/16-inch drill bit all the way into the hole.*

c) *With the drill bit touching the lip of the fork leg where the fork leg fits around the axle, tighten the pinch bolt nuts to 25 to 30 ft-lbs. Make sure the drill bit is in continuous contact with the fork leg all during this Step.*

d) *Remove the drill bit.*

14 On 1973 through 1999 models, coat the caliper pins (that allow the caliper to move back-and-forth) with high temperature grease. On all models, tighten the mounting bolts to the specified torque. **Note:** *On 2000 and later models, loosely tighten the upper (long) mounting bolt, then tighten the lower mounting bolt to 28 to 38 ft-lbs, then tighten the upper mounting bolt to 28 to 38 ft-lbs.*

15 After the calipers are installed, the brake system must be bled as described in Section 10.

8 Front disc brake caliper - overhaul

1 The caliper should not be disassembled unless it leaks fluid around the piston(s) or doesn't operate properly. If the piston travel on early models (Section 5) is not as specified, the piston will have to be removed and inspected. Before disassembling the caliper, read through the entire procedure and make sure you have the correct caliper rebuild kit. Also, you'll need some new, clean brake fluid of the recommended type and some clean rags. **Note:** *Disassembly, overhaul and reassembly of the brake caliper must be done in a spotlessly clean work area to avoid contamination and possible failure of the brake hydraulic system components. If such a work area isn't available, have the caliper rebuilt by a dealer service department or a motorcycle repair shop.*

Disassembly (single-piston front calipers)

1973

2 Remove the caliper as described in Section 7 but DO NOT disconnect the hydraulic brake line.

3 Remove the brake pads as described in Section 5.

4 Slowly pump the brake lever until the piston doesn't move any further.

5 Disconnect the brake line from the caliper and plug the line.

6 Pull the piston boot away from the groove in the piston, then remove the piston from the bore in the caliper.

7 Remove the snap-ring from the piston, then pull off the backing plate, the wave spring, the friction ring and the O-ring.

8 Unscrew the bleeder valve from the caliper.

1974 through 1977

9 Remove the caliper and the brake pads as described in Sections 5 and 7.

10 Disconnect the brake line from the caliper and plug it.

11 Remove the rubber boot, then, using two screwdrivers, pry the piston out of the caliper bore.

12 Check the friction ring at the end of the piston **(see illustration 5.5a)**. If it's damaged, remove it and install a new one.

13 Carefully pry the O-ring out of the caliper bore with a wood or plastic tool.

14 Unscrew the bleeder valve from the caliper.

1978 through 1983

15 Remove the caliper and brake pads as described in Sections 5 and 7. Disconnect the brake line from the caliper and plug it.

16 Carefully pry the piston out of the caliper, then remove the boot **(see illustration)**. If the piston cannot be pried out, place the caliper face down on a clean work surface. Position a clean towel under the piston and apply low pressure air to the inlet hole to force the piston out.

17 Carefully remove the seal from the caliper bore **(see illustration 5.7)**. Use a wood or plastic tool to remove the seal (to avoid scratching the caliper bore).

1984 through 1999

18 Remove the caliper and brake pads as described in Sections 5 and 7. Disconnect the brake line from the caliper and discard the washers.

19 Pry out the boot retainer by inserting a small screwdriver into the notch at the bottom of the piston bore.

20 Note how it's installed, then remove the rubber piston boot.

21 Place the caliper face down on a clean work surface. Position a clean towel under the piston and apply low pressure air to the inlet hole to force the piston out.

22 Remove the seal from the caliper bore with a wood or plastic tool.

23 Note how they're installed, then remove the threaded bushing from the caliper and pull the pin boot out.

24 Remove the O-rings from the mounting bolt/pin holes.

Inspection and assembly (single-piston front calipers)

25 Clean all the brake components (except the pads) with brake system cleaner (available at auto parts stores) or clean brake fluid.

 Warning: Do not, under any circumstances, use petroleum-based solvents to clean brake parts.

If compressed air is available, use it to dry the parts thoroughly.

26 Check the caliper bores and the outside of the pistons for scratches, nicks and score marks. If damage is evident, the caliper must be replaced with a new one.

27 Reassembly of the components is done in reverse order of disassembly. **Note:** *Harley caliper kits come with the correct lubricant for assembling the caliper, silicone grease for the piston. Apply it to the piston during assembly.*

 Warning: It's OK to use DOT 5 brake fluid as a cleaner, but do not use it as an assembly lubricant. It will cause an increase in pedal or lever travel.

28 Install the brake pads as described in Section 5, connect the brake line and install the caliper (see Section 7).

29 Bleed the system (see Section 10).

6

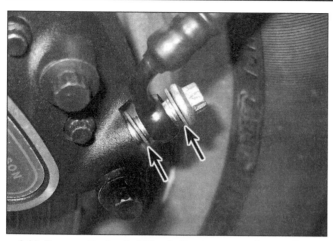

8.30 Remove the banjo fitting bolt; use new sealing washers (arrows) on installation

8.32 This is the JIMS special tool used for piston removal with four-piston calipers

Disassembly (four-piston front calipers)

30 **Note:** *If you're planning to overhaul the caliper and don't have a source of com-*

8.35 Gently blow low-pressure compressed air into the fluid outlet to push the pistons out

pressed air to blow out the piston, leave the brake hose connected and use the bike's hydraulic system instead as described in Step 32. Remove the brake hose banjo fitting bolt and separate the hose from the caliper **(see illustration)**. Discard the sealing washers. Plug the end of the hose or wrap a plastic bag tightly around it and secure the bag with a rubber band to prevent excessive fluid loss and contamination.

31 Remove the caliper mounting bolts and take the caliper off the fork leg **(see illustration 5.15a or 5.15b)**.

32 If you're planning to overhaul the caliper and don't have a source of compressed air to blow out the piston, use the bike's hydraulic system instead. To do this, remove the pads and caliper as described in this Section and Section 2, leaving the brake hose connected. Operate the brake lever to force the pistons out of the cylinder. Block two pistons in the brake pad cavity, then push the remaining pistons almost all the way out. There's a special JIMS tool designed for this purpose **(see illustration)**.

 TOOL TiP *You can also place a block of wood in the brake pad cavity between two opposing pistons, then push the remaining pistons almost all the way out. Use a C-clamp to retain the pistons that start out first while you push the other ones almost all the way out. Remove the wood or special tool and operate the brake lever to push the pistons out.*

Once one piston comes out, you'll no longer have hydraulic pressure to push out the remaining pistons, but it should be possible to remove them by hand at this point. If it isn't, or if the pistons won't move at all, the pistons may be seized, in which case the caliper should be replaced with a new one.

Note: *Brake fluid will run out of the caliper if you remove the pistons in this manner. It's a good idea to hold the caliper over a pan while an assistant operates the brake lever.*

33 Remove the brake pads from the caliper (see Section 5, if necessary).

34 Clean the exterior of the caliper with denatured alcohol or brake system cleaner.

35 If you didn't force out the piston with

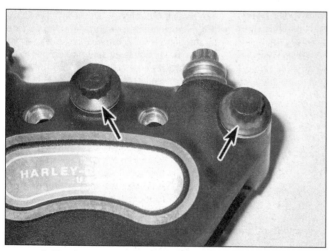

8.36a Remove the caliper bridge bolts (arrows) . . .

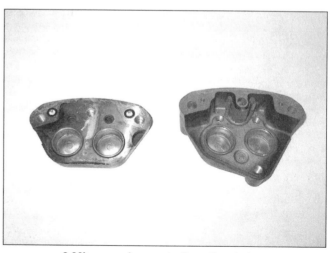

8.36b . . . and separate the caliper halves

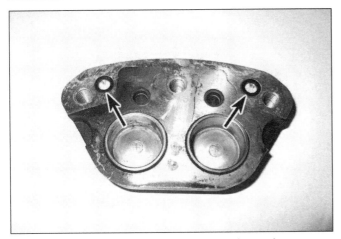

8.37a Remove the crossover O-rings (arrows) . . .

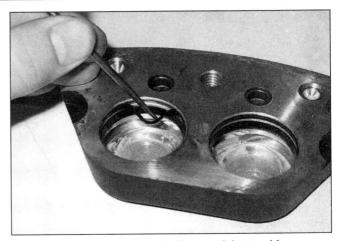

8.37b . . . and remove the piston and dust seal from their grooves

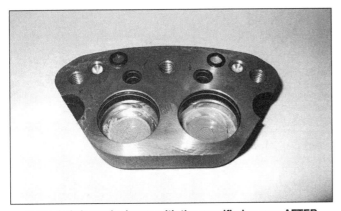

8.41a Lubricate the bores with the specified grease AFTER installing the seals without lubrication

8.41b Make sure the pistons are squarely aligned with their bores . . .

the bike's hydraulic system in Step 32, place a block of wood between the pistons to act as a cushion, then use compressed air, directed into the fluid inlet, to remove the pistons (see illustration). Use only enough air pressure to ease the pistons out of the bore. If a piston is blown out, even with the wood in place, it may be damaged.

 Warning: Never place your fingers in front of a piston in an attempt to catch or protect it when applying compressed air, as serious injury could occur.

36 Remove the caliper bridge bolts and separate the caliper halves (see illustrations).
37 Using a wood or plastic tool, remove the crossover O-rings, dust seals and piston seals from the caliper bores (see illustrations). Metal tools may cause bore damage.

Inspection (four-piston calipers)

38 Clean the pistons and bores with denatured alcohol or brake system cleaner and blow dry them with filtered, unlubricated compressed air. Inspect the surface of the piston for nicks and burrs and loss of plating.

Check the caliper bore, too. If surface defects are present, the caliper must be replaced. If the caliper is in bad shape, the master cylinder should also be checked.

Assembly (four-piston calipers)

39 Install the new piston seals in their grooves in the caliper bores (don't lubricate them). Make sure they seat completely and aren't twisted. Note: Harley caliper kits come with the correct lubricant for assembling the caliper, silicone grease for the piston. Apply it to the piston during assembly. Assemble all other parts without lubricant.

 Warning: It's OK to use DOT 5 brake fluid as a cleaner, but do not use it as an assembly lubricant. It will cause an increase in pedal or lever travel.

40 Install the dust boots, again without lubrication, in the grooves in the caliper bores.
41 Lightly coat the outside of the piston with silicone grease (GE Versilube G322L, supplied in the Harley-Davidson overhaul kit, or the equivalent). Lightly coat the caliper bore and seals with the same grease (see

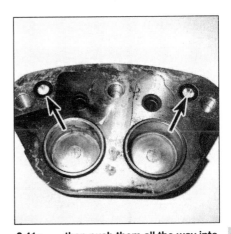

8.41c . . . then push them all the way into the inner half and install the crossover O-ring (arrows) . . .

illustration). Start the pistons into their bores, making sure they're not tilted (see illustration). Push each piston all the way into the caliper bore, using a C-clamp if necessary (see illustrations). Note: If the pistons are difficult to install, make sure the seals haven't slipped out of their bores.

6

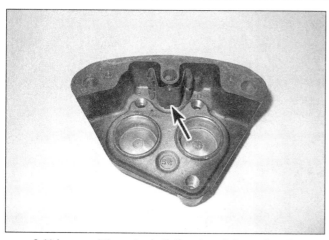

8.41d ... and the outer half, then install the anti-rattle clip (arrow)

8.42 If the bleed valve was removed (arrow), install it

42   If the bleed valve was removed, install it **(see illustration)**. Install the anti-rattle clip in the outer caliper housing **(see illustration 8.41d)**.

43   Install two new crossover O-rings in their grooves in the caliper housing **(see illustration 8.41c)**.

44   Assemble the caliper halves, installing the bridge bolts loosely. Verify that the anti-rattle clip is still in position, then tighten the bridge bolts to the torque listed in this Chapter's Specifications.

45   Refer to Section 5 and install the pads in the caliper.

9   Front disc brake master cylinder - removal and installation

1   If the master cylinder is leaking fluid, or if the lever doesn't feel firm when the brake is applied, and bleeding the brakes doesn't help, the master cylinder should be overhauled or replaced with a new one.

1973 through 1981

2   Turn the handlebars so the master cylinder is as level as possible and remove the cover and gasket. Disconnect the brake line from the master cylinder and catch the fluid in a container.

3   Remove the handlebar switch assembly and disconnect the brake light wires.

4   Remove the snap-ring and pivot pin so the handlebar brake lever can be removed. It'll pull out with the brake lever pin, plunger, spring, washers and dust wiper.

1982 through 1995

5   Open the bleeder valve on the front caliper and attach a piece of hose to the valve. Place the other end of the hose in a clean container and slowly pump the handlebar brake lever to drain the brake fluid.

6   Remove the bolt attaching the brake line to the master cylinder. Discard the washers on either side of the brake line **(see illustration)**.

7   Remove the cover and gasket from the master cylinder.

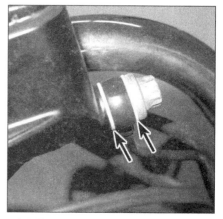

9.6 Unscrew the banjo fitting bolt and remove the sealing washers (arrows)

8   Remove the snap-ring securing the pivot pin, then lift out the pivot pin. Separate the brake lever and the reaction pin from the master cylinder.

9   Remove the master cylinder clamp and detach the assembly from the handlebars.

9.11 Place a wedge between the handle and bracket (arrow)

9.12 Remove the mounting bolts (arrows)

9.14 Secure the pivot pin with the snap-ring (arrow)

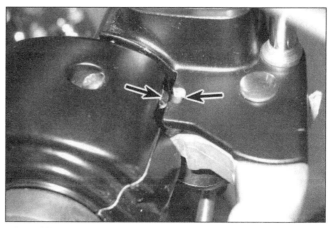

9.16 Align the notch in the bracket with the tab on the throttle housing (arrows)

1996 and later

10   Perform Steps 5 and 6 to drain the brake fluid from the master cylinder.

11   Make a wedge of cardboard 5/32-inch thick (wood or plastic will also work). Pull the brake lever and slip the wedge between the end of the lever and its bracket on the front side of the master cylinder (this protects the brake light switch plunger and boot) **(see illustration)**.

12   Remove the two Torx screws and washers that secure the master cylinder clamp to the cylinder **(see illustration)**. Separate the clamp from the cylinder body and remove the master cylinder from the handlebar.

All models

13   If you're working on a 1995 or earlier model, apply a light coat of anti-seize compound to the reaction pin and insert it into the large hole in the brake lever. Connect the lever to the master cylinder, aligning the plunger (pushrod and switch on 1982 and earlier models) with the hole in the pin.

14   Install the pivot pin and secure it with

the snap-ring **(see illustration)**.

15   On 1973 through 1981 models, attach the brake light wires and assemble the handlebar switch.

16   On 1982 and later models, clamp the master cylinder to the handlebars, aligning the notch in the bracket with the tab on the throttle housing **(see illustration)**.

17   Make sure the relief port in the master cylinder is uncovered when the brake lever is released.

18   Connect the brake line to the master cylinder - use new washers on 1982 and later models.

19   Fill the master cylinder with the recommended brake fluid as described in Chapter 1 and bleed the system (see Section 10).

10 Disc brakes - bleeding

1   Bleeding the brake is simply the process of removing all the air bubbles from the brake fluid reservoir, the hose and the brake

caliper. Bleeding is necessary whenever a brake system hydraulic connection is loosened, when a component or hose is replaced, or when the master cylinder or caliper is overhauled. Leaks in the system may also allow air to enter, but leaking brake fluid will reveal their presence and warn you of the need for repair.

2   To bleed the brake, you will need some new, clean brake fluid of the recommended type (see Chapter 1), a length of clear vinyl or plastic tubing, a small container partially filled with clean brake fluid, some rags and a wrench to fit the brake caliper bleed valve.

3   Cover the fuel tank and other painted components to prevent damage in the event that brake fluid is spilled.

4   Remove the reservoir cap and slowly pump the brake lever a few times, until no air bubbles can be seen floating up from the holes at the bottom of the reservoir. Doing this bleeds the air from the master cylinder end of the line. Reinstall the reservoir cap.

5   Attach one end of the clear vinyl or plastic tubing to the brake caliper bleeder valve and submerge the other end in the brake fluid in the container **(see illustration)**.

10.5a Here's the bleed valve on a typical single-piston front caliper (rear similar) . . .

10.5b . . . and here's a four-piston front caliper (rear similar)

6

11.3a On models with a drum brake, remove the brake adjusting nut . . .

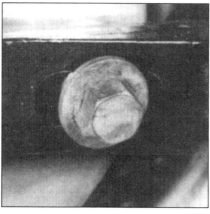

11.3b . . . and the backing plate anchor bolt (if equipped)

11.4a On 1970 through 1988 models, unscrew the axle nut (arrow) and pull out the axle

6   Remove the reservoir cap and check the fluid level. Do not allow the fluid level to drop below the lower mark during the bleeding process.

7   Carefully pump the brake lever three or four times and hold it while opening the caliper bleeder valve. When the valve is opened, brake fluid will flow out of the caliper into the clear tubing and the lever will move toward the handlebar.

8   Retighten the bleeder valve, then release the brake lever gradually. Repeat the process until no air bubbles are visible in the brake fluid leaving the caliper and the lever is firm when applied. Remember to add fluid to the reservoir as the level drops. Use only new, clean brake fluid of the recommended type. Never reuse the fluid lost during bleeding.

9   Replace the reservoir cap, wipe up any spilled brake fluid and check the entire system for leaks. **Note:** *If bleeding is difficult, it may be necessary to let the brake fluid in the system stabilize for a few hours (it may be aerated). Repeat the bleeding procedure when the tiny bubbles in the system have settled out.*

10   If you're working on a four-piston rear caliper, repeat the procedure for the other bleed valve.

If it's not possible to produce a firm feel to the lever or pedal, the fluid may be aerated. Let the brake fluid in the system stabilize for a few hours, then repeat the procedure when the tiny bubbles in the system have settled out. Also check to make sure that there are no "high spots" in the brake hose where air bubbles can become trapped - this will occur most often in an incorrectly mounted hose union, but also can be caused by bleeding the brakes while some of the brake system components are at such an angle to encourage this. Reversing the angle or moving the affected component around will normally dislodge any trapped air.

11.4b On 1989 and later models, remove and discard the cotter pin (arrow), unscrew the nut and remove the washer

11 Rear wheel - removal and installation

Removal

1   Raise the rear of the motorcycle and support it securely on blocks so the tire is at least four inches off the ground (it must be stable from side-to-side so it won't tip over).

2   On chain drive models, rotate the rear wheel until the master link on the chain is positioned on the teeth of the rear sprocket (see Chapter 5). Remove the master link and disengage the chain from the rear wheel; lay the chain onto paper to prevent it picking up dirt from the ground. On belt drive models, first loosen the axle nut as described below, fully release the belt adjusters and push the wheel fully forward in the swingarm; this will create enough slack to allow the belt to be slipped off the sprocket.

3   On 1970 through 1978 models, unscrew the adjusting nut from the brake rod or cable and disconnect the rear brake operating lever **(see illustration)**. Remove the backing plate anchor bolt, if equipped **(see illustration)**.

4   On 1970 through 1988 models, remove the axle nut and any washers that are used **(see illustration)**. On 1989 and later models, remove and discard the cotter pin, then unscrew the nut and remove the washer **(see illustration)**.

5   Tap the end of the axle with a soft-face hammer to loosen it, then pull it out of the rear hub and swingarm. On drum brake models, an axle spacer must be removed from the left side.

6   Remove the wheel from the swingarm.

Installation

7   Apply a thin coat of anti-seize compound to the axle before installing the rear wheel.

8   Position the wheel in the swingarm. On 1979 and later models, guide the brake disc into the caliper. Lift the wheel until the axle can be inserted through the swingarm and rear hub. Install all of the associated components with the axle in the reverse order of removal **(see illustration)**. Attach the brake rod or cable to the actuating lever on 1970 through 1978 models.

9   On chain drive models position the ends of the chain adjacent to each other on the rear sprocket and insert the master link

11.8 Install the spacer on the left side of the wheel before inserting the axle (drum brake models)

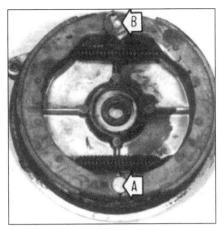

12.7 Location of the rear drum brake pivot stud (A) and operating shaft (B)

with its closed end facing in the normal direction of wheel travel. On belt drive models, slip the belt over the sprocket.

10   Adjust the drive chain or belt as described in Chapter 1.

11   Tighten the axle nut to the specified torque. On 1989 and later models, install a new cotter pin. Bend one end up against the axle and the other end down against one of the nut flats.

12   On 1970 through 1978 models, adjust the rear brake as described in Section 12.

13   Check the rear wheel bearing end play and compare it to the Specifications in this Chapter. If end play doesn't fall within the specified limits it will be necessary to install a different length hub bearing spacer on models through mid-1991, or a different thickness spacer shim on models from mid-1991-on. Refer to Section 20 for access to spacer or shim and to a Harley-Davidson dealer for the appropriate replacement part.

12 Rear drum brake - inspection and brake shoe replacement

 Warning: The dust created as the brake shoes wear is harmful to your health. Never blow it out with compressed air and don't inhale any of it. An approved filtering mask should be worn when working on the brakes. Do not, under any circumstances, use petroleum-based solvents to clean brake parts. Use brake cleaner or denatured alcohol only!

1   Drum brakes don't normally require frequent maintenance, but they should be checked periodically to ensure proper operation. If the linkage is properly adjusted, if the brake shoes aren't contaminated or worn out and if the return springs are in good condition, the brakes should work fine.

2   Check the brake pedal for proper operation. It shouldn't bind when depressed and

should return completely when released.

3   If the brake doesn't operate properly, make sure nothing is interfering with the pedal or brake rod/cable and lubricate the pedal pivot. If the brakes still don't operate or return properly, the problem is in the shoe actuating mechanism.

4   If the brake shoe wear check (Chapter 1) indicates the shoes are near the wear limit, refer to Section 11 and remove the rear wheel. Measure the thickness of the brake shoe lining and compare it to the Specifications in Chapter 1. If the shoes have worn beyond the allowable limits, or if they're worn unevenly, they must be replaced with new ones.

5   If the linings are acceptable as far as thickness is concerned, check them for glazing, high spots and hard areas. A light touch-up with a file or emery paper will restore them to usable condition. If the linings are extremely glazed, they probably have been dragging. Be sure to adjust the pedal free play to prevent further glazing.

6   Occasionally the linings may become contaminated with grease from the wheel bearing or brake cam. If this happens, and it's not too severe, cleaning the shoes with brake system solvent (available at auto parts stores) may restore them. However, the best approach is to replace the shoes with new ones.

7   To remove the shoes from the backing plate, unscrew the operating lever retaining nut and pull off the lever and washer. Unscrew the pivot stud nut (anchor bolt on 1973 through 1978 models) and remove the washer **(see illustration)**. On 1970 through 1972 models a locating block is used; 1973 models have a spacer that must be removed next.

8   Gently tap the end of the operating shaft with a soft-face hammer and detach the brake shoes, springs, pivot stud and operating shaft/washer, as an assembly, from the brake backing plate.

9   Separate the springs from the brake shoes and check the springs for cracks and distortion. Replace the springs with new

ones if they're cracked, bent or stretched.

10   Clean the backing plate to remove brake dust and dirt. Also, clean the operating shaft and pivot stud. If compressed air is available, use it to dry the parts thoroughly.

11   Check the operating shaft and pivot stud and the holes in the backing plate for excessive wear. Place the operating shaft in position in the backing plate and make sure it turns smoothly without binding. If excessive side play is evident, the operating shaft and/or backing plate will have to be replaced with new parts. Also check the shoe contact area on the operating shaft for wear.

12   Apply a thin coat of high-temperature grease to the operating shaft and pivot stud and attach the shoes to the pivot and shaft with one spring. Place the spring in the groove that's closest to the backing plate.

13   Place the washer over the operating shaft and install the assembly in the backing plate.

14   Install the locating block (or spacer), the nut and lock washer (anchor bolt and washer), the operating lever and the nut and washer that secure it to the backing plate.

15   Attach the remaining spring to the brake shoes.

16   Clean the brake drum out with a wet rag.

17   Check the drum for rough spots, rust and excessive wear (if the outer edge of the drum has a pronounced ridge, excessive wear has occurred). Measure the diameter of the drum at several places to determine if it's worn out-of-round. Excessive wear and out-of-roundness indicate the need for a new hub/drum. Slight rough spots can be removed with fine emery paper. Use one of the brake shoes as a sanding block so low spots aren't created in the drum.

18   Insert the brake shoe/backing plate assembly into the brake drum and install the rear wheel as described in Section 11.

19   Insert the brake rod or cable through the operating lever and install the adjusting nut. Tighten the adjusting nut so the brake begins to make contact when the brake pedal is depressed 1-1/4 inches.

20   If the brake drags after the brake pedal is released, and the pedal is adjusted correctly, the brake shoes should be centered in the drum. Loosen the pivot stud nut or bolt and the axle nut. Spin the wheel and apply the brake. While the wheel is spinning, tighten the pivot stud nut or bolt and the axle nut. Check the brake pedal adjustment again.

6

13 Rear disc brake - brake pad replacement

Inspection

Caution: Do not operate the brake pedal while the caliper is apart - the piston will be forced out of the caliper. Always

13.1 Remove the caliper mounting bolts (A) and the clamp (B) securing the brake line to the swingarm (1979 through 1981 models)

13.5 On late 1987 and later models, the rear brake caliper is attached to the bracket and slides on two mounting (pin) bolts

replace both pads in the rear brake caliper at the same time; never replace only one pad.

Pad removal

1979 through 1981

1   Loosen the large bolt on the back side of the caliper. Unscrew the two Allen-head

bolts securing the caliper to the mounting bracket. Remove the clamp securing the brake line to the swingarm (see illustration).
2   Detach the caliper from the mounting bracket and remove the large bolt from the back side. Separate the two halves of the caliper and pull the pads and plates off the pins.

13.6 Brake pad components (late 1987 through 1999)

1   Wire retainer clip
2   Outer brake pad
3   Inner brake pad
4   Pad shim (2)
5   Bracket
6   Rubber bushing (2)

13.8 Unscrew the pad retaining pins (arrows)

1982 through early 1987

3   Remove the two Allen-head bolts securing the caliper to the bracket and detach the caliper.
4   Slide the brake pads out of position.

Late 1987 through 1999

Note: *On some models you may have to remove the lower shock absorber mounting bolt and pivot the shock out of the way to remove the rear caliper mounting bolt.*
5   Remove the caliper mounting (pin) bolts (see illustration), then pull the caliper up and off the brake disc and pads. This may be difficult due to the piston clearing the pin on the back of the moving pad. If so, rock the caliper back and forth on the bracket to ease the piston back in its bore.
6   Carefully note how it's installed, then remove the wire retainer clip from the back side of the bracket (see illustration). Slide the outer brake pad off the bracket.
7   Slide the inner pad off toward the wheel and detach the pad shims from the bracket.

2000 and later

8   If necessary, remove the left saddlebag for access. Unscrew the pad retaining pins with a 12-point, 1/4-inch socket, the pull out the pins and slide the pads out of the caliper (see illustration).

Pad installation

9   Before installing the new pads, clean the brake disc with brake system cleaner (available at auto parts stores), lacquer thinner or acetone.

⚠️ *Warning: Do not use petroleum-based solvents.*

10   Push the piston into the caliper bore as far as possible before installing the new brake pads.

1979 through 1981

11   Slide the outer plate over the pins on

13.11 Slide the outer plate onto the guide pins, then . . .

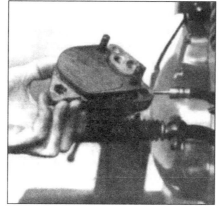

13.12a . . . place the outer brake pad over the guide pins . . .

13.12b . . . followed by the inner brake pad . . .

the outer caliper (see illustration).

12   Install the new brake pads and the inner plate over the guide pins (see illustrations).

13   Attach the inner caliper half to the outer half and install the bolt in the back side of the caliper finger-tight (see illustration).

14   Position the caliper over the rear disc and attach it to the mounting bracket. The two Allen-head mounting bolts should be coated with anti-seize compound before installation. Use new locknuts on the mounting bolts. If new locknuts aren't available, coat the threads of the bolts with thread locking compound.

1982 through early 1987

15   Attach the pad spring to the top of the caliper with the long tab above the piston. The short tab must be hooked above the ridge on the caliper casting, opposite the piston, to hold the spring in place.

16   Position the pads on the bracket and attach the caliper to the bracket without turning the pins. The flat sides of the pin heads should be parallel with the opening in the bracket.

17   Install the caliper mounting bolts and tighten them to the torque listed in this Chapter's Specifications.

Late 1987 through 1999

Caution: Ensure only the correct parts are fitted when replacing pads, discs or shims. Modifications to the pad and disc material from 1992-on and redesign of the shims and pad shape from mid-1991 prevent the mixing of early and late components.

18   On all models through mid-1991 position the pad shims on the mounting bracket with the tabs seated in the holes (see illustration 13.6). From mid-1991 fit the shims so that their looped ends are positioned outwards (towards the piston) and hold them in place while the pads and wire retainer are installed (see illustration).

19   Slide the inner pad onto the shims from the wheel side. Slide the outer pad on from the outside.

20   Insert the wire retainer clip ends into the mounting bracket holes and position the clip over the outer brake pad (see illustration 13.6).

Caution: Make sure the pads are still riding on the shims after the retainer clip is installed.

21   Make sure the mounting (pin) bolts are clean so the caliper can move freely. Carefully lower the caliper over the pads and disc

and align the holes, then install the mounting bolts.

22   Tighten the mounting bolts to the torque listed in this Chapter's Specifications. Connect the lower end of the shock absorber and install the mounting bolt if it was removed.

2000 and later

23   The curved edge of the friction material on both pads faces the rear of the motorcycle. Pad sets are interchangeable for all calipers, right front (if so equipped); left front and rear. On the rear caliper, the pad with two square tabs goes on the outboard side of the caliper, while the pad with one square tab goes on the inboard side. Position the pads tightly against the anti-rattle clip and install the pad pins. You should hear the pad pins tap when they engage the inside caliper housing. Tighten the pad pins to 180 to 200 inch-lbs. *Note: If the pad pins won't go in, make sure you've installed one pad that has two square tabs and one pad that has one square tab (not two pads with one tab or two pads with two tabs). Make sure the pads are installed in the correct locations (inboard or outboard side) and facing the proper direction.*

13.12c . . . and the inner plate

13.13 Connect the inner caliper to the outer caliper (don't forget to tighten the bolt after the caliper is installed)

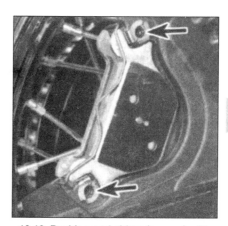

13.18 Position pad shims (arrows) with looped ends outward - mid-1991 through 1999

6

All models

24   Check the brake fluid level in the master cylinder and add some if necessary (see Chapter 1).

14 Rear disc brake caliper - removal, overhaul and installation

1   If the caliper is leaking fluid around the piston, it should be removed and overhauled to restore braking performance. Before disassembling the caliper, read through the entire procedure and make sure you have the correct caliper rebuild kit. Also, you'll need some new, clean brake fluid of the recommended type and some clean rags. **Note:** *Disassembly, overhaul and reassembly of the brake caliper must be done in a spotlessly clean work area to avoid contamination and possible failure of the brake hydraulic system components. If such a work area isn't available, have the caliper rebuilt by a dealer service department or a motorcycle repair shop.*
2   Remove the caliper as described in Section 13.

1979 through 1981

3   Disconnect the brake line from the caliper and plug the end. Do not lose the hose seat.
4   Separate the two halves of the caliper and remove the brake pads.
5   Carefully pry the piston out of the caliper, then remove the rubber boot.
6   To avoid scratching the bore, use a wood or plastic tool to remove the seal.

1982 through early 1987

7   Remove the brake pads from the caliper.
8   Detach the rubber boots from the upper and lower pins, then remove the pins from the caliper.
9   Note how the pad spring is installed on the caliper body, then remove it.
10   Pry the retaining wire out of the caliper and remove the piston boot.
11   Try to withdraw the piston and seal from the caliper bore. If it can't easily be removed, pump the brake pedal slowly until the piston is forced out as far as possible. Detach the brake line from the caliper and place the caliper on a workbench with the piston facing down. Place a clean rag under the piston and apply low air pressure to the brake line inlet hole (a bicycle tire pump should work for this). The air pressure should be enough to force the piston out of the bore, but it may be necessary to tap lightly around the caliper with a soft-face hammer at the same time. Remove the seal from the bore with a wood or plastic tool.

Late 1987 through 1999

12   Detach the retaining wire and remove the rubber boot from the caliper.

13   Slowly pump the brake pedal until the piston doesn't move any further.
14   Disconnect the brake line from the caliper and plug the line.
15   Remove the piston and seal from the caliper. You may have to force the piston out of the caliper with air pressure (see Step 11).
16   Remove the rubber bushings from the mounting bracket bores. If they're worn or damaged, install new ones.

2000 and later

17   If necessary, remove the left saddlebag for access.
18   Unscrew the pad retaining pins and remove the pads from the caliper **(see illustration 13.8).**
19   If you're removing the caliper for overhaul, press the brake pedal to force the pistons out of their bores.
20   Remove the brake line banjo bolt and both sealing washers.
21   Pull the rear axle out of the caliper and wheel (see Section 11).
22   Lift the caliper off the motorcycle. The notch in the lower left corner of the caliper must clear the tab on the swingarm.
23   Remove the caliper bridge bolts and separate the caliper halves.

All models

24   Clean all the brake components (except the pads) with brake system cleaner (available at auto parts stores), isopropyl alcohol or clean brake fluid.

 Warning: Do not, under any circumstances, use petroleum-based solvents to clean brake parts.

If compressed air is available, use it to dry the parts thoroughly.
25   Check the caliper bore(s) and the outside of the piston(s) for scratches, nicks and score marks. If damage is evident, the caliper must be replaced with a new one.
26   Reassembly of the components is done in reverse order of disassembly. Be sure to lubricate all of the components with clean brake fluid during assembly and install new seals and O-rings.
27   Carefully insert the piston(s) as far as possible into the bore(s). If you're working on a 1982 through 1987 model, install the boot and retaining wire.
28   On 1979 through 1981 models, begin reassembly as described in Section 13.
29   On 1982 through early 1987 models, attach the pad spring to the caliper with the long tab extending above the piston. The short tab should be hooked above the ridge on the caliper casting to hold the spring in place. Lubricate the pins and pin bores with silicone grease and install the pins. The pin with the nylon sleeve fits in the top hole. Turn the pins so the flat edges on the heads are parallel with the opening in the bracket.
30   If you're working on a 2000 or later model, assemble the caliper halves, using new O-rings in the crossover passages.

Install the three bridge bolts and tighten to 28 to 38 ft-lbs. Install the caliper, making sure the notch in the lower left of the caliper housing fits inside the tab on the swingarm. Also make sure the full length of the rubber bumper on the caliper contacts the underside of the caliper mount. Install the rear axle (see Section 11) and adjust drive belt tension as described in Chapter 1.
31   Reattach the brake hose and complete reassembly as described in Section 13. **Note:** *If the brake hose is attached to the caliper with a banjo fitting and bolt, use new sealing washers when installing the bolt. The replacement washers must be the same type as the originals (some are zinc-plated copper, while some are steel with a rubber O-ring). Be sure to tighten the banjo fitting bolt to the correct torque - it's different, depending on the type of washers used.*
32   Fill the master cylinder with the recommended brake fluid and bleed the system as described in Chapter 1.

15 Rear disc brake master cylinder - removal and installation

1   If the master cylinder is leaking fluid, or if the pedal doesn't feel firm when the brake is applied - and bleeding the brakes doesn't help - master cylinder overhaul or replacement is recommended.

Removal

2   Disconnect the master cylinder-to-caliper brake line from the master cylinder and plug the end. On models through early 1987, use a flare-nut wrench, if possible, to avoid rounding off the fitting. Late 1987 and later models have a banjo fitting and bolt, so a flare-nut wrench isn't necessary.

Caution: If DOT 3 brake fluid, used on early models, is spilled on a painted surface, wipe it off immediately or the paint will be damaged.

15.6 Unscrew the flare nut and remove the two mounting bolts (through early 1987)

15.8 Master cylinder mounting details (late 1987 and later)

A   Pushrod locknut   C   Mounting bolts
B   Banjo fitting

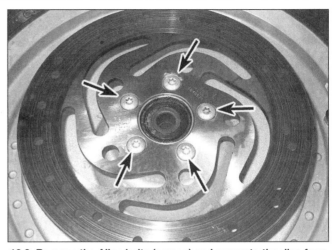

16.3 Remove the Allen bolts (arrows) and separate the disc from the hub

1979

3   Remove the snap-ring from the clevis pin, then remove the clevis pin and the pushrod from the outer pivot arm.
4   Remove the two mounting bolts and lockwashers, then detach the master cylinder.
5   Remove the cover and gasket from the top of the master cylinder and drain the brake fluid out.

1980 through early 1987

6   Unscrew the two master cylinder mounting bolts and pull the master cylinder off the pushrod (see **illustration**).
7   Remove the cover and the gasket from the top of the master cylinder and drain the brake fluid out.

Late 1987 and later

8   Back off the adjuster locknut on the threaded brake pedal rod **(see illustration)**.
9   Remove the two Allen-head bolts and detach the master cylinder from the sprocket cover on the engine. Free the steel brake line from its clamp on the rear sprocket cover bolt.
10   Turn the internal master cylinder pushrod (that the pedal rod threads into) until the master cylinder is free.
11   Clean the exterior of the master cylinder, then thread the brake line banjo bolt back into the fitting. The bolt will protect the sealing surface in the master cylinder cartridge body during disassembly.

Installation

1979 through early 1987

12   Insert the pushrod carefully through the dust boot, into the piston assembly.
13   Attach the pushrod and clevis pin to the outer pivot arm and secure the clevis pin with the snap-ring (1979 models only).

Late 1987 and later

14   Attach the master cylinder to the threaded pedal rod (see Step 10).

All models

15   Position the master cylinder on the engine and install the mounting bolts. Tighten the bolts to the torque listed in this Chapter's Specifications.
16   Connect the brake line to the master cylinder and fill the reservoir with brake fluid. If a banjo fitting is used, be sure to install new washers of the correct type (DO NOT interchange zinc-plated copper washers with steel/rubber washers) and tighten the banjo bolt to the torque listed in this Chapter's Specifications - the torque is different, depending on the type of
washers used.
17   Bleed the brakes as described in Section 10.
18   Adjust the brake pedal (see Chapter 1).

16 Rear brake disc - inspection, removal and installation

1   Disc inspection is the same as for front discs, described in Section 6. Attach the dial indicator to the frame when measuring runout. If necessary, remove the saddlebag for access to the disc.
2   Remove the rear wheel as described in Section 11.
3   The brake disc is attached to the rear hub with five bolts. Remove the bolts and detach the brake disc from the hub **(see illustration)**.
4   Before installing the disc, be sure the threads on the bolts and in the hub are clean and undamaged. It is recommended that new screws be used when installing the disc; unless the new screws are supplied with a patch of locking compound on them, apply a few drops of thread-locking compound yourself. Install the bolts and tighten them in a criss-cross pattern until the specified torque is reached. **Note:** *New bolts containing the locking patch can be removed and installed up to three times, then they should be replaced.*

17 Tubeless tires - general information

1   Tubeless tires are generally safer than tube-type tires but if problems do occur they require special repair techniques.
2   The force required to break the seal between the rim and the bead of the tire is substantial, and is usually beyond the capabilities of an individual working with normal tire irons.
3   Also, repair of the punctured tire and replacement on the wheel rim requires special tools, skills and experience that the average do-it-yourselfer lacks.
4   For these reasons, if a puncture or flat occurs with a tubeless tire, the wheel should be removed from the motorcycle and taken to a dealer service department or a motorcycle repair shop for repair or replacement of the tire.

18 Tube tires - removal and installation

1   To properly remove and install tires, you will need at least two motorcycle tire irons, some water and a tire pressure gauge.
2   Begin by removing the wheel from the motorcycle. If the tire is going to be re-used, mark it next to the valve stem, wheel balance weight or rim lock.
3   Deflate the tire by removing the valve stem core. When it is fully deflated, push the bead of the tire away from the rim on both sides. In some extreme cases, this can only be accomplished with a bead breaking tool, but most often it can be carried out with tire irons. Riding on a deflated tire to break the bead is not recommended, as damage to the rim and tire will occur.
4   Dismounting a tire is easier when the tire is warm, so an indoor tire change is recom-

6

mended in cold climates. The rubber gets very stiff and is difficult to manipulate when cold.

5   Place the wheel on a thick pad or old blanket. This will help keep the wheel and tire from slipping around.

6   Once the bead is completely free of the rim, lubricate the inside edge of the rim and the tire bead with soap and water or rubber lubricant (do not use any type of petroleum-based lubricant, as it will cause the tire to deteriorate). Remove the locknut and push the tire valve through the rim.

7   Insert one of the tire irons under the bead of the tire at the valve stem and lift the bead up over the rim. This should be fairly easy. Take care not to pinch the tube as this is done. If it is difficult to pry the bead up, make sure that the rest of the bead opposite the valve stem is in the dropped center section of the rim.

8   Hold the tire iron down with the bead over the rim, then move about 1 or 2 inches to either side and insert the second tire iron. Be careful not to cut or slice the bead or the tire may split when inflated. Also, take care not to catch or pinch the inner tube as the second tire iron is levered over. For this reason, tire irons are recommended over screwdrivers or other implements.

9   With a small section of the bead up over the rim, one of the levers can be removed and reinserted 1 or 2 inches farther around the rim until about 1/4 of the tire bead is above the rim edge. Make sure that the rest of the bead is in the dropped center of the rim. At this point, the bead can usually be pulled up over the rim by hand.

10   Once all of the first bead is over the rim, the inner tube can be withdrawn from the tire and rim. Push in on the valve stem, lift up on the tire next to the stem, reach inside the tire and carefully pull out the tube. It is usually not necessary to completely remove the tire from the rim to repair the inner tube. It is sometimes recommended though, because checking for foreign objects in the tire is difficult while it is still mounted on the rim.

11   To remove the tire completely, make sure the bead is broken all the way around on the remaining edge, then stand the tire and wheel up on the tread and grab the wheel with one hand. Push the tire down over the same edge of the rim while pulling the rim away from the tire. If the bead is correctly positioned in the dropped center of the rim, the tire should roll off and separate from the rim very easily. If tire irons are used to work this last bead over the rim, the outer edge of the rim may be marred. If a tire iron is necessary, be sure to pad the rim as described earlier.

12   Refer to Section 19 for inner tube repair procedures.

13   Mounting a tire is basically the reverse of removal. Some tires have a balance mark and/or directional arrows molded into the tire sidewall. Look for these marks so that the tire can be installed properly. The dot should be aligned with the valve stem.

14   If the tire was not removed completely to repair or replace the inner tube, the tube should be inflated just enough to make it round. Sprinkle it with talcum powder, which acts as a dry lubricant, then carefully lift up the tire edge and install the tube with the valve stem next to the hole in the rim. Once the tube is in place, push the valve stem through the rim and start the locknut on the stem.

15   Lubricate the tire bead, then push it over the rim edge and into the dropped center section opposite the inner tube valve stem. Work around each side of the rim, carefully pushing the bead over the rim. The last section may have to be levered on with tire irons. If so, take care not to pinch the inner tube as this is done.

16   Once the bead is over the rim edge, check to see that the inner tube valve stem is pointing to the center of the hub. If it's angled slightly in either direction, rotate the tire on the rim to straighten it out. Run the locknut the rest of the way onto the stem but don't tighten it completely.

17   Inflate the tube to approximately 1-1/2 times the pressure listed in the Chapter 1 Specifications and check to make sure the guidelines on the tire sidewalls are the same distance from the rim around the circumference of the tire.

 Warning: Do not over inflate the tube or the tire may burst, causing serious injury.

18   After the tire bead is correctly seated on the rim, allow the tire to deflate. Replace the valve core and inflate the tube to the recommended pressure, then tighten the valve stem locknut securely and tighten the cap.

19 Tubes - repair

1   Tire tube repair requires a patching kit that's usually available from motorcycle dealers, accessory stores or auto parts stores. Be sure to follow the directions supplied with the kit to ensure a safe repair. Patching should be done only when a new tube is unavailable. Replace the tube as soon as possible. Sudden deflation can cause loss of control and an accident.

2   To repair a tube, remove it from the tire, inflate and immerse it in a sink or tub full of water to pinpoint the leak. Mark the position of the leak, then deflate the tube. Dry it off and thoroughly clean the area around the puncture.

3   Most tire patching kits have a buffer to rough up the area around the hole for proper adhesion of the patch. Roughen an area slightly larger than the patch, then apply a thin coat of the patching cement to the roughened area. Allow the cement to dry until tacky, then apply the patch.

4   It may be necessary to remove a protective covering from the top surface of the

patch after it has been attached to the tube. Keep in mind that tubes made from synthetic rubber may require a special patch and adhesive if a satisfactory bond is to be achieved.

5   Before replacing the tube, check the inside of the tire to make sure the object that caused the puncture is not still inside. Also check the outside of the tire, particularly the tread area, to make sure nothing is projecting through the tire that may cause another puncture. Check the rim for sharp edges or damage. Make sure the rubber trim band is in good condition and properly installed before inserting the tube.

20 Wheel bearings - inspection and maintenance

1   Drum brake models (1970 through 1972) use open ball bearings. Disc brake models use tapered roller bearings (1973 through 1999) or sealed ball bearings (2000 and later). Sealed ball bearings can be inspected, but not repacked. If the grease has leaked out of them, they must be replaced with new ones.

2   Support the bike securely so it can't be knocked over during this procedure. Remove the wheel (see Section3 or 11).

3   If the wheel is equipped with a brake disc or sprocket, set the wheel on blocks so as not to allow the weight of the wheel to rest on the brake disc or sprocket.

Front wheel (drum brake models)

4   Pry the seal out of the left side of the hub.

5   Lift the brake backing plate and shoe assembly out to expose the right-hand bearing. Remove the snap-ring that secures the bearing in the hub.

6   Drive the left-hand bearing into the hub as far as possible with a punch or a large socket. This will force the right-hand bearing out of position, along with the spacer that separates the bearings.

7   Remove the spacer, then drive the left bearing out from inside the hub.

8   Thoroughly clean the bearings and the inside of the hub with high-flash point solvent and blow them dry with compressed air, if available.

 Warning: Do not spin the bearings with compressed air. They may fly apart and cause injury.

9   Check the bearings for scoring, flaking, pitting, chips, rust and the bluish tint that indicates overheating. Replace the bearings as a set (both bearings, including rollers and outer races) if any of these conditions is found.

10   Pack the wheel bearings with grease from the open side of the bearing. Apply a

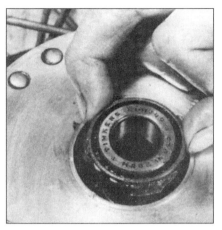

20.22a Install the spacer . . .

20.22b . . . followed by the grease-
packed bearing . . .

20.22c . . . and the seal in each
side of the hub

liberal amount of grease to the inside of the hub and insert the bearings.

11   After the left bearing is in place, be sure to install the spacer separating the bearings.

Front wheel (disc brake models)

Tapered roller bearings (1973 through 1999)

12   If you haven't already done so, remove the speedometer drive housing and collar.

13   Remove the brake disc(s) (see Section 6) if they block access to the wheel bearings.

14   Pry out the grease seal from each side of the wheel and remove the bearing inner races and spacer sleeve. On mid-1991 through 1999 models, remove the spacer shim and shouldered spacer from the left side of the wheel.

15   Thoroughly clean the outer races and the inside of the hub with high-flash point solvent and blow them dry with compressed air, if available.

16   Thoroughly clean the bearings with high-flash point solvent and blow them dry with compressed air, if available.

⚠️ **Warning: Do not spin the bearings with compressed air. They may fly apart and cause injury.**

17   Check the bearing rollers and outer races for scoring, flaking, pitting, chips, rust and the bluish tint that indicates overheating. Replace the bearings as a set (both bearings, including rollers and outer races) if any of these conditions is found.

18   If the bearing outer races need to be replaced, insert a soft metal drift through the hub and position it against the outer race of the opposite bearing. Tap on the drift with a hammer to drive the outer race out, working around the outer race in a circle as you tap. Insert the drift from the opposite side and drive out the remaining outer race in the same manner.

19   Lubricate new outer races with clean

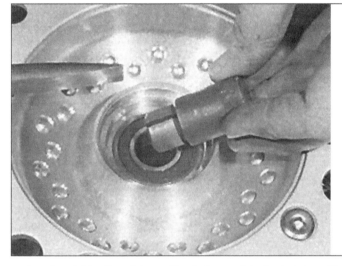

20.25a The slotted end of the removed head fits inside the bearing; the wedge end of the remover shaft spreads the head and locks it to the bearing

engine oil and drive them into position in the hub.

20   Coat the outer races with high quality wheel bearing grease. Pack the inner races with the same grease, making sure to work the grease into the spaces between the rollers. A bearing packer and grease gun, available from many auto parts stores, will make the job easier.

21   On the left side of the wheel, install the spacer shim, then install the shoulder washer with its shoulder facing outward. Install the bearing inner race against the shoulder washer, then drive in a new grease seal with its open side facing into the hub. The grease seal should be flush with the hub to as much as 0.020-inch recessed when installed. Pack the space between the grease seal and bearing inner race with wheel bearing grease.

22   On the right side of the wheel, install the spacer sleeve in the hub, seating it in the bore on the opposite side of the hub **(see illustration)**. Be sure the spacer sleeve goes straight in and is not cocked in the bore. Install the bearing inner race against the spacer sleeve **(see illustration)**, then drive in a new grease seal with its open side facing

into the hub **(see illustration)**. The grease seal should be flush with the hub to as much as 0.020-inch recessed when installed. Pack the space between the grease seal and bearing inner race with wheel bearing grease.

23   Insert the hub spacer into the grease seal on the right side, with its chamfer facing into the hub.

24   The remainder of installation is the reverse of the removal steps.

Sealed ball bearings (2000 and later)

25   Insert a brass drift from the right side of the hub and tap evenly around the inner race of the opposite bearing to remove it. Remove the bearing spacer, then remove the remaining bearing in the same way. **Note 1:** *If there isn't room to insert a drift into the hub and push the spacer out of the way so you can catch the edge of the bearing with the drift, use a bearing remover tool. These can be ordered from aftermarket tool suppliers such as K and L supply, or fabricated from readily available hardware (a large bolt and a length of steel rod)* **(see illustrations)**. **Note 2:** *Bearing removal requires applying force to*

20.25b Tap the slotted end of the remover head into the bearing

20.30a Remove the rear wheel bearing locknut, seal and outer spacer . . .

the unsupported inner race, which may damage the bearings. For this reason, the wheel bearings must be replaced with new ones whenever they're removed.

26   Thoroughly clean the inside of the hub with high-flash point solvent and blow it out with compressed air, if available.

27   Drive in the new bearings with a bearing driver or a socket the same diameter as the bearing outer race. Don't forget to install the spacer after you've installed the first bearing.

28   The remainder of installation is the reverse of the removal steps. Install new snap-rings and make sure they seat securely in their grooves.

Rear wheel

1970 through 1978

29   Loosen the bearing locknut on the left side of the hub. It's staked into place and may be difficult to turn initially.

30   Remove the locknut, seal and outer spacer from the hub **(see illustration)**. Next, drive out the left bearing and remove the washer and bearing spacer **(see illustrations)**.

31   Flip the wheel over and, working from the inside of the hub, drive the right bearing out. Remove the washer.

32   Service and install the bearings as described in Steps 9 through 11. Don't forget the spacer and washers. After it's tightened securely, stake the locknut with a hammer and punch.

1979 through 1983

33   Remove the snap-rings and washers from both sides of the hub.

34   Carefully pry out both seals and remove the spacers. Note that one spacer is longer than the other.

35   Remove the bearings and the spacer from the center of the hub. Refer to Steps 8 and 9 above. If replacement is necessary, the races must be pressed out of the hub. The bearings and races must be replaced as matched sets.

36   Install the spacer in the center of the hub, then pack the bearings full of grease and install them. The seals must be installed so they are 3/16 to 1/4-inch below the edge of the hub. Apply grease to the outer edge of the seals before they're pressed into the hub.

37   The short spacer should be installed on the disc side of the hub; the long spacer on the other side.

38   Install the washers and snap-rings (be sure the sharp edge of each snap-ring faces out).

1984 and later

39   Later models are very similar to 1979 through 1983 models, except they don't have snap-rings holding the bearings in the hub.

21 Brake pedal - removal and installation

Drum brake models

1   The brake pedal on drum brake models is on the left side of the motorcycle. Mark the position of the pedal on the splined shaft before removing it.

2   Unscrew the pedal spring bolt and

20.30b . . . then drive out the bearing . . .

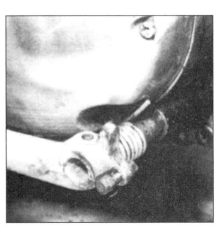

20.30c . . . and remove the center spacer

21.2 On drum brake models, release the return spring tension before removing the brake pedal

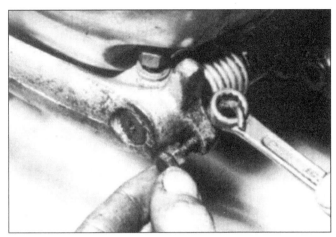

21.3 On drum brake models, tension the return spring while installing the brake pedal

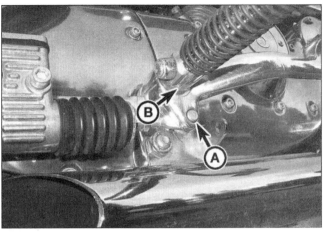

21.4a Typical disc brake pedal installation (except Custom)

A   Pivot pin   B   Footpeg bracket

remove the pedal pinch bolt, nut and lock-washer completely. Pull the pedal off the shaft, carefully releasing the spring tension as you do so **(see illustration)**.

3   Installation is the reverse of the removal Steps. Use a box wrench to tension the spring while you install the pedal **(see illustration)**. Tighten the bolts securely, but don't overtighten them and strip the threads.

Disc brake models

4   Remove the cotter pin from the brake pedal pivot shaft **(see illustrations)**. Pull the pivot shaft out of the brake pedal and master cylinder pushrod.

5   Remove the footpeg pivot bolt and nut **(see illustration 21.4a or 21.4b)**. Unbolt the footpeg bracket, then slide the pedal off the shaft.

6   Installation is the reverse of the removal Steps.

21.4b Typical disc brake pedal installation (Custom)

A   Pivot pin
B   Footpeg bracket

6

Notes

TIRE CHANGING SEQUENCE - TUBED TIRES

A Deflate tire. After pushing tire beads away from rim flanges push tire bead into well of rim at point opposite valve. Insert tire lever next to valve and work bead over edge of rim.

Use two levers to work bead over edge of rim. Note use of rim protectors

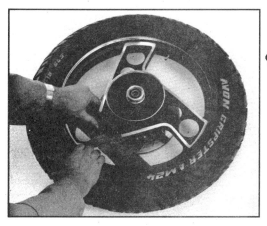

 Remove inner tube from tire

When first bead is clear, remove tire as shown

 To install, partially inflate inner tube and insert in tire

Work first bead over rim and feed valve through hole in rim. Partially screw on retaining nut to hold valve in place.

 Check that inner tube is positioned correctly and work second bead over rim using tire levers. Start at a point opposite valve.

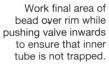 Work final area of bead over rim while pushing valve inwards to ensure that inner tube is not trapped.

Notes

Chapter 7
Frame and bodywork

Contents

Degrees of difficulty

Easy, suitable for novice with little experience		**Fairly easy,** suitable for beginner with some experience		**Fairly difficult,** suitable for competent DIY mechanic		**Difficult,** suitable for experienced DIY mechanic	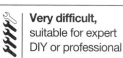	**Very difficult,** suitable for expert DIY or professional	

1 General information

The machines covered by this manual use a backbone frame made of steel tubing. This Chapter covers the procedures necessary to remove and install the fenders, side covers and other body parts. Since many service and repair operations on these motorcycles require removal of the side covers and/or other body parts, the procedures are grouped here and referred to from other Chapters.

2 Frame - inspection and repair

1   The Harley-Davidson models covered by this manual have a duplex tube, full cradle frame with a single top tube running from the steering head to the seat tube. Unlike many other designs, the twin tubes are very close together so the engine tends to straddle the frame rather than sit in it.
2   The frame is unlikely to require attention unless accident damage has occurred. In most cases, frame replacement is the only satisfactory remedy for such damage. A few frame specialists have the jigs and other equipment necessary for straightening frames to the required standard of accuracy, but even then there's no sure way of determining exactly how much the frame was overstressed.
3   After the machine has accumulated a lot of miles, it's a good idea to examine the frame closely for cracks at the welded joints. Rust can also cause weakness at the joints. Loose engine mount bolts can cause enlargement of the holes and cracks at the mounting tabs. Minor damage can often be repaired by welding, depending on the extent and nature of the damage.
4   Remember, an out-of-alignment frame

will cause handling problems. If misalignment is suspected as the result of an accident, you will have to strip the machine completely so the frame can be thoroughly checked.

3 Seat - removal and installation

1   The seat is attached with a bolt at the front, passing through lugs on the seat and the frame. There's also a bolt securing the rear of the seat directly to the rear fender.
2   1979 and later models must have the seat removed to gain access to the battery and other electrical components, as well as the return line to the oil tank.
3   Remove the bolt that secures the rear of the seat to the rear fender. It equipped, slide the passenger strap toward the front of the seat **(see illustration)**. Lift the rear of the

7

3.3a Pull the passenger strap (if equipped) forward to release the seat

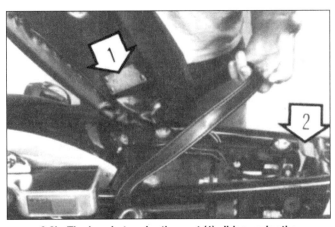

3.3b The bracket under the seat (1) slides under the protrusion on the frame (2)

seat and withdraw the seat to the rear. The front of the seat is held in place with a bracket that slides over a protrusion on the frame **(see illustration)**.

4   Installation of the seat is the reverse of removal.

4   Footpegs and brackets - removal and installation

1   If it's only necessary to detach the footpeg from the bracket, remove the nut and pivot pin, slide out the pin(s) and detach the footpeg from the bracket. Installation is the reverse of removal.

2   If it's necessary to remove the bracket from the frame, remove the bracket mounting bolt, which is exposed when the footpeg is removed.

3   Installation is the reverse of removal.

5   Jiffy stand (sidestand) - maintenance

1   The sidestand pivots in a bracket

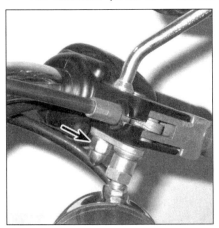

6.1 Unscrew the acorn nut (arrow) and lift the mirror off

welded to the frame. An extension spring ensures that the stand is held in the retracted position.

2   Make sure the pivot bolt is securely fastened and the extension spring is in good condition and not over stretched. An accident is almost certain to occur if the stand extends while the machine is in motion.

3   To remove the stand, unhook its spring and remove the cotter pin, washer and pivot pin. Slide the stand down out of the bracket.

4   Installation is the reverse of the removal steps, with the following additions:

a) Be sure the side of the stop labeled DOWN goes downward.

b) Use a new cotter pin.

6   Rear view mirrors - removal and installation

1   To remove a mirror, unscrew its mounting nut from below **(see illustration)**. Lift the mirror from the bracket on the handlebar and remove the spacer (if equipped).

2   Installation is the reverse of removal. Position the mirror.

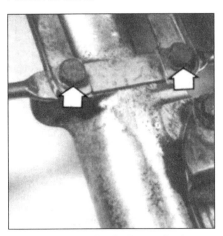

8.2 The front fender is attached to the inside of the forks with two bolts (arrows) on each side

7   Side cover - removal and installation

1   The side cover (on the left side) covers the ignition module. To remove a cover, unscrew the three mounting bolts, then lift the cover off.

2   Installation is the reverse of the removal steps.

8   Front fender - removal and installation

1   Remove the front wheel (see Chapter 6).

2   Unbolt the fender from the fork legs and take it off **(see illustration)**.

3   Installation is the reverse of the removal steps. Tighten the fender mounting bolts securely, but don't overtighten them and strip the threads.

9   Rear fender - removal and installation

1   Remove the seat (see Section 3).

2   Disconnect the negative cable from the battery. Disconnect the electrical connectors for the brake/taillight and rear turn signals under the seat. Free the circuit breakers from their mounting clips.

3   Working inside the fender, remove the rear turn signal mounting bolts. Pull the turn signals and their wires through the holes in the fender.

4   Remove the fender mounting bolts and nuts and lift the fender out

5   Installation is the reverse of the removal steps. If you're installing a new fender, drill out the pop rivets that secure the circuit breaker clips and fender extension with a 1/4-inch drill, then rivet the clips and fender extension to the new fender.

Chapter 8
Electrical system

Contents

Degrees of difficulty

Easy, suitable for novice with little experience	**Fairly easy,** suitable for beginner with some experience	**Fairly difficult,** suitable for competent DIY mechanic	**Difficult,** suitable for experienced DIY mechanic	**Very difficult,** suitable for expert DIY or professional

Specifications

Battery

Voltage...	12-volts
Electrolyte specific gravity (at 80-degrees-F)*	
100 per cent charge	1.250 to 1.270
75 per cent charge	1.220 to 1.240
50 per cent charge	1.190 to 1.210
25 per cent charge	1.160 to 1.180
Ground connection..	Negative
Applies to fillable batteries only	

Fuses and circuit breakers

1970 through 1985	Not specified
1986 through 1993	
Main..	30 amps
Ignition..	15 amps
Lighting...	15 amps
Accessory..	15 amps
1994 through 1996	
Main..	50 amps
Ignition..	15 amps
Accessory..	15 amps
Lighting...	10 amps
Instruments	10 amps

8

Fuses and circuit breakers (continued)

1997

Main	30 amps
Ignition	15 amps
Accessory	15 amps
Lighting	10 amps
Instruments	10 amps

1998

Main	30 amps
Ignition fuse	15 amps
Accessory fuse	15 amps
Lighting fuse	10 amps
Instruments fuse	10 amps

1999 and later

Main	30 amps
Ignition fuse	15 amps
Accessory fuse	15 amps
Lighting fuse	15 amps
Instruments fuse	15 amps

Generator

Type	Two brush
Minimum brush length	1/2-inch (12.7 mm)
Starter motor brush length (minimum)	
1970 through 1980	
Prestolite	1/4-inch (6.35 mm)
Hitachi	0.438 inch (11.13 mm)
1979 and later	0.354 inch (8.99 mm)

Bulbs (1970 through 1983)*

Headlight	
1970 through 1978	45/35 watts
1979 through 1983	50/35 watts
Brake/taillight	
1970 through 1978	32/4 cp
1979 through 1983	32/3 cp
Generator warning light	4 cp
Oil pressure warning light	4 cp
High beam indicator light	2 cp
Speedometer/tachometer lights	2 cp
Turn signal lights	32 cp

*For 1984 and later bulb specifications, consult a Harley-Davidson dealer.

Torque specifications

Starter through-bolts	
1970 through 1978	20 to 25 inch-lbs (2.3 to 2.8 Nm)
1979 and 1980	60 to 80 inch-lbs (6.8 to 9 Nm)
Starter mounting bolts (1981 and later)	13 to 20 ft-lbs (18 to 27 Nm)
Battery cable-to-starter terminal (1979 and 1980)	65 to 80 inch-lbs (7.3 to 9 Nm)
Alternator stator Torx screws	30 to 40 inch-lbs (3.4 to 4.5 Nm)
Alternator rotor bolts (1981 and later)	90 to 110 inch-lbs (10 to 12 Nm)

1 General information

All models covered in this manual are equipped with a 12-volt electrical system. The charging system on early models (through early 1984) is made up of a two-pole, two-brush DC generator, driven by the timing gears. The output of the generator is controlled by a voltage regulator to keep the battery charged and to meet the requirements of the motorcycle. Since the generator output is DC, there's no need for a rectifier.

On late 1984 and later models, the charging system consists of an alternator and a rectifier/regulator. On models through 1990 the alternator stator is bolted to the transmission access cover, behind the clutch on the left-hand side of the engine, and the rotor is mounted on the rear of the clutch outer drum. From 1991 the alternator stator is mounted on the left crankcase at the front, and the rotor is bolted to the rear of the primary drive sprocket. The rectifier/regulator is attached to the frame downtubes in front of the engine, where it's cooled by airflow as the machine is moving.

A large capacity battery is installed on models with an electric starter. A solenoid relay provides power to the starter motor directly from the battery. The solenoid is controlled by a switch on the handlebars.

Keep in mind that electrical parts, once purchased, can't normally be returned. To avoid unnecessary expense, make very sure the defective component has been positively identified before buying a replacement part.

Caution: When working on the electrical system, the battery should be disconnected to avoid accidentally causing a short circuit in the system. Always disconnect the negative cable first, followed by the positive cable.

2 Electrical troubleshooting - general information

A typical electrical circuit consists of an electrical component, any switches, relays, motors, fuses or circuit breakers related to that component and the wiring and connectors that link the component to both the battery and the frame. To help pinpoint electrical circuit problems, wiring diagrams are included at the end of the manual.

Before tackling any troublesome electrical circuit, first study the appropriate wiring diagram to get a complete understanding of what makes up the circuit. Trouble spots, for instance, can often be narrowed down by noting if other components related to the cir-

cuit are operating properly. If several components or circuits fail at one time, chances are the problem is in a fuse or ground connection, because several circuits are often routed through the same ones.

Electrical problems usually stem from simple causes, such as loose or corroded connections, a blown fuse or a bad relay. Visually check the condition of all fuses, wires and connections in a problem circuit before troubleshooting it.

If test instruments are going to be utilized, use the diagram to plan ahead of time where to make the connections in order to accurately pinpoint the trouble spot.

The basic items needed for electrical troubleshooting include a battery and bulb test circuit or a continuity tester, a test light and a jumper wire. A multimeter capable of reading volts, ohms and amps is a very useful alternative and performs the functions of all of the above, and is necessary for performing more extensive tests and checks where specific voltage, current or resistance values are needed.

 Refer to Troubleshooting Equipment in the Reference section for details of how to use electrical test equipment.

3 Charging system check - general information

1   If the battery loses its charge even thought the bike is being ridden, the charging system should be checked first, followed by testing of the individual components (the generator/regulator or alternator/regulator/rectifier). Before beginning the checks, make sure the battery is fully charged and all system connections are clean and tight (particularly the battery cables).

2   Checking the output of the charging system and the operation of the components in the system requires special electrical test equipment. A voltmeter and ammeter or a multimeter are the absolute minimum tools required. In addition, an ohmmeter is generally required for checking the remainder of the electrical system.

3   When making the checks, follow the procedures carefully to prevent incorrect connections and short circuits - irreparable damage to electrical system components may result if a short circuit occurs. Because of the special tools and expertise required, checking the electrical system normally should be left to a dealer service department or a reputable motorcycle repair shop.

4 Battery - check, maintenance and charging

Check and maintenance

1   The battery on models through 1996 has removable filler caps that allow the addition of water to the electrolyte. Later models are equipped with a sealed, maintenance-free battery. Never remove the cap strip or attempt to add water to a sealed battery.

2   Most battery damage is caused by heat, vibration and/or low electrolyte level. Keep the battery securely mounted and make sure the charging system is functioning correctly. On models through 1996, check the electrolyte level frequently. Refer to Chapter 1 for the electrolyte level checking procedure.

3   On maintenance free batteries, condition is indicated by the battery's open circuit voltage. To check this, disconnect the battery negative cable, then the positive cable. Connect the positive terminal of a voltmeter to the battery positive terminal and the voltmeter's negative terminal to the negative terminal of the battery. Readings are as follows:

a) *13 volts - 100 percent charged*
b) *12.8 volts - 75 percent charged*
c) *12.5 volts - 50 percent charged*
d) *12.2 volts - 25 percent charged*

4   On models through 1996, check around the base of the battery for sediment, which is the result of sulfation caused by low electrolyte levels. These deposits will cause internal short circuits, which can quickly discharge the battery. On all models, look for cracks in the case. Replace the battery if either of these conditions are found.

5   Check the battery terminals and the cable ends for tightness and corrosion. If corrosion is evident, remove the cables from the battery and clean the terminals and cable ends with a wire brush or a knife and emery cloth. Reconnect the cables and apply a thin coat of petroleum jelly to the connections to slow further corrosion.

6   The battery case should be kept clean to prevent current leakage, which can discharge the battery over a period of time (especially when it sits unused). Wash the outside of the case with a solution of baking soda and water.

Caution: Do not get any baking soda solution in the battery cells. Rinse the battery thoroughly, then dry it.

7   If acid has been spilled on the frame or battery box, neutralize it with the baking soda and water solution, dry it thoroughly, then touch up any damaged paint. Make sure the battery vent tube is directed away from the frame and the final drive chain or belt and isn't kinked or pinched.

8   If the motorcycle sits unused for long periods of time, refer to Section 5 and charge the battery approximately once every month.

Charging

9   If the machine sits idle for extended periods of time or if the charging system malfunctions, the battery can be charged from an external source.

10   To charge the battery properly, you will need a charger of the correct rating. If you're working on a fillable battery, you'll also need a hydrometer, a clean rag and a syringe for adding distilled water to the battery cells.

11   The maximum charging rate for any battery is 1/10 of the rated amp/hour capacity. For example, the maximum charging rate for a 22 amp/hour battery would be 2.2 amps; the maximum rate for the 1997 maintenance free battery, which is rated at 18 amp/hours, is 1.8 amps. If the battery is charged at a higher rate, it could be damaged.

12   Don't allow the battery to be subjected to a so-called quick charge (high rate of charge over a short period of time) unless you're prepared to buy a new battery. The heat this generates can warp the plates inside the battery. If they touch each other, the resulting short will ruin the battery.

13   When charging the battery, always remove it from the machine before hooking it to the charger. If you're working on a fillable battery, be sure to check the electrolyte level and add distilled water to any cells that are low before you start charging the battery.

14   If you're working on a fillable battery, loosen the cell caps and cover the top of the battery with a clean rag. Hook up the battery charger leads (positive to battery positive and negative to battery negative). Then - and only then - plug in the battery charger.

> ⚠ **Warning: Remember, the hydrogen gas escaping from a battery coil is explosive, so keep open flames and sparks well away from the area. Also, the electrolyte is extremely corrosive and will damage anything it comes in contact with.**

15   If you're working on a fillable battery, allow the battery to charge until the specific gravity is as specified. The charger must be unplugged and disconnected from the battery when making specific gravity checks.

16   If you're working on a 1997 through 1999 maintenance free battery, charge at a constant 1.8 amps for the following periods of time, depending on the open circuit voltage obtained in Section 4:

a) *12.8 volts - three to five hours*
b) *12.5 volts - four to seven hours*
c) *12.2 volts - ten hours*

If you're working on a 2000 or later maintenance free battery (1.9 amp/hour rating), a constant current charger is not recommended. Instead, vary the charging time according to both the open circuit voltage and the amperage of the charger, as follows.

a) *3 amp charger:*
   12.6 volts - 1-3/4 hours
   12.3 volts - 3-1/2 hours
   12.0 volts - 5 hours
   11.8 volts - 6 hours, 40 minutes
b) *6 amp charger:*
   12.6 volts - 50 minutes
   12.3 volts - 1-3/4 hours
   12.0 volts - 2-1/2 hours
   11.8 volts - 3 hours, 20 minutes
c) *10 amp charger:*
   12.6 volts - 30 minutes
   12.3 volts -1 hour
   12.0 volts - 1-1/2 hours
   11.8 volts - 2 hours
d) *20 amp charger:*
   12.6 volts - 15 minutes
   12.3 volts - 30 minutes
   12.0 volts - 45 minutes
   11.8 volts - 1 hour

17   If the battery gets warm to the touch or gases excessively, the charging rate is too high. Either disconnect the charger and let the battery cool down or lower the charging rate to prevent damage to the battery.

18   If one or more of the cells do not show an increase in specific gravity after a long slow charge (fillable batteries only) or if the battery as a whole doesn't seem to want to take a charge, it's time for a new battery.

19   When the battery is fully charged, unplug the charger first, then disconnect the charger leads from the battery. Install the cell caps (fillable batteries only) and wipe any electrolyte off the outside of the battery case.

5   Battery - removal and installation

Caution: Be extremely careful when handling or working around the battery. The electrolyte is very caustic and an explosive gas is given off when the battery is being charged.

1970 through 1978

1   Loosen the nuts securing the battery retaining strap and release the strap from the bottom of the battery box **(see illustrations)**.

2   Tilt the side cover to clear the frame and release it.

3   Disconnect the battery cables (negative cable first) and lift the battery out of the motorcycle. Note how the vent hose is routed.

1979 and later

4   Remove the seat as described in Chapter 7. Disconnect the battery cables from the battery (negative cable first).

5   Remove the top cover from the battery.

6   Remove the battery retaining strap and carefully lift the battery out of the motorcycle. The battery may be stuck to the rubber anti-vibration pad it rests on. If so, simply rock it from side-to-side until the seal is broken. Note how the vent hose is routed.

7   Be sure to correct any problems and charge the battery if necessary before reinstalling it in the machine. Refer to Sections 4 and 5 for additional battery maintenance and charging procedures.

8   Install the battery by reversing the removal sequence. Be very careful not to pinch or otherwise restrict the battery vent tube, as the battery may build up enough internal pressure during normal charging system operation to explode.

 Battery corrosion can be kept to a minimum by applying a layer of petroleum jelly or battery terminal (dielectric) grease to the terminals after the cables have been connected.

6   Fuses and circuit breakers - check and replacement

1   All models use one or more circuit breakers. These open in response to an electrical overload, then reset themselves as they cool down. If the condition that caused the overload still exists, the circuit breaker will open again.

5.1a On early models, loosen the retainer nuts . . .

5.1b . . . then remove the retainer and pull the battery out to the side

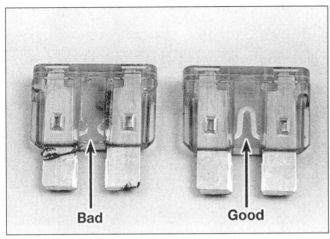

6.5 A blown fuse can be identified by a break in the element (plug-in type shown) - be sure to replace a blown fuse with one of the same amperage rating

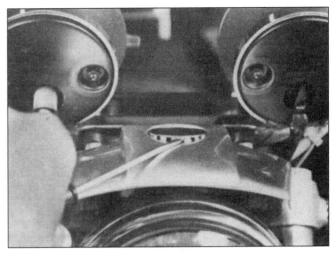

7.3a Pry out the plug . . .

2   1970 through 1972 models use a single circuit breaker in the battery positive cable. 1973 through 1978 models use separate circuit breakers for the lighting, accessory and ignition circuits. 1979 through 1993 models use these three circuit breakers, plus one main breaker in the battery positive cable. 1994 through 1997 models use five circuit breakers: main, ignition, lights, accessories and instruments.

3   1998 and later models use a main circuit breaker, with fuses for the ignition, lighting, accessory and instrument circuits.

4   Circuit breakers and fuses are located under the seat. To replace a circuit breaker, disconnect the negative cable from the battery. Disconnect the cables or wires from the circuit breaker, then remove it from the vehicle, install a new one and connect the cables or wires.

5   Blown fuses can be identified by a break in the metal element inside the fuse (see illustration). To replace a cylindrical glass fuse, pry it out of its clips and push in a new one. To replace a mini-fuse (plug-in type), pull it out of its terminals and push in a new one.

 Warning: Never bridge fuse terminals with wire or any other metal, and never replace a fuse with one of a higher-than-rated amperage. This will allow overheating, which could cause melted wires, ruined components or a fire.

7   Headlight bulb - adjustment and replacement

Adjustment

1   An improperly adjusted headlight may cause problems for oncoming traffic or provide poor, unsafe illumination of the road ahead. Before adjusting the headlight, be sure to consult local traffic laws and regulations.

2   To set up the headlight, the machine should be placed on level ground at least 25 feet from a wall in its normal position (off the stand and with a rider on the seat). On high beam, the top of the beam on the wall should be at the same height as the top of the headlight.

3   To adjust the beam, pry the decorative plug out, loosen the headlight adjusting locknut and twist the headlight assembly up or down to aim the beam (see illustrations).

4   Tighten the locknut and recheck the aim.

5   Install the decorative plug.

Replacement

6   Models through 1991 have a sealed beam headlight, and 1992 and later models have a quartz bulb headlight. The sealed beam unit comprises the reflector, glass and bulb as a single unit, whereas the quartz bulb can be replaced separately from the reflector unit.

7   To gain access to the bulb, remove the screw through the chrome plated clamp that surrounds the headlight (see illustration). Take off the clamp, then pry the headlight unit away from the rubber mount.

8   Lift the headlight out of the housing until the wire harness connector can be unplugged from the rear (see illustration).

7.3b . . . to get at the headlight adjusting locknut (arrow)

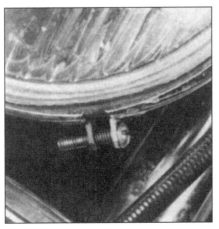

7.7 Loosen the clamp screw to remove the headlight (early models) . . .

7.8 . . . and unplug the wire harness connector from the rear of the headlight

8

9   Where a quartz bulb is fined, release the wire clip from its slot and hinge the clip backward. Holding the bulb by its wire connector terminals, withdraw it from the reflector **(see illustration)**.

Caution: When installing a new bulb, do not touch its glass envelope - bulb life will be shortened by skin contact.

10   Attach the wire connector to the rear of the new headlight and position the headlight in the housing.

11   Install the chrome plated clamp and tighten the screw securely.

12   Adjustment should not have been altered while changing the headlight. If necessary, adjust the headlight as described above.

8   Taillight and turn signal bulbs - replacement

1   Remove the screws securing the plastic lens cover to the taillight or the turn signal and detach the cover **(see illustrations)**.

2   Push in on the bulb and simultaneously turn it counterclockwise.

3   Replace the bulb with a new one of the same type by pushing it into the socket and turning it clockwise. **Note:** *The taillight bulb is a two filament bulb. The pins at the base of the bulb are offset so the bulb can only be inserted into the socket one way. If the bulb will not go into the socket, pull it out and rotate it 180-degrees, then reinsert it into the socket.*

4   Place the lens in position on the housing. Be sure the rubber seal is in good condition and makes contact all around the perimeter of the lens. Secure the lens with the two mounting screws.

9   Generator/alternator - check

1   The generator or alternator can be tested without removing it from the motorcycle. **Note:** *For all tests to be accurate, the battery must be in good condition and fully charged.*

Generator

1970 through 1978
Refer to illustration 9.2

2   On 1970 through 1977 models, test the circuit to the generator warning light to be sure it isn't grounded. Remove the wire or wires from the regulator terminal marked D or GEN and position them so they don't make contact with any part of the machine. Turn the ignition on and note whether the warning light glows. If it does, there's a short circuit somewhere in the wiring, which is probably the cause of the generator malfunction. Reconnect the wire to the regulator

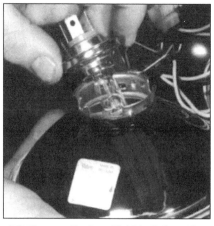

7.9 Remove the headlight bulb from the reflector (1992 and later models)

after making this test.

Caution: Never ground either the F terminal (XL models) or the BT terminal (XLCH models) before the wires to the terminal are disconnected. Failure to observe this precaution will result in permanent damage to the regulator.

3   If the light doesn't glow, or if the test is being made on a 1978 model, remove the wire from the F or field terminal of the generator. Connect a short jumper wire to the terminal, and ground the other end of the jumper wire to some convenient part of the frame. A good ground connection is important. Disconnect the wire from terminal A of the generator and attach the positive lead from an ammeter to the A terminal on the generator.

4   Start the engine and run it at approximately 2000 rpm. Momentarily connect the negative lead of the ammeter to the positive terminal of the battery or to the terminal marked BAT on the regulator. If a reading of 10-amps or more is obtained, the generator is operating properly. If a somewhat lower reading or no reading at all is obtained, the generator should be removed from the engine for additional checks.

1979 and later

5   Disconnect the wires from terminals A and F of the generator. Connect the positive lead of a voltmeter, adjusted to 1 O-volts on the DC scale, to terminal A. Connect the negative lead of the voltmeter to ground.

6   Start the engine and run it at 2000 rpm. The voltmeter should read a minimum of 2.0-to-2.5 volts DC. if the meter registers the correct output, the generator is in good condition.

7   If zero or very little voltage is registered on the voltmeter, polarize the generator and test the output again. To polarize the generator while it's still installed on the engine, connect one end of a jumper wire to the terminal on the generator armature (A) then momentarily touch the other end of the jumper wire to the positive terminal of the battery.

8   If the voltmeter still registers zero or

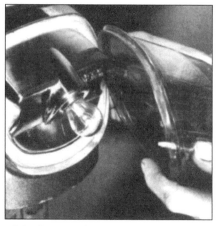

8.1a Remove the lens for access to the tail/brakelight bulb

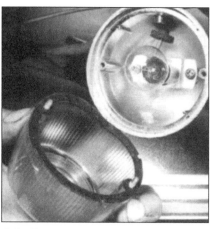

8.1b Turn signals through mid-2003 have bayonet-type bulbs (late 2003 models have wedge-type bulbs)

very low voltage, the generator will have to be disassembled and repaired.

9   With the voltmeter connected to the generator and the engine running at 2000 rpm, momentarily (not more than 10 seconds) connect a jumper wire to terminal F. The voltage should be 25-to-30 volts DC. If not, the generator will have to be disassembled and repaired.

Alternator

10   Checking of the alternator output requires access to test equipment not normally available to the home mechanic, plus a degree of skill to determine the alternator's condition from the results. It is recommended that the motorcycle be taken to a Harley-Davidson dealer service department for testing on the approved load tester.

11   It is, however, possible to perform a continuity check of the alternator windings as described in Steps 12 and 13. No test details are supplied by the manufacturer for the regulator/rectifier unit; if failure is suspected it can only be tested by the substitution of a new unit. Note that many regulator faults are due to poor ground contact at the unit mounting.

10.1a Label the wires and terminals, then detach the wires from the generator

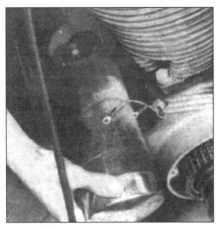

10.1b Tilt the generator while removing it to give the oil thrower clearance

10.2 Check the brushes for wear and damage

12   Disconnect the alternator at the wiring harness connector, just to the rear of the left side of the engine (models through 1990) or just down from the regulator/rectifier (1991 and later models). Connect an ohmmeter (selector switch on the R x 1 scale) between one of the stator pins in the engine side of the connector and a good ground on the engine - there should be no continuity, i.e. infinite resistance. Repeat this test between the other pin in the connector and ground. Any reading other than infinite resistance indicates a grounded stator, which must be replaced.

13   Connect the ohmmeter between both pins on the engine side of the wire harness connector. Very low resistance should be indicated (0.2-to-0.4 ohm). If the resistance is much higher, or no meter needle movement occurs, the stator must be replaced.

10 Generator/alternator - removal, overhaul and installation

Generator removal

1   After disconnecting the two wires **(see illustration)**, the generator can be removed from the engine by removing the two long screws that pass through the timing cover and secure the generator in position. Be careful when the generator is being lifted from the engine, so the oil slinger on the end of the driveshaft will clear the idler gear **(see illustration)**.

Generator overhaul

1970 through 1981

2   Remove the brush strap from the generator and examine the brushes for wear, broken wires or a tendency to stick in the holders **(see illustrations)**. The brushes must be replaced with new ones when the longest side measures 1/2-inch or less.

3   The brush holder mounting plate can be removed from the generator by unscrewing

the commutator end cover nuts and washers and the two long through-bolts that hold the generator together. You'll need to disconnect the two black brush wires and the positive brush cable.

4   Remove the brushes from the holders, then make sure they slide in the holders without binding. If necessary, the brush holders can be cleaned with solvent to remove accumulated carbon dust. Clean the commutator at the same time; don't use harsh abrasives such as emery cloth.

1982 and later

5   Remove the two long through-bolts and detach the rear cover from the generator. **Note:** *There are several thrust washers between the end cover and the rear bearing. Be sure none of them are lost because they must be reinstalled during reassembly of the generator.*

6   Separate the brush holder mounting plate and the body assembly from the front cover. Inspect the brushes for wear and broken wires. Measure the length of the brushes. If the length of the longest side is 1/2-inch or less, the brushes should be replaced as a set.

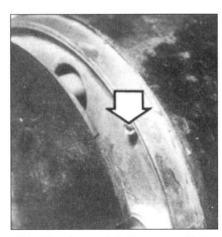

10.9 Align the notch in the cover with the locating pin (arrow) during reassembly

7   Check the brush springs for wear. The springs should exert a constant even pressure on the brushes. Replace the springs, if necessary, with new ones.

All models

8   If no reason has been found for malfunctioning of the generator at this point, take it to a Harley-Davidson dealer service department or an auto electric shop. The more detailed inspection required demands equipment and expertise the home mechanic isn't likely to have.

9   Reassemble the generator in the reverse order of disassembly. Be sure to align the notch in the end cover with the locating pin in the main body **(see illustration)**.

Generator installation

10   Installation is the reverse of removal.

11   After the generator is assembled and installed, it must be polarized to be sure it will charge correctly. If the generator isn't polarized, permanent damage may occur to the generator and the regulator.

12   On 1970 through 1977 models, momentarily bridge the BAT and GEN terminals of the regulator with a jumper wire. This should be done after all of the electrical connections have been made, but before the engine has been started for the first time.

13   On 1978 and later models, the generator can be polarized on the motorcycle or on the workbench. While on the workbench, connect the positive battery cable to the armature terminal of the generator. Momentarily (not more than 10 seconds) connect the negative battery cable to the field terminal of the generator. If the generator is installed on the motorcycle, connect a jumper wire to the armature terminal of the generator and momentarily touch the other end of the jumper wire to the positive battery terminal.

14   The generator should be polarized any time a new one is installed, the wires are disconnected or after extended periods of non-use.

8

10.17 The rotor is bolted to the back of the primary sprocket on 1991 and later models

10.20 The stator is secured by four screws (1991 and later location shown) - stator wiring must be clamped to the casing

11.4 On early models, the regulator is mounted under the left side cover; on later models it's mounted at the front between the frame members

Alternator removal

15 Access to the alternator is gained by removing the primary chaincase cover as described in Chapter 2 and withdrawing the engine sprocket, clutch and primary chain as a complete unit. **Note:** *You may notice slight drag from the rotor magnets as the stator and rotor separate.*

16 On models through 1990, to separate the rotor from the back of the clutch unit, remove the large snap ring. Unscrew the four Torx screws to release the stator from the transmission access cover and release its wiring.

17 On 1991 and later models, remove the bolts holding the rotor to the engine sprocket and press the engine sprocket boss out of the rotor (take care to support both components while this is done) **(see illustration).** The stator is retained to the left crankcase half by four Torx screws, but first disconnect the wiring at the connector just below the regulator/rectifier, free it from any ties and withdraw it from between the gearcase. **Note:** *Due to the difficulty in threading the wiring back through the casing on installation, a length of string or a spare wire should be drawn temporarily into place as the wiring is removed.*

Alternator inspection

18 Clean all traces of dirt or metallic particles which have become attached to the rotor magnets.

Caution: *Do not drop the rotor - damage to its magnetism will result.*

19 Clean the stator coils with contact cleaner and check for signs of damage. If the stator coil test in Section 9 has indicated a coil failure the stator must be replaced.

Alternator installation

20 Install the stator, first making sure its wiring is routed correctly and secured by any clamps provided (see illustration). On 1991

and later models, it will be necessary to insert the grommet in the crankcase, and route the wiring across the top of the case, then down through the gearcase (use of string or spare wire as a guide will make this easier) and tie it to the inner side of the frame tube; take care to position it well forward of the gearcase mounting lug to avoid contact with the drive belt/chain. On all models, use new Torx screws to secure the stator and tighten them evenly to the torque listed in this Chapter's Specifications. These screws contain a locking patch, and can be used once only.

21 On models through 1990 the manufacturer advises that a new snap-ring is used when installing the rotor on the clutch unit.

22 When reassembling the rotor and engine sprocket on 1991 and later models, align the bolt holes and press the two components together, applying pressure to the rotor boss, not its periphery. Apply thread-locking compound to each bolt and tighten to the torque listed in this Chapter's Specifications.

23 Refit the primary drive and clutch as described in Chapter 2, followed by the chaincase. Replenish the transmission oil supply.

11 Regulator - general information, removal and installation

1 The usual signs of a defective regulator include a battery that will not remain charged, the need to fill the battery more often than usual, or lights that increase significantly in intensity as engine speed increases. If these signs pass unnoticed or ignored, the battery and the regulator itself will suffer permanent damage.

2 Sophisticated test equipment is required to check the regulator for proper operation. This is especially true of Bosch

regulators, which are factory set and sealed.

3 If the regulator is suspected of being defective, take it to a dealer and have it checked. Normally the regulator doesn't require attention during routine maintenance, although Delco-Remy regulators may benefit from an occasional cleaning of the points. The cleaning and adjusting of the points should be left to a Harley-Davidson dealer service department or an auto electric shop.

4 The regulator is mounted on the left side or front of the bike **(see illustration).** Label and disconnect the wires, remove the mounting screws and take it off.

5 Installation is the reverse of the removal Steps.

12 Starter motor and solenoid - removal and installation

Removal

1 Disconnect the negative cable from the battery.

1970 through 1980

2 Disconnect the large cable from the starter motor and loosen the clamp on the starter body.

3 Remove the starter motor end cover and the mounting bracket. This will permit access to the two long through bolts that retain the starter motor to the rear of the primary chaincase **(see illustrations).** When these two bolts have been loosened, the starter motor can be removed as a complete unit **(see illustrations).**

4 Moving to the left-hand side of the machine, remove the primary chaincase (see Chapter 2) and press in the spring loaded plunger of the starter solenoid so the pin that normally seats in the retainer cap can be removed **(see illustration).** Lift off the cup and spring. The solenoid itself can now be

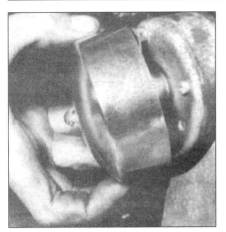

12.3a Remove the end cover from 1980 and earlier starters (it's held by a single screw) . . .

12.3b . . . and take off the mounting bracket, then . . .

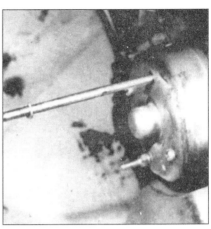

12.3c . . . unscrew the long through-bolts

removed from the back of the chaincase by disconnecting the wire and removing the two mounting bolts **(see illustration)**.

5   Remove the single countersunk screw found in the top of the chaincase casting, immediately above the clutch. This will release the solenoid reaction lever which, when removed, will permit the starter drive

assembly to be lifted out, together with the casting bolted to the back of the primary chaincase. Don't lose the bronze washer on the end of the shaft.

1981 and later

6   Remove the left footpeg, footpeg bracket and the shift lever.
7   Remove the primary chaincase cover

on the left side of the motorcycle as described in Section 4, Step 20. Without disconnecting the clutch cable, pivot the chaincase cover out of the way so the starter mounting bolts are accessible.
8   Disconnect the wires from the starter motor and the solenoid **(see illustration)**.
9   Remove the exhaust system to gain clearance to remove the starter motor. On some models it's necessary to remove the rear exhaust pipe only.
10   Remove the starter motor mounting bolts from inside the primary chaincase and detach the starter motor from the engine **(see illustration)**.

Installation

1970 through 1980 models
11   On 1970 through 1980 models, attach the housing containing the starter drive assembly to the back of the chaincase. The starter drive assembly and solenoid reaction lever should be assembled first. Attach the starter solenoid and bolt the whole assembly in place. Install the spring, cap and pin.
12   Install the starter motor, securing it to the back of the chaincase with the two long through-bolts. Install the mounting bracket, then the end cover.

12.3d The starter motor can now be detached

12.4a Press in the spring-loaded plunger and withdraw the pin (arrow)

12.4b The solenoid can be unscrewed from the rear of the primary chaincase

12.8 Starter motor wires - 1981 and later models (arrow)

12.10 Starter motor mounting bolts - 1981 and later models (arrows)

13.1a Remove the screws . . .

13.1b . . . and detach the cover
from the starter motor

13.2 Disengage the spring to release
the brush from the holder

13   Reconnect the starter motor wire to the terminal and route the cable like it was originally. Place the retaining clamp around the starter motor body before attaching the wire. It's held by the single bolt that also retains the rear valve lifter assembly in place.

1981 and later models

14   Slip the starter motor with a new gasket into position in the primary chaincase. Insert the two mounting bolts into the front of the starter motor and through the chaincase. The short starter mounting bolt is installed at the upper left corner of the chaincase.
15   Connect the battery cable and the solenoid wire to the solenoid.

All models

16   If the engine is in the frame, install the primary chaincase (see Chapter 2) and top up the transmission oil. Install the exhaust and reconnect the battery negative cable.

---

13 Starter motor and drive - disassembly, inspection and reassembly

Starter motor

1970 through 1980

1   Remove the end cover from the rear of the starter motor (see illustrations).
2   Check the length of the brushes and compare the measurement to the Specifications (see illustration). If necessary, replace the brushes with a new set. Make sure the brushes can move freely in the holders. If they aren't free to move, remove them and clean the holders with solvent to remove any carbon deposits that may be built-up. Clean the commutator with solvent at the same time. Do not use a harsh abrasive such as emery cloth on the commutator.
3   To replace the brushes on a Prestolite starter, remove the terminal and brush assembly from the main body shell. Install a

new terminal and brush assembly. The other two brushes can be removed from the field coils by cutting the brush lead wire where it connects to the field coil lead.
4   File the old coil connection until the coil lead is thoroughly cleaned. Strip the insulation from the coil lead as far as necessary to make a new solder connection.
5   Solder the leads from the new brushes to the field coil lead with rosin flux. Be sure the new lead is in the same position as the original lead. Do not use too much heat or solder, otherwise the leads will become flow coated with solder and lose their flexibility.
6   To replace the brushes in Hitachi starters, the brush leads must be unsoldered from the brush holder. Solder the new brushes into position on the brush holder. Do not use too much heat or solder, otherwise the leads will become flow coated with solder and lose their flexibility.

1981 and later

7   Release the field coil wire from the unit. Remove the two long bolts which pass from the end cover to the housing. Remove the two screws from the end cover and withdraw the cover, complete with large O-ring on 1200 models.
8   Release the springs from the ends of the brushes with a wire hook, then lift the brush assembly off the commutator. Slide the new brush assembly over the commutator and position the brushes in the holder. Use a wire hook to attach the springs to the ends of the brushes.
9   Inspect the brushes and commutator as described in Step 2.

All models

10   If the starter motor has been used a lot, the mica insulation between the individual copper segments of the commutator may need servicing. The commutator must be undercut 11/32-inch by an automotive electric shop or a Harley-Davidson dealer service department.
11   Other defects in the starter motor

require professional attention or the installation of a new unit.
12   Be sure the brush leads do not contact the body of the motor before reinstalling the starter motor on the motorcycle.

Starter drive assembly

Inspection

13   The Bendix-type drive shaft and gear assembly located between the starter motor and the ring gear on the clutch engage the starter motor drive gear with the clutch ring gear when the starter motor button is depressed. It also ensures the drive is disengaged as soon as the engine starts or when the starter motor button is released.
14   Examine all the components of the starter drive assembly. Look for worn or broken teeth on the gears and damage to the worm drive gear in the drive gear. The gear must move freely on the worm, without tilting or binding at any point. All worn parts must be replaced - they cannot be repaired.
15   To disassemble the starter drive assembly on 1970 through 1980 models, remove the bronze thrust washer and place the nut on the end of the shaft in a vise, between two soft metal clamps. The nut has a left-hand thread and will unscrew. There is a bearing race behind it. The gear and reaction collar assembly will then pull off. To disassemble this sub-assembly, remove the snap-ring from the inner end of the shaft.
16   When reassembling, give the worm drive gear a liberal coat of moly-base grease and make sure the sliding gear moves freely when the assembly is complete.
17   To remove the starter drive assembly on 1981 and later models, remove the two mounting bolts from the drive end, along with the washers, lock washers and O-rings.
18   The starter drive, idler gear and bearing can be removed from the starter housing. Check the condition of the O-ring in the groove of the starter housing.
19   Clean the drive components and apply high-temperature grease to them.

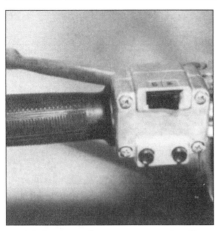

15.1 Remove the screws securing the switch to the handlebar

16.1 Unscrew the knurled ring around the ignition switch or release the switch from the bracket (models through 1991)

16.2 Release the retaining ring (A) and locknut (B) to free the switch (1992 and later models)

14 Starter solenoid - check

1970 through 1980

1   Disconnect the negative cable from the battery, followed by the positive cable. Remove the wires from the solenoid.
2   Connect solenoid terminals A and C to a 12-volt battery; A to the positive terminal and C to the negative terminal. Terminal A is the upper large stud; terminal C is the lower large stud. Attach a jumper wire to the positive terminal of the battery and touch the other end of the jumper wire to terminal C of the solenoid. The solenoid should make a clicking sound. If a click or heavy spark at the terminal doesn't occur, the solenoid is defective and must be replaced with a new one.

1981 and later

3   Disconnect the wire from terminal C on the solenoid.
4   Connect terminal 50 (on the solenoid) to the positive terminal of a 12-volt battery. Connect the negative terminal of the battery to terminal C and to the body of the solenoid. The starter gear should pull-in forcefully. If not, the solenoid is defective and must be replaced with a new one.
5   Disconnect the negative cable from terminal C. The starter gear should remain in the pulled-in position. If not, the solenoid is defective and must be replaced with a new one.
6   Connect terminals C and 50 to the positive terminal of the 12-volt battery. Ground the negative terminal of the battery on the solenoid body. Disconnect the test lead from terminal 50. This should result in the starter gear returning to its original position. If the gear doesn't return to its original position, the solenoid is defective and must be replaced with a new one.

7   Replacement of the solenoid on 1981 and later models requires disassembly of the starter motor and should be left to a Harley-Davidson dealer service department.

15 Handlebar switches - removal and installation

1   Generally speaking, the handlebar switches give little trouble, but if necessary they can be removed by separating the sections that form a split clamp around the handlebars **(see illustration)**.
2   To prevent the possibility of a short circuit, disconnect the battery before removing the switches.
3   Most troubles are caused by dirty contacts, which can be cleaned with an aerosol contact cleaner specially formulated for this purpose.
4   Repair of the switches is usually impractical. In the event of damage or pronounced wear of some internal part, the switch should be replaced with a new one.

16 Ignition and light switch - removal and installation

 Warning: Disconnect the battery negative cable before working on the switch.

1   The main switch that controls both the ignition system and the lights is attached to the top engine mounting bracket on the left side of the motorcycle. On models through 1991, the switch is attached to a plate by a knurled ring. Once the ring is unscrewed, the switch can be pressed through the plate and removed from the rear after its wires have been disconnected **(see illustration)**.
2   On 1992 and later models unscrew the

retaining ring from the front of the switch and remove the locknut from the stud on its underside **(see illustration)**. Lift the switch assembly and its seal away from the engine bracket and remove the switch cover. Disconnect the wires from the switch.
3   If the switch malfunctions, replace it with a new one - repair isn't possible. Note that if the switch is replaced, the ignition key will have to be replaced also.
4   The switch doesn't normally require attention and it should never be oiled. If the switch is oiled, there's a risk of oil reaching the electrical contacts and acting as an insulator.

17 Horn-adjustment

1   The horn is equipped with an adjusting screw on the back side so the volume can be varied.
2   To adjust the tone or volume, turn the screw 1/2 turn in either direction and check the sound. If the sound is weaker or lost altogether, turn the screw in the opposite direction. Continue adjusting until the desired note and volume are achieved.
3   If the horn malfunctions and can't be restored by adjustment, install a new one. Horn repair isn't possible, because the assembly is riveted together.

18 Brake light switches - adjustment

Rear brake light switch

1   The switch on drum brake models is bolted to a small lug on the right side of the lower frame tube, close to the rear wheel. The plunger-type switch is actuated by a small right angle bracket that's clamped to

8

18.1 Location of the brake light switch on rear drum brake models

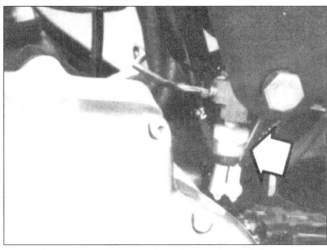

18.3 On rear disc brake models, the rear brake light switch is mounted below the oil tank

18.4 Detach the switch (arrow) from the master cylinder and disconnect its wires

19.3 Remove the upper two Allen-head bolts to release the instrument bracket, then . . .

the rear brake operating rod (see illustration).

2   To adjust the point at which the switch operates and the brake light comes on, the screw through the bracket should be loosened and the bracket moved up-or-down the rod, as required. Moving it to the rear of the machine makes the light operate later, since the switch is in the off position while the plunger is depressed.

3   The brake light switch on rear disc brake models is located on the left side of the frame, just below the oil tank (see illustration). The rear disc brake is self-compensating so adjustment of the switch isn't necessary or possible.

Front brake light switch

4   Early models with front drum brakes have the brake light switch incorporated in the brake cable. Later disc brake models have the brake light switch built into the master cylinder (see illustration). Since the disc brakes are self-compensating, the switch doesn't require adjustment.

19 Warning light bulbs - replacement

Early models

1   Two separate warning lights are mounted in a small display panel, just above the headlight. The left light is the generator charging light and the right light is the oil pressure warning light. Both lights should illuminate as soon as the ignition switch is turned on, but should go out soon after the engine is started.

2   Access to the bulbs is from the back of the panel, which the bulbs fit into.

3   Remove the upper two Allen-head bolts securing the handlebar clamp (see illustration). Carefully loosen the lower two bolts until the instrument bracket can be slid out from under the clamp. Hold the handlebars so they don't slip out of position while the clamp is loose.

4   Pry the plug out of the top of the warn-

ing light panel and loosen the headlight adjusting nut.

5   Remove the two bolts securing the warning light panel and lift the panel off (see illustration). Be careful - there are washers between the panel and mounting bracket

19.5 . . . remove the bolts securing the warning light panel

19.11 Warning light pulls out of housing on later models

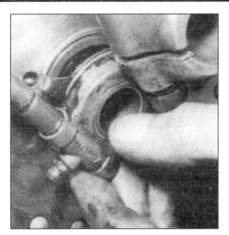

20.2a Lower the front wheel and disengage the speedometer drive unit from the wheel hub

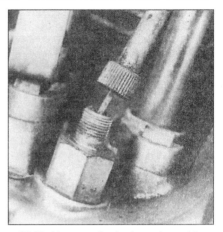

20.2b Unscrew the tachometer cable from the timing cover

which may be lost when the panel is removed.

6   Unplug the defective light and install a new bulb.

7   Place the panel in position with the washers under it and install the bolts.

8   Slide the instrument mounting bracket into place between the handlebar mounting clamps. Insert the two upper mounting bolts and begin to tighten them. Be sure the nuts at the bottom of the upper yoke that the bolts thread into are in position.

9   Place the handlebars at the desired level and tighten the mounting bolts securely.

Later models

10   Each warning light is a sealed assembly; bulb replacement is not possible.

11   To remove a defective light, first remove the headlamp reflector for access to the warning light wiring connector. Disconnect the wiring and any ground connections. Pry the inner cover from the warning light display and withdraw the defective light unit from the housing or instrument bracket **(see illustration)**.

12   Installation is the reverse of the removal procedure.

Speedometer and tachometer illumination

13   Refer to Section for 20 details.

---

20 Instruments - removal, installation and replacement

Removal

1   A speedometer is standard equipment. Some models are equipped with a tachometer as well.

2   If the gauge is equipped with a mechanical drive cable, detach it from the front wheel hub (speedometer) or timing cover (tachometer) **(see illustrations)**. Disconnect the other end of the cable from the back of

the gauge.

3   If the gauge is electronic, remove the plate from the back of the gauge to expose the electrical connector, then disconnect it.

4   If the gauge is mounted directly to the top of the fork leg, unbolt from the top of the fork leg and remove it **(see illustration)**.

5   If the gauge is mounted in a bracket, free the rear cushion and pull the gauge out of the bracket. You can also unbolt the bracket from the handlebar retainer **(see illustration 19.3)**.

Installation

6   Installation is the reverse of the removal Steps.

Bulb replacement

Note: *Electronic instruments are illuminated by light-emitting diodes which can't be replaced separately from the gauge.*

7   Remove the gauge as described above.

8   Pull the bulb holders from the gauge. Early models use bayonet-type bulbs which are twisted counterclockwise to remove. Later models use wedge-type bulbs which are pulled directly out and pushed in.

Speed sensor replacement (electronic speedometer)

9   The speed sensor used with electronic speedometers is mounted in the crankcase and picks up its signal from the fifth gear mainshaft.

10   The manufacturer's recommended test procedure includes substituting a known good speed sensor. If you don't have a speed sensor you can borrow, diagnosis of the speed sensor should be done by a dealer service department or other qualified shop.

11   To remove the sensor, remove the seat (see Chapter 7). Disconnect the sensor connector and free the harness from any retainers. Unbolt the sensor from the crankcase (on the right side, below the starter) and take it out.

12   Installation is the reverse of the removal Steps.

20.4 The instruments are bolted to the top of each fork leg on some early models

---

21 Evaporative emission control system - solenoid test

1992 and later California models

1   The solenoid is clamped to the rear of the air cleaner baseplate and operates a butterfly valve located in the bottom of the air cleaner housing. A mechanical linkage connects the two components. If operating normally, it will shut the valve when the engine is stopped (ignition switch in OFF position), open it with the pull-in winding when the starter circuit is operated, and keep it open with its hold-in winding while the engine is running.

2   To test the two windings, trace the wiring up to the connector and separate it at this point. Making the tests on the solenoid side of the connector, use an ohmmeter to measure the resistance between the pull-in winding wires (black/red and gray/black on early models; green and black on later models). A reading of 4 to 6 ohms should be

8

obtained. Take another reading between the hold-in winding wires (white and black on early models; white/black and black on later models). A reading of 21 to 27 ohms should be obtained.

3   If either resistance reading is widely different from that specified, the solenoid is defective and must be replaced.

4   If the windings prove sound, yet the butterfly valve still fails to operate normally, make continuity checks along the supply and ground circuits to isolate the problem - it will most likely be due to a corroded connector or broken wire.

22 Turn signal relay/cancel unit-location

Models through 1990

1   The turn signal relay is in the headlamp shell. Remove the headlamp sealed beam unit as described in Section 7 for access. If a problem occurs in the turn signal circuit which cannot be traced to the bulbs, handlebar switches or associated wiring, the relay must be replaced.

2   When installing a new relay, check that it fits into its clip and will not contact the headlamp unit.

1991 and later models

3   The self-canceling circuit comprises the cancel relay (bolted to the rear of the ignition module bracket), the reed switch in the speedometer head and the handlebar switches. The relay automatically cancels the turn signals after receiving distance information from the reed switch, or on manual control via either handlebar switch. An internal circuit of the relay provides a hazard flasher function.

4   Various tests can be made on the relay if it is suspected of failure, but first check that the fault is not due to a blown bulb, poor ground connection, corrosion or damaged wiring - these are more likely than a failed relay.

5   If the fault only affects one side of the system, check for battery voltage (12 volts DC) at the harness side of the relay block connector. Connect the positive voltmeter probe to the white/brown terminal (right-

23.2 the early oil pressure switch (shown) is mounted in the engine; on later models, it's in the oil filter mount

hand side) or white/violet terminal (left-hand side) and the negative probe to ground. With the ignition switch ON, press the appropriate turn signal switch. If battery voltage is shown on the meter the switch is proved good and the fault lies in the relay or lamp wiring.

6   If the complete system fails, including the hazard function, check for battery voltage at the orange wire terminal of the connector with the ignition switch ON. If battery voltage is shown, the relay is defective, although make sure that its ground wire is sound. No battery voltage indicates a power supply problem; refer to the wiring diagrams at the end of this Chapter and work back through the system to identify the cause.

7   If the turn signals work, but will not cancel, check the reed switch operation. Connect an ohmmeter between the white/green wire of the relay connector and ground. With the front wheel raised, have someone spin it while you observe the meter; it should vary from zero to infinity if the reed switch is functioning correctly.

23 Oil pressure switch - check and replacement

1   If the oil pressure warning light fails to operate properly, check the oil level and make sure it is correct.

2   If the oil level is correct, disconnect the wire from the oil pressure switch, which is located on the right side of the crankcase

(early models) or on the oil filter mount (later models) **(see illustration)**. Turn the ignition switch ON and ground the end of the wire. If the light comes on, the oil pressure switch is defective and must be replaced with a new one.

3   If the light does not come on, check the oil pressure warning light LED or bulb, the wiring between the oil pressure switch and the light, and between the light and the fuse (see the wiring diagrams at the end of this manual).

4   To replace the switch, unscrew the switch from its mount. Coat the threads of the new switch with electrically conductive sealant, then screw the unit into its hole and tighten it securely.

5   Run the engine and check for leaks.

24 Wiring diagrams - general information

Prior to troubleshooting a circuit, check the fuse to make sure it's in good condition. Make sure the battery is fully charged and check the cable connections (Sections 4, 5 and 6).

When checking a circuit, make sure all connectors are clean, with no broken or loose terminals or wires. When unplugging a connector, do not pull on the wires. Pull only on the connector housings themselves. Refer to the accompanying table for the wire color codes.

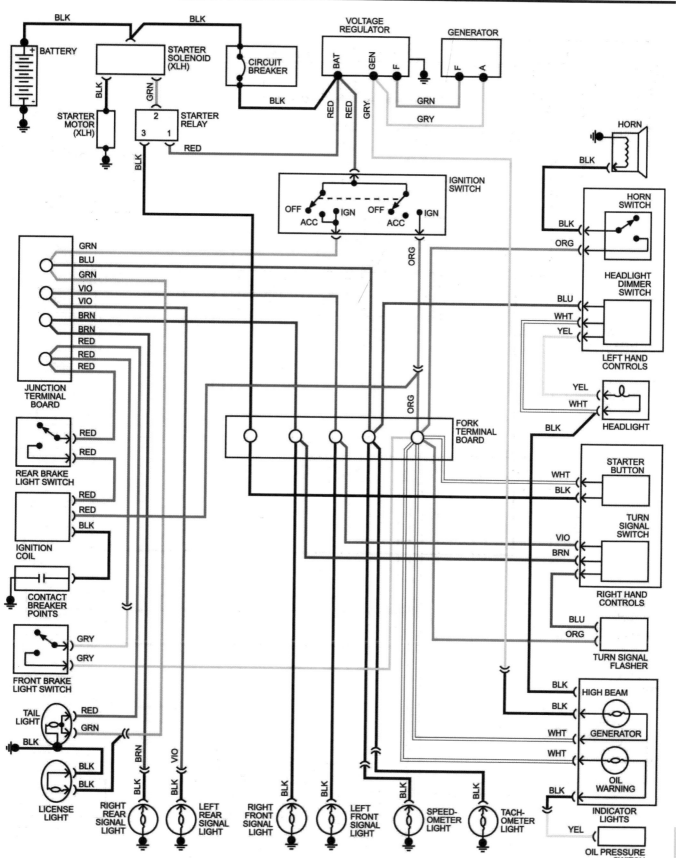

Wiring diagram - 1970 through 1972

8

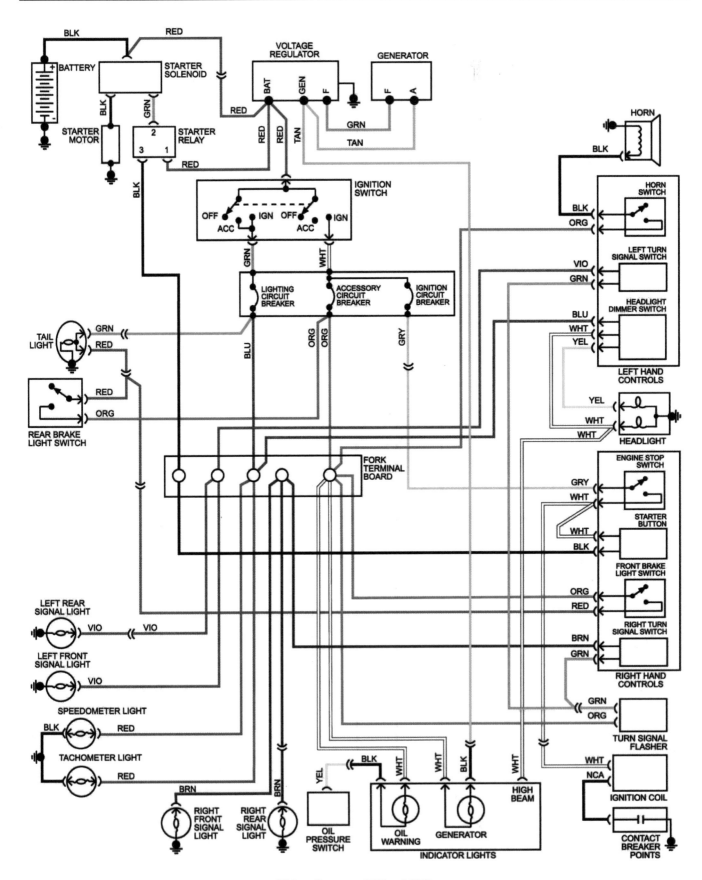

Wiring diagram - 1973 and 1974

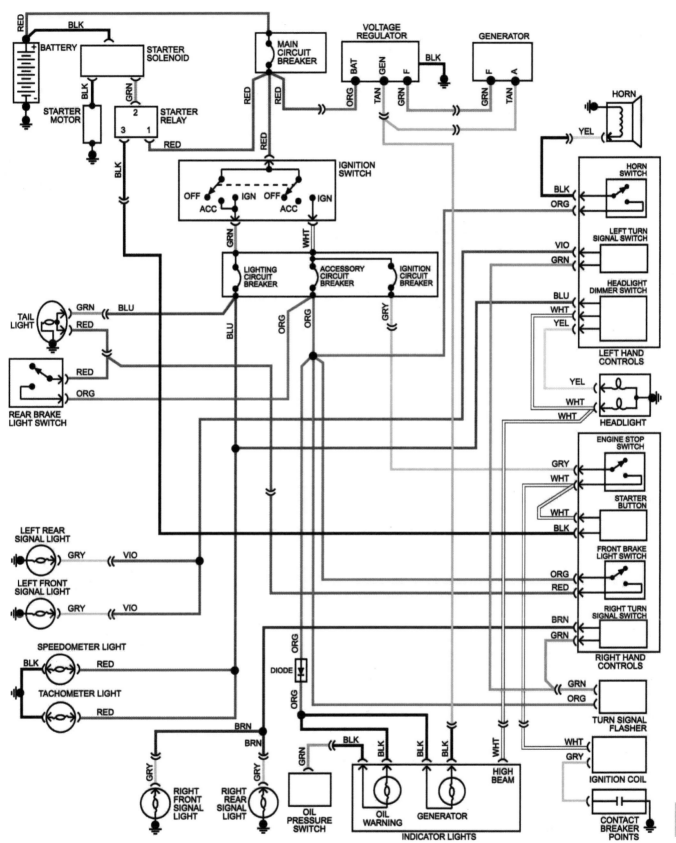

Wiring diagram - 1975 through 1979

8

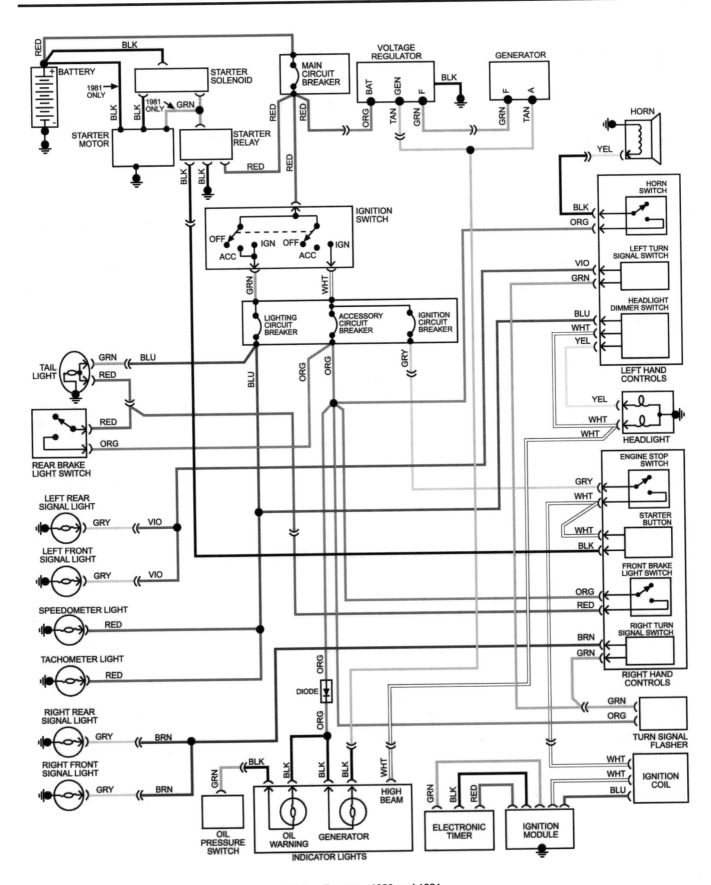

Wiring diagram - 1980 and 1981

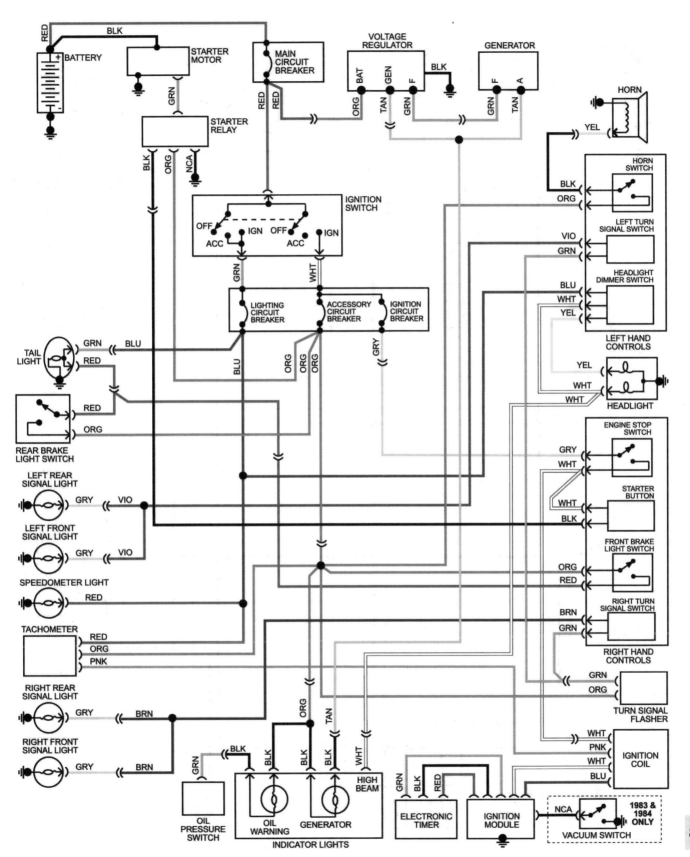

Wiring diagram - 1982 through early 1984

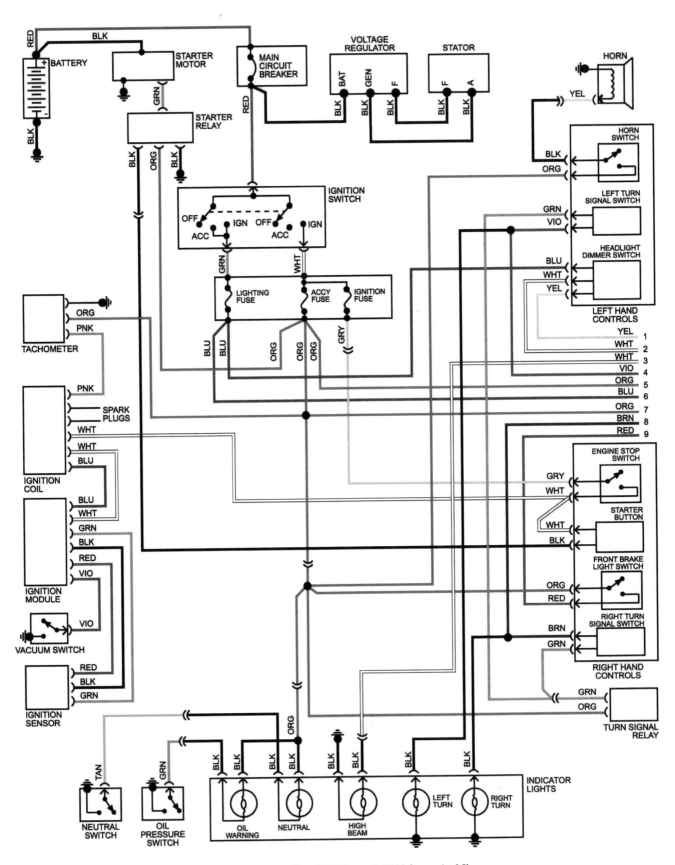

Wiring diagram - late 1984 through 1990 (page 1 of 2)

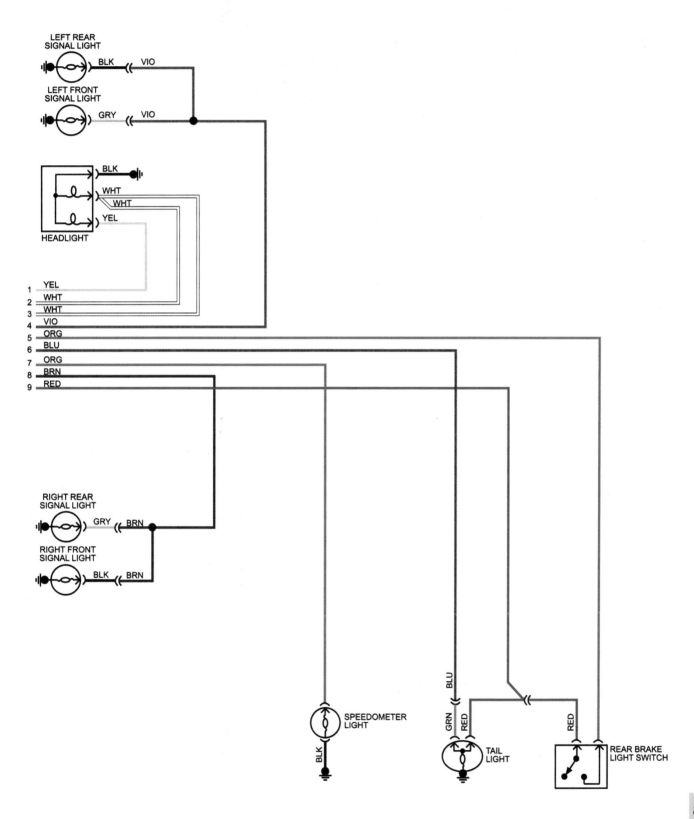

Wiring diagram - late 1984 through 1990 (page 2 of 2)

8

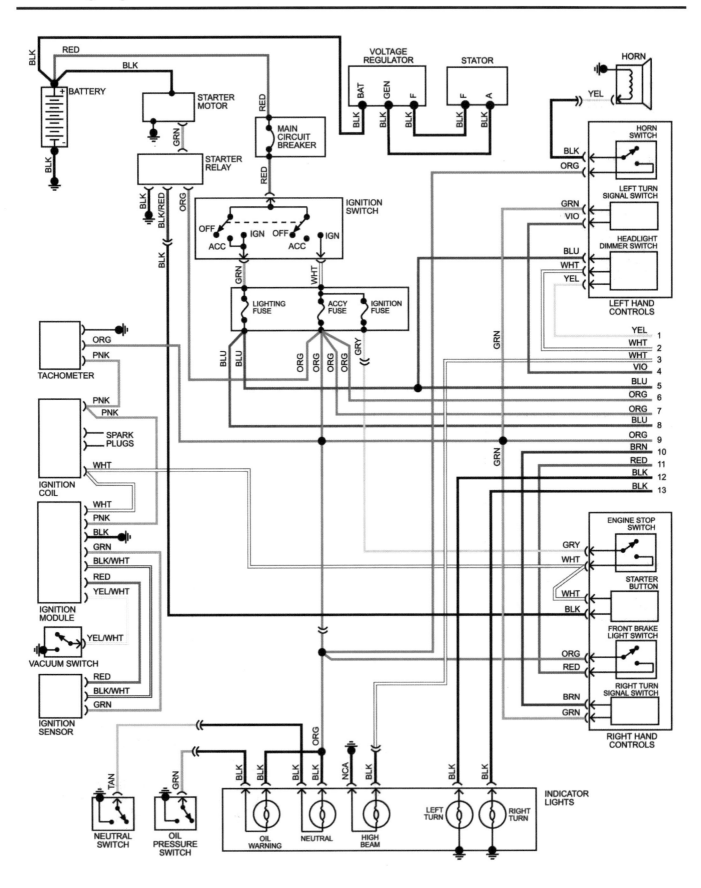

Wiring diagram - 1991 (page 1 of 2)

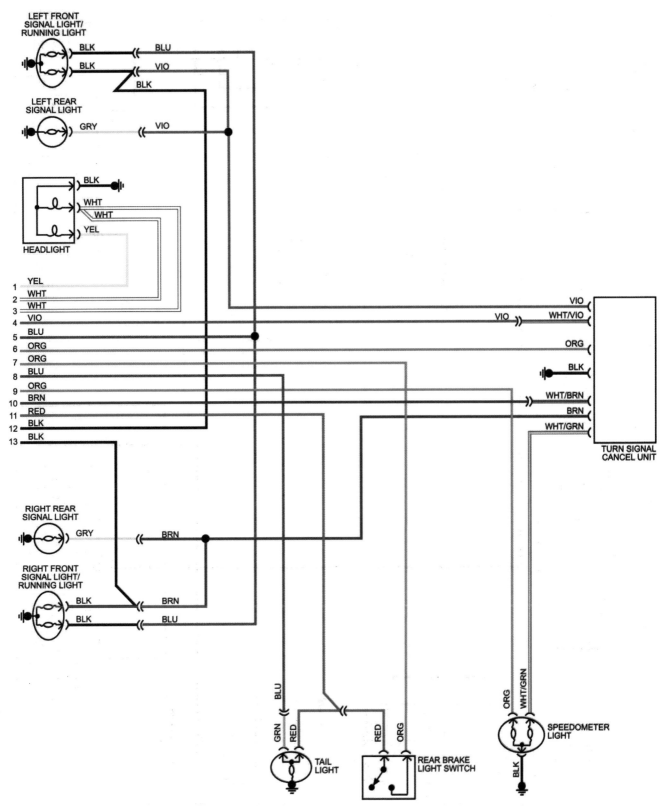

Wiring diagram - 1991 (page 2 of 2)

8

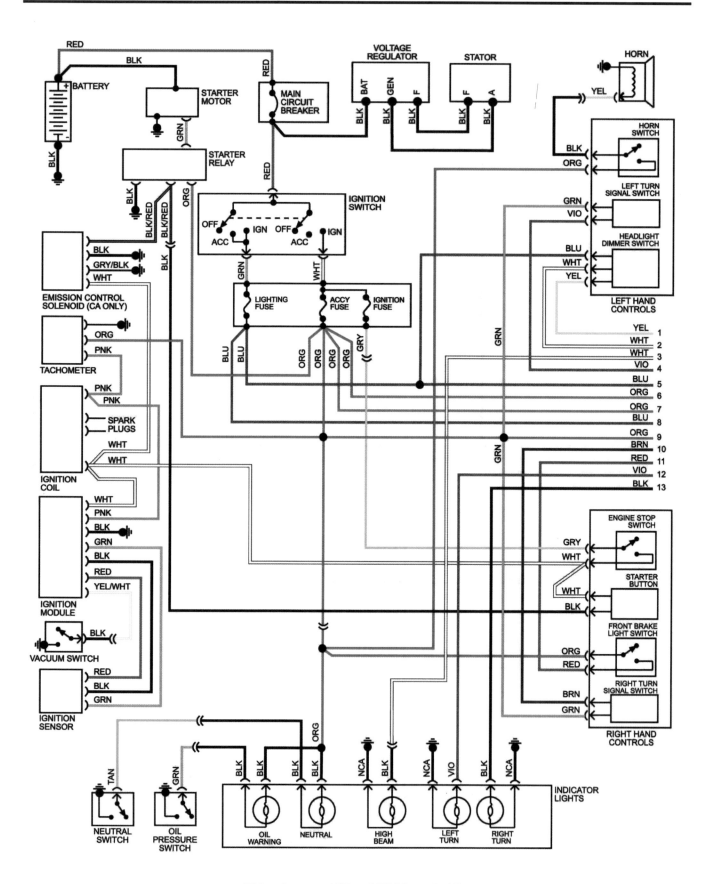

Wiring diagram - 1992 and 1993 (page 1 of 2)

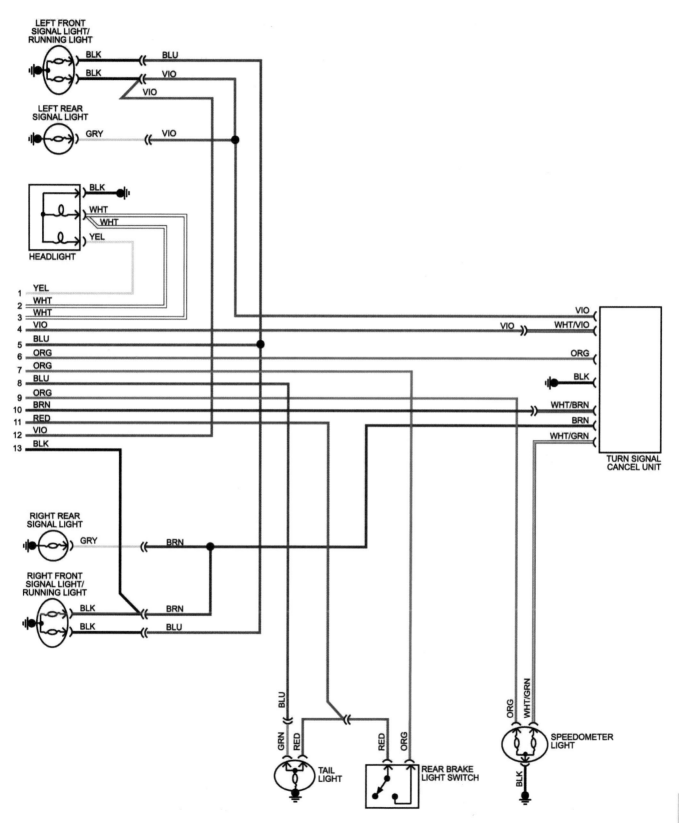

Wiring diagram - 1992 and 1993 (page 2 of 2)

8

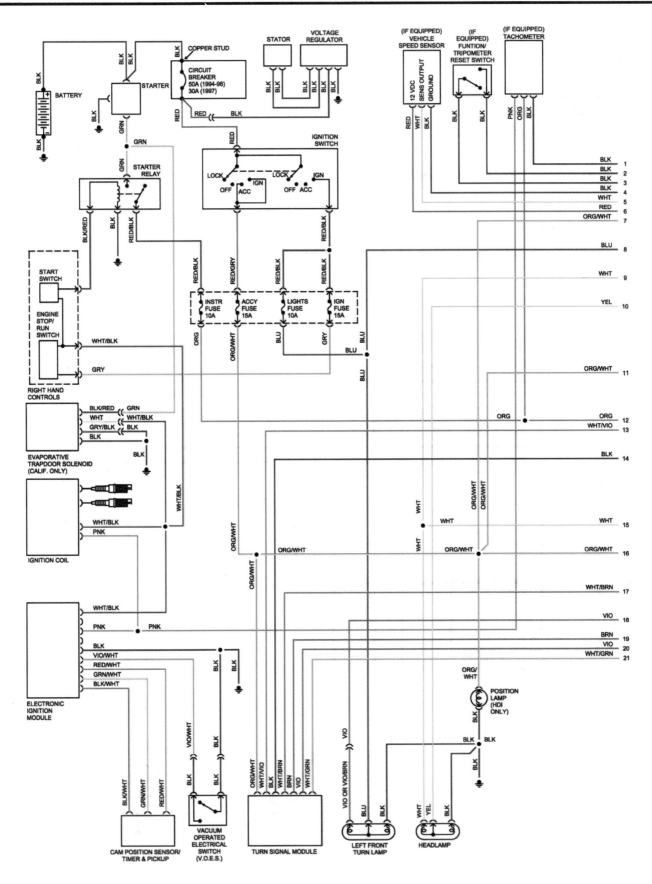

Wiring diagram - 1994 through 1997 (page 1 of 2)

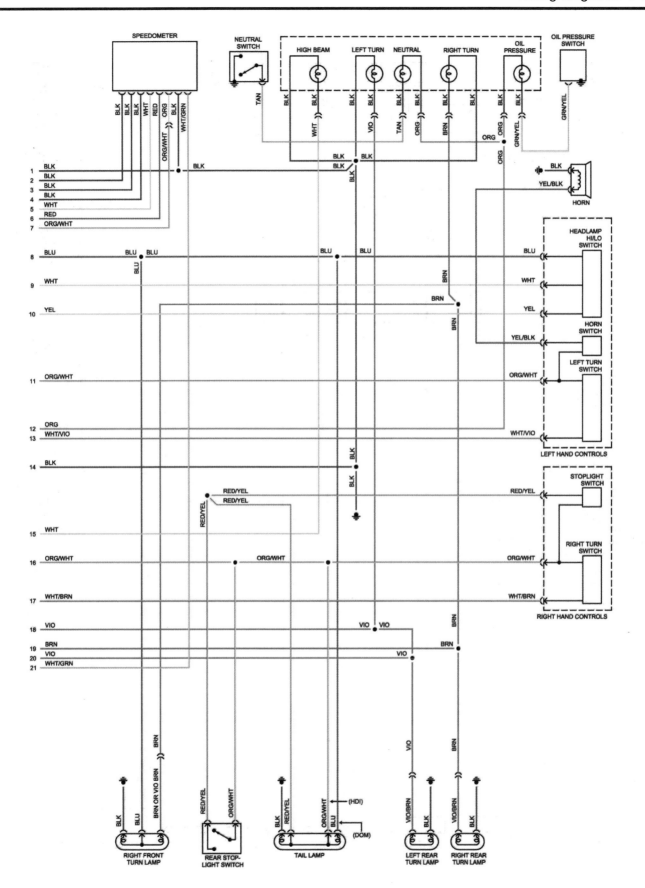

Wiring diagram - 1994 through 1997 (page 2 of 2)

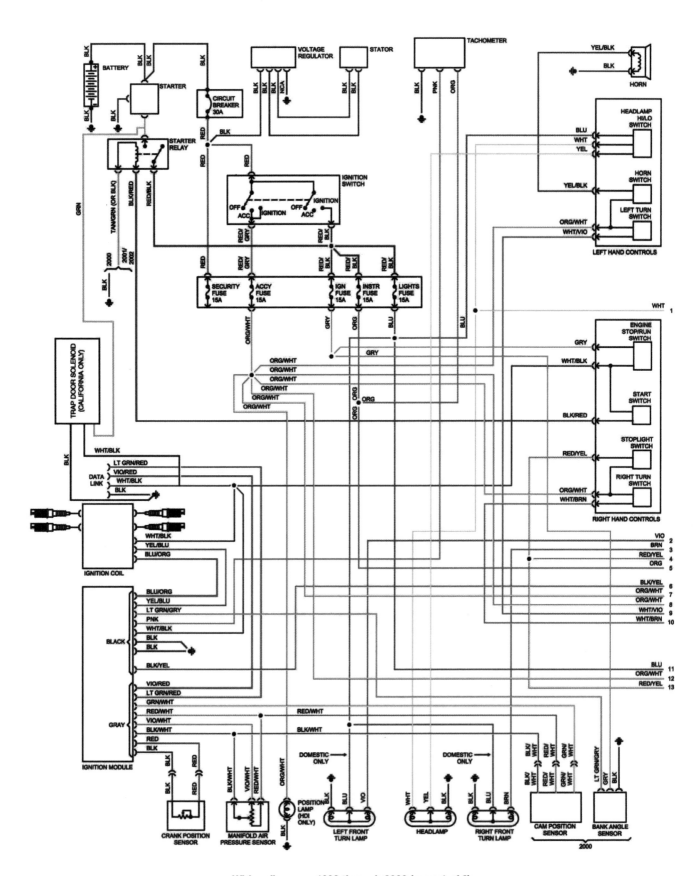

Wiring diagram - 1998 through 2003 (page 1 of 2)

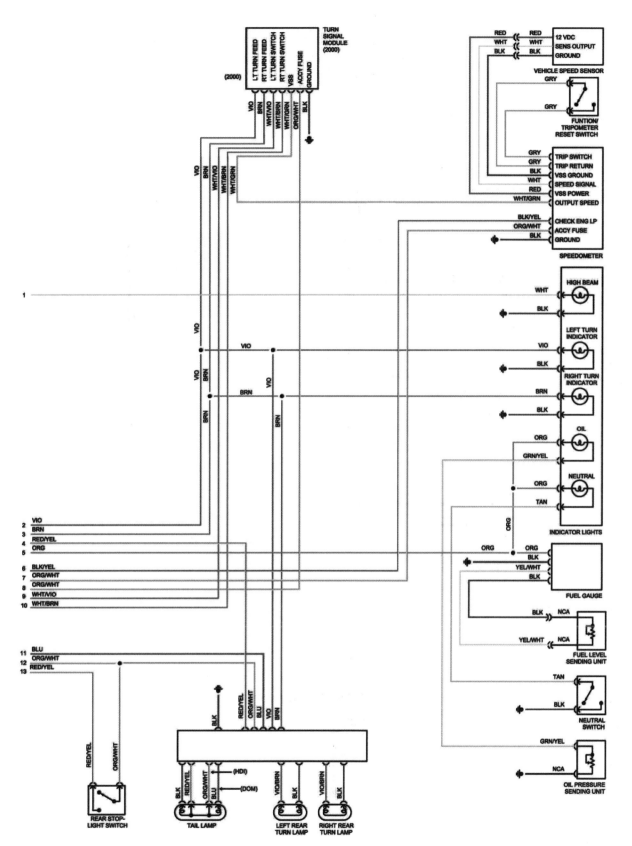

Wiring diagram - 1998 through 2003 (page 2 of 2)

1200S ignition circuit shown. See following diagram for ignition circuit on all except 1200S models.

8

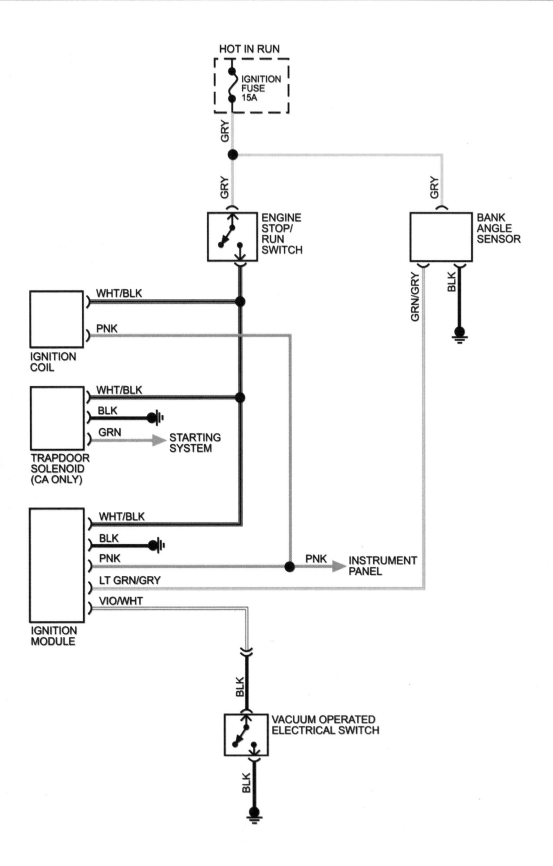

Ignition circuit diagram - 1998 through 2003, all models except 1200S

Dimensions and weights

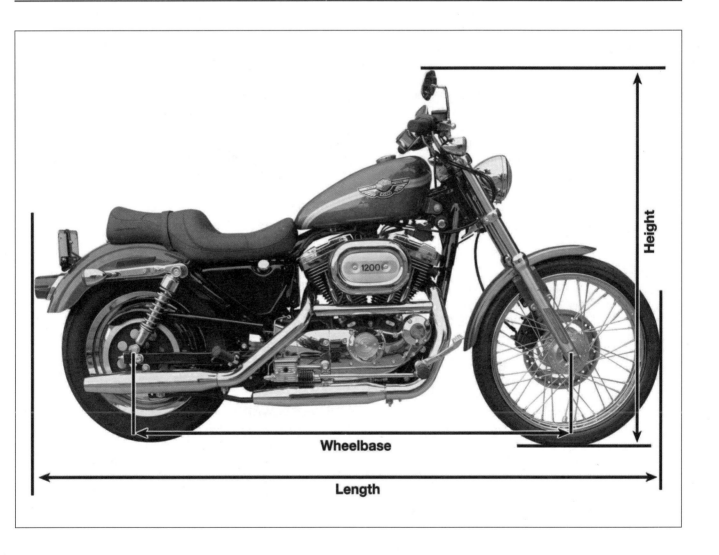

Wheelbase

1970 through 1978	58.5 inches (1485.9 mm)
1979 through 1981	
XLH and XLCH.........	58.5 inches (1485.9 mm)
XLS..........................	59.6 inches (1513.84 mm)
1982	
XLH	60 inches (1524 mm)
XLS..........................	60.75 inches (1543.05 mm)
1983	
XLH and XLX............	60 inches (1524 mm)
XLS..........................	60.75 inches (1543.05 mm)
1984 and 1985..............	60 inches (1524 mm)
1986 through 1989	
883cc (except Hugger) and 1200cc	60 inches (1524 mm)
Hugger 883cc	60.5 inches (1536.7 mm)
1990..............................	Not available
1991	
XLH 883, XLH 883 Deluxe, XLH 1200	60.2 inches (1529.08 mm)
XLH 883 Hugger	60.5 inches (1536.7 mm)
1992 through 1994	
XLH 883	60.2 inches (1529.08 mm)
XLH 883 Hugger, XLH 883 Deluxe, XLH 1200	59.0 inches (1498.6 mm)
1995 through 1998	
XLH 883	60.2 inches (1529.08 mm)
XLH 883 Hugger, XLH 1200, XL1200C, XL1200S..............	59.0 inches (1498.6 mm)
1999 through 2001	
XLH 883 and XLH 1200, XL 1200S............	60.2 inches (1529.08 mm)
XLH 883 Hugger, XL 883C, XL 1200C	59 inches (1498.6 mm)
2002 and later	
XLH 883, XL 883C, XL 883R, XLH 1200, XL 1200C	60 inches (1524 mm)
XLH 883 Hugger	59 inches (1498.6 mm)
XL 1200S..................	60.2 inches (1529.08 mm)

Overall length

1970 through 1976	87.25 inches (2216.15 mm)
1977 and 1978..............	87.75 inches (2946.4 mm)
1979 through 1981	
XLH and XLCH.........	88 inches (2235.2 mm)
XLS..........................	89.6 inches (2275.84 mm)
1982	
XLH	60 inches (1524 mm)
XLS..........................	60.75 inches (1543.05 mm)
1983 through 1989	87.5 inches (2222.5 mm)
1990	Not available
1991	87.6 inches (2225.04 mm)
1992 through 1994	
XLH 883	87.6 inches (2225.04 mm)
XLH 883 Hugger, XLH 883 Deluxe, XLH 1200	87.25 inches (2216.15 mm)
1995 through 1998	
XLH 883 and XLH 1200	87.6 inches (2225.04 mm)
XLH 883 Hugger, XL 1200C, XL 1200S............	87.25 inches (2216.15 mm)
1999 through 2001	
XLH 883, XLH 1200, XL 1200S............	87.6 inches (2225.04 mm)
XLH 883 Hugger, XL 883C, XL 1200C	87.25 inches (2216.15 mm)
2002 and later	
XLH 883, XL 883R, XLH 1200	88.1 inches (2237.74 mm)
XLH 883 Hugger	88 inches (2235.2 mm)
XL 883C, XL 1200C .	89.0 inches (2260.6)
XL 1200S..................	88.5 inches (2159.4 mm)

Overall width

1970 through 1976	
XL and XLH	33 inches (838.2 mm)
XLCH........................	32 inches (812.8 mm)
1977 and 1978..............	35 inches (889 mm)

1979 through 1981
 XLH and XLCH......... 33.8 inches
 XLS.......................... 29.2 inches
1982 through 1985 .... 33 inches (838.2 mm)
1986 through 1989
 883cc (except Hugger) and
  1200cc .... 33 inches (838.2 mm)
 Hugger 883cc .... 32 inches
1990 .... Not available
1991 through 1993
 XLH 883 .... 32 inches (812.8 mm)
 XLH 883 Hugger, XLH 883 Deluxe,
  XLH 1200 .... 33 inches (838.2 mm)
1994
 XLH 883 .... 33 inches (838.2 mm)
 XLH 883 Hugger, XLH 883 Deluxe,
  XLH 1200 .... 35 inches (889 mm)
1995 and 1996
 XLH 883, XLH 1200 . 33 inches (838.2 mm)
 XLH 883 Hugger, XL 1200C,
  XL 1200S............. 35 inches (889 mm)
1997 and 1998
 XLH 883 .... 33 inches (838.2 mm)
 XLH 883 Hugger, XLH 883 Deluxe,
  XLH 1200 .... 35 inches (889 mm)
1999 through 2001
 XLH 883 .... 33 inches (838.2 mm)
 XLH 883 Hugger, XL 883C, XLH 1200, XL 1200C,
  XL 1200S............. 35.0 inches
2002 and later
 XLH 883, XL 883R,
  XL 1200S............. 33 inches (838.2 mm)
 XLH 883 Hugger, XL 883C, XLH 1200,
  XL 1200C .... 35 inches (889 mm)

Overall height

1970 through 1976
 XL and XLH .... 40.5 inches (1028.7 mm)
 XLCH...................... 42 inches (1066.8 mm)

1977 and 1978............. 48 inches (1219.2 mm)
1979 through 1981
 XLH and XLCH......... 46.5 inches (1181.1 mm)
 XLS.......................... 42.5 inches (1079.5 mm)
1982
 XLH .... 48.5 inches (1231.9 mm)
 XLS.......................... 50.5 inches (1282.7 mm)
1983 through 1985
 XLH .... 48.5 inches (1231.9 mm)
 XLS.......................... 47.5 inches (1206.5 mm)
 XLX......................... 45 inches (1143 mm)
1986 through 1989
 883cc Hugger, 1100cc,
  1200cc .... 49.75 inches (1263.65 mm)
 883cc (except Hugger) 47.5 inches (1206.5 mm)
1990 .... Not available
1991 through 1993
 XLH 883 .... 47.5 inches (1206.5 mm)
 XLH 883 Hugger, XLH 883 Deluxe,
  XLH 1200 .... 49.75 inches (1263.65 mm)
1994
 XLH 883 and XLH 883
  Deluxe .... 47.5 inches (1206.5 mm)
 XLH 883 Hugger,
  XLH 1200 .... 49.75 inches (1263.65 mm)
1995 through 1998
 XLH 883 and
  XLH 1200 .... 47.5 inches (1206.5 mm)
 XLH 883 Hugger, XL1200C,
  XL 1200S............. 49.75 inches (1263.65 mm)
1999 through 2001
 XLH 883 .... 47.5 inches (1206.5 mm)
 XLH 883 Hugger, XLH 883C, XLH 1200, XL 1200C,
  XL 1200S............. 49.75 inches (1263.65 mm)
2002 and later
 XLH 883, XL 883R.... 47.5 inches (1206.5 mm)
 XLH 883 Hugger, XL 883C, XLH 1200,
  XL 1200C .... 49.75 inches (1263.65 mm)
 XL 1200S................. 49.5 inches (1257.3 mm)

Ground clearance

1970 and 1972
  XL and XLH .... 6.75 inches (171.45 mm)
  XLCH .... 6.5 inches (165.1 mm)
1973 through 1977 .... 7.25 inches (184.15 mm)
1979 through 1981
  XLH and XLCH .... 6.9 inches (175.26 mm)
  XLS .... 6.8 inches
1982
  XLH .... 6.75 inches (171.45 mm)
  XLS .... 7.5 inches (184.15 mm)
1983 through 1985 .... 6.75 inches (171.45 mm)
1986 through 1989
  883cc (except Hugger), 1100cc,
    1200cc .... 6.75 inches (171.45 mm)
  883cc Hugger .... 5.9 inches (149.86 mm)
1990 .... Not available
1991
  XLH 883 .... 6.75 inches (171.45 mm)
  XLH 883 Hugger, XLH 883 Deluxe,
    XLH 1200 .... 5.9 inches (149.86 mm)
1992
  XLH 883 .... 6.75 inches (171.45 mm)
  XLH 883 Hugger, XLH 883 Deluxe,
    XLH 1200 .... 4.5 inches (114.3 mm)
1993 .... 6.75 inches (171.45 mm)
1994
  XLH 883 .... 6.75 inches (171.45 mm)
  XLH 883 Hugger, XLH 883 Deluxe,
    XLH 1200 .... 4.5 inches (114.3 mm)
1995 and 1996
  XLH 883, XLH 1200,
    XL 1200S .... 6.7 inches (170.18 mm)
  XLH 883 Hugger,
    XL 1200C 4.5 inches (114.3 mm)
1997 and 1998
  XLH 883, XLH 1200, XL 1200C,
    XL 1200S .... 6.7 inches (170.18 mm)
  XLH 883 Hugger ...... 4.5 inches (114.3 mm)

1999 through 2001
  XLH 883, XL 883C, XLH 1200, XL 1200C,
    XL 1200S .... 6.7 inches (170.18 mm)
  XLH 883 Hugger ...... 4.5 inches (114.3 mm)
2002 and later
  XLH 883, XL 883R, XLH 1200,
    XL1200S .... 6.7 inches (170.18 mm)
  XL 883C
    2002 .... 6.7 inches (170.18 mm)
    2003 .... 4.7 inches (119.38 m)
  XLH 883 Hugger,
    XL 1200C .... 4.7 inches (119.38 m)

Weight (shipped from factory)

1970 through 1978 .... Not specified
1979 through 1981
  XLH .... 522 lbs (237 kg)
  XLCH .... 513 lbs (233.9 kg)
  XLS .... 527 lbs (239.26 kg)
1982
  XLH .... 512 lbs (232.49 kg)
  XLS .... 525 lbs (238.35 kg)
1983
  XLH .... 512 lbs (232.49 kg)
  XLS .... 523 lbs (237.44 kg)
  XLX .... 492 lbs (223.37 kg)
Early 1984
  XLH .... 489 lbs (222.00 kg)
  XLS .... 491 lbs (222.91 kg)
  XLX .... 481 lbs (218.37 kg)

Late 1984 and 1985
  XLH .... 476 lbs (216.1 kg)
  XLS .... 491 lbs (222.91 kg)
  XLX .... 468 lbs (212.47 kg)
1986 through 1989
  883cc .... 463 lbs (210.2 kg)
  1100cc and 1200cc . 457 lbs (207.48 kg)
1990 .... Not available

1991 and 1992
  XLH 883,
    XLH 883 Hugger.. 472 lbs (214.29 kg)
  XLH 883 Deluxe .... 484 lbs (219.74 kg)
  XLH 1200 .... 470 lbs (213.38 kg)
1993
  XLH 883, XLH 883
    Hugger .... 472 lbs (214.29 kg)
  XLH 883 Deluxe,
    XLH 1200 .... 484 lbs (219.74 kg)
1994
  XLH 883 .... 488 lbs (221.55 kg)
  XLH 883 Hugger ...... 485 lbs (220.19 kg)
  XLH 883 Deluxe .... 494 lbs (224.28 kg)
  XLH 1200 .... 490 lbs (222.46 kg)
1995 and 1996
  XLH 883 .... 488 lbs (221.55 kg)
  XLH 883 Hugger ...... 485 lbs (220.19 kg)
  XLH 1200 .... 490 lbs (222.46 kg)
  XL 1200C .... 483 lbs (219.28 kg)
  XL 1200S................. 497 lbs (225.64 kg)
1997 and 1998
  XLH 883 .... 488 lbs (221.55 kg)
  XLH 883 Hugger ...... 485 lbs (220.19 kg)
  XLH 1200 .... 494 lbs (224.28 kg)
  XL 1200C .... 483 lbs (219.28 kg)
  XL 1200S................. 497 lbs (225.64 kg)
1999 through 2001
  XLH 883 .... 488 lbs (221.55 kg)
  XLH 883 Hugger ...... 485 lbs (220.19 kg)
  XL 8883C .... 489 lbs (222.00 kg)
  XLH 1200 .... 494 lbs (224.28 kg)
  XL 1200C
    1999 .... 483 lbs (219.28 kg)
    2000 .... 491 lbs (222.91 kg)
  XL 1200S................. 497 lbs (225.64 kg)

2002 and later
  XLH 883
    2002 .... 488 lbs (221.55 kg)
    2003 .... 489 lbs (222.00 kg)
  XLH 883 Hugger ...... 486 lbs (220.64 kg)
  XL 883C .... 489 lbs (222.0 kg)
  XL 883R .... 503 lbs (228.36 kg)
  XLH 1200 and
    XL 1200C .... 491 lbs (222.91 kg)
  XL 1200S................. 501 lbs (227.45 kg)

Horsepower

1970 and 1971............. 58 hp (43.25 kw) at 6800 rpm
1972 through 1977 .... 61 hp (45.48 kw) at 6200 rpm
1978 .... 59.5 hp (44.37 kw)
                             at 6400 rpm
1979 through 1985 .... Not specified
1986 through 1989
  883 cc .... 52 hp (38.78 kw) at 6000 rpm
  1100 cc .... 62 hp (46.23 kw) at 6000 rom
  1200 cc .... 68 hp (50.71 kw) at 6000 rpm
1990 .... Not available
1991 and 1992
  883 cc .... 55 hp (41.01 kw) at 6000 rpm
  1200 cc .... 64 hp (47.72 kw) at 5200 rpm
1993 through 1997
  883 cc .... 55 hp (41.01 kw) at 6000 rpm
  1200 cc .... 65 hp (48.47 kw) at 5200 rpm
1998 through 2002
  883 cc .... 57 hp (41.54 kw) at 6000 rpm
  1200 cc
    Except 1200S...... 66 hp (49.22 kw) at 5200 rpm
    1200S................. 69 hp (51.45 kw) at 5500 rpm
2003 .... Not specified

Buying tools

A good set of tools is a fundamental requirement for servicing and repairing a motorcycle. Although there will be an initial expense in building up enough tools for servicing, this will soon be offset by the savings made by doing the job yourself. As experience and confidence grow, additional tools can be added to enable the repair and overhaul of the motorcycle. Many of the special tools are expensive and not often used so it may be preferable to rent them, or for a group of friends or motorcycle club to join in the purchase.

As a rule, it is better to buy more expensive, good quality tools. Cheaper tools are likely to wear out faster and need to be replaced more often, nullifying the original savings.

> ⚠️ **Warning: To avoid the risk of a poor quality tool breaking in use, causing injury or damage to the component being worked on, always aim to purchase tools which meet the relevant national safety standards.**

The following lists of tools do not represent the manufacturer's service tools, but serve as a guide to help the owner decide which tools are needed for this level of work. In addition, items such as an electric drill, hacksaw, files, soldering iron and a workbench equipped with a vise, may be needed. Although not classed as tools, a selection of bolts, screws, nuts, washers and pieces of tubing always come in useful.

For more information about tools, refer to the Haynes *Motorcycle Workshop Practice Techbook* (Bk. No. 3470).

Manufacturer's service tools

Inevitably certain tasks require the use of a service tool. Where possible an alternative tool or method of approach is recommended, but sometimes there is no option if personal injury or damage to the component is to be avoided. Where required, service tools are referred to in the relevant procedure.

Service tools can be purchased from JIMS Tools (www.JIMUSA.com) or Motion Pro (www.MotionPro.com). Some of the commonly-used tools, such as rotor pullers, are available in aftermarket form from mail-order motorcycle tool and accessory suppliers.

Maintenance and minor repair tools

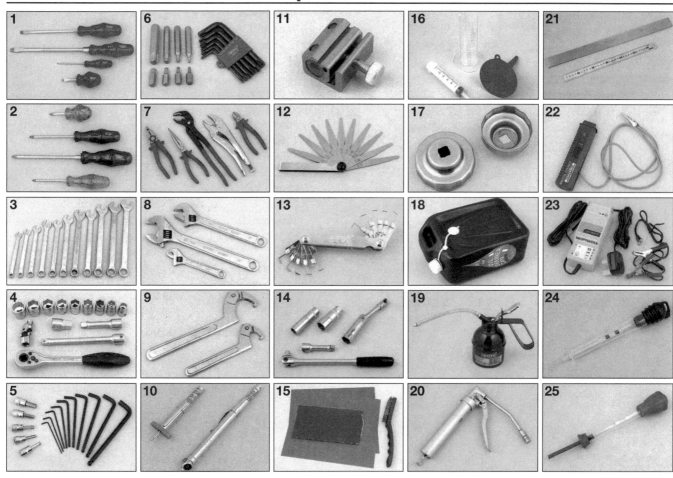

1 Set of flat-bladed screwdrivers
2 Set of Phillips head screwdrivers
3 Combination open-end and box wrenches
4 Socket set (3/8 inch or 1/2 inch drive)
5 Set of Allen keys or bits
6 Set of Torx keys or bits
7 Pliers, cutters and self-locking grips (vise grips)
8 Adjustable wrenches
9 C-spanners
10 Tread depth gauge and tire pressure gauge
11 Cable oiler clamp
12 Feeler gauges
13 Spark plug gap measuring tool
14 Spark plug wrench or deep plug sockets
15 Wire brush and emery paper
16 Calibrated syringe, measuring cup and funnel
17 Oil filter adapters
18 Oil drainer can or tray
19 Pump type oil can
20 Grease gun
21 Straight-edge and steel ruler
22 Continuity tester
23 Battery charger
24 Hydrometer (for battery specific gravity check)
25 Anti-freeze tester (for liquid-cooled engines)

Repair and overhaul tools

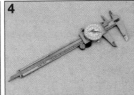

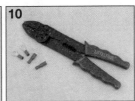

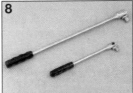

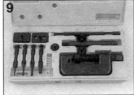

1 *Torque wrench (small and mid-ranges)*
2 *Conventional, plastic or soft-faced hammers*
3 *Impact driver set*
4 *Vernier caliper*
5 *Snap-ring pliers (internal and external, or combination)*
6 *Set of cold chisels and punches*
7 *Selection of pullers*
8 *Breaker bars*
9 *Chain breaking/ riveting tool set*
10 *Wire stripper and crimper tool*
11 *Multimeter (measures amps, volts and ohms)*
12 *Stroboscope (for dynamic timing checks)*
13 *Hose clamp (wingnut type shown)*
14 *Clutch holding tool*
15 *One-man brake/clutch bleeder kit*

Special tools

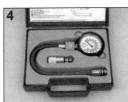

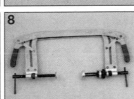
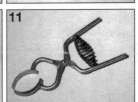
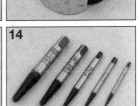

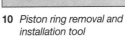
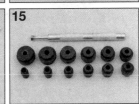

1 *Micrometers (external type)*
2 *Telescoping gauges*
3 *Dial gauge*
4 *Cylinder compression gauge*
5 *Vacuum gauges (left) or manometer (right)*
6 *Oil pressure gauge*
7 *Plastigage kit*
8 *Valve spring compressor (4-stroke engines)*
9 *Piston pin drawbolt tool*
10 *Piston ring removal and installation tool*
11 *Piston ring clamp*
12 *Cylinder bore hone (stone type shown)*
13 *Stud extractor*
14 *Screw extractor set*
15 *Bearing driver set*

1 Workshop equipment and facilities

The workbench

● Work is made much easier by raising the bike up on a ramp - components are much more accessible if raised to waist level. The hydraulic or pneumatic types seen in the dealer's workshop are a sound investment if you undertake a lot of repairs or overhauls **(see illustration 1.1)**.

1.1 Hydraulic motorcycle ramp

● If raised off ground level, the bike must be supported on the ramp to avoid it falling. Most ramps incorporate a front wheel locating clamp which can be adjusted to suit different diameter wheels. When tightening the clamp, take care not to mark the wheel rim or damage the tire - use wood blocks on each side to prevent this.
● Secure the bike to the ramp using tie-downs **(see illustration 1.2)**. If the bike has only a sidestand, and hence leans at a dangerous angle when raised, support the bike on an auxiliary stand.

1.2 Tie-downs are used around the passenger footrests to secure the bike

● Auxiliary (paddock) stands are widely available from mail order companies or motorcycle dealers and attach either to the wheel axle or swingarm pivot **(see illustration 1.3)**. If the motorcycle has a centerstand, you can support it under the crankcase to prevent it toppling while either wheel is removed **(see illustration 1.4)**.

1.3 This auxiliary stand attaches to the swingarm pivot

1.4 Always use a block of wood between the engine and jack head when supporting the engine in this way

Fumes and fire

● Refer to the Safety first! page at the beginning of the manual for full details. Make sure your workshop is equipped with a fire extinguisher suitable for fuel-related fires (Class B fire - flammable liquids) - it is not sufficient to have a water-filled extinguisher.
● Always ensure adequate ventilation is available. Unless an exhaust gas extraction system is available for use, ensure that the engine is run outside of the workshop.
● If working on the fuel system, make sure the workshop is ventilated to avoid a build-up of fumes. This applies equally to fume build-up when charging a battery. Do not smoke or allow anyone else to smoke in the workshop.

Fluids

● If you need to drain fuel from the tank, store it in an approved container marked as suitable for the storage of gasoline **(see illustration 1.5)**. Do not store fuel in glass jars or bottles.

1.5 Use an approved can only for storing gasoline

● Use proprietary engine degreasers or solvents which have a high flash-point, such as kerosene, for cleaning off oil, grease and dirt - never use gasoline for cleaning. Wear rubber gloves when handling solvent and engine degreaser. The fumes from certain solvents can be dangerous - always work in a well-ventilated area.

Dust, eye and hand protection

● Protect your lungs from inhalation of dust particles by wearing a filtering mask over the nose and mouth. Many frictional materials still contain asbestos which is dangerous to your health. Protect your eyes from spouts of liquid and sprung components by wearing a pair of protective goggles **(see illustration 1.6)**.

1.6 A fire extinguisher, goggles, mask and protective gloves should be at hand in the workshop

● Protect your hands from contact with solvents, fuel and oils by wearing rubber gloves. Alternatively apply a barrier cream to your hands before starting work. If handling hot components or fluids, wear suitable gloves to protect your hands from scalding and burns.

What to do with old fluids

● Old cleaning solvent, fuel, coolant and oils should not be poured down domestic drains or onto the ground. Package the fluid up in old oil containers, label it accordingly, and take it to a garage or disposal facility. Contact your local disposal company for location of such sites.

Note: It is illegal to dump oil down the drain. Check with your local auto parts store, disposal facility or environmental agency to see if they accept the oil for recycling.

2 Fasteners -
screws, bolts and nuts

Fastener types and applications

Bolts and screws

● Fastener head types are either of hexagonal, Torx or splined design, with internal and external versions of each type (see illustrations 2.1 and 2.2); splined head fasteners are not in common use on motorcycles. The conventional slotted or Phillips head design is used for certain screws. Bolt or screw length is always measured from the underside of the head to the end of the item (see illustration 2.11).

2.1 Internal hexagon/Allen (A), Torx (B) and splined (C) fasteners, with corresponding bits

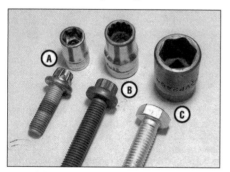

2.2 External Torx (A), splined (B) and hexagon (C) fasteners, with corresponding sockets

● Certain fasteners on the motorcycle have a tensile marking on their heads, the higher the marking the stronger the fastener. High tensile fasteners generally carry a 10 or higher marking. Never replace a high tensile fastener with one of a lower tensile strength.

Washers (see illustration 2.3)

● Plain washers are used between a fastener head and a component to prevent damage to the component or to spread the load when torque is applied. Plain washers can also be used as spacers or shims in certain assemblies. Copper or aluminum plain washers are often used as sealing washers on drain plugs.

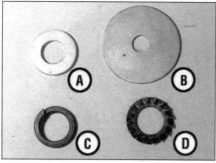

2.3 Plain washer (A), penny washer (B), spring washer (C) and serrated washer (D)

● The split-ring spring washer works by applying axial tension between the fastener head and component. If flattened, it is fatigued and must be replaced. If a plain (flat) washer is used on the fastener, position the spring washer between the fastener and the plain washer.

● Serrated star type washers dig into the fastener and component faces, preventing loosening. They are often used on electrical ground connections to the frame.

● Cone type washers (sometimes called Belleville) are conical and when tightened apply axial tension between the fastener head and component. They must be installed with the dished side against the component and often carry an OUTSIDE marking on their outer face. If flattened, they are fatigued and must be replaced.

● Tab washers are used to lock plain nuts or bolts on a shaft. A portion of the tab washer is bent up hard against one flat of the nut or bolt to prevent it loosening. Due to the tab washer being deformed in use, a new tab washer should be used every time it is removed.

● Wave washers are used to take up endfloat on a shaft. They provide light springing and prevent excessive side-to-side play of a component. Can be found on rocker arm shafts.

Nuts and cotter pins

● Conventional plain nuts are usually six-sided (see illustration 2.4). They are sized by thread diameter and pitch. High tensile nuts carry a number on one end to denote their tensile strength.

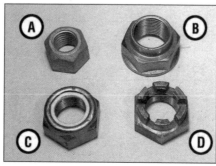

2.4 Plain nut (A), shouldered locknut (B), nylon insert nut (C) and castellated nut (D)

● Self-locking nuts either have a nylon insert, two spring metal tabs, or a shoulder which is staked into a groove in the shaft - their advantage over conventional plain nuts is a resistance to loosening due to vibration. The nylon insert type can be used a number of times, but must be replaced when the friction of the nylon insert is reduced, i.e. when the nut spins freely on the shaft. The spring tab type can be reused unless the tabs are damaged. The shouldered type must be replaced every time it is removed.

● Cotter pins are used to lock a castellated nut to a shaft or to prevent loosening of a plain nut. Common applications are wheel axles and brake torque arms. Because the cotter pin arms are deformed to lock around the nut a new cotter pin must always be used on installation - always use the correct size cotter pin which will fit snugly in the shaft hole. Make sure the cotter pin arms are correctly located around the nut (see illustrations 2.5 and 2.6).

2.5 Bend cotter pin arms as shown (arrows) to secure a castellated nut

2.6 Bend cotter pin arms as shown to secure a plain nut

Caution: If the castellated nut slots do not align with the shaft hole after tightening to the torque setting, tighten the nut until the next slot aligns with the hole - never loosen the nut to align its slot.

● R-pins (shaped like the letter R), or slip pins as they are sometimes called, are sprung and can be reused if they are otherwise in good condition. Always install R-pins with their closed end facing forwards (see illustration 2.7).

**2.7 Correct fitting of R-pin.
Arrow indicates forward direction**

Snap-rings (see illustration 2.8)

● Snap-rings are used to retain components on a shaft or in a housing and have corresponding external or internal ears to permit removal. Parallel-sided (machined) snap-rings can be installed either way round in their groove, whereas stamped snap-rings (which have a chamfered edge on one face) must be installed with the chamfer facing away from the direction of thrust load **(see illustration 2.9)**.

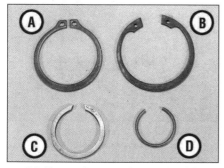

**2.8 External stamped snap-ring (A),
internal stamped snap-ring (B), machined
snap-ring (C) and wire snap-ring (D)**

● Always use snap-ring pliers to remove and install snap-rings; expand or compress them just enough to remove them. After installation, rotate the snap-ring in its groove to ensure it is securely seated. If installing a snap-ring on a splined shaft, always align its opening with a shaft channel to ensure the snap-ring ends are well supported and unlikely to catch **(see illustration 2.10)**.

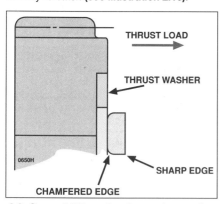

2.9 Correct fitting of a stamped snap-ring

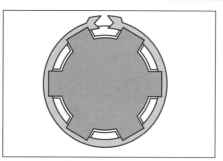

**2.10 Align snap-ring opening
with shaft channel**

● Snap-rings can wear due to the thrust of components and become loose in their grooves, with the subsequent danger of becoming dislodged in operation. For this reason, replacement is advised every time a snap-ring is disturbed.
● Wire snap-rings are commonly used as piston pin retaining clips. If a removal tang is provided, long-nosed pliers can be used to dislodge them, otherwise careful use of a small flat-bladed screwdriver is necessary. Wire snap-rings should be replaced every time they are disturbed.

Thread diameter and pitch

● Diameter of a male thread (screw, bolt or stud) is the outside diameter of the threaded portion **(see illustration 2.11)**. Most motorcycle manufacturers use the ISO (International Standards Organization) metric system expressed in millimeters. For example, M6 refers to a 6 mm diameter thread. Sizing is the same for nuts, except that the thread diameter is measured across the valleys of the nut.
● Pitch is the distance between the peaks of the thread **(see illustration 2.11)**. It is expressed in millimeters, thus a common bolt size may be expressed as 6.0 x 1.0 mm (6 mm thread diameter and 1 mm pitch). Generally pitch increases in proportion to thread diameter, although there are always exceptions.
● Thread diameter and pitch are related for conventional fastener applications and the accompanying table can be used as a guide. Additionally, the AF (Across Flats), wrench or socket size dimension of the bolt or nut **(see illustration 2.11)** is linked to thread and pitch specification. Thread pitch can be measured with a thread gauge **(see illustration 2.12)**.

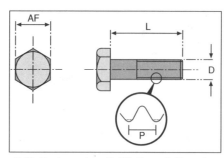

**2.11 Fastener length (L), thread diameter
(D), thread pitch (P) and head size (AF)**

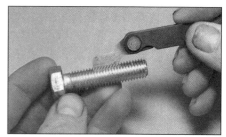

**2.12 Using a thread gauge
to measure pitch**

AF size	Thread diameter x pitch (mm)
8 mm	M5 x 0.8
8 mm	M6 x 1.0
10 mm	M6 x 1.0
12 mm	M8 x 1.25
14 mm	M10 x 1.25
17 mm	M12 x 1.25

● The threads of most fasteners are of the right-hand type, i.e. they are turned clockwise to tighten and counterclockwise to loosen. The reverse situation applies to left-hand thread fasteners, which are turned counter-clockwise to tighten and clockwise to loosen. Left-hand threads are used where rotation of a component might loosen a conventional right-hand thread fastener.

Seized fasteners

● Corrosion of external fasteners due to water or reaction between two dissimilar metals can occur over a period of time. It will build up sooner in wet conditions or in countries where salt is used on the roads during the winter. If a fastener is severely corroded it is likely that normal methods of removal will fail and result in its head being ruined. When you attempt removal, the fastener thread should be heard to crack free and unscrew easily - if it doesn't, stop there before damaging something.
● A smart tap on the head of the fastener will often succeed in breaking free corrosion which has occurred in the threads **(see illustration 2.13)**.
● An aerosol penetrating fluid (such as WD-40) applied the night beforehand may work its way down into the thread and ease removal. Depending on the location, you may be able to make up a modeling-clay well around the fastener head and fill it with penetrating fluid.

**2.13 A sharp tap on the head of a fastener
will often break free a corroded thread**

● If you are working on an engine internal component, corrosion will most likely not be a problem due to the well lubricated environment. However, components can be very tight and an impact driver is a useful tool in freeing them **(see illustration 2.14)**.

2.14 Using an impact driver to free a fastener

● Where corrosion has occurred between dissimilar metals (e.g. steel and aluminum alloy), the application of heat to the fastener head will create a disproportionate expansion rate between the two metals and break the seizure caused by the corrosion. Whether heat can be applied depends on the location of the fastener - any surrounding components likely to be damaged must first be removed **(see illustration 2.15)**. Heat can be applied using a paint stripper heat gun or clothes iron, or by immersing the component in boiling water - wear protective gloves to prevent scalding or burns to the hands.

2.15 Using heat to free a seized fastener

● As a last resort, it is possible to use a hammer and cold chisel to work the fastener head unscrewed **(see illustration 2.16)**. This will damage the fastener, but more importantly extreme care must be taken not to damage the surrounding component.

Caution: Remember that the component being secured is generally of more value than the bolt, nut or screw - when the fastener is freed, do not unscrew it with force, instead work the fastener back and forth when resistance is felt to prevent thread damage.

2.16 Using a hammer and chisel to free a seized fastener

Broken fasteners and damaged heads

● If the shank of a broken bolt or screw is accessible you can grip it with self-locking grips. The knurled wheel type stud extractor tool or self-gripping stud puller tool is particularly useful for removing the long studs which screw into the cylinder mouth surface of the crankcase or bolts and screws from which the head has broken off **(see illustration 2.17)**. Studs can also be removed by locking two nuts together on the threaded end of the stud and using a wrench on the lower nut **(see illustration 2.18)**.

2.17 Using a stud extractor tool to remove a broken crankcase stud

2.18 Two nuts can be locked together to unscrew a stud from a component

● A bolt or screw which has broken off below or level with the casing must be extracted using a screw extractor set. Centerpunch the fastener to centralize the drill bit, then drill a hole in the fastener **(see illustration 2.19)**. Select a drill bit which is approximately half to three-quarters the

2.19 When using a screw extractor, first drill a hole in the fastener . . .

diameter of the fastener and drill to a depth which will accommodate the extractor. Use the largest size extractor possible, but avoid leaving too small a wall thickness otherwise the extractor will merely force the fastener walls outwards wedging it in the casing thread.

● If a spiral type extractor is used, thread it counterclockwise into the fastener. As it is screwed in, it will grip the fastener and unscrew it from the casing **(see illustration 2.20)**.

2.20 . . . then thread the extractor counterclockwise into the fastener

● If a taper type extractor is used, tap it into the fastener so that it is firmly wedged in place. Unscrew the extractor (counter-clockwise) to draw the fastener out.

> ⚠ *Warning: Stud extractors are very hard and may break off in the fastener if care is not taken - ask a machine shop about spark erosion if this happens.*

● Alternatively, the broken bolt/screw can be drilled out and the hole retapped for an oversize bolt/screw or a diamond-section thread insert. It is essential that the drilling is carried out squarely and to the correct depth, otherwise the casing may be ruined - if in doubt, entrust the work to a machine shop.

● Bolts and nuts with rounded corners cause the correct size wrench or socket to slip when force is applied. Of the types of wrench/socket available always use a six-point type rather than an eight or twelve-point type - better grip

2.21 Comparison of surface drive box wrench (left) with 12-point type (right)

is obtained. Surface drive wrenches grip the middle of the hex flats, rather than the corners, and are thus good in cases of damaged heads **(see illustration 2.21)**.

● Slotted-head or Phillips-head screws are often damaged by the use of the wrong size screwdriver. Allen-head and Torx-head screws are much less likely to sustain damage. If enough of the screw head is exposed you can use a hacksaw to cut a slot in its head and then use a conventional flat-bladed screwdriver to remove it. Alternatively use a hammer and cold chisel to tap the head of the fastener around to loosen it. Always replace damaged fasteners with new ones, preferably Torx or Allen-head type.

HAYNES HiNT

A dab of valve grinding compound between the screw head and screwdriver tip will often give a good grip.

Thread repair

● Threads (particularly those in aluminum alloy components) can be damaged by overtightening, being assembled with dirt in the threads, or from a component working loose and vibrating. Eventually the thread will fail completely, and it will be impossible to tighten the fastener.

● If a thread is damaged or clogged with old locking compound it can be renovated with a thread repair tool (thread chaser) **(see illustrations 2.22 and 2.23)**; special thread

2.22 A thread repair tool being used to correct an internal thread

2.23 A thread repair tool being used to correct an external thread

chasers are available for spark plug hole threads. The tool will not cut a new thread, but clean and true the original thread. Make sure that you use the correct diameter and pitch tool. Similarly, external threads can be cleaned up with a die or a thread restorer file **(see illustration 2.24)**.

2.24 Using a thread restorer file

● It is possible to drill out the old thread and retap the component to the next thread size. This will work where there is enough surrounding material and a new bolt or screw can be obtained. Sometimes, however, this is not possible - such as where the bolt/screw passes through another component which must also be suitably modified, also in cases where a spark plug or oil drain plug cannot be obtained in a larger diameter thread size.

● The diamond-section thread insert (often known by its popular trade name of Heli-Coil) is a simple and effective method of replacing the thread and retaining the original size. A kit can be purchased which contains the tap, insert and installing tool **(see illustration 2.25)**. Drill out the damaged thread with the size drill specified **(see illustration 2.26)**. Carefully retap the thread **(see illustration 2.27)**. Install the

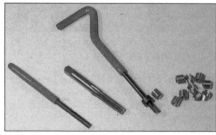

2.25 Obtain a thread insert kit to suit the thread diameter and pitch required

2.26 To install a thread insert, first drill out the original thread . . .

2.27 . . . tap a new thread . . .

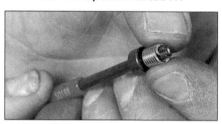

2.28 . . . fit insert on the installing tool . . .

2.29 . . . and thread into the component . . .

2.30 . . . break off the tang when complete

insert on the installing tool and thread it slowly into place using a light downward pressure **(see illustrations 2.28 and 2.29)**. When positioned between a 1/4 and 1/2 turn below the surface withdraw the installing tool and use the break-off tool to press down on the tang, breaking it off **(see illustration 2.30)**.

● There are epoxy thread repair kits on the market which can rebuild stripped internal threads, although this repair should not be used on high load-bearing components.

Thread locking and sealing compounds

● Locking compounds are used in locations where the fastener is prone to loosening due to vibration or on important safety-related items which might cause loss of control of the motorcycle if they fail. It is also used where important fasteners cannot be secured by other means such as lockwashers or cotter pins.

● Before applying locking compound, make sure that the threads (internal and external) are clean and dry with all old compound removed. Select a compound to suit the component being secured - a non-permanent general locking and sealing type is suitable for most applications, but a high strength type is needed for permanent fixing of studs in castings. Apply a drop or two of the compound to the first few threads of the fastener, then thread it into place and tighten to the specified torque. Do not apply excessive thread locking compound otherwise the thread may be damaged on subsequent removal.

● Certain fasteners are impregnated with a dry film type coating of locking compound on their threads. Always replace this type of fastener if disturbed.

● Anti-seize compounds, such as copper-based greases, can be applied to protect threads from seizure due to extreme heat and corrosion. A common instance is spark plug threads and exhaust system fasteners.

3 Measuring tools and gauges

Feeler gauges

● Feeler gauges (or blades) are used for measuring small gaps and clearances (see illustration 3.1). They can also be used to measure endfloat (sideplay) of a component on a shaft where access is not possible with a dial gauge.

● Feeler gauge sets should be treated with care and not bent or damaged. They are etched with their size on one face. Keep them clean and very lightly oiled to prevent corrosion build-up.

3.1 Feeler gauges are used for measuring small gaps and clearances - thickness is marked on one face of gauge

● When measuring a clearance, select a gauge which is a light sliding fit between the two components. You may need to use two gauges together to measure the clearance accurately.

Micrometers

● A micrometer is a precision tool capable of measuring to 0.01 or 0.001 of a millimeter. It should always be stored in its case and not in the general toolbox. It must be kept clean and never dropped, otherwise its frame or measuring anvils could be distorted resulting in inaccurate readings.

● External micrometers are used for measuring outside diameters of components and have many more applications than internal micrometers. Micrometers are available in different size ranges, typically 0 to 25 mm, 25 to 50 mm, and upwards in 25 mm steps; some large micrometers have interchangeable anvils to allow a range of measurements to be taken. Generally the largest precision measurement you are likely to take on a motorcycle is the piston diameter.

● Internal micrometers (or bore micrometers) are used for measuring inside diameters, such as valve guides and cylinder bores. Telescoping gauges and small hole gauges are used in conjunction with an external micrometer, whereas the more expensive internal micrometers have their own measuring device.

External micrometer

Note: *The conventional analogue type instrument is described. Although much easier to read, digital micrometers are considerably more expensive.*

● Always check the calibration of the micrometer before use. With the anvils closed (0 to 25 mm type) or set over a test gauge (for

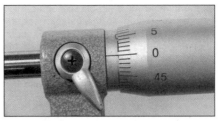

3.2 Check micrometer calibration before use

the larger types) the scale should read zero **(see illustration 3.2)**; make sure that the anvils (and test piece) are clean first. Any discrepancy can be adjusted by referring to the instructions supplied with the tool. Remember that the micrometer is a precision measuring tool - don't force the anvils closed, use the ratchet (4) on the end of the micrometer to close it. In this way, a measured force is always applied.

● To use, first make sure that the item being measured is clean. Place the anvil of the micrometer (1) against the item and use the thimble (2) to bring the spindle (3) lightly into contact with the other side of the item **(see illustration 3.3)**. Don't tighten the thimble down because this will damage the micrometer - instead use the ratchet (4) on the end of the micrometer. The ratchet mechanism applies a measured force preventing damage to the instrument.

● The micrometer is read by referring to the linear scale on the sleeve and the annular scale on the thimble. Read off the sleeve first to obtain the base measurement, then add the fine measurement from the thimble to obtain the overall reading. The linear scale on the sleeve represents the measuring range of the micrometer (eg 0 to 25 mm). The annular scale

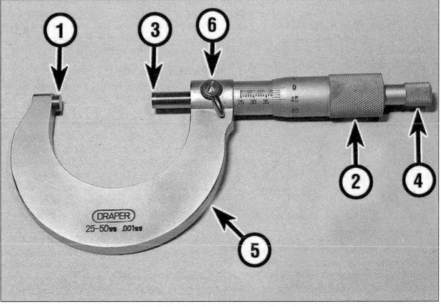

3.3 Micrometer component parts

1 Anvil	3 Spindle	5 Frame
2 Thimble	4 Ratchet	6 Locking lever

on the thimble will be in graduations of 0.01 mm (or as marked on the frame) - one full revolution of the thimble will move 0.5 mm on the linear scale. Take the reading where the datum line on the sleeve intersects the thimble's scale. Always position the eye directly above the scale otherwise an inaccurate reading will result.

In the example shown the item measures 2.95 mm **(see illustration 3.4)**:

Linear scale	2.00 mm
Linear scale	0.50 mm
Annular scale	0.45 mm
Total figure	**2.95 mm**

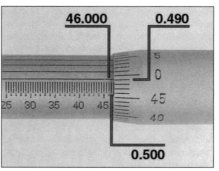

3.5 **Micrometer reading of 46.99 mm on linear and annular scales . . .**

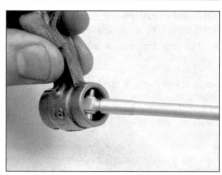

3.7 **Expand the telescoping gauge in the bore, lock its position . . .**

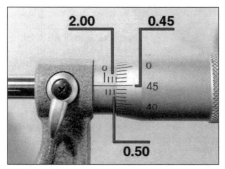

3.4 **Micrometer reading of 2.95 mm**

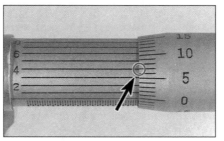

3.6 **. . . and 0.004 mm on vernier scale**

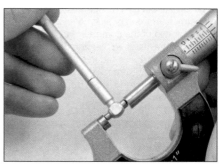

3.8 **. . . then measure the gauge with a micrometer**

Most micrometers have a locking lever (6) on the frame to hold the setting in place, allowing the item to be removed from the micrometer.
● Some micrometers have a vernier scale on their sleeve, providing an even finer measurement to be taken, in 0.001 increments of a millimeter. Take the sleeve and thimble measurement as described above, then check which graduation on the vernier scale aligns with that of the annular scale on the thimble **Note:** *The eye must be perpendicular to the scale when taking the vernier reading - if necessary rotate the body of the micrometer to ensure this.* Multiply the vernier scale figure by 0.001 and add it to the base and fine measurement figures.

In the example shown the item measures 46.994 mm **(see illustrations 3.5 and 3.6)**:

Linear scale (base)	46.000 mm
Linear scale (base)	00.500 mm
Annular scale (fine)	00.490 mm
Vernier scale	00.004 mm
Total figure	**46.994 mm**

Internal micrometer

● Internal micrometers are available for measuring bore diameters, but are expensive and unlikely to be available for home use. It is suggested that a set of telescoping gauges and small hole gauges, both of which must be used with an external micrometer, will suffice for taking internal measurements on a motorcycle.
● Telescoping gauges can be used to

measure internal diameters of components. Select a gauge with the correct size range, make sure its ends are clean and insert it into the bore. Expand the gauge, then lock its position and withdraw it from the bore **(see illustration 3.7)**. Measure across the gauge ends with a micrometer **(see illustration 3.8)**.
● Very small diameter bores (such as valve guides) are measured with a small hole gauge. Once adjusted to a slip-fit inside the component, its position is locked and the gauge withdrawn for measurement with a micrometer **(see illustrations 3.9 and 3.10)**.

Vernier caliper

Note: *The conventional linear and dial gauge type instruments are described. Digital types are easier to read, but are far more expensive.*
● The vernier caliper does not provide the precision of a micrometer, but is versatile in being able to measure internal and external diameters. Some types also incorporate a depth gauge. It is ideal for measuring clutch plate friction material and spring free lengths.
● To use the conventional linear scale vernier, loosen off the vernier clamp screws (1) and set its jaws over (2), or inside (3), the item to be measured **(see illustration 3.11)**. Slide the jaw into contact, using the thumbwheel (4) for fine movement of the sliding scale (5) then tighten the clamp screws (1). Read off the main scale (6) where the zero on the sliding scale (5) intersects it, taking the whole number to the left of the zero; this provides the base measurement. View along the sliding scale and select the division which

3.9 **Expand the small hole gauge in the bore, lock its position . . .**

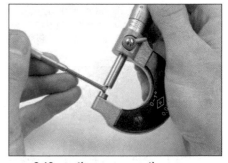

3.10 **. . . then measure the gauge with a micrometer**

lines up exactly with any of the divisions on the main scale, noting that the divisions usually represents 0.02 of a millimeter. Add this fine measurement to the base measurement to obtain the total reading.

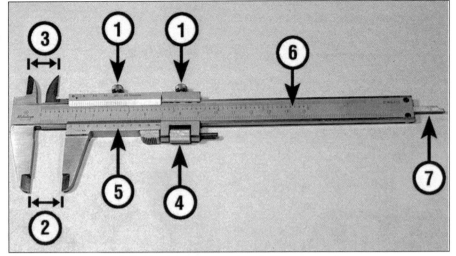

3.11 Vernier component parts (linear gauge)

1 Clamp screws   3 Internal jaws   5 Sliding scale   7 Depth gauge
2 External jaws   4 Thumbwheel   6 Main scale

In the example shown the item measures 55.92 mm (see illustration 3.12):

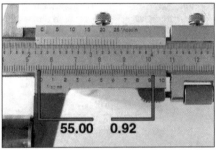

3.12 Vernier gauge reading of 55.92 mm

Base measurement	55.00 mm
Fine measurement	00.92 mm
Total figure	**55.92 mm**

● Some vernier calipers are equipped with a dial gauge for fine measurement. Before use, check that the jaws are clean, then close them fully and check that the dial gauge reads zero. If necessary adjust the gauge ring accordingly. Slacken the vernier clamp screw (1) and set its jaws over (2), or inside (3), the item to be measured (see illustration 3.13). Slide the jaws into contact, using the thumbwheel (4) for fine movement. Read off the main scale (5) where the edge of the sliding scale (6) intersects it, taking the whole number to the left of the zero; this provides the base measurement. Read off the needle position on the dial gauge (7) scale to provide the fine measurement; each division represents 0.05 of a millimeter. Add this fine measurement to the base measurement to obtain the total reading.

In the example shown the item measures 55.95 mm (see illustration 3.14):

Base measurement	55.00 mm
Fine measurement	00.95 mm
Total figure	**55.95 mm**

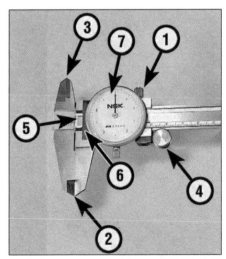

3.13 Vernier component parts (dial gauge)

1 Clamp screw   5 Main scale
2 External jaws   6 Sliding scale
3 Internal jaws   7 Dial gauge
4 Thumbwheel

3.14 Vernier gauge reading of 55.95 mm

Plastigage

● Plastigage is a plastic material which can be compressed between two surfaces to measure the oil clearance between them. The width of the compressed Plastigage is measured against a calibrated scale to determine the clearance.

● Common uses of Plastigage are for measuring the clearance between crankshaft journal and main bearing inserts, between crankshaft journal and big-end bearing inserts, and between camshaft and bearing surfaces. The following example describes big-end oil clearance measurement.

● Handle the Plastigage material carefully to prevent distortion. Using a sharp knife, cut a length which corresponds with the width of the bearing being measured and place it carefully across the journal so that it is parallel with the shaft (see illustration 3.15). Carefully install both bearing shells and the connecting rod. Without rotating the rod on the journal tighten its bolts or nuts (as applicable) to the specified torque. The connecting rod and bearings are then disassembled and the crushed Plastigage examined.

3.15 Plastigage placed across shaft journal

● Using the scale provided in the Plastigage kit, measure the width of the material to determine the oil clearance (see illustration 3.16). Always remove all traces of Plastigage after use using your fingernails.

Caution: Arriving at the correct clearance demands that the assembly is torqued correctly, according to the settings and sequence (where applicable) provided by the motorcycle manufacturer.

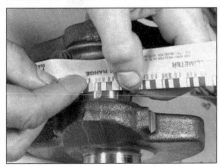

3.16 Measuring the width of the crushed Plastigage

Dial gauge or DTI (Dial Test Indicator)

● A dial gauge can be used to accurately measure small amounts of movement. Typical uses are measuring shaft runout or shaft endfloat (sideplay) and setting piston position for ignition timing on two-strokes. A dial gauge set usually comes with a range of different probes and adapters and mounting equipment.

● The gauge needle must point to zero when at rest. Rotate the ring around its periphery to zero the gauge.

● Check that the gauge is capable of reading the extent of movement in the work. Most gauges have a small dial set in the face which records whole millimeters of movement as well as the fine scale around the face periphery which is calibrated in 0.01 mm divisions. Read off the small dial first to obtain the base measurement, then add the measurement from the fine scale to obtain the total reading.

In the example shown the gauge reads 1.48 mm (see illustration 3.17):

Base measurement	1.00 mm
Fine measurement	0.48 mm
Total figure	**1.48 mm**

3.17 Dial gauge reading of 1.48 mm

● If measuring shaft runout, the shaft must be supported in vee-blocks and the gauge mounted on a stand perpendicular to the shaft. Rest the tip of the gauge against the center of the shaft and rotate the shaft slowly while watching the gauge reading (see illustration 3.18). Take several measurements along the length of the shaft and record the

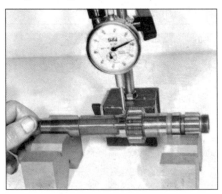

3.18 Using a dial gauge to measure shaft runout

maximum gauge reading as the amount of runout in the shaft. **Note:** *The reading obtained will be total runout at that point - some manufacturers specify that the runout figure is halved to compare with their specified runout limit.*

● Endfloat (sideplay) measurement requires that the gauge is mounted securely to the surrounding component with its probe touching the end of the shaft. Using hand pressure, push and pull on the shaft noting the maximum endfloat recorded on the gauge (see illustration 3.19).

3.19 Using a dial gauge to measure shaft endfloat

● A dial gauge with suitable adapters can be used to determine piston position BTDC on two-stroke engines for the purposes of ignition timing. The gauge, adapter and suitable length probe are installed in the place of the spark plug and the gauge zeroed at TDC. If the piston position is specified as 1.14 mm BTDC, rotate the engine back to 2.00 mm BTDC, then slowly forwards to 1.14 mm BTDC.

Cylinder compression gauges

● A compression gauge is used for measuring cylinder compression. Either the rubber-cone type or the threaded adapter type can be used. The latter is preferred to ensure a perfect seal against the cylinder head. A 0 to 300 psi (0 to 20 Bar) type gauge (for gasoline engines) will be suitable for motorcycles.

● The spark plug is removed and the gauge either held hard against the cylinder head (cone type) or the gauge adapter screwed into the cylinder head (threaded type) (see illustration 3.20). Cylinder compression is measured with the engine turning over, but not running - carry out the compression test as described in

3.20 Using a rubber-cone type cylinder compression gauge

Troubleshooting Equipment. The gauge will hold the reading until manually released.

Oil pressure gauge

● An oil pressure gauge is used for measuring engine oil pressure. Most gauges come with a set of adapters to fit the thread of the take-off point (see illustration 3.21). If the take-off point specified by the motorcycle manufacturer is an external oil pipe union, make sure that the specified replacement union is used to prevent oil starvation.

3.21 Oil pressure gauge and take-off point adapter (arrow)

● Oil pressure is measured with the engine running (at a specific rpm) and often the manufacturer will specify pressure limits for a cold and hot engine.

Straight-edge and surface plate

● If checking the gasket face of a component for warpage, place a steel rule or precision straight-edge across the gasket face and measure any gap between the straight-edge and component with feeler gauges (see illustration 3.22). Check diagonally across the component and between mounting holes (see illustration 3.23).

3.22 Use a straight-edge and feeler gauges to check for warpage

3.23 Check for warpage in these directions

● Checking individual components for warpage, such as clutch plain (metal) plates, requires a perfectly flat plate or piece of plate glass and feeler gauges.

4 Torque and leverage

What is torque?

● Torque describes the twisting force around a shaft. The amount of torque applied is determined by the distance from the center of the shaft to the end of the lever and the amount of force being applied to the end of the lever; distance multiplied by force equals torque.

● The manufacturer applies a measured torque to a bolt or nut to ensure that it will not loosen in use and to hold two components securely together without movement in the joint. The actual torque setting depends on the thread size, bolt or nut material and the composition of the components being held.

● Too little torque may cause the fastener to loosen due to vibration, whereas too much torque will distort the joint faces of the component or cause the fastener to shear off. Always stick to the specified torque setting.

Using a torque wrench

● Check the calibration of the torque wrench and make sure it has a suitable range for the job. Torque wrenches are available in Nm (Newton-meters), kgf m (kilograms-force meter), lbf ft (pounds-feet), lbf in (inch-pounds). Do not confuse lbf ft with lbf in.

● Adjust the tool to the desired torque on the scale (see illustration 4.1). If your torque wrench is not calibrated in the units specified, carefully convert the figure (see *Conversion Factors*). A manufacturer sometimes gives a torque setting as a range (8 to 10 Nm) rather than a single figure - in this case set the tool midway between the two settings. The same torque may be expressed as 9 Nm ± 1 Nm. Some torque wrenches have a method of locking the setting so that it isn't inadvertently altered during use.

● Install the bolts/nuts in their correct location and secure them lightly. Their threads must be clean and free of any old locking compound. Unless specified the threads and flange should be dry - oiled threads are necessary in certain circumstances and the manufacturer will take this into account in the specified torque figure. Similarly, the manufacturer may also specify the application of thread-locking compound.

● Tighten the fasteners in the specified sequence until the torque wrench clicks, indicating that the torque setting has been reached. Apply the torque again to double-check the setting. Where different thread diameter fasteners secure the component, as a rule tighten the larger diameter ones first.

● When the torque wrench has been finished with, release the lock (where applicable) and fully back off its setting to zero - do not leave the torque wrench tensioned. Also, do not use a torque wrench for loosening a fastener.

Angle-tightening

● Manufacturers often specify a figure in degrees for final tightening of a fastener. This usually follows tightening to a specific torque setting.

● A degree disc can be set and attached to the socket (see illustration 4.2) or a protractor can be used to mark the angle of movement on the bolt/nut head and the surrounding casting (see illustration 4.3).

4.2 Angle tightening can be accomplished with a torque-angle gauge ...

4.1 Set the torque wrench index mark to the setting required, in this case 12 Nm

4.3 ... or by marking the angle on the surrounding component

Loosening sequences

● Where more than one bolt/nut secures a component, loosen each fastener evenly a little at a time. In this way, not all the stress of the joint is held by one fastener and the components are not likely to distort.

● If a tightening sequence is provided, work in the REVERSE of this, but if not, work from the outside in, in a criss-cross sequence (see illustration 4.4).

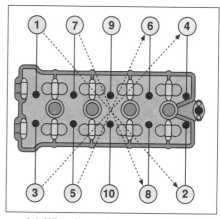

4.4 When loosening, work from the outside inwards

Tightening sequences

● If a component is held by more than one fastener it is important that the retaining bolts/nuts are tightened evenly to prevent uneven stress build-up and distortion of sealing faces. This is especially important on high-compression joints such as the cylinder head.

● A sequence is usually provided by the manufacturer, either in a diagram or actually marked in the casting. If not, always start in the center and work outwards in a criss-cross pattern (see illustration 4.5). Start off by securing all bolts/nuts finger-tight, then set the torque wrench and tighten each fastener by a small amount in sequence until the final torque is reached. By following this practice,

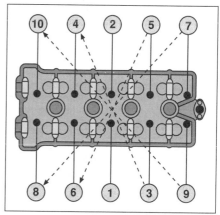

4.5 When tightening, work from the inside outwards

the joint will be held evenly and will not be distorted. Important joints, such as the cylinder head and big-end fasteners often have two- or three-stage torque settings.

Applying leverage

● Use tools at the correct angle. Position a socket or wrench on the bolt/nut so that you pull it towards you when loosening. If this can't be done, push the wrench without curling your fingers around it **(see illustration 4.6)** - the wrench may slip or the fastener loosen suddenly, resulting in your fingers being crushed against a component.

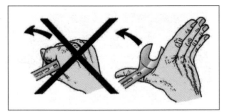

4.6 If you can't pull on the wrench to loosen a fastener, push with your hand open

● Additional leverage is gained by extending the length of the lever. The best way to do this is to use a breaker bar instead of the regular length tool, or to slip a length of tubing over the end of the wrench or socket.
● If additional leverage will not work, the fastener head is either damaged or firmly corroded in place (see *Fasteners*).

5 Bearings

Bearing removal and installation

Drivers and sockets

● Before removing a bearing, always inspect the casing to see which way it must be driven out - some casings will have retaining plates or a cast step. Also check for any identifying markings on the bearing and, if installed to a certain depth, measure this at this stage. Some roller bearings are sealed on one side - take note of the original installed position.
● Bearings can be driven out of a casing using a bearing driver tool (with the correct size head) or a socket of the correct diameter. Select the driver head or socket so that it contacts the outer race of the bearing, not the balls/rollers or inner race. Always support the casing around the bearing housing with wood blocks, otherwise there is a risk of fracture. The bearing is driven out with a few blows on the driver or socket from a heavy mallet. Unless access is severely restricted (as with wheel bearings), a pin-punch is not recommended unless it is moved around the bearing to keep it square in its housing.

● The same equipment can be used to install bearings. Make sure the bearing housing is supported on wood blocks and line up the bearing in its housing. Install the bearing as noted on removal - generally they are installed with their marked side facing outwards. Tap the bearing squarely into its housing using a driver or socket which bears only on the bearing's outer race - contact with the bearing balls/rollers or inner race will destroy it **(see illustrations 5.1 and 5.2).**
● Check that the bearing inner race and balls/rollers rotate freely.

5.1 Using a bearing driver against the bearing's outer race

5.2 Using a large socket against the bearing's outer race

Pullers and slide-hammers

● Where a bearing is pressed on a shaft a puller will be required to extract it **(see illustration 5.3).** Make sure that the puller clamp or legs fit securely behind the bearing and are unlikely to slip out. If pulling a bearing

5.3 This bearing puller clamps behind the bearing and pressure is applied to the shaft end to draw the bearing off

off a gear shaft for example, you may have to locate the puller behind a gear pinion if there is no access to the race and draw the gear pinion off the shaft as well **(see illustration 5.4).**

> *Caution: Ensure that the puller's center bolt locates securely against the end of the shaft and will not slip when pressure is applied. Also ensure that puller does not damage the shaft end.*

5.4 Where no access is available to the rear of the bearing, it is sometimes possible to draw off the adjacent component

● Operate the puller so that its center bolt exerts pressure on the shaft end and draws the bearing off the shaft.
● When installing the bearing on the shaft, tap only on the bearing's inner race - contact with the balls/rollers or outer race will destroy the bearing. Use a socket or length of tubing as a drift which fits over the shaft end **(see illustration 5.5).**

5.5 When installing a bearing on a shaft use a piece of tubing which bears only on the bearing's inner race

● Where a bearing locates in a blind hole in a casing, it cannot be driven or pulled out as described above. A slide-hammer with a knife-edged bearing puller attachment will be required. The puller attachment passes through the bearing, and when tightened, expands to fit firmly behind the bearing **(see illustration 5.6).** By operating the slide-hammer part of the tool the bearing is jarred out of its housing **(see illustration 5.7).**
● It is possible, if the bearing is of reasonable weight, for it to drop out of its housing if the casing is heated as described opposite. If this

5.6 Expand the bearing puller so that it locks behind the bearing . . .

5.7 . . . attach the slide hammer to the bearing puller

method is attempted, first prepare a work surface which will enable the casing to be tapped face down to help dislodge the bearing - a wood surface is ideal since it will not damage the casing's gasket surface. Wearing protective gloves, tap the heated casing several times against the work surface to dislodge the bearing under its own weight **(see illustration 5.8)**.

5.8 Tapping a casing face down on wood blocks can often dislodge a bearing

● Bearings can be installed in blind holes using the driver or socket method described above.

Drawbolts

● Where a bearing or bushing is set in the eye of a component, such as a suspension linkage arm or connecting rod small-end, removal by drift may damage the component. Furthermore, a rubber bushing in a shock absorber eye cannot successfully be driven out of position. If access is available to a hydraulic press, the task is straightforward. If not, a drawbolt can be fabricated to extract the bearing or bushing.

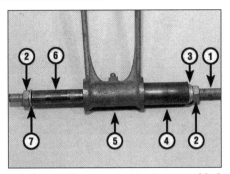

5.9 Drawbolt component parts assembled on a suspension arm

1 Bolt or length of threaded bar
2 Nuts
3 Washer (external diameter greater than tubing internal diameter)
4 Tubing (internal diameter sufficient to accommodate bearing)
5 Suspension arm with bearing
6 Tubing (external diameter slightly smaller than bearing)
7 Washer (external diameter slightly smaller than bearing)

5.10 Drawing the bearing out of the suspension arm

● To extract the bearing/bushing you will need a long bolt with nut (or piece of threaded bar with two nuts), a piece of tubing which has an internal diameter larger than the bearing/bushing, another piece of tubing which has an external diameter slightly smaller than the bearing/bushing, and a selection of washers **(see illustrations 5.9 and 5.10)**. Note that the pieces of tubing must be of the same length, or longer, than the bearing/bushing.
● The same kit (without the pieces of tubing) can be used to draw the new bearing/bushing back into place **(see illustration 5.11)**.

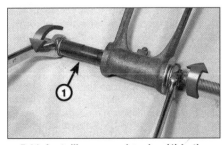

5.11 Installing a new bearing (1) in the suspension arm

Temperature change

● If the bearing's outer race is a tight fit in the casing, the aluminum casing can be heated to release its grip on the bearing. Aluminum will expand at a greater rate than the steel bearing outer race. There are several ways to do this, but avoid any localized extreme heat (such as a blow torch) - aluminum alloy has a low melting point.
● Approved methods of heating a casing are using a domestic oven (heated to 100°C/200°F) or immersing the casing in boiling water **(see illustration 5.12)**. Low temperature range localized heat sources such as a paint stripper heat gun or clothes iron can also be used **(see illustration 5.13)**. Alternatively, soak a rag in boiling water, wring it out and wrap it around the bearing housing.

> ⚠ **Warning: All of these methods require care in use to prevent scalding and burns to the hands. Wear protective gloves when handling hot components.**

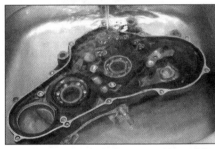

5.12 A casing can be immersed in a sink of boiling water to aid bearing removal

5.13 Using a localized heat source to aid bearing removal

● If heating the whole casing note that plastic components, such as the neutral switch, may suffer - remove them beforehand.
● After heating, remove the bearing as described above. You may find that the expansion is sufficient for the bearing to fall out of the casing under its own weight or with a light tap on the driver or socket.
● If necessary, the casing can be heated to aid bearing installation, and this is sometimes the recommended procedure if the motorcycle manufacturer has designed the housing and bearing fit with this intention.

● Installation of bearings can be eased by placing them in a freezer the night before installation. The steel bearing will contract slightly, allowing easy insertion in its housing. This is often useful when installing steering head outer races in the frame.

Bearing types and markings

● Plain shell bearings, ball bearings, needle roller bearings and tapered roller bearings will all be found on motorcycles (see illustrations 5.14 and 5.15). The ball and roller types are usually caged between an inner and outer race, but uncaged variations may be found.

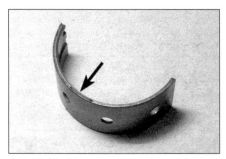

5.14 Shell bearings are either plain or grooved. They are usually identified by color code (arrow)

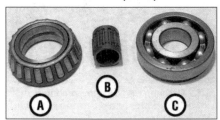

5.15 Tapered roller bearing (A), needle roller bearing (B) and ball journal bearing (C)

● Shell bearings (often called inserts) are usually found at the crankshaft main and connecting rod big-end where they are good at coping with high loads. They are made of a phosphor-bronze material and are impregnated with self-lubricating properties.
● Ball bearings and needle roller bearings consist of a steel inner and outer race with the balls or rollers between the races. They require constant lubrication by oil or grease and are good at coping with axial loads. Taper roller bearings consist of rollers set in a tapered cage set on the inner race; the outer race is separate. They are good at coping with axial loads and prevent movement along the shaft - a typical application is in the steering head.
● Bearing manufacturers produce bearings to ISO size standards and stamp one face of the bearing to indicate its internal and external diameter, load capacity and type (see illustration 5.16).
● Metal bushings are usually of phosphor-bronze material. Rubber bushings are used in suspension mounting eyes. Fiber bushings have also been used in suspension pivots.

5.16 Typical bearing marking

Bearing troubleshooting

● If a bearing outer race has spun in its housing, the housing material will be damaged. You can use a bearing locking compound to bond the outer race in place if damage is not too severe.
● Shell bearings will fail due to damage of their working surface, as a result of lack of lubrication, corrosion or abrasive particles in the oil (see illustration 5.17). Small particles of dirt in the oil may embed in the bearing material whereas larger particles will score the bearing and shaft journal. If a number of short journeys are made, insufficient heat will be generated to drive off condensation which has built up on the bearings.

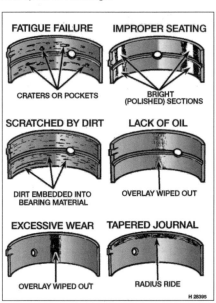

5.17 Typical bearing failures

● Ball and roller bearings will fail due to lack of lubrication or damage to the balls or rollers. Tapered-roller bearings can be damaged by overloading them. Unless the bearing is sealed on both sides, wash it in kerosene to remove all old grease then allow it to dry. Make a visual inspection looking to dented balls or rollers, damaged cages and worn or pitted races (see illustration 5.18).
● A ball bearing can be checked for wear by listening to it when spun. Apply a film of light oil to the bearing and hold it close to the ear - hold the outer race with one hand and spin the inner

5.18 Example of ball journal bearing with damaged balls and cages

5.19 Hold outer race and listen to inner race when spun

race with the other hand (see illustration 5.19). The bearing should be almost silent when spun; if it grates or rattles it is worn.

6 Oil seals

Oil seal removal and installation

● Oil seals should be replaced every time a component is dismantled. This is because the seal lips will become set to the sealing surface and will not necessarily reseal.
● Oil seals can be pried out of position using a large flat-bladed screwdriver (see illustration 6.1). In the case of crankcase seals, check first that the seal is not lipped on the inside, preventing its removal with the crankcases joined.

6.1 Pry out oil seals with a large flat-bladed screwdriver

● New seals are usually installed with their marked face (containing the seal reference code) outwards and the spring side towards the fluid being retained. In certain cases, such as a two-stroke engine crankshaft seal, a double lipped seal may be used due to there being fluid or gas on each side of the joint.

● Use a bearing driver or socket which bears only on the outer hard edge of the seal to install it in the casing - tapping on the inner edge will damage the sealing lip.

Oil seal types and markings

● Oil seals are usually of the single-lipped type. Double-lipped seals are found where a liquid or gas is on both sides of the joint.
● Oil seals can harden and lose their sealing ability if the motorcycle has been in storage for a long period - replacement is the only solution.
● Oil seal manufacturers also conform to the ISO markings for seal size - these are molded into the outer face of the seal **(see illustration 6.2)**.

6.2 These oil seal markings indicate inside diameter, outside diameter and seal thickness

7 Gaskets and sealants

Types of gasket and sealant

● Gaskets are used to seal the mating surfaces between components and keep lubricants, fluids, vacuum or pressure contained within the assembly. Aluminum gaskets are sometimes found at the cylinder joints, but most gaskets are paper-based. If the mating surfaces of the components being joined are undamaged the gasket can be installed dry, although a dab of sealant or grease will be useful to hold it in place during assembly.
● RTV (Room Temperature Vulcanizing) silicone rubber sealants cure when exposed to moisture in the atmosphere. These sealants are good at filling pits or irregular gasket faces, but will tend to be forced out of the joint under very high torque. They can be used to replace a paper gasket, but first make sure that the width of the paper gasket is not essential to the shimming of internal components. RTV sealants should not be used on components containing gasoline.
● Non-hardening, semi-hardening and hard setting liquid gasket compounds can be used with a gasket or between a metal-to-metal joint. Select the sealant to suit the application: universal non-hardening sealant can be used on virtually all joints; semi-hardening on joint faces which are rough or damaged; hard setting sealant on joints which require a permanent bond and are subjected to high temperature and pressure. **Note:** *Check first if the paper gasket has a bead of sealant*

impregnated in its surface before applying additional sealant.
● When choosing a sealant, make sure it is suitable for the application, particularly if being applied in a high-temperature area or in the vicinity of fuel. Certain manufacturers produce sealants in either clear, silver or black colors to match the finish of the engine. This has a particular application on motorcycles where much of the engine is exposed.
● Do not over-apply sealant. That which is squeezed out on the outside of the joint can be wiped off, whereas an excess of sealant on the inside can break off and clog oilways.

Breaking a sealed joint

● Age, heat, pressure and the use of hard setting sealant can cause two components to stick together so tightly that they are difficult to separate using finger pressure alone. Do not resort to using levers unless there is a pry point provided for this purpose **(see illustration 7.1)** or else the gasket surfaces will be damaged.
● Use a soft-faced hammer **(see illustration 7.2)** or a wood block and conventional hammer to strike the component near the mating surface. Avoid hammering against cast extremities since they may break off. If this method fails, try using a wood wedge between the two components.

Caution: If the joint will not separate, double-check that you have removed all the fasteners.

7.1 If a pry point is provided, apply gentle pressure with a flat-bladed screwdriver

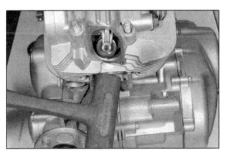

7.2 Tap around the joint with a soft-faced mallet if necessary - don't strike cooling fins

Removal of old gasket and sealant

● Paper gaskets will most likely come away complete, leaving only a few traces stuck on

Most components have one or two hollow locating dowels between the two gasket faces. If a dowel cannot be removed, do not resort to gripping it with pliers - it will almost certainly be distorted. Install a close-fitting socket or Phillips screwdriver into the dowel and then grip the outer edge of the dowel to free it.

the sealing faces of the components. It is imperative that all traces are removed to ensure correct sealing of the new gasket.
● Very carefully scrape all traces of gasket away making sure that the sealing surfaces are not gouged or scored by the scraper **(see illustrations 7.3, 7.4 and 7.5)**. Stubborn deposits can be removed by spraying with an aerosol gasket remover. Final preparation of

7.3 Paper gaskets can be scraped off with a gasket scraper tool . . .

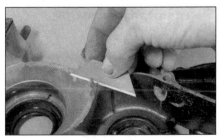

7.4 . . . a knife blade . . .

7.5 . . . or a household scraper

7.6 Fine abrasive paper is wrapped around a flat file to clean up the gasket face

7.7 A kitchen scourer can be used on stubborn deposits

the gasket surface can be made with very fine abrasive paper or a plastic kitchen scourer **(see illustrations 7.6 and 7.7)**.
● Old sealant can be scraped or peeled off components, depending on the type originally used. Note that gasket removal compounds are available to avoid scraping the components clean; make sure the gasket remover suits the type of sealant used.

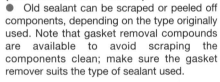

8 Chains

Breaking and joining final drive chains

● Drive chains for all but small bikes are continuous and do not have a clip-type connecting link. The chain must be broken using a chain breaker tool and the new chain securely riveted together using a new soft rivet-type link. Never use a clip-type connecting link instead of a rivet-type link, except in an emergency. Various chain breaking and riveting tools are available, either as separate tools or combined as illustrated in the accompanying photographs - read the instructions supplied with the tool carefully.

> ⚠ **Warning: The need to rivet the new link pins correctly cannot be overstressed - loss of control of the motorcycle is very likely to result if the chain breaks in use.**

● Rotate the chain and look for the soft link. The soft link pins look like they have been

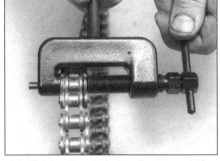

8.1 Tighten the chain breaker to push the pin out of the link . . .

8.2 . . . withdraw the pin, remove the tool . . .

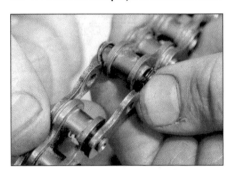

8.3 . . . and separate the chain link

deeply center-punched instead of peened over like all the other pins **(see illustration 8.9)** and its sideplate may be a different color. Position the soft link midway between the sprockets and assemble the chain breaker tool over one of the soft link pins **(see illustration 8.1)**. Operate the tool to push the pin out through the chain **(see illustration 8.2)**. On an O-ring chain, remove the O-rings **(see illustration 8.3)**. Carry out the same procedure on the other soft link pin.

> *Caution: Certain soft link pins (particularly on the larger chains) may require their ends to be filed or ground off before they can be pressed out using the tool.*

● Check that you have the correct size and strength (standard or heavy duty) new soft link - do not reuse the old link. Look for the size marking on the chain sideplates **(see illustration 8.10)**.
● Position the chain ends so that they are engaged over the rear sprocket. On an O-ring

8.4 Insert the new soft link, with O-rings, through the chain ends . . .

8.5 . . . install the O-rings over the pin ends . . .

8.6 . . . followed by the sideplate

chain, install a new O-ring over each pin of the link and insert the link through the two chain ends **(see illustration 8.4)**. Install a new O-ring over the end of each pin, followed by the sideplate (with the chain manufacturer's marking facing outwards) **(see illustrations 8.5 and 8.6)**. On an unsealed chain, insert the link through the two chain ends, then install the sideplate with the chain manufacturer's marking facing outwards.
● Note that it may not be possible to install the sideplate using finger pressure alone. If using a joining tool, assemble it so that the plates of the tool clamp the link and press the sideplate over the pins **(see illustration 8.7)**. Otherwise, use two small sockets placed over

8.7 Push the sideplate into position using a clamp

8.8 Assemble the chain riveting tool over one pin at a time and tighten it fully

8.9 Pin end correctly riveted (A), pin end unriveted (B)

the rivet ends and two pieces of the wood between a C-clamp. Operate the clamp to press the sideplate over the pins.

● Assemble the joining tool over one pin (following the manufacturer's instructions) and tighten the tool down to spread the pin end securely **(see illustrations 8.8 and 8.9)**. Do the same on the other pin.

> ⚠️ **Warning: Check that the pin ends are secure and that there is no danger of the sideplate coming loose. If the pin ends are cracked the soft link must be replaced.**

Final drive chain sizing

● Chains are sized using a three digit number, followed by a suffix to denote the chain type **(see illustration 8.10)**. Chain type is either standard or heavy duty (thicker sideplates), and also unsealed or O-ring/X-ring type.

● The first digit of the number relates to the pitch of the chain, ie the distance from the center of one pin to the center of the next pin **(see illustration 8.11)**. Pitch is expressed in eighths of an inch, as follows:

8.10 Typical chain size and type marking

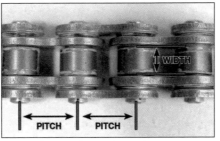

8.11 Chain dimensions

Sizes commencing with a 4 (for example 428) have a pitch of 1/2 inch (12.7 mm)

Sizes commencing with a 5 (for example 520) have a pitch of 5/8 inch (15.9 mm)

Sizes commencing with a 6 (for example 630) have a pitch of 3/4 inch (19.1 mm)

● The second and third digits of the chain size relate to the width of the rollers, for example the 525 shown has 5/16 inch (7.94 mm) rollers **(see illustration 8.11)**.

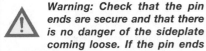

9 Hoses

Clamping to prevent flow

● Small-bore flexible hoses can be clamped to prevent fluid flow while a component is worked on. Whichever method is used, ensure that the hose material is not permanently distorted or damaged by the clamp.

a) A brake hose clamp available from auto parts stores **(see illustration 9.1)**.
b) A wingnut type hose clamp **(see illustration 9.2)**.

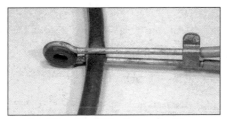

9.1 Hoses can be clamped with an automotive brake hose clamp . . .

9.2 . . . a wingnut type hose clamp . . .

c) Two sockets placed on each side of the hose and held with straight-jawed self-locking pliers **(see illustration 9.3)**.
d) Thick card stock on each side of the hose held between straight-jawed self-locking pliers **(see illustration 9.4)**.

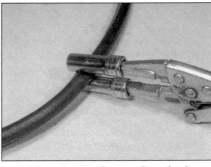

9.3 . . . two sockets and a pair of self-locking grips . . .

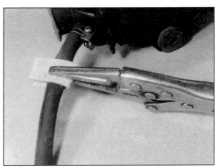

9.4 . . . or thick card and self-locking grips

Freeing and fitting hoses

● Always make sure the hose clamp is moved well clear of the hose end. Grip the hose with your hand and rotate it while pulling it off the union. If the hose has hardened due to age and will not move, slit it with a sharp knife and peel its ends off the union **(see illustration 9.5)**.

● Resist the temptation to use grease or soap on the unions to aid installation; although it helps the hose slip over the union it will equally aid the escape of fluid from the joint. It is preferable to soften the hose ends in hot water and wet the inside surface of the hose with water or a fluid which will evaporate.

9.5 Cutting a coolant hose free with a sharp knife

Length (distance)

Inches (in)	X	25.4	= Millimeters (mm)	X	0.0394	= Inches (in)
Feet (ft)	X	0.305	= Meters (m)	X	3.281	= Feet (ft)
Miles	X	1.609	= Kilometers (km)	X	0.621	= Miles

	X	25.4	= Millimeters (mm)	X	0.0394	= Inches (in)
Inches (in)	X	25.4	= Millimeters (mm)	X	0.0394	= Inches (in)
Feet (ft)	X	0.305	= Meters (m)	X	3.281	= Feet (ft)
Miles	X	1.609	= Kilometers (km)	X	0.621	= Miles

Volume (capacity)

Cubic inches (cu in; in^3)	X	16.387	= Cubic centimeters (cc; cm^3)	X	0.061	= Cubic inches (cu in; in^3)
Imperial pints (Imp pt)	X	0.568	= Liters (l)	X	1.76	= Imperial pints (Imp pt)
Imperial quarts (Imp qt)	X	1.137	= Liters (l)	X	0.88	= Imperial quarts (Imp qt)
Imperial quarts (Imp qt)	X	1.201	= US quarts (US qt)	X	0.833	= Imperial quarts (Imp qt)
US quarts (US qt)	X	0.946	= Liters (l)	X	1.057	= US quarts (US qt)
Imperial gallons (Imp gal)	X	4.546	= Liters (l)	X	0.22	= Imperial gallons (Imp gal)
Imperial gallons (Imp gal)	X	1.201	= US gallons (US gal)	X	0.833	= Imperial gallons (Imp gal)
US gallons (US gal)	X	3.785	= Liters (l)	X	0.264	= US gallons (US gal)

Mass (weight)

Ounces (oz)	X	28.35	= Grams (g)	X	0.035	= Ounces (oz)
Pounds (lb)	X	0.454	= Kilograms (kg)	X	2.205	= Pounds (lb)

Force

Ounces-force (ozf; oz)	X	0.278	= Newtons (N)	X	3.6	= Ounces-force (ozf; oz)
Pounds-force (lbf; lb)	X	4.448	= Newtons (N)	X	0.225	= Pounds-force (lbf; lb)
Newtons (N)	X	0.1	= Kilograms-force (kgf; kg)	X	9.81	= Newtons (N)

Pressure

Pounds-force per square inch (psi; lbf/in^2; lb/in^2)	X	0.070	= Kilograms-force per square centimeter (kgf/cm^2; kg/cm^2)	X	14.223	= Pounds-force per square inch (psi; lbf/in^2; lb/in^2)
Pounds-force per square inch (psi; lbf/in^2; lb/in^2)	X	0.068	= Atmospheres (atm)	X	14.696	= Pounds-force per square inch (psi; lbf/in^2; lb/in^2)
Pounds-force per square inch (psi; lbf/in^2; lb/in^2)	X	0.069	= Bars	X	14.5	= Pounds-force per square inch (psi; lbf/in^2; lb/in^2)
Pounds-force per square inch (psi; lbf/in^2; lb/in^2)	X	6.895	= Kilopascals (kPa)	X	0.145	= Pounds-force per square inch (psi; lbf/in^2; lb/in^2)
Kilopascals (kPa)	X	0.01	= Kilograms-force per square centimeter (kgf/cm^2; kg/cm^2)	X	98.1	= Kilopascals (kPa)

Torque (moment of force)

Pounds-force inches (lbf in; lb in)	X	1.152	= Kilograms-force centimeter (kgf cm; kg cm)	X	0.868	= Pounds-force inches (lbf in; lb in)
Pounds-force inches (lbf in; lb in)	X	0.113	= Newton meters (Nm)	X	8.85	= Pounds-force inches (lbf in; lb in)
Pounds-force inches (lbf in; lb in)	X	0.083	= Pounds-force feet (lbf ft; lb ft)	X	12	= Pounds-force inches (lbf in; lb in)
Pounds-force feet (lbf ft; lb ft)	X	0.138	= Kilograms-force meters (kgf m; kg m)	X	7.233	= Pounds-force feet (lbf ft; lb ft)
Pounds-force feet (lbf ft; lb ft)	X	1.356	= Newton meters (Nm)	X	0.738	= Pounds-force feet (lbf ft; lb ft)
Newton meters (Nm)	X	0.102	= Kilograms-force meters (kgf m; kg m)	X	9.804	= Newton meters (Nm)

Vacuum

Inches mercury (in. Hg)	X	3.377	= Kilopascals (kPa)	X	0.2961	= Inches mercury
Inches mercury (in. Hg)	X	25.4	= Millimeters mercury (mm Hg)	X	0.0394	= Inches mercury

Power

Horsepower (hp)	X	745.7	= Watts (W)	X	0.0013	= Horsepower (hp)

Velocity (speed)

Miles per hour (miles/hr; mph)	X	1.609	= Kilometers per hour (km/hr; kph)	X	0.621	= Miles per hour (miles/hr; mph)

Fuel consumption*

Miles per gallon, Imperial (mpg)	X	0.354	= Kilometers per liter (km/l)	X	2.825	= Miles per gallon, Imperial (mpg)
Miles per gallon, US (mpg)	X	0.425	= Kilometers per liter (km/l)	X	2.352	= Miles per gallon, US (mpg)

Temperature

Degrees Fahrenheit = (°C x 1.8) + 32

Degrees Celsius (Degrees Centigrade; °C) = (°F − 32) x 0.56

*It is common practice to convert from miles per gallon (mpg) to liters/100 kilometers (l/100km),
where mpg (Imperial) x l/100 km = 282 and mpg (US) x l/100 km = 235

A number of chemicals and lubricants are available for use in motorcycle maintenance and repair. They include a wide variety of products ranging from cleaning solvents and degreasers to lubricants and protective sprays for rubber, plastic and vinyl.

• **Contact point/spark plug cleaner** is a solvent used to clean oily film and dirt from points, grime from electrical connectors and oil deposits from spark plugs. It is oil free and leaves no residue. It can also be used to remove gum and varnish from carburetor jets and other orifices.

• **Carburetor cleaner** is similar to contact point/spark plug cleaner but it usually has a stronger solvent and may leave a slight oily residue. It is not recommended for cleaning electrical components or connections.

• **Brake system cleaner** is used to remove brake dust, grease and brake fluid from the brake system, where clean surfaces are absolutely necessary. It leaves no residue and often eliminates brake squeal caused by contaminants.

• **Silicone-based lubricants** are used to protect rubber parts such as hoses and grommets, and are used as lubricants for hinges and locks.

• **Multi-purpose grease** is an all purpose lubricant used wherever grease is more practical than a liquid lubricant such as oil. Some multi-purpose grease is colored white and specially formulated to be more resistant to water than ordinary grease.

• **Gear oil** (sometimes called gear lube) is a specially designed oil used in transmissions and final drive units, as well as other areas where high friction, high temperature lubrication is required. It is available in a number of viscosities (weights) for various applications.

• **Motor oil**, of course, is the lubricant specially formulated for use in the engine. It normally contains a wide variety of additives to prevent corrosion and reduce foaming and wear. Motor oil comes in various weights (viscosity ratings) from 5 to 80. The recommended weight of the oil depends on the seasonal temperature and the demands on the engine. Light oil is used in cold climates and under light load conditions; heavy oil is used in hot climates where high loads are encountered. Multi-viscosity oils are designed to have characteristics of both light and heavy oils and are available in a number of weights from 5W-20 to 20W-50.

• **Gasoline additives** perform several functions, depending on their chemical makeup. They usually contain solvents that help dissolve gum and varnish that build up on carburetor and inlet parts. They also serve to break down carbon deposits that form on the inside surfaces of the combustion chambers. Some additives contain upper cylinder lubricants for valves and piston rings.

• **Brake and clutch fluid** is a specially formulated hydraulic fluid that can withstand the heat and pressure encountered in break/clutch systems. Care must be taken that this fluid does not come in contact with painted surfaces or plastics. An opened container should always be resealed to prevent contamination by water or dirt.

• **Chain lubricants** are formulated especially for use on motorcycle final drive chains. A good chain lube should adhere well and have good penetrating qualities to be effective as a lubricant inside the chain and on the side plates, pins and rollers. Most chain lubes are either the foaming type or quick drying type and are usually marketed as sprays. Take care to use a lubricant marked as being suitable for O-ring chains.

• **Degreasers** are heavy duty solvents used to remove grease and grime that may accumulate on the engine and frame components. They can be sprayed or brushed on and, depending on the type, are rinsed with either water or solvent.

• **Solvents** are used alone or in combination with degreasers to clean parts and assemblies during repair and overhaul. The home mechanic should use only solvents that are non-flammable and that do not produce irritating fumes.

• **Gasket sealing compounds** may be used in conjunction with gaskets, to improve their sealing capabilities, or alone, to seal metal-to-metal joints. Many gasket sealers can withstand extreme heat, some are impervious to gasoline and lubricants, while others are capable of filling and sealing large cavities. Depending on the intended use, gasket sealers either dry hard or stay relatively soft and pliable. They are usually applied by hand, with a brush or are sprayed on the gasket sealing surfaces.

• **Thread locking compound** is an adhesive locking compound that prevents threaded fasteners from loosening because of vibration. It is available in a variety of types for different applications.

• **Moisture dispersants** are usually sprays that can be used to dry out electrical components such as the fuse block and wiring connectors. Some types an also be used as treatment for rubber and as a lubricant for hinges, cables and locks.

• **Waxes and polishes** are used to help protect painted and plated surfaces from the weather. Different types of paint may require the use of different types of wax polish. Some polishes utilize a chemical or abrasive cleaner to help remove the top layer of oxidized (dull) paint on older vehicles. In recent years, many non-wax polishes (that contain a wide variety of chemicals such as polymers and silicones) have been introduced. These non-wax polishes are usually easier to apply and last longer than conventional waxes and polishes.

Preparing for storage

Before you start

If repairs or an overhaul is needed, see that this is carried out now rather than left until you want to ride the bike again.

Give the bike a good wash and scrub all dirt from its underside. Make sure the bike dries completely before preparing for storage.

Engine

● Remove the spark plug(s) and lubricate the cylinder bores with approximately a teaspoon of motor oil using a spout-type oil can **(see illustration 1)**. Reinstall the spark plug(s). Crank the engine over a couple of times to coat the piston rings and bores with oil. If the bike has a kickstart, use this to turn the engine over. If not, flick the kill switch to the OFF position and crank the engine over on the starter **(see illustration 2)**. If the nature of the ignition system prevents the starter operating with the kill switch in the OFF position, remove the spark plugs and fit them back in

their caps; ensure that the plugs are grounded against the cylinder head when the starter is operated **(see illustration 3)**.

> ⚠ **Warning: It is important that the plugs are grounded away from the spark plug holes otherwise there is a risk of atomized fuel from the cylinders igniting.**

> **HAYNES HiNT** *On a single cylinder four-stroke engine, you can seal the combustion chamber completely by positioning the piston at TDC on the compression stroke.*

● Drain the carburetor(s) otherwise there is a risk of jets becoming blocked by gum deposits from the fuel **(see illustration 4)**.

● If the bike is going into long-term storage, consider adding a fuel stabilizer to the fuel in the tank. If the tank is drained completely, corrosion of its internal surfaces may occur if left unprotected for a long period. The tank can be treated with a rust preventative especially for this purpose. Alternatively, remove the tank and pour half a liter of motor oil into it, install the filler cap and shake the tank to coat its internals with oil before draining off the excess. The same effect can also be achieved by spraying WD-40 or a similar water-dispersant around the inside of the tank via its flexible nozzle.

● Make sure the cooling system contains the correct mix of antifreeze. Antifreeze also contains important corrosion inhibitors.

● The air intakes and exhaust can be sealed off by covering or plugging the openings. Ensure that you do not seal in any condensation; run the engine until it is hot, then switch off and allow to cool. Tape a piece

Squirt a drop of motor oil into each cylinder

Flick the kill switch to OFF . . .

. . . and ensure that the metal bodies of the plugs (arrows) are grounded against the cylinder head

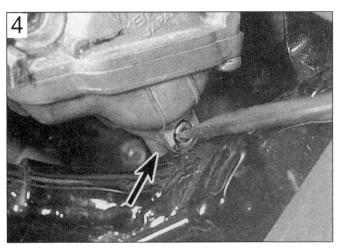

Connect a hose to the carburetor float chamber drain stub (arrow) and unscrew the drain screw

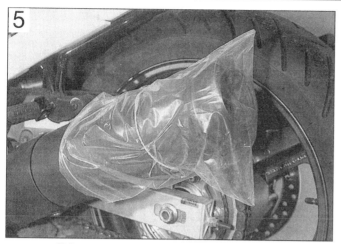

Exhausts can be sealed off with a plastic bag

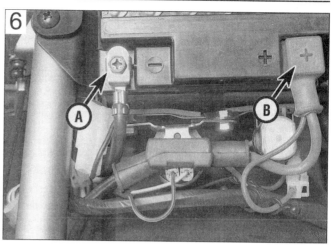

Disconnect the negative lead (A) first, followed by the positive lead (B)

of thick plastic over the silencer end(s) **(see illustration 5)**. Note that some advocate pouring a tablespoon of motor oil into the silencer(s) before sealing them off.

Battery

● Remove it from the bike - in extreme cases of cold the battery may freeze and crack its case **(see illustration 6)**.
● Check the electrolyte level and top up if necessary (conventional refillable batteries). Clean the terminals.
● Store the battery off the motorcycle and away from any sources of fire. Position a wooden block under the battery if it is to sit on the ground.
● Give the battery a trickle charge for a few hours every month **(see illustration 7)**.

Tires

● Place the bike on its centerstand or an auxiliary stand which will support the motorcycle in an upright position. Position wood blocks under the tires to keep them off the ground and to provide insulation from damp. If the bike is being put into long-term storage, ideally both tires should be off the

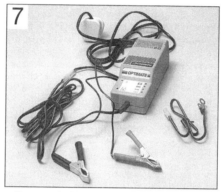

Use a suitable battery charger - this kit also assesses battery condition

ground; not only will this protect the tires, but will also ensure that no load is placed on the steering head or wheel bearings.
● Deflate each tire by 5 to 10 psi, no more or the beads may unseat from the rim, making subsequent inflation difficult on tubeless tires.

Pivots and controls

● Lubricate all lever, pedal, stand and

footrest pivot points. If grease nipples are fitted to the rear suspension components, apply lubricant to the pivots.
● Lubricate all control cables.

Cycle components

● Apply a wax protectant to all painted and plastic components. Wipe off any excess, but don't polish to a shine. Where fitted, clean the screen with soap and water.
● Coat metal parts with Vaseline (petroleum jelly). When applying this to the fork tubes, do not compress the forks otherwise the seals will rot from contact with the Vaseline.
● Apply a vinyl cleaner to the seat.

Storage conditions

● Aim to store the bike in a shed or garage which does not leak and is free from damp.
● Drape an old blanket or bedspread over the bike to protect it from dust and direct contact with sunlight (which will fade paint). Beware of tight-fitting plastic covers which may allow condensation to form and settle on the bike.

Getting back on the road

Engine and transmission

● Change the oil and replace the oil filter. If this was done prior to storage, check that the oil hasn't emulsified - a thick whitish substance which occurs through condensation.
● Remove the spark plugs. Using a spout-type oil can, squirt a few drops of oil into the cylinder(s). This will provide initial lubrication as the piston rings and bores comes back into contact. Service the spark plugs, or buy new ones, and install them in the engine.

● Check that the clutch isn't stuck on. The plates can stick together if left standing for some time, preventing clutch operation. Engage a gear and try rocking the bike back and forth with the clutch lever held against the handlebar. If this doesn't work on cable-operated clutches, hold the clutch lever back against the handlebar with a strong rubber band or cable tie for a couple of hours **(see illustration 8)**.
● If the air intakes or silencer end(s) were blocked off, remove the plug or cover used.
● If the fuel tank was coated with a rust

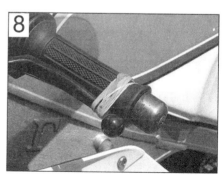

Hold the clutch lever back against the handlebar with rubber bands or a cable tie

preventative, oil or a stabilizer added to the fuel, drain and flush the tank and dispose of the fuel sensibly. If no action was taken with the fuel tank prior to storage, it is advised that the old fuel is disposed of since it will go bad over a period of time. Refill the fuel tank with fresh fuel.

Frame and running gear

● Oil all pivot points and cables.
● Check the tire pressures. They will definitely need inflating if pressures were reduced for storage.
● Lubricate the final drive chain (where applicable).
● Remove any protective coating applied to the fork tubes (stanchions) since this may well destroy the fork seals. If the fork tubes weren't protected and have picked up rust spots, remove them with very fine abrasive paper and refinish with metal polish.
● Check that both brakes operate correctly. Apply each brake hard and check that it's not possible to move the motorcycle forwards, then check that the brake frees off again once released. Brake caliper pistons can stick due to corrosion around the piston head, or on the sliding caliper types, due to corrosion of the slider pins. If the brake doesn't free after repeated operation, take the caliper off for examination. Similarly drum brakes can stick

due to a seized operating cam, cable or rod linkage.
● If the motorcycle has been in long-term storage, replace the brake fluid and clutch fluid (where applicable).
● Depending on where the bike has been stored, the wiring, cables and hoses may have been nibbled by rodents. Make a visual check and investigate disturbed wiring loom tape.

Battery

● If the battery has been previously removed and given top up charges it can simply be reconnected. Remember to connect the positive cable first and the negative cable last.
● On conventional refillable batteries, if the battery has not received any attention, remove it from the motorcycle and check its electrolyte level. Top up if necessary then charge the battery. If the battery fails to hold a charge and a visual check show heavy white sulfation of the plates, the battery is probably defective and must be replaced. This is particularly likely if the battery is old. Confirm battery condition with a specific gravity check.
● On sealed (MF) batteries, if the battery has not received any attention, remove it from the motorcycle and charge it according to the information on the battery case - if the battery fails to hold a charge it must be replaced.

Starting procedure

● If a kickstart is fitted, turn the engine over a couple of times with the ignition OFF to distribute oil around the engine. If no kickstart is fitted, flick the engine kill switch OFF and the ignition ON and crank the engine over a couple of times to work oil around the upper cylinder components. If the nature of the ignition system is such that the starter won't work with the kill switch OFF, remove the spark plugs, fit them back into their caps and ground their bodies on the cylinder head. Reinstall the spark plugs afterwards.
● Switch the kill switch to RUN, operate the choke and start the engine. If the engine won't start don't continue cranking the engine - not only will this flatten the battery, but the starter motor will overheat. Switch the ignition off and try again later. If the engine refuses to start, go through the troubleshooting procedures in this manual. **Note:** *If the bike has been in storage for a long time, old fuel or a carburetor blockage may be the problem. Gum deposits in carburetors can block jets - if a carburetor cleaner doesn't prove successful the carburetors must be dismantled for cleaning.*

● Once the engine has started, check that the lights, turn signals and horn work properly.

● Treat the bike gently for the first ride and check all fluid levels on completion. Settle the bike back into the maintenance schedule.

This Section provides an easy reference-guide to the more common faults that are likely to afflict your machine. Obviously, the opportunities are almost limitless for faults to occur as a result of obscure failures, and to try and cover all eventualities would require a book. Indeed, a number have been written on the subject.

Successful troubleshooting is not a mysterious 'black art' but the application of a bit of knowledge combined with a systematic and logical approach to the problem. Approach any troubleshooting by first accurately identifying the symptom and then checking through the list of possible causes, starting with the simplest or most obvious and progressing in stages to the most complex. Take nothing for granted, but above all apply liberal quantities of common sense.

The main symptom of a fault is given in the text as a major heading below which are listed the various systems or areas which may contain the fault. Details of each possible cause for a fault and the remedial action to be taken are given. Further information should be sought in the relevant Chapter.

1 Engine doesn't start or is difficult to start

☐ Starter motor doesn't rotate
☐ Starter motor rotates but engine does not turn over
☐ Starter works but engine won't turn over (seized)
☐ No fuel flow
☐ Engine flooded
☐ No spark or weak spark
☐ Compression low
☐ Stalls after starting
☐ Rough idle

2 Poor running at low speed

☐ Spark weak
☐ Fuel/air mixture incorrect
☐ Compression low
☐ Poor acceleration

3 Poor running or no power at high speed

☐ Firing incorrect
☐ Fuel/air mixture incorrect
☐ Compression low
☐ Knocking or pinging
☐ Miscellaneous causes

4 Overheating

☐ Engine overheats
☐ Firing incorrect
☐ Fuel/air mixture incorrect
☐ Compression too high
☐ Engine load excessive
☐ Lubrication inadequate
☐ Miscellaneous causes

5 Clutch problems

☐ Clutch slipping
☐ Clutch not disengaging completely

6 Gearchanging problems

☐ Doesn't go into gear, or lever doesn't return
☐ Jumps out of gear
☐ Overselects

7 Abnormal engine noise

☐ Knocking or pinging
☐ Piston slap or rattling
☐ Valve noise
☐ Other noise

8 Abnormal driveline noise

☐ Clutch noise
☐ Transmission noise
☐ Final drive noise

9 Abnormal frame and suspension noise

☐ Front end noise
☐ Shock absorber noise
☐ Brake noise

10 Oil pressure warning light comes on

☐ Engine lubrication system
☐ Electrical system

11 Excessive exhaust smoke

☐ White smoke
☐ Black smoke

12 Poor handling or stability

☐ Handlebar hard to turn
☐ Handlebar shakes or vibrates excessively
☐ Handlebar pulls to one side
☐ Poor shock absorbing qualities

13 Braking problems

☐ Brakes are spongy, don't hold
☐ Brake lever or pedal pulsates
☐ Brakes drag

14 Electrical problems

☐ Battery dead or weak
☐ Battery overcharged

1 Engine doesn't start or is difficult to start

Starter motor doesn't rotate

☐ Engine kill switch OFF.
☐ Fuse blown. Check main circuit breaker (Chapter 8).
☐ Battery voltage low. Check and recharge battery (Chapter 8).
☐ Starter motor defective. Make sure the wiring to the starter is secure. Make sure the starter solenoid clicks when the start button is pushed. If the solenoid clicks, then the fault is in the wiring or motor.
☐ Starter solenoid faulty. Check it according to the procedure in Chapter 8.
☐ Starter switch not contacting. The contacts could be wet, corroded or dirty. Disassemble and clean the switch (Chapter 8).
☐ Wiring open or shorted. Check all wiring connections and harnesses to make sure that they are dry, tight and not corroded. Also check for broken or frayed wires that can cause a short to ground (see wiring diagram, Chapter 8).
☐ Ignition (main) switch defective. Check the switch according to the procedure in Chapter 8. Replace the switch with a new one if it is defective.
☐ Engine kill switch defective. Check for wet, dirty or corroded contacts. Clean or replace the switch as necessary (Chapter 8).

Starter motor rotates but engine does not turn over

☐ Starter pinion gear defective. Inspect and repair or replace (Chapter 8).
☐ Damaged starter jackshaft. Inspect and replace the damaged parts (Chapter 8).

Starter works but engine won't turn over (seized)

☐ Seized engine caused by one or more internally damaged components. Failure due to wear, abuse or lack of lubrication. Damage can include seized valves, rocker arms, lifters, camshafts, pistons, crankshaft or connecting rod bearings. Refer to Chapter 2 for engine disassembly.

No fuel flow

☐ No fuel in tank.
☐ Fuel tank breather hose obstructed.
☐ Fuel filter is blocked (see Chapter 1).

Engine flooded

☐ Starting technique incorrect. Under normal circumstances the machine should start with little or no throttle. When the engine is cold, the choke should be operated (carburetor models) and the engine started without opening the throttle. When the engine is at operating temperature, only a very slight amount of throttle should be necessary.

No spark or weak spark

☐ Ignition switch OFF.
☐ Engine kill switch turned to the OFF position.
☐ Battery voltage low. Check and recharge the battery as necessary (Chapter 8).
☐ Spark plugs dirty, defective or worn out. Locate reason for fouled plugs using spark plug condition chart and follow the plug maintenance procedures (Chapter 1).
☐ Spark plug caps or secondary (HT) wiring faulty. Check condition. Replace either or both components if cracks or deterioration are evident (Chapter 4).

☐ Spark plug caps not making good contact. Make sure that the plug caps fit snugly over the plug ends.
☐ Ignition HT coils defective. Check the coils, referring to Chapter 4.
☐ ECM defective. Refer to Chapter 4 for details.
☐ Crankshaft or camshaft position sensor defective. Check the unit, referring to Chapter 4 for details.
☐ Ignition or kill switch shorted. This is usually caused by water, corrosion, damage or excessive wear. The switches can be disassembled and cleaned with electrical contact cleaner. If cleaning does not help, replace the switches (Chapter 8).
☐ Wiring shorted or broken between:

a) Ignition (main) switch and engine kill switch (or blown fuse, tripped breaker)
b) ECM and engine kill switch
c) ECM and ignition HT coils
d) Ignition HT coils and spark plugs
e) ECM and camshaft position sensor.

☐ Make sure that all wiring connections are clean, dry and tight. Look for chafed and broken wires (Chapters 4 and 8).

Compression low

☐ Spark plugs loose. Remove the plugs and inspect their threads. Reinstall and tighten to the specified torque (Chapter 1).
☐ Cylinder head not sufficiently tightened down. If the cylinder head is suspected of being loose, then there's a chance that the gasket or head is damaged if the problem has persisted for any length of time. The head bolts should be tightened to the proper torque in the correct sequence (Chapter 2).
☐ Cylinder and/or piston worn. Excessive wear will cause compression pressure to leak past the rings. This is usually accompanied by worn rings as well. A top-end overhaul is necessary (Chapter 2).
☐ Piston rings worn, weak, broken, or sticking. Broken or sticking piston rings usually indicate a lubrication or fuelling problem that causes excess carbon deposits or seizures to form on the pistons and rings. Top-end overhaul is necessary (Chapter 2).
☐ Piston ring-to-groove clearance excessive. This is caused by excessive wear of the piston ring lands. Piston replacement is necessary (Chapter 2).
☐ Cylinder head gasket damaged. If a head is allowed to become loose, or if excessive carbon build-up on the piston crown and combustion chamber causes extremely high compression, the head gasket may leak. Retorquing the head is not always sufficient to restore the seal, so gasket replacement is necessary (Chapter 2).
☐ Cylinder head warped. This is caused by overheating or improperly tightened head bolts. Machine shop resurfacing or head replacement is necessary (Chapter 2).
☐ Valve spring broken or weak. Caused by component failure or wear; the springs must be replaced (Chapter 2).
☐ Valve not seating properly. This is caused by a bent valve (from over-revving burned valve or seat (improper fuelling) or an accumulation of carbon deposits on the seat (from fuelling or lubrication problems). The valves must be cleaned and/or replaced and the seats serviced if possible (Chapter 2).

1 Engine doesn't start or is difficult to start (continued)

Stalls after starting

☐ Improper choke action. Make sure the choke linkage shaft is getting a full stroke and staying in the out position (Chapter 3).
☐ Ignition malfunction. See Chapter 4.
☐ Carburetor malfunction. See Chapter 3.
☐ Fuel contaminated. The fuel can be contaminated with either dirt or water, or can change chemically if the machine is allowed to sit for several months or more. Drain the tank (Chapter 3).
☐ Intake air leak. Check for loose intake manifold and damaged/disconnected vacuum hoses (Chapter 3).
☐ Engine idle speed incorrect. On carburetor models, turn idle adjusting screw until the engine idles at the specified rpm (Chapter 1).

Rough idle

☐ Ignition malfunction. See Chapter 4.
☐ Idle speed incorrect. See Chapter 1.
☐ Carburetor malfunction. See Chapter 3.
☐ Fuel contaminated. The fuel can be contaminated with either dirt or water, or can change chemically if the machine is allowed to sit for several months or more. Drain the tank (Chapter 3).
☐ Intake air leak. Check for loose intake manifold and damaged/disconnected vacuum hoses. Replace the intake ducts if they are split or deteriorated (Chapter 3).
☐ Air filter clogged. Replace the air filter element (Chapter 1).

2 Poor running at low speeds

Spark weak

☐ Battery voltage low. Check and recharge battery (Chapter 8).
☐ Spark plugs fouled, defective or worn out. Refer to Chapter 1 for spark plug maintenance.
☐ Spark plug cap or HT wiring defective. Refer to Chapters 1 and 4 for details on the ignition system.
☐ Spark plug caps not making contact.
☐ Incorrect spark plugs. Wrong type, heat range or cap configuration. Check and install correct plugs listed in Chapter 1.
☐ ECM faulty. See Chapter 3.
☐ Pick-up coil defective. See Chapter 3.
☐ Ignition coil defective. See Chapter 4.

Fuel/air mixture incorrect

☐ Pilot jet or air passage blocked. Remove and overhaul the carburetor (if equipped) (Chapter 3).
☐ Air filter clogged, poorly sealed or missing (Chapter 1).
☐ Air filter housing poorly sealed. Look for cracks, holes or loose clamps and replace or repair defective parts.
☐ Fuel tank breather hose obstructed.
☐ Intake air leak. Check for loose intake manifold and damaged/disconnected vacuum hoses. Replace the intake ducts if they are split or deteriorated (Chapter 3).

Compression low

☐ Spark plugs loose. Remove the plugs and inspect their threads. Reinstall and tighten to the specified torque (Chapter 1).
☐ Cylinder head not sufficiently tightened down. If the cylinder head is suspected of being loose, then there's a chance that the gasket and head are damaged if the problem has persisted for any length of time. The head bolts should be tightened to the proper torque in the correct sequence (Chapter 2).
☐ Cylinder and/or piston worn. Excessive wear will cause compression pressure to leak past the rings. This is usually accompanied by worn rings as well. A top-end overhaul is necessary (Chapter 2).

☐ Piston rings worn, weak, broken, or sticking. Broken or sticking piston rings usually indicate a lubrication or fuelling problem that causes excess carbon deposits or seizures to form on the pistons and rings. Top-end overhaul is necessary (Chapter 2).
☐ Piston ring-to-groove clearance excessive. This is caused by excessive wear of the piston ring lands. Piston replacement is necessary (Chapter 2).
☐ Cylinder head gasket damaged. If a head is allowed to become loose, or if excessive carbon build-up on the piston crown and combustion chamber causes extremely high compression, the head gasket may leak. Retorquing the head is not always sufficient to restore the seal, so gasket replacement is necessary (Chapter 2).
☐ Cylinder head warped. This is caused by overheating or improperly tightened head bolts. Machine shop resurfacing or head replacement is necessary (Chapter 2).
☐ Valve spring broken or weak. Caused by component failure or wear; the springs must be replaced (Chapter 2).
☐ Valve not seating properly. This is caused by a bent valve (from over-revving or improper valve adjustment), burned valve or seat (improper fuelling) or an accumulation of carbon deposits on the seat (from fuelling, lubrication problems). The valves must be cleaned and/or replaced and the seats serviced if possible (Chapter 2).

Poor acceleration

☐ Carburetor fault. Remove and overhaul the carburetor (Chapter 3).
☐ Engine oil viscosity too high. Using a heavier oil than that recommended in Chapter 1 can damage the oil pump or lubrication system and cause drag on the engine.
☐ Brakes dragging. Usually caused by debris which has entered the brake piston seals, or from a warped disc or bent axle. Repair as necessary (Chapter 6).

3 Poor running or no power at high speed

Firing incorrect

☐ Air filter restricted. Clean or replace filter (Chapter 1).
☐ Spark plugs fouled, defective or worn out. See Chapter 1 for spark plug maintenance.
☐ Spark plug caps or HT wiring defective. See Chapters 1 and 4 for details of the ignition system.
☐ Spark plug caps not in good contact. See Chapter 4.
☐ Incorrect spark plugs. Wrong type, heat range or cap configuration. Check and install correct plugs listed in Chapter 1.
☐ ECM defective. See Chapter 4.
☐ Camshaft position sensor defective. See Chapter 4.
☐ Ignition coils defective. See Chapter 4.

Fuel/air mixture incorrect

☐ Carburetor fault. Remove and overhaul the carburetor (Chapter 3).
☐ Air filter clogged, poorly sealed, or missing (Chapter 1).
☐ Air filter housing poorly sealed. Look for cracks, holes or loose clamps, and replace or repair defective parts.
☐ Fuel tank breather hose obstructed.
☐ Intake air leak. Check for loose intake manifold and damaged/disconnected vacuum hoses. Replace the intake ducts if they are split or deteriorated (Chapter 4).

Compression low

☐ Spark plugs loose. Remove the plugs and inspect their threads. Reinstall and tighten to the specified torque (Chapter 1).
☐ Cylinder head not sufficiently tightened down. If the cylinder head is suspected of being loose, then there's a chance that the gasket and head are damaged if the problem has persisted for any length of time. The head bolts should be tightened to the proper torque in the correct sequence (Chapter 2).
☐ Cylinder and/or piston worn. Excessive wear will cause compression pressure to leak past the rings. This is usually accompanied by worn rings as well. A top-end overhaul is necessary (Chapter 2).
☐ Piston rings worn, weak, broken, or sticking. Broken or sticking piston rings usually indicate a lubrication or fuelling problem that causes excess carbon deposits or seizures to form on the pistons and rings. Top-end overhaul is necessary (Chapter 2).
☐ Piston ring-to-groove clearance excessive. This is caused by excessive wear of the piston ring lands. Piston replacement is necessary (Chapter 2).
☐ Cylinder head gasket damaged. If a head is allowed to become loose, or if excessive carbon build-up on the piston crown and combustion chamber causes extremely high compression, the head gasket may leak. Retorquing the head is not always sufficient to restore the seal, so gasket replacement is necessary (Chapter 2).
☐ Cylinder head warped. This is caused by overheating or improperly tightened head bolts. Machine shop resurfacing or head replacement is necessary (Chapter 2).
☐ Valve spring broken or weak. Caused by component failure or wear; the springs must be replaced (Chapter 2).
☐ Valve not seating properly. This is caused by a bent valve (from over-revving), burned valve or seat (improper fuelling) or an accumulation of carbon deposits on the seat (from fuelling or lubrication problems). The valves must be cleaned and/or replaced and the seats serviced if possible (Chapter 2).

Knocking or pinging

☐ Carbon build-up in combustion chamber. Use of a fuel additive that will dissolve the adhesive bonding the carbon particles to the crown and chamber is the easiest way to remove the build-up. Otherwise, the cylinder head will have to be removed and decarbonized (Chapter 2).
☐ Incorrect or poor quality fuel. Old or improper grades of fuel can cause detonation. This causes the piston to rattle, thus the knocking or pinging sound. Drain old fuel and always use the recommended fuel grade.
☐ Spark plug heat range incorrect. Uncontrolled detonation indicates the plug heat range is too hot. The plug in effect becomes a glow plug, raising cylinder temperatures. Install the proper heat range plug (Chapter 1).
☐ Improper air/fuel mixture. This will cause the cylinders to run hot, which leads to detonation. An intake air leak can cause this imbalance. See Chapter 3.

Miscellaneous causes

☐ Throttle valve doesn't open fully. Adjust the throttle grip freeplay (Chapter 1).
☐ Clutch slipping. May be caused by loose or worn clutch components. Refer to Chapter 2 for clutch overhaul procedures.
☐ Engine oil viscosity too high. Using a heavier oil than the one recommended in Chapter 1 can damage the oil pump or lubrication system and cause drag on the engine.
☐ Brakes dragging. Usually caused by debris which has entered the brake piston seals, or from a warped disc or drum, or bent axle. Repair as necessary.

4 Overheating

Firing incorrect

- ☐ Spark plugs fouled, defective or worn out. See Chapter 1 for spark plug maintenance.
- ☐ Incorrect spark plugs.
- ☐ ECM defective. See Chapter 4.
- ☐ Camshaft position sensor faulty. See Chapter 4.
- ☐ Faulty ignition coil. See Chapter 4.

Fuel/air mixture incorrect

- ☐ Carburetor fault. Remove and overhaul the carburetor (Chapter 3).
- ☐ Air filter clogged, poorly sealed, or missing (Chapter 1).
- ☐ Air filter housing poorly sealed. Look for cracks, holes or loose clamps, and replace or repair defective parts.
- ☐ Fuel tank breather hose obstructed.
- ☐ Intake air leak. Check for loose carburetor intake duct retaining clips and damaged/disconnected vacuum hoses. Replace the intake ducts if they are split or deteriorated (Chapter 3).

Compression too high

- ☐ Carbon build-up in combustion chamber. Use of a fuel additive that will dissolve the adhesive bonding the carbon particles to the piston crown and chamber is the easiest way to remove the build-up. Otherwise, the cylinder head will have to be removed and decarbonized (Chapter 2).
- ☐ Improperly machined head surface or installation of incorrect gasket during engine assembly.

Engine load excessive

- ☐ Clutch slipping. Can be caused by damaged, loose or worn clutch components. Refer to Chapter 2 for overhaul procedures.
- ☐ Engine oil level too high. The addition of too much oil will cause pressurization of the crankcase and inefficient engine operation. Check Specifications and drain to proper level (Chapter 1).
- ☐ Engine oil viscosity too high. Using a heavier oil than the one recommended in Chapter 1 can damage the oil pump or lubrication system as well as cause drag on the engine.
- ☐ Brakes dragging. Usually caused by debris which has entered the brake piston seals, or from a warped disc or drum, or bent axle. Repair as necessary.

Lubrication inadequate

- ☐ Engine oil level too low. Friction caused by intermittent lack of lubrication or from oil that is overworked can cause overheating. The oil provides a definite cooling function in the engine. Check the oil level (Chapter 1).
- ☐ Poor quality engine oil or incorrect viscosity or type. Oil is rated not only according to viscosity but also according to type. Some oils are not rated high enough for use in this engine. Check the Specifications section and change to the correct oil (Chapter 1).

Miscellaneous causes

- ☐ Modification to exhaust system. Most aftermarket exhaust systems cause the engine to run leaner, which makes it run hotter.

5 Clutch problems

Clutch slipping

- ☐ Clutch cable freeplay incorrectly adjusted (Chapter 1).
- ☐ Friction plates worn or warped. Overhaul the clutch assembly (Chapter 2).
- ☐ Metal plates warped (Chapter 2).
- ☐ Clutch diaphragm spring broken or weak. An old or heat-damaged (from slipping clutch) spring should be replaced with a new one (Chapter 2).
- ☐ Clutch pushrod bent. Check and, if necessary, replace (Chapter 2).
- ☐ Clutch center or housing unevenly worn. This causes improper engagement of the plates. Replace the damaged or worn parts (Chapter 2).

Clutch not disengaging completely

- ☐ Clutch cable freeplay incorrectly adjusted (Chapter 1).
- ☐ Clutch plates warped or damaged. This will cause clutch drag, which in turn will cause the machine to creep. Overhaul the clutch assembly (Chapter 2).
- ☐ Clutch spring tension uneven. Usually caused by a sagged or broken spring. Check and replace the diaphragm spring (Chapter 2).
- ☐ Engine oil deteriorated. Old, thin, worn out oil will not provide proper lubrication for the plates, causing the clutch to drag. Replace the oil and filter (Chapter 1).
- ☐ Engine oil viscosity too high. Using a heavier oil than recommended in Chapter 1 can cause the plates to stick together, putting a drag on the engine. Change to the correct weight oil (Chapter 1).
- ☐ Clutch housing bearing seized. Lack of lubrication, severe wear or damage can cause the bearing to seize on the input shaft. Overhaul of the clutch, and perhaps transmission, may be necessary to repair the damage (Chapter 2).

6 Gearchanging problems

Doesn't go into gear or lever doesn't return

- ☐ Clutch not disengaging. See above.
- ☐ Shift fork(s) bent or seized. Often caused by dropping the machine or from lack of lubrication. Overhaul the transmission (Chapter 2).
- ☐ Gear(s) stuck on shaft. Most often caused by a lack of lubrication or excessive wear in transmission bearings and bushings. Overhaul the transmission (Chapter 2).
- ☐ Gear shift drum binding. Caused by lubrication failure or excessive wear. Replace the drum and bearing (Chapter 2).
- ☐ Gear shift lever pawl spring weak or broken (Chapter 2).
- ☐ Gear shift lever broken. Splines stripped out of lever or shaft, caused by allowing the lever to get loose or from dropping the machine. Replace necessary parts (Chapter 2).
- ☐ Gear shift mechanism stopper arm broken or worn. Full engagement and rotary movement of shift drum results. Replace the arm (Chapter 2).

- ☐ Stopper arm spring broken. Allows arm to float, causing sporadic shift operation. Replace spring (Chapter 2).

Jumps out of gear

- ☐ Shift fork(s) worn. Overhaul the transmission (Chapter 2).
- ☐ Gear groove(s) worn. Overhaul the transmission (Chapter 2).
- ☐ Gear dogs or dog slots worn or damaged. The gears should be inspected and replaced. No attempt should be made to service the worn parts.

Overselects

- ☐ Stopper arm spring weak or broken (Chapter 2).
- ☐ Return spring post broken or distorted (Chapter 2).

7 Abnormal engine noise

Knocking or pinging

- ☐ Carbon build-up in combustion chamber. Use of a fuel additive that will dissolve the adhesive bonding the carbon particles to the piston crown and chamber is the easiest way to remove the build-up. Otherwise, the cylinder head will have to be removed and decarbonized (Chapter 2).
- ☐ Incorrect or poor quality fuel. Old or improper fuel can cause detonation. This causes the pistons to rattle, thus the knocking or pinging sound. Drain the old fuel and always use the recommended grade fuel (Chapter 3).
- ☐ Spark plug heat range incorrect. Uncontrolled detonation indicates that the plug heat range is too hot. The plug in effect becomes a glow plug, raising cylinder temperatures. Install the proper heat range plug (Chapter 1).
- ☐ Improper air/fuel mixture. This will cause the cylinders to run hot and lead to detonation. Blocked carburetor jets or an air leak can cause this imbalance. See Chapter 3.

Piston slap or rattling

- ☐ Cylinder-to-piston clearance excessive. Caused by improper assembly. Inspect and overhaul top-end parts (Chapter 2).
- ☐ Connecting rod bent. Caused by over-revving, trying to start a badly flooded engine or from ingesting a foreign object into the combustion chamber. Replace the damaged parts (Chapter 2).
- ☐ Piston pin or piston pin bore worn or seized from wear or lack of lubrication. Replace damaged parts (Chapter 2).
- ☐ Piston ring(s) worn, broken or sticking. Overhaul the top-end (Chapter 2).
- ☐ Piston seizure damage. Usually from lack of lubrication or overheating. Replace the pistons and cylinders, as necessary (Chapter 2).

- ☐ Connecting rod bearing clearance excessive. Caused by excessive wear or lack of lubrication. Replace worn parts.

Valve noise

- ☐ Hydraulic lifter worn or damaged. Inspect and replace as necessary (Chapter 2).
- ☐ Valve spring broken or weak. Check and replace weak valve springs (Chapter 2).
- ☐ Camshaft or rocker arms worn or damaged. Lack of lubrication at high rpm is usually the cause of damage. Insufficient oil or failure to change the oil at the recommended intervals are the chief causes. Inspect and replace as necessary. Rocker arm bushings can be replaced separately (Chapter 2).

Other noise

- ☐ Cylinder head gasket leaking.
- ☐ Exhaust pipe leaking at cylinder head connection. Caused by improper fit of pipe(s) or loose exhaust nuts. All exhaust fasteners should be tightened evenly and carefully. Failure to do this will lead to a leak.
- ☐ Crankshaft runout excessive. Caused by a bent crankshaft (from over-revving) or damage from an upper cylinder component failure. Can also be attributed to dropping the machine on either of the crankshaft ends.
- ☐ Engine mounting bolts loose. Tighten all engine mount bolts (Chapter 2).
- ☐ Crankshaft bearings worn (Chapter 2).
- ☐ Camchain, tensioner or guides worn. Replace according to the procedure in Chapter 2.

8 Abnormal driveline noise

Clutch and primary drive noise

☐ Clutch outer drum/friction plate clearance excessive (Chapter 2).
☐ Loose or damaged clutch pressure plate and/or bolts (Chapter 2).
☐ Loose or damaged primary chain (Chapter 1).

Transmission noise

☐ Bearings worn. Also includes the possibility that the shafts are worn. Overhaul the transmission (Chapter 2).
☐ Gears worn or chipped (Chapter 2).
☐ Metal chips jammed in gear teeth. Probably pieces from a broken gear or shift mechanism that were picked up by the gears. This will cause early bearing failure (Chapter 2).

☐ Transmission oil level too low. Causes a howl from transmission (Chapter 1).

Final drive noise

☐ Belt not adjusted properly (Chapter 1).
☐ Front or rear sprocket loose. Tighten fasteners (Chapter 6).
☐ Sprockets worn. Replace sprockets (Chapter 6).
☐ Rear sprocket warped. Replace sprockets (Chapter 6).

9 Abnormal frame and suspension noise

Front end noise

☐ Low fluid level or improper viscosity oil in forks. This can sound like spurting and is usually accompanied by irregular fork action (Chapter 5).
☐ Spring weak or broken. Makes a clicking or scraping sound. Fork oil, when drained, will have a lot of metal particles in it (Chapter 5).
☐ Steering head bearings loose or damaged. Clicks when braking. Check and adjust or replace as necessary (Chapters 1 and 5).
☐ Triple clamps loose. Make sure all clamp bolts are tightened to the specified torque (Chapter 5).
☐ Fork tube bent. Good possibility if machine has been dropped. Replace tube with a new one (Chapter 5).
☐ Front axle bolt or axle pinch bolts loose. Tighten them to the specified torque (Chapter 6).
☐ Loose or worn wheel bearings. Check and replace as needed (Chapter 6).

Shock absorber noise

☐ Fluid level incorrect. Indicates a leak caused by defective seal. Shock will be covered with oil. Replace shock (Chapter 5).
☐ Defective shock absorber with internal damage. This is in the body of the shock and can't be remedied. The shock must be replaced with a new one (Chapter 5).

☐ Bent or damaged shock body. Replace the shock with a new one (Chapter 5).

Brake noise

☐ Squeal caused by dust on brake pads. Usually found in combination with glazed pads. Clean using brake cleaning solvent (Chapter 6).
☐ Contamination of brake pads or shoes. Oil, brake fluid or dirt causing brake to chatter or squeal. Clean or replace pads (Chapter 6).
☐ Pads or shoes glazed. Caused by excessive heat from prolonged use or from contamination. Do not use sandpaper/emery cloth or any other abrasive to roughen the pad surfaces as abrasives will stay in the pad material and damage the disc. A very fine flat file can be used, but pad replacement is suggested as a cure (Chapter 6).
☐ Disc warped. Can cause a chattering, clicking or intermittent squeal. Usually accompanied by a pulsating lever and uneven braking. Replace the disc (Chapter 6).
☐ Loose or worn wheel bearings. Check and replace as needed (Chapter 6).

10 Oil pressure warning light comes on

Engine lubrication system

☐ Engine oil pump defective or failed relief valve. Inspect (Chapter 2).
☐ Engine oil level low. Inspect for leak or other problem causing low oil level and add recommended oil (Chapter 1).
☐ Engine oil viscosity too low. Very old, thin oil or an improper weight of oil used in the engine. Change to correct oil (Chapter 1).

Electrical system

☐ Oil pressure switch defective. Check the switch according to the procedure in Chapter 8. Replace it if it is defective.
☐ Oil pressure indicator light circuit defective. Check for pinched, shorted, disconnected or damaged wiring (Chapter 8).

11 Excessive exhaust smoke

White smoke

☐ Piston oil ring worn. The ring may be broken or damaged, causing oil from the crankcase to be pulled past the piston into the combustion chamber. Replace the rings with new ones (Chapter 2).

☐ Cylinders worn, cracked, or scored. Caused by overheating or oil starvation. Install a new cylinder (Chapter 2).

☐ Valve oil seal damaged or worn. Replace oil seals with new ones (Chapter 2).

☐ Valve guide worn. Perform a complete valve job (Chapter 2).

☐ Engine oil level too high, which causes the oil to be forced past the rings. Drain oil to the proper level (Chapter 1).

☐ Head gasket broken between oil return and cylinder. Causes oil to be pulled into the combustion chamber. Replace the head gasket and check the head for warpage (Chapter 2).

☐ Abnormal crankcase pressurization, which forces oil past the rings. Clogged breather is usually the cause.

Black smoke

☐ Air filter clogged. Clean or replace the element (Chapter 1).

☐ Carburetor flooding. Remove and overhaul the carburetor (Chapter 3).

☐ Main jet too large. Remove and overhaul the carburetor(s) (Chapter 3).

☐ Choke cable stuck (Chapter 3).

☐ Fuel level too high. Check the fuel level (Chapter 3).

12 Poor handling or stability

Handlebar hard to turn

☐ Steering head bearing adjuster nut too tight. Check adjustment as described in Chapter 5.

☐ Bearings damaged. Roughness can be felt as the bars are turned from side-to-side. Replace bearings and races (Chapter 5).

☐ Races dented or worn. Denting results from wear in only one position (e.g., straight ahead), from a collision or hitting a pothole or from dropping the machine. Replace races and bearings (Chapter 5).

☐ Steering stem lubrication inadequate. Causes are grease getting hard from age or being washed out by high pressure car washes. Disassemble steering head and repack bearings (Chapter 5).

☐ Steering stem bent. Caused by a collision, hitting a pothole or by dropping the machine. Replace damaged part. Don't try to straighten the steering stem (Chapter 5).

☐ Front tire air pressure too low (Chapter 1).

Handlebar shakes or vibrates excessively

☐ Tires worn or out of balance (Chapter 6).

☐ Swingarm bearings worn. Replace worn bearings (Chapter 5).

☐ Wheel rim(s) warped or damaged. Inspect wheels for runout (Chapter 6).

☐ Wheel bearings worn. Worn front or rear wheel bearings can cause poor tracking. Worn front bearings will cause wobble (Chapter 6).

☐ Handlebar clamp bolts loose (Chapter 5).

☐ Fork yoke bolts loose. Tighten them to the specified torque (Chapter 5).

☐ Engine mounting bolts loose. Will cause excessive vibration with increased engine rpm (Chapter 2).

Handlebar pulls to one side

☐ Frame bent. Definitely suspect this if the machine has been dropped. May or may not be accompanied by cracking near the bend. Replace the frame (Chapter 7).

☐ Wheels out of alignment. Caused by improper location of axle spacers or from bent steering stem or frame (Chapters 5 and 7).

☐ Swingarm bent or twisted. Caused by age (metal fatigue) or impact damage. Replace the arm (Chapter 5).

☐ Steering stem bent. Caused by impact damage or by dropping the motorcycle. Replace the steering stem (Chapter 5).

☐ Fork tube bent. Disassemble the forks and replace the damaged parts (Chapter 5).

☐ Fork oil level uneven. Check and add or drain as necessary (Chapter 1).

Poor shock absorbing qualities

Too hard:
a) Fork oil level excessive (Chapter 1).
b) Fork oil viscosity too high. Use a lighter oil (see the Specifications in Chapter 1).
c) Fork tube bent. Causes a harsh, sticking feeling (Chapter 5).
d) Shock shaft or body bent or damaged (Chapter 5).
e) Fork internal damage (Chapter 5).
f) Shock internal damage.
g) Tire pressure too high (Chapter 1).
Too soft:
a) Fork or shock oil insufficient and/or leaking (Chapter 1).
b) Fork oil level too low (Chapter 5).
c) Fork oil viscosity too light (Chapter 5).
d) Fork springs weak or broken (Chapter 5).
e) Shock internal damage or leakage (Chapter 5).

13 Braking problems

Brakes are spongy, don't hold

- ☐ Air in brake line. Caused by inattention to master cylinder fluid level or by leakage. Locate problem and bleed brakes (Chapter 6).
- ☐ Pad or disc worn (Chapters 1 and 6).
- ☐ Brake fluid leak. See paragraph 1.
- ☐ Contaminated pads. Caused by contamination with oil, grease, brake fluid, etc. Clean or replace pads. Clean disc thoroughly with brake cleaner (Chapter 7).
- ☐ Brake fluid deteriorated. Fluid is old or contaminated. Drain system, replenish with new fluid and bleed the system (Chapter 6).
- ☐ Master cylinder internal parts worn or damaged causing fluid to bypass (Chapter 6).
- ☐ Master cylinder bore scratched by foreign material or broken spring. Repair or replace master cylinder (Chapter 6).
- ☐ Disc warped. Replace disc (Chapter 6).

Brake lever or pedal pulsates

- ☐ Disc or drum warped. Replace (Chapter 6).

- ☐ Axle bent. Replace axle (Chapter 6).
- ☐ Brake caliper bolts loose (Chapter 6).
- ☐ Wheel warped or otherwise damaged (Chapter 6).
- ☐ Wheel bearings damaged or worn (Chapter 6).

Brakes drag

- ☐ Master cylinder piston seized. Caused by wear or damage to piston or cylinder bore (Chapter 6).
- ☐ Lever binding. Check pivot and lubricate (Chapter 6).
- ☐ Brake caliper piston seized in bore. Caused by wear or ingestion of dirt past deteriorated seal (Chapter 6).
- ☐ Brake caliper mounting bracket pins corroded. Clean off corrosion and lubricate (Chapter 6).
- ☐ Brake pad damaged. Material separated from backing plate. Usually caused by faulty manufacturing process or from contact with chemicals. Replace pads (Chapter 6).
- ☐ Pads or shoes improperly installed (Chapter 6).

14 Electrical problems

Battery dead or weak

- ☐ Battery faulty. Caused by sulfated plates which are shorted through sedimentation. Also, broken battery terminal making only occasional contact (Chapter 8).
- ☐ Battery cables making poor contact (Chapter 8).
- ☐ Load excessive. Caused by addition of high wattage lights or other electrical accessories.
- ☐ Ignition (main) switch defective. Switch either grounds internally or fails to shut off system. Replace the switch (Chapter 8).
- ☐ Regulator/rectifier defective (Chapter 8).
- ☐ Alternator stator coil open or shorted (Chapter 8).
- ☐ Wiring faulty. Wiring grounded or connections loose in ignition, charging or lighting circuits (Chapter 8).

Battery overcharged

- ☐ Regulator/rectifier defective. Overcharging is noticed when battery gets excessively warm (Chapter 8).
- ☐ Battery defective. Replace battery with a new one (Chapter 8).
- ☐ Battery amperage too low, wrong type or size. Install manufacturer's specified amp-hour battery to handle charging load (Chapter 8).

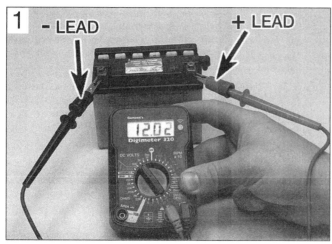

Measuring open-circuit battery voltage

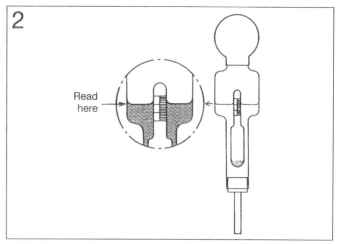

Float-type hydrometer for measuring battery specific gravity

Checking engine compression

● Low compression will result in exhaust smoke, heavy oil consumption, poor starting and poor performance. A compression test will provide useful information about an engine's condition and if performed regularly, can give warning of trouble before any other symptoms become apparent.

● A compression gauge will be required, along with an adapter to suit the spark plug hole thread size. Note that the screw-in type gauge/adapter set up is preferable to the rubber cone type.

● Compression testing procedures for the motorcycles covered in this manual are described in Chapter 2.

Checking battery open-circuit voltage

> ⚠ **Warning:** The gases produced by the battery are explosive - never smoke or create any sparks in the vicinity of the battery. Never allow the electrolyte to contact your skin or clothing - if it does, wash it off and seek immediate medical attention.

● Before any electrical fault is investigated the battery should be checked.

● You'll need a dc voltmeter or multimeter to check battery voltage. Check that the leads are inserted in the correct terminals on the meter, red lead to positive (+), black lead to

negative (-). Incorrect connections can damage the meter.

● A sound, fully-charged 12 volt battery should produce between 12.3 and 12.6 volts across its terminals (12.8 volts for a maintenance-free battery). On machines with a 6 volt battery, voltage should be between 6.1 and 6.3 volts.

1 Set a multimeter to the 0 to 20 volts dc range and connect its probes across the battery terminals. Connect the meter's positive (+) probe, usually red, to the battery positive (+) terminal, followed by the meter's negative (-) probe, usually black, to the battery negative terminal (-) **(see illustration 1)**.

2 If battery voltage is low (below 10 volts on a 12 volt battery or below 4 volts on a six volt battery), charge the battery and test the voltage again. If the battery repeatedly goes flat, investigate the motorcycle's charging system.

Checking battery specific gravity (SG)

> ⚠ **Warning:** The gases produced by the battery are explosive - never smoke or create any sparks in the vicinity of the battery. Never allow the electrolyte to contact your skin or clothing - if it does, wash it off and seek immediate medical attention.

● The specific gravity check gives an indication of a battery's state of charge.

● A hydrometer is used for measuring specific gravity. Make sure you purchase one which has a small enough hose to insert in the aperture of a motorcycle battery.

● Specific gravity is simply a measure of the electrolyte's density compared with that of water. Water has an SG of 1.000 and fully-

charged battery electrolyte is about 26% heavier, at 1.260.

● Specific gravity checks are not possible on maintenance-free batteries. Testing the open-circuit voltage is the only means of determining their state of charge.

1 To measure SG, remove the battery from the motorcycle and remove the first cell cap. Draw some electrolyte into the hydrometer and note the reading **(see illustration 2)**. Return the electrolyte to the cell and install the cap.

2 The reading should be in the region of 1.260 to 1.280. If SG is below 1.200 the battery needs charging. Note that SG will vary with temperature; it should be measured at 20°C (68°F). Add 0.007 to the reading for every 10°C above 20°C, and subtract 0.007 from the reading for every 10°C below 20°C. Add 0.004 to the reading for every 10°F above 68°F, and subtract 0.004 from the reading for every 10°F below 68°F.

3 When the check is complete, rinse the hydrometer thoroughly with clean water.

Checking for continuity

● The term continuity describes the uninterrupted flow of electricity through an electrical circuit. A continuity check will determine whether an **open-circuit** situation exists.

● Continuity can be checked with an ohmmeter, multimeter, continuity tester or battery and bulb test circuit **(see illustrations 3, 4 and 5)**.

● All of these instruments are self-powered by a battery, therefore the checks are made with the ignition OFF.

● As a safety precaution, always disconnect the battery negative (-) lead before making checks, particularly if ignition switch checks are being made.

● If using a meter, select the appropriate

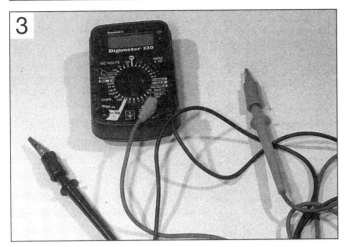

Digital multimeter can be used for all electrical tests

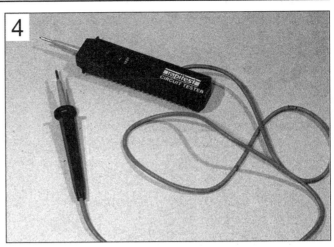

Battery-powered continuity tester

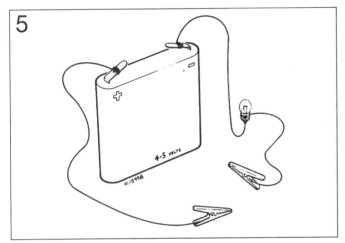

Battery and bulb test circuit

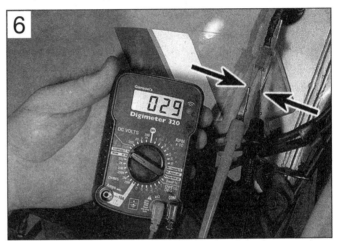

Continuity check of front brake light switch using a meter - note cotter pins used to access connector terminals

ohms scale and check that the meter reads infinity (∞). Touch the meter probes together and check that meter reads zero; where necessary adjust the meter so that it reads zero.

● After using a meter, always switch it OFF to conserve its battery.

Switch checks

1 If a switch is at fault, trace its wiring up to the wiring connectors. Separate the wire connectors and inspect them for security and condition. A build-up of dirt or corrosion here will most likely be the cause of the problem - clean up and apply a water dispersant such as WD40.

2 If using a test meter, set the meter to the ohms x 10 scale and connect its probes across the wires from the switch **(see illustration 6)**. Simple ON/OFF type switches, such as brake light switches, only have two wires whereas combination switches, like the ignition switch, have many internal links.

Study the wiring diagram to ensure that you are connecting across the correct pair of wires. Continuity (low or no measurable resistance - 0 ohms) should be indicated with the switch ON and no continuity (high resistance) with it OFF.

3 Note that the polarity of the test probes doesn't matter for continuity checks, although care should be taken to follow specific test procedures if a diode or solid-state component is being checked.

4 A continuity tester or battery and bulb circuit can be used in the same way. Connect its probes as described above **(see illustration 7)**. The light should come on to indicate continuity in the ON switch position, but should extinguish in the OFF position.

Wiring checks

● Many electrical faults are caused by damaged wiring, often due to incorrect routing or chaffing on frame components.
● Loose, wet or corroded wire connectors

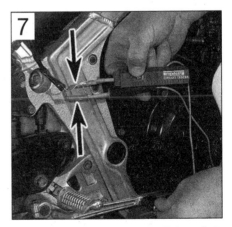

Continuity check of rear brake light switch using a continuity tester

can also be the cause of electrical problems, especially in exposed locations.

Continuity check of front brake light switch sub-harness

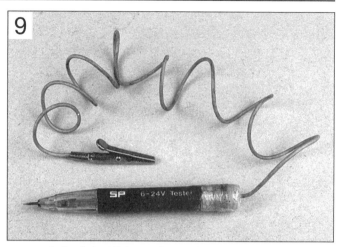

A simple test light can be used for voltage checks

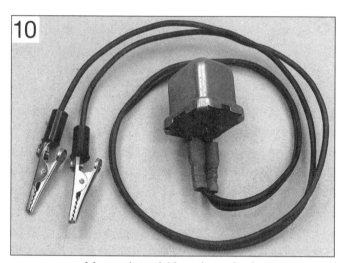

A buzzer is useful for voltage checks

Checking for voltage at the rear brake light power supply wire using a meter . . .

1 A continuity check can be made on a single length of wire by disconnecting it at each end and connecting a meter or continuity tester across both ends of the wire (see illustration 8).
2 Continuity (low or no resistance - 0 ohms) should be indicated if the wire is good. If no continuity (high resistance) is shown, suspect a broken wire.

Checking for voltage

● A voltage check can determine whether current is reaching a component.
● Voltage can be checked with a dc voltmeter, multimeter set on the dc volts scale, test light or buzzer (see illustrations 9 and 10). A meter has the advantage of being able to measure actual voltage.
● When using a meter, check that its leads are inserted in the correct terminals on the meter, red to positive (+), black to negative (-). Incorrect connections can damage the meter.
● A voltmeter (or multimeter set to the dc volts scale) should always be connected in parallel (across the load). Connecting it in series will destroy the meter.
● Voltage checks are made with the ignition ON.
1 First identify the relevant wiring circuit by referring to the wiring diagram at the end of this manual. If other electrical components share the same power supply (ie are fed from the same fuse), take note whether they are working correctly - this is useful information in deciding where to start checking the circuit.
2 If using a meter, check first that the meter leads are plugged into the correct terminals on the meter (see above). Set the meter to the dc volts function, at a range suitable for the battery voltage. Connect the meter red probe (+) to the power supply wire and the black probe to a good metal ground on the motor-

cycle's frame or directly to the battery negative (-) terminal (see illustration 11). Battery voltage should be shown on the meter with the ignition switched ON.
3 If using a test light or buzzer, connect its positive (+) probe to the power supply terminal and its negative (-) probe to a good ground on the motorcycle's frame or directly to the battery negative (-) terminal (see illustration 12). With the ignition ON, the test light should illuminate or the buzzer sound.
4 If no voltage is indicated, work back towards the fuse continuing to check for voltage. When you reach a point where there is voltage, you know the problem lies between that point and your last check point.

Checking the ground

● Ground connections are made either

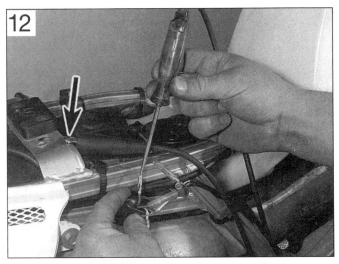

... or a test light - note the ground connection to the frame (arrow)

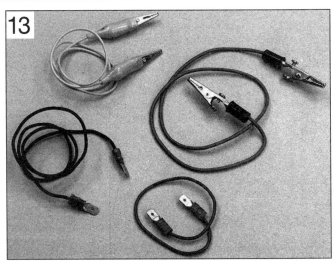

A selection of jumper wires for making ground checks

directly to the engine or frame (such as sensors, neutral switch etc. which only have a positive feed) or by a separate wire into the ground circuit of the wiring harness. Alternatively a short ground wire is sometimes run directly from the component to the motorcycle's frame.
● Corrosion is often the cause of a poor ground connection.
● If total failure is experienced, check the security of the main ground lead from the negative (-) terminal of the battery and also the main ground point on the wiring harness. If corroded, dismantle the connection and clean all surfaces back to bare metal.
1 To check the ground on a component, use an insulated jumper wire to temporarily bypass its ground connection **(see illustration 13)**. Connect one end of the jumper wire between the ground terminal or

metal body of the component and the other end to the motorcycle's frame.
2 If the circuit works with the jumper wire installed, the original ground circuit is faulty. Check the wiring for open-circuits or poor connections. Clean up direct ground connections, removing all traces of corrosion and remake the joint. Apply petroleum jelly to the joint to prevent future corrosion.

Tracing a short-circuit

● A short-circuit occurs where current shorts to ground bypassing the circuit components. This usually results in a blown fuse.

● A short-circuit is most likely to occur where the insulation has worn through due to wiring chafing on a component, allowing a direct path to ground on the frame.
1 Remove any body panels necessary to access the circuit wiring.
2 Check that all electrical switches in the circuit are OFF, then remove the circuit fuse and connect a test light, buzzer or voltmeter (set to the dc scale) across the fuse terminals. No voltage should be shown.
3 Move the wiring from side to side while observing the test light or meter. When the test light comes on, buzzer sounds or meter shows voltage, you have found the cause of the short. It will usually shown up as damaged or burned insulation.
4 Note that the same test can be performed on each component in the circuit, even the switch.

Notes

A

ABS (Anti-lock braking system) A system, usually electronically controlled, that senses incipient wheel lockup during braking and relieves hydraulic pressure at wheel which is about to skid.

Aftermarket Components suitable for the motorcycle, but not produced by the motorcycle manufacturer.

Allen key A hexagonal wrench which fits into a recessed hexagonal hole.

Alternating current (ac) Current produced by an alternator. Requires converting to direct current by a rectifier for charging purposes.

Alternator Converts mechanical energy from the engine into electrical energy to charge the battery and power the electrical system.

Ampere (amp) A unit of measurement for the flow of electrical current. Current = Volts ÷ Ohms.

Ampere-hour (Ah) Measure of battery capacity.

Angle-tightening A torque expressed in degrees. Often follows a conventional tightening torque for cylinder head or main bearing fasteners **(see illustration)**.

Angle-tightening cylinder head bolts

Antifreeze A substance (usually ethylene glycol) mixed with water, and added to the cooling system, to prevent freezing of the coolant in winter. Antifreeze also contains chemicals to inhibit corrosion and the formation of rust and other deposits that would tend to clog the radiator and coolant passages and reduce cooling efficiency.

Anti-dive System attached to the fork lower leg (slider) to prevent fork dive when braking hard.

Anti-seize compound A coating that reduces the risk of seizing on fasteners that are subjected to high temperatures, such as exhaust clamp bolts and nuts.

API American Petroleum Institute. A quality standard for 4-stroke motor oils.

Asbestos A natural fibrous mineral with great heat resistance, commonly used in the composition of brake friction materials. Asbestos is a health hazard and the dust created by brake systems should never be inhaled or ingested.

ATF Automatic Transmission Fluid. Often used in front forks.

ATU Automatic Timing Unit. Mechanical device for advancing the ignition timing on early engines.

ATV All Terrain Vehicle. Often called a Quad.

Axial play Side-to-side movement.

Axle A shaft on which a wheel revolves. Also known as a spindle.

B

Backlash The amount of movement between meshed components when one component is held still. Usually applies to gear teeth.

Ball bearing A bearing consisting of a hardened inner and outer race with hardened steel balls between the two races.

Bearings Used between two working surfaces to prevent wear of the components and a build-up of heat. Four types of bearing are commonly used on motorcycles: plain shell bearings, ball bearings, tapered roller bearings and needle roller bearings.

Bevel gears Used to turn the drive through 90°. Typical applications are shaft final drive and camshaft drive **(see illustration)**.

BHP Brake Horsepower. The British measure-ment for engine power output. Power output is now usually expressed in kilowatts (kW).

Bevel gears are used to turn the drive through 90°

Bias-belted tire Similar construction to radial tire, but with outer belt running at an angle to the wheel rim.

Big-end bearing The bearing in the end of the connecting rod that's attached to the crankshaft.

Bleeding The process of removing air from a hydraulic system via a bleed nipple or bleed screw.

Bottom-end A description of an engine's crankcase components and all components contained therein.

BTDC Before Top Dead Center in terms of piston position. Ignition timing is often expressed in terms of degrees or millimeters BTDC.

Bush A cylindrical metal or rubber component used between two moving parts.

Burr Rough edge left on a component after machining or as a result of excessive wear.

C

Cam chain The chain which takes drive from the crankshaft to the camshaft(s).

Canister The main component in an evaporative emission control system (California market only); contains activated charcoal granules to trap vapors from the fuel system rather than allowing them to vent to the atmosphere.

Castellated Resembling the parapets along the top of a castle wall. For example, a castellated wheel axle or spindle nut.

Catalytic converter A device in the exhaust system of some machines which

Cush drive rubber segments dampen out transmission shocks

converts certain pollutants in the exhaust gases into less harmful substances.

Charging system Description of the components which charge the battery, ie the alternator, rectifer and regulator.

Clearance The amount of space between two parts. For example, between a piston and a cylinder, between a bearing and a journal, etc.

Coil spring A spiral of elastic steel found in various sizes throughout a vehicle, for example as a springing medium in the suspension and in the valve train.

Compression Reduction in volume, and increase in pressure and temperature, of a gas, caused by squeezing it into a smaller space.

Compression damping Controls the speed the suspension compresses when hitting a bump.

Compression ratio The relationship between cylinder volume when the piston is at top dead center and cylinder volume when the piston is at bottom dead center.

Continuity The uninterrupted path in the flow of electricity. Little or no measurable resistance.

Continuity tester Self-powered bleeper or test light which indicates continuity.

Cp Candlepower. Bulb rating commonly found on US motorcycles.

Crossply tire Tire plies arranged in a criss-cross pattern. Usually four or six plies used, hence 4PR or 6PR in tire size codes.

Cush drive Rubber damper segments fitted between the rear wheel and final drive sprocket to absorb transmission shocks **(see illustration)**.

D

Degree disc Calibrated disc for measuring piston position. Expressed in degrees.

Dial gauge Clock-type gauge with adapters for measuring runout and piston position. Expressed in mm or inches.

Diaphragm The rubber membrane in a master cylinder or carburetor which seals the upper chamber.

Diaphragm spring A single sprung plate often used in clutches.

Direct current (dc) Current produced by a dc generator.

Decarbonization The process of removing carbon deposits - typically from the combustion chamber, valves and exhaust port/system.

Detonation Destructive and damaging explosion of fuel/air mixture in combustion chamber instead of controlled burning.

Diode An electrical valve which only allows current to flow in one direction. Commonly used in rectifiers and starter interlock systems.

Disc valve (or rotary valve) An induction system used on some two-stroke engines.

Double-overhead camshaft (DOHC) An engine that uses two overhead camshafts, one for the intake valves and one for the exhaust valves.

Drivebelt A toothed belt used to transmit drive to the rear wheel on some motorcycles. A drivebelt has also been used to drive the camshafts. Drivebelts are usually made of Kevlar.

Driveshaft Any shaft used to transmit motion. Commonly used when referring to the final driveshaft on shaft drive motorcycles.

E

ECU (Electronic Control Unit) A computer which controls (for instance) an ignition system, or an anti-lock braking system.

EGO Exhaust Gas Oxygen sensor. Some-times called a Lambda sensor.

Electrolyte The fluid in a lead-acid battery.

EMS (Engine Management System) A computer controlled system which manages the fuel injection and the ignition systems in an integrated fashion.

Endfloat The amount of lengthways movement between two parts. As applied to a crankshaft, the distance that the crankshaft can move side-to-side in the crankcase.

Endless chain A chain having no joining link. Common use for cam chains and final drive chains.

EP (Extreme Pressure) Oil type used in locations where high loads are applied, such as between gear teeth.

Evaporative emission control system Describes a charcoal filled canister which stores fuel vapors from the tank rather than allowing them to vent to the atmosphere. Usually only fitted to California models and referred to as an EVAP system.

Expansion chamber Section of two-stroke engine exhaust system so designed to improve engine efficiency and boost power.

F

Feeler blade or gauge A thin strip or blade of hardened steel, ground to an exact thickness, used to check or measure clearances between parts.

Final drive Description of the drive from the transmission to the rear wheel. Usually by chain or shaft, but sometimes by belt.

Firing order The order in which the engine cylinders fire, or deliver their power strokes, beginning with the number one cylinder.

Flooding Term used to describe a high fuel level in the carburetor float chambers, leading to fuel overflow. Also refers to excess fuel in the combustion chamber due to incorrect starting technique.

Free length The no-load state of a component when measured. Clutch, valve and fork spring lengths are measured at rest, without any preload.

Freeplay The amount of travel before any action takes place. The looseness in a linkage, or an assembly of parts, between the initial application of force and actual movement. For example, the distance the rear brake pedal moves before the rear brake is actuated.

Fuel injection The fuel/air mixture is metered electronically and directed into the engine intake ports (indirect injection) or into the cylinders (direct injection). Sensors supply information on engine speed and conditions.

Fuel/air mixture The charge of fuel and air going into the engine. See Stoichiometric ratio.

Fuse An electrical device which protects a circuit against accidental overload. The typical fuse contains a soft piece of metal which is calibrated to melt at a predetermined current flow (expressed as amps) and break the circuit.

G

Gap The distance the spark must travel in jumping from the center electrode to the side electrode in a spark plug. Also refers to the distance between the ignition rotor and the pickup coil in an electronic ignition system.

Gasket Any thin, soft material - usually cork, cardboard, asbestos or soft metal - installed between two metal surfaces to ensure a good seal. For instance, the cylinder head gasket seals the joint between the block and the cylinder head.

Gauge An instrument panel display used to monitor engine conditions. A gauge with a movable pointer on a dial or a fixed scale is an analog gauge. A gauge with a numerical readout is called a digital gauge.

Gear ratios The drive ratio of a pair of gears in a gearbox, calculated on their number of teeth.

Glaze-busting see **Honing**

Grinding Process for renovating the valve face and valve seat contact area in the cylinder head.

Ground return The return path of an electrical circuit, utilizing the motorcycle's frame.

Gudgeon pin The shaft which connects the connecting rod small-end with the piston. Often called a piston pin or wrist pin.

H

Helical gears Gear teeth are slightly curved and produce less gear noise that straight-cut gears. Often used for primary drives.

Helicoil A thread insert repair system. Commonly used as a repair for stripped spark plug threads **(see illustration)**.

Installing a Helicoil thread insert in a cylinder head

Honing A process used to break down the glaze on a cylinder bore (also called glaze-busting). Can also be carried out to roughen a rebored cylinder to aid ring bedding-in.

HT (High Tension) Description of the electrical circuit from the secondary winding of the ignition coil to the spark plug.

Hydraulic A liquid filled system used to transmit pressure from one component to another. Common uses on motorcycles are brakes and clutches.

Hydrometer An instrument for measuring the specific gravity of a lead-acid battery.

Hygroscopic Water absorbing. In motorcycle applications, braking efficiency will be reduced if DOT 3 or 4 hydraulic fluid absorbs water from the air - care must be taken to keep new brake fluid in tightly sealed containers.

I

lbf ft Pounds-force feet. An imperial unit of torque. Sometimes written as ft-lbs.

lbf in Pound-force inch. An imperial unit of torque, applied to components where a very low torque is required. Sometimes written as inch-lbs.

IC Abbreviation for Integrated Circuit.

Ignition advance Means of increasing the timing of the spark at higher engine speeds. Done by mechanical means (ATU) on early engines or electronically by the ignition control unit on later engines.

Ignition timing The moment at which the spark plug fires, expressed in the number of crankshaft degrees before the piston reaches the top of its stroke, or in the number of millimeters before the piston reaches the top of its stroke.

Infinity (∞) Description of an open-circuit electrical state, where no continuity exists.

Inverted forks (upside down forks) The sliders or lower legs are held in the yokes and the fork tubes or stanchions are connected to the wheel axle (spindle). Less unsprung weight and stiffer construction than conventional forks.

J

JASO Japan Automobile Standards Organ-ization. JASO MA is a standard for motorcycle oil equivalent to API SJ, but designed to prevent problems with wet-type motorcycle clutches.

Joule The unit of electrical energy.

Journal The bearing surface of a shaft.

K

Kickstart Mechanical means of turning the engine over for starting purposes.

Only usually fitted to mopeds, small capacity motorcycles and off-road motorcycles.

Kill switch Handebar-mounted switch for emergency ignition cut-out. Cuts the ignition circuit on all models, and additionally prevent starter motor operation on others.

km Symbol for kilometer.

kmh Abbreviation for kilometers per hour.

L

Lambda sensor A sensor fitted in the exhaust system to measure the exhaust gas oxygen content (excess air factor). Also called oxygen sensor.

Lapping see **Grinding**.

LCD Abbreviation for Liquid Crystal Display.

LED Abbreviation for Light Emitting Diode.

Liner A steel cylinder liner inserted in an aluminum alloy cylinder block.

Locknut A nut used to lock an adjustment nut, or other threaded component, in place.

Lockstops The lugs on the lower triple clamp (yoke) which abut those on the frame, preventing handlebar-to-fuel tank contact.

Lockwasher A form of washer designed to prevent an attaching nut from working loose.

LT Low Tension Description of the electrical circuit from the power supply to the primary winding of the ignition coil.

M

Main bearings The bearings between the crankshaft and crankcase.

Maintenance-free (MF) battery A sealed battery which cannot be topped up.

Manometer Mercury-filled calibrated tubes used to measure intake tract vacuum. Used to synchronize carburetors on multi-cylinder engines.

Tappet shims are measured with a micrometer

Micrometer A precision measuring instru-ment that measures component outside diameters **(see illustration)**.

MON (Motor Octane Number) A measure of a fuel's resistance to knock.

Monograde oil An oil with a single viscosity, eg SAE80W.

Monoshock A single suspension unit linking the swingarm or suspension linkage to the frame.

mph Abbreviation for miles per hour.

Multigrade oil Having a wide viscosity range (eg 10W40). The W stands for Winter, thus the viscosity ranges from SAE10 when cold to SAE40 when hot.

Multimeter An electrical test instrument with the capability to measure voltage, current and resistance. Some meters also incorporate a continuity tester and buzzer.

N

Needle roller bearing Inner race of caged needle rollers and hardened outer race. Examples of uncaged needle rollers can be found on some engines. Commonly used in rear suspension applications and in two-stroke engines.

Nm Newton meters.

NOx Oxides of Nitrogen. A common toxic pollutant emitted by gasoline engines at higher temperatures.

O

Octane The measure of a fuel's resistance to knock.

OE (Original Equipment) Relates to components fitted to a motorcycle as standard or replacement parts supplied by the motorcycle manufacturer.

Ohm The unit of electrical resistance. Ohms = Volts 4 Current.

Ohmmeter An instrument for measuring electrical resistance.

Oil cooler System for diverting engine oil outside of the engine to a radiator for cooling purposes.

Oil injection A system of two-stroke engine lubrication where oil is pump-fed to the engine in accordance with throttle position.

Open-circuit An electrical condition where there is a break in the flow of electricity - no continuity (high resistance).

O-ring A type of sealing ring made of a special rubber-like material; in use, the O-ring is compressed into a groove to provide the sealing action.

Oversize (OS) Term used for piston and ring size options fitted to a rebored cylinder.

Overhead cam (sohc) engine An engine with single camshaft located on top of the cylinder head.

Overhead valve (ohv) engine An engine with the valves located in the cylinder head, but with the camshaft located in the engine block or crankcase.

Oxygen sensor A device installed in the exhaust system which senses the oxygen content in the exhaust and converts this information into an electric current. Also called a Lambda sensor.

P

Plastigage A thin strip of plastic thread, available in different sizes, used for measuring clearances. For example, a strip of Plastigage is laid across a bearing journal. The parts are assembled and dismantled; the width of the crushed strip indicates the clearance between journal and bearing.

Polarity Either negative or positive ground, determined by which battery lead is connected to the frame (ground return). Modern motorcycles are usually negative ground.

Pre-ignition A situation where the fuel/air mixture ignites before the spark plug fires. Often due to a hot spot in the combustion chamber caused by carbon build-up. Engine has a tendency to 'run-on'.

Pre-load (suspension) The amount a spring is compressed when in the unloaded state. Preload can be applied by gas, spacer or mechanical adjuster.

Premix The method of engine lubrication on some gasoline two-stroke engines. Engine oil is mixed with the gasoline in the fuel tank in a specific ratio. The fuel/oil mix is sometimes referred to as "petrol".

Primary drive Description of the drive from the crankshaft to the clutch. Usually by gear or chain.

PS Pferdestärke - a German interpretation of BHP.

PSI Pounds-force per square inch. Imperial measurement of tire pressure and cylinder pressure measurement.

PTFE Polytetrafluroethylene. A low friction substance.

Pulse secondary air injection system A process of promoting the burning of excess fuel present in the exhaust gases by routing fresh air into the exhaust ports.

Q

Quartz halogen bulb Tungsten filament surrounded by a halogen gas. Typically used for the headlight (see illustration).

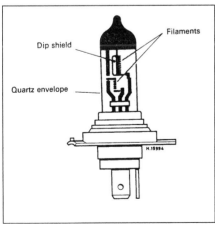

Quartz halogen headlight bulb construction

R

Rack-and-pinion A pinion gear on the end of a shaft that mates with a rack (think of a geared wheel opened up and laid flat). Sometimes used in clutch operating systems.

Radial play Up and down movement about a shaft.

Radial ply tires Tire plies run across the tire (from bead to bead) and around the circumference of the tire. Less resistant to tread distortion than other tire types.

Radiator A liquid-to-air heat transfer device designed to reduce the temperature of the coolant in a liquid cooled engine.

Rake A feature of steering geometry - the angle of the steering head in relation to the vertical (see illustration).

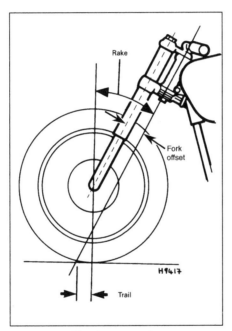

Steering geometry

Rebore Providing a new working surface to the cylinder bore by boring out the old surface. Necessitates the use of oversize piston and rings.

Rebound damping A means of controlling the oscillation of a suspension unit spring after it has been compressed. Resists the spring's natural tendency to bounce back after being compressed.

Rectifier Device for converting the ac output of an alternator into dc for battery charging.

Reed valve An induction system commonly used on two-stroke engines.

Regulator Device for maintaining the charging voltage from the generator or alternator within a specified range.

Relay A electrical device used to switch heavy current on and off by using a low current auxiliary circuit.

Resistance Measured in ohms. An electrical component's ability to pass electrical current.

RON (Research Octane Number) A measure of a fuel's resistance to knock.

rpm revolutions per minute.

Runout The amount of wobble (in-and-out movement) of a wheel or shaft as it's rotated. The amount a shaft rotates `out-of-true'. The out-of-round condition of a rotating part.

S

SAE (Society of Automotive Engineers) A standard for the viscosity of a fluid.

Sealant A liquid or paste used to prevent leakage at a joint. Sometimes used in conjunction with a gasket.

Service limit Term for the point where a component is no longer useable and must be replaced.

Shaft drive A method of transmitting drive from the transmission to the rear wheel.

Shell bearings Plain bearings consisting of two shell halves. Most often used as big-end and main bearings in a four-stroke engine. Often called bearing inserts.

Shim Thin spacer, commonly used to adjust the clearance or relative positions between two parts. For example, shims inserted into or under tappets or followers to control valve clearances. Clearance is adjusted by changing the thickness of the shim.

Short-circuit An electrical condition where current shorts to ground bypassing the circuit components.

Skimming Process to correct warpage or repair a damaged surface, eg on brake discs or drums.

Slide-hammer A special puller that screws into or hooks onto a component such as a shaft or bearing; a heavy sliding handle on the shaft bottoms against the end of the shaft to knock the component free.

Small-end bearing The bearing in the upper end of the connecting rod at its joint with the gudgeon pin.

Snap-ring A ring-shaped clip used to prevent endwise movement of cylindrical parts and shafts. An internal snap-ring is installed in a groove in a housing; an external snap-ring fits into a groove on the outside of a cylindrical piece such as a shaft. Also known as a snap-ring.

Spalling Damage to camshaft lobes or bearing journals shown as pitting of the working surface.

Specific gravity (SG) The state of charge of the electrolyte in a lead-acid battery. A measure of the electrolyte's density compared with water.

Straight-cut gears Common type gear used on gearbox shafts and for oil pump and water pump drives.

Stanchion The inner sliding part of the front forks, held by the yokes. Often called a fork tube.

Stoichiometric ratio The optimum chemical air/fuel ratio for a gasoline engine, said to be 14.7 parts of air to 1 part of fuel.

Sulphuric acid The liquid (electrolyte) used in a lead-acid battery. Poisonous and extremely corrosive.

Surface grinding (lapping) Process to correct a warped gasket face, commonly used on cylinder heads.

T

Tapered-roller bearing Tapered inner race of caged needle rollers and separate tapered outer race. Examples of taper roller bearings can be found on steering heads.

Tappet A cylindrical component which transmits motion from the cam to the valve stem, either directly or via a pushrod and rocker arm. Also called a cam follower.

TCS Traction Control System. An electron-ically-controlled system which senses wheel spin and reduces engine speed accordingly.

TDC Top Dead Center denotes that the piston is at its highest point in the cylinder.

Thread-locking compound Solution applied to fastener threads to prevent loosening. Select type to suit application.

Thrust washer A washer positioned between two moving components on a shaft. For example, between gear pinions on gearshaft.

Timing chain See **Cam Chain**.

Timing light Stroboscopic lamp for carrying out ignition timing checks with the engine running.

Top-end A description of an engine's cylinder block, head and valve gear components.

Torque Turning or twisting force about a shaft.

Torque setting A prescribed tightness specified by the motorcycle manufacturer to ensure that the bolt or nut is secured correctly. Undertightening can result in the bolt or nut coming loose or a surface not being sealed. Overtightening can result in stripped threads, distortion or damage to the component being retained.

Torx key A six-point wrench.

Tracer A stripe of a second color applied to a wire insulator to distinguish that wire from another one with the same color insulator. For example, Br/W is often used to denote a brown insulator with a white tracer.

Trail A feature of steering geometry. Distance from the steering head axis to the tire's central contact point.

Triple clamps The cast components which extend from the steering head and support the fork stanchions or tubes. Often called fork yokes.

Turbocharger A centrifugal device, driven by exhaust gases, that pressurizes the intake air. Normally used to increase the power output from a given engine displacement.

TWI Abbreviation for Tire Wear Indicator. Indicates the location of the tread depth indicator bars on tires.

U

Universal joint or U-joint (UJ) A double-pivoted connection for transmitting power from a driving to a driven shaft through an angle. Typically found in shaft drive assemblies.

Unsprung weight Anything not supported by the bike's suspension (ie the wheel, tires, brakes, final drive and bottom (moving) part of the suspension).

V

Vacuum gauges Clock-type gauges for measuring intake tract vacuum. Used for carburetor synchronization on multi-cylinder engines.

Valve A device through which the flow of liquid, gas or vacuum may be stopped, started or regulated by a moveable part that opens, shuts or partially obstructs one or more ports or passageways. The intake and exhaust valves in the cylinder head are of the poppet type.

Valve clearance The clearance between the valve tip (the end of the valve stem) and the rocker arm or tappet/follower. The valve clearance is measured when the valve is closed. The correct clearance is important - if too small the valve won't close fully and will burn out, whereas if too large noisy operation will result.

Valve lift The amount a valve is lifted off its seat by the camshaft lobe.

Valve timing The exact setting for the opening and closing of the valves in relation to piston position.

Vernier caliper A precision measuring instrument that measures inside and outside dimensions. Not quite as accurate as a micrometer, but more convenient.

VIN Vehicle Identification Number. Term for the bike's engine and frame numbers.

Viscosity The thickness of a liquid or its resistance to flow.

Volt A unit for expressing electrical "pressure" in a circuit. Volts = current x ohms.

W

Water pump A mechanically-driven device for moving coolant around the engine.

Watt A unit for expressing electrical power. Watts = volts x current.

Wet liner arrangement

Wear limit see **Service limit**

Wet liner A liquid-cooled engine design where the pistons run in liners which are directly surrounded by coolant **(see illustration)**.

Wheelbase Distance from the center of the front wheel to the center of the rear wheel.

Wiring harness or loom Describes the electrical wires running the length of the motorcycle and enclosed in tape or plastic sheathing. Wiring coming off the main harness is usually referred to as a sub harness.

Woodruff key A key of semi-circular or square section used to locate a gear to a shaft. Often used to locate the alternator rotor on the crankshaft.

Wrist pin Another name for gudgeon or piston pin.

Notes

Note: *References throughout this index are in the form - "Chapter number"•"Page number"*

V

W

Notes